Geoff Tibballs is the author of the bestselling *Mammoth Book of Jokes* and *The Mammoth Book of Dirty Jokes* as well as many other books including *Business Blunders* and *Legal Blunders*. A former journalist and press officer, he is now a full-time writer who lists his hobbies as sport, eating, drinking and avoiding housework. he lives in Nottingham, England, with his wife and daughters.

Recent Mammoth titles

The Mammoth Book of Hard Bastards
The Mammoth Book of Dracula
The Mammoth Book of Best New Erotica 10
The Mammoth Book of Best British Crime 8
The Mammoth Book of Tattoo Art
The Mammoth Book of Bob Dylan
The Mammoth Book of Mixed Martial Arts
The Mammoth Book of Codeword Puzzles
The Mammoth Book of Hot Romance
The Mammoth Book of Historical Crime Fiction
The Mammoth Book of Best New SF 24
The Mammoth Book of Gorgeous Guys
The Mammoth Book of Really Silly Jokes
The Mammoth Book of Best New Horror 22
The Mammoth Book of Undercover Cops
The Mammoth Book of Weird News
The Mammoth Book of Antarctic Journeys
The Mammoth Book of Muhammad Ali
The Mammoth Book of The Best of Best New Erotica
The Mammoth Book of Best British Crime 9
The Mammoth Book of Conspiracies
The Mammoth Book of Lost Symbols
The Mammoth Book of Nebula Awards SF
The Mammoth Book of Sex Scandals
The Mammoth Book of Body Horror
The Mammoth Book of Steampunk
The Mammoth Book of New CSI
The Mammoth Book of Gangs
The Mammoth Book of SF Wars
The Mammoth Book of Ghost Romance

THE MAMMOTH BOOK OF

One-Liners

Geoff Tibballs

ROBINSON   RUNNING PRESS
PHILADELPHIA · LONDON

Constable & Robinson Ltd
55–56 Russell Square
London WC1B 4HP
www.constablerobinson.com

First published in the UK as *The Mammoth Book of One-Liners*
by Robinson, an imprint of Constable & Robinson Ltd, 2012

A copy of the British Library Cataloguing in
Publication Data is available from the British Library

UK ISBN: 978-1-78033-390-8 (paperback)
UK ISBN: 978-1-78033-536-0 (ebook)

Printed and bound in the UK

13 5 7 9 10 8 6 4 2

First published in the United States in 2012 as *The Mammoth Book of 10,000 Zingers*
by Running Press Book Publishers, a Member of the Perseus Books Group

Books published by Running Press are available at special discounts for bulk purchases in the United
States by corporations, institutions, and other organizations. For more information, please contact
the Special Markets Department at the Perseus Books Group, 2300 Chestnut Street, Suite 200,
Philadelphia, PA 19103, or call (800) 810-4145, ext. 5000, or e-mail special.markets@perseusbooks.
com.

US ISBN: 978-0-7624-4595-0
US Library of Congress Control Number: 2011939123

9   8   7   6   5   4   3   2   1
Digit on the right indicates the number of this printing

Running Press Book Publishers
2300 Chestnut Street
Philadelphia, PA 19103-4371

Visit us on the web!
www.runningpress.com

Printed and bound in the UK

CONTENTS

INTRODUCTION

Thanks to clever and imaginative stand-up comedians such as Milton Jones, Tim Vine, Steven Wright and Jimmy Carr, one- and two-line jokes have never been more popular. They are easy to remember and can be slipped effortlessly into most conversations and speeches. You can't help thinking that the Queen's annual Christmas message, Lincoln's Gettysburg Address and the opening speech of Shakespeare's *Richard III* would all have benefited from the odd one-liner: "Now is the winter of our discount tents, so hurry while stocks last . . ." Well, you get the idea.

I have collected over 10,000 quickfire jokes for this book, covering more than 300 different subjects and featuring a wealth of new material alongside some favourite old classics. They range from surreal observations to subtle wordplay and include what must surely be a candidate for the world's shortest joke: "Pretentious? *Moi*?"

The jokes come so thick and fast that if you happen not to like one particular gag, before you have time to draw breath another arrives that is hopefully more to your taste. Which reminds me: "Did you hear about the artist who was so bad it was a wonder he could draw breath?"

I'll get my coat.

Thanks to Duncan Proudfoot and Becca Allen at Constable & Robinson, as well as Lynn Curtis and Andy Armitage.

Geoff Tibballs, 2012

ACCIDENTS

A truckload of onions overturned on the highway. Motorists are advised to look for a hard shoulder to cry on.

Did you hear about the man who fell into a lens-grinding machine and made a spectacle of himself?

In the 15 years that I've been driving, I've never been involved in an accident. I've seen a few in the rear-view mirror though.

My grandfather broke his leg after standing on a doormat. I probably should have explained to him the concept of a helter-skelter. *Milton Jones*

Did you hear about the old lady who accidentally plugged her electric blanket into the toaster? She spent the night popping out of bed.

Kids in the back seat cause accidents; accidents in the back seat cause kids.

Did you hear about the man who bent down to pick up a sieve and strained himself?

A truck carrying copies of *Roget's Thesaurus* crashed yesterday, shedding its load across the highway. Onlookers are said to be stunned, bewildered, dumbfounded, astonished, amazed, shocked and flabbergasted.

Did you hear about the butcher who backed into the bacon slicer and got a little behind in his orders?

After I lost a hand in an accident, my girlfriend was really frustrated. She's a palm reader and wants to know what happens next.

My friend has swallowed some Lego. The doctors aren't too worried, but he's shitting bricks.

People think I'm weird because I swallowed an abacus, but it's what's inside that counts.

Did you hear about the man who accidentally mixed his Viagra with his iron pills? Now he can't stop pointing north.

A truck carrying a load of Vicks vapour rub has overturned on the motorway. Police say there will be no congestion for eight hours.

Did you hear about the man who lost his left arm and his left leg in a factory accident? He's all right now.

What happened when the metalworker spilled boiling acetic acid and molten copper on himself?
He suffered verdigris burns.

I've just poured superglue into a non-stick pan. Someone's going to be wrong.

Arriving at the scene of a car crash, a paramedic asks the driver: "Are you badly hurt?" "I don't know," says the driver. "I haven't spoken to my lawyer yet."

I heard that most accidents happen within two miles of home, so I moved.

A truck carrying a consignment of glue has spilled its load on the motorway. Drivers are being advised to stick to the inside lane.

I read a story about a man who lost a leg after ignoring a shark warning. I bet he's kicking himself now.

Did you hear about the man who got hit in the head with a can of soda? He was lucky it was a soft drink.

Every time my wife has an accident in the kitchen, I get it for dinner.

A TV weatherman broke both his arms and legs. He had to call in from hospital to explain about the four casts.

An ambulance is a vehicle used to show lawyers where the accident is.

I saw a poor old lady fall over today on the ice. At least I presume she was poor – she only had $2.50 in her purse.

Did you hear about the carpenter who accidentally sat on his electric drill and was bored to tears?

I saw a headline: "Two People Die In Collision". How fast must they have been walking?

Did you hear about the man who fell into an upholstery machine? He is now completely recovered.

With hindsight, I wouldn't have sat on that cactus.

Did you hear about the boarding house that blew up? Roomers are still flying.

Last night I reached for my liquid Viagra but accidentally drank from a bottle of Tipp-ex instead. I woke up this morning with a huge correction.
Alan Davies

Explosion at a Yorkshire pie factory: 3.14159265 dead.

Paramedic: "Are you hurt? Give me your name so we can tell your family."
Accident victim: "My family already knows my name."

I spilt some stain remover on my shirt. I don't know how I'm going to get it out.

"What do you mean I was lucky?" asked the woman after being hit by a bicycle. The cyclist replied: "I usually drive a bus."

My friend lost his voice and both legs in a car accident, but he doesn't make a song and dance about it.

Why didn't the boy tell his mother that he'd been eating glue?
Because his lips were sealed.

"It was an accident, officer," said the woman. "I was cleaning my fingernails with a hunting knife when my husband ran into me. Backwards. Seventeen times."

A man falls from an eighth-floor window. Seeing him lying on the ground, a cop asks: "What happened?" "I don't know," says the man. "I just got here."

A unicorn and a Cyclops: that's an accident waiting to happen.

Hans and Klaus went mountain climbing with their mother, but she slipped and fell 1,500 feet. Klaus yelled: "Look, Hans! No Ma!"

My identical twin was run over by a steamroller last year. He's not been the same since.

Did you hear about the man who swallowed dozens of Scrabble tiles? The doctor said they would eventually just pass naturally, but not in so many words.

Humpty Dumpty had a great fall – and a pretty good spring and summer, too.

Traffic cop: "How did the accident happen?"
Driver: "My wife fell asleep on the back seat."

I recently broke a mirror and got seven years' bad luck. But my lawyer thinks he can get me five. *Steven Wright*

Did you hear about the man who was run over by a mobile library? As he lay in the road groaning in agony, the librarian rushed up to him and said: "Shhhh!"

ACCOUNTANCY

Did you hear about the constipated accountant? He couldn't budget, so he had to work it out with a pencil and paper.

Why is it tough to do inventories in Afghanistan?
Because of the tally ban.

How do you know when you've got a good tax accountant?
He has a loophole named after him.

Who was the world's first accountant?
Adam: he turned a leaf and made an entry.

What do accountants do to liven up their office party?
Invite a funeral director.

What do you call an accountant without a spreadsheet?
Lost.

What's the most depraved thing a group of young accountants can do?
Go into town and gang-audit someone.

How do you define an extrovert accountant?
One who looks at your shoes while he's talking to you rather than his own.

What is an actuary?
An accountant without the sense of humour.

What does it mean when an accountant is drooling out of both sides of his mouth?
His desk is level.

How do you know when an accountant is on vacation?
He doesn't wear a tie to work and comes in at 8.31.

Why do some accountants become actuaries?
They find bookkeeping too exciting.

Why did God invent economists?
So that accountants would have someone to laugh at.

What's the definition of an accountant?
Someone who solves a problem you didn't know you had in a way you don't understand.

What do you call an accountant who is seen talking to someone?
Popular.

What's an accountant's idea of trashing his hotel room?
Refusing to fill out the guest comment card.

Accountant: "So how is your personal growth?"
Client: "Well, I had an erection last night."

Why was smoke coming from the accountant's office?
He had been cooking the books.

Why did the auditor cross the road?
He looked in the file and that's what they did last year.

Why did he cross back?
So he could charge the client for travel expenses.

What does an accountant say when you ask him the time?
"It's 9.14 a.m. and 26 seconds . . . no, wait, 27 seconds . . . no, wait, 28 seconds . . . no, wait . . ."

Did you hear about the accountant who went to see a psychiatrist because he kept hearing strange invoices?

Accountant after reading nursery rhymes to his young child: "No, son, when Little Bo Peep lost her sheep it wouldn't be tax-deductible, but I like your thinking."

What do accountants suffer from that ordinary people don't?
Depreciation.

How do you drive an accountant insane?
Tie him to a chair, stand in front of him and fold up a road map the wrong way.

What's an accountant's favourite chat-up line?
"Mmmm, nice assets."

Did you hear about the accountant who is shy and retiring? He's half a million shy, and that's why he's retiring.

Why did the accountant pay twice as much for sex as the lawyer?
He used the double-entry system.

Employee to boss: "Sir, the good news is that the auditors have been through the books thoroughly. The bad news is they want 15 per cent to keep quiet."

Conversation between two accountants at a cocktail party: ". . . and ninthly . . ."

If an accountant's wife has trouble sleeping, what does she say?
"Darling, tell me about your work."

ACTING

I was once cast as Oliver in a silent interpretation of *Oliver Twist*. It was brilliant, I couldn't ask for more.

Why don't actors stare out of the window in the morning?
Because if they did, they'd have nothing to do in the afternoon.

How can you tell the dumbest actress on a movie?
She's the one sleeping with the writer.

Mike: "Who was that Hollywood actress who stabbed a guy? Reese . . .?"
Marty: "Witherspoon?"
Mike: "No, with a knife."

I remember when I played Noah in a school play. Ah, those memories are flooding back.

An actor is someone who makes $500,000 a year some weeks.

A woman is staring at an actor. Eventually he goes over and says: "You think you know me, don't you? You've probably seen me in the movies." "Oh," she says. "Where do you sit?"

How do you get an actor off your front porch?
Pay him for the pizza.

Actor: "Yes, madam, I am on TV on and off. How do you like me?"
Woman: "Off."

The play had a happy ending – everyone was glad it was over.

I went for an audition the other day; they were casting 13 people to be clouds. Unfortunately 14 turned up, so it was overcast.

An actor is a man with an infinite capacity for taking praise.

A boy was performing in a school play when he fell through a hole in the floor. His father turned to his mother and said: "Don't worry, it's just a stage he's going through."

I once worked as a porn actor, but I left when I didn't get a raise.

Did you hear about the Hollywood actress who wanted to get a divorce in the same dress her mother got divorced in?

Mike: "Why do you keep applauding such a lousy play?"
Marty: "To stay awake."

I come from a long line of actors. It's called the dole queue.

What did the actor say when he learnt that his agent had gone round to his house and murdered his wife and children?
"My agent came to my house?!"

I'll never forget my first words in the theatre. "Peanuts. Popcorn." *Henny Youngman*

I'm hoping someone will tell me when my days of acting in pantomime are behind me.

Wife: "What do you want to do tonight? Stay at home?"
Husband: "No, I've got a tickly cough. Let's go to the theatre."

I saw the play under adverse conditions – the curtain was up.

What happens when a ghost haunts a theatre?
The actors get stage fright.

Did you hear about the actress who auditioned for *The Vagina Monologues*? She dried.

His mother egged him on to be an actor, but his first audience egged him off.

I've always had the theatre in my veins. Sometimes I wish I had blood.

An agent is someone who believes an actor takes 85 per cent of *his* money.

Director: "The play was a great success, but the audience was a failure."

How can you tell when an airplane is full of actors?
When the engine stops, the whining continues.

Mike: "I was once in a play called *Breakfast in Bed*."
Marty: "Did you have a big role?"
Mike: "No, just toast and marmalade."

Why did the actor turn down a movie role as a juggler?
He didn't have the balls to do it.

You're driving along the road and see your director and a fellow actor crossing the street in front of you. Which one do you hit first, and why?
Your director: business before pleasure.

ADDICTION

Did you hear about the man who phoned Gamblers Anonymous for help with his fruit machine addiction? They asked him if he wanted to hold.

If you're addicted to meths, you've either got a drug problem or you're a South African who loves numbers.

My wife threatened to leave me because of my addiction to the game *Football Manager*. So I fined her two weeks' wages and put her on the transfer list.

I'm so addicted to eating cabbages that to wean me off them I've had to get a cabbage patch.

My wife made fun of me because of my addiction to the metric system. So I beat her to within 2.54 centimetres of her life.

I said to my girlfriend: "Do you think my addiction to golf is driving a wedge between us?"

Doctor: "You should stop taking those pills. They could become addictive."
Patient: "Nonsense. I've been taking them for 14 years."

I've developed a taste for fabric conditioner. My doctor says it's just Comfort eating.

My girlfriend dumped me because she said I'm addicted to plants. I asked: "Where's this stemming from, petal?"

I'm addicted to placebos. I'd give them up, but it wouldn't make any difference. *Steven Wright*

My mate keeps drinking brake fluid, but he says he's not addicted because he can stop whenever he wants.

I used to be addicted to soap, but I'm clean now.

My wife said she was leaving me, because of my addiction to rhyming. I nearly choked on my tea, what terrible timing!

ADULTERY

I'm always frank with my sexual partners. Don't want them knowing my real name, do I?

A mistress is what goes in between a mister and a mattress.

A man arrives home to find his wife in bed with another man. "Who is this guy?" he yells. "That's a fair question," says the wife, turning to her lover. "What is your name?"

My mother ran off with the milkman when I was five years old. Watching them drive away together on his float was the worst hour and a half of my life.

What do you call a woman who knows where her husband is every night?
A widow.

My girlfriend and I have been experiencing communication problems. Every time I ring, her husband answers the phone.

I asked him: "Who said you could fool around with my wife?" He said: "Everybody." – *Rodney Dangerfield*

I've been sleeping with my girlfriend and her twin, but luckily I can tell them apart. Her brother has a moustache.

Husband: "I've just been told that our milkman has made love to every woman in this street except one."
Wife: "I bet it's that stuck-up cow at number 17."

I cheated on my wife at a funeral. It was a black-tie affair.

A man needs a mistress just to break the monogamy.

Tiger Woods never lied to his wife. Whenever she asked where he was going, he said: "To play a round."

A wife answers the phone. "It must have been from a ship," she tells her husband, "because it was some woman wanting to know if the coast is clear."

What do you call a man who doesn't cheat on his wife when he's away on business?
An astronaut.

A man comes home from work to find a note from his wife. It says: "I've run off with a surrealist. Your dinner's in the piano."

If I had a pound for every time my wife has accused me of being unfaithful, I could have bought my girlfriend that gold necklace she likes.

Mike: "Oh, no, here come my wife and my mistress!"
Marty: "What a coincidence! I was going to say the same thing!"

How does a woman know when a man is cheating on her?
He has two baths a week.

Wife: "For Pete's sake, I'm getting sick and tired of you accusing me of cheating on you!"
Husband: "Who's Pete?"

Guns don't kill people. Husbands who come home early kill people.

I'll never be unfaithful to my wife for the reason that I love my house very much. **Bob Monkhouse**

What's the difference between a Western girl and an Arab girl?
A Western girl gets stoned *before* she commits adultery.

Husband: "I have never had an affair. Can you say the same?"
Wife: "Yes, but not with such a straight face."

My wife ran off with my best friend last week. I'm going to miss him.

A long line of men are queuing to get into Heaven when a loud roar comes from the front. "Why are they cheering?" asks a man at the back. A voice replies: "They're not counting adultery!"

I nearly had an affair with Amanda Lynn, but there were strings attached.

After years of suspicion, I'm now convinced my wife is having an affair. We've moved 300 miles away, but we've still got the same window cleaner!

Do infants enjoy infancy as much as adults enjoy adultery?

Mike: "I emailed my wife to say I'd be home early, but when I walked in the house I found her in bed with another man. Why? Why?"
Marty: "Maybe she didn't read your email."

What's the most vulnerable part of a cheating man?
His wallet.

A new survey says people who live in the countryside are more likely to cheat on their partners. It comes to something when you can't even trust your own family. *Frank Skinner*

My wife's been seeing a psychiatrist – and a butcher, a postman, a builder and a policeman.

My wife caught me in bed with her sister. Well, she said she wanted a surprise for her birthday.

I'm so angry! I found out today that both my wife and my girlfriend have been cheating on me.

Husband to wife: "You haven't nagged me all evening, honey. Is there someone else?"

Why did the unfaithful husband fall over?
He was on a guilt trip.

Coming home early from work, I saw a guy jogging naked. I said: "Why are you doing that?" He said: "Because you've come home early."

ADVERTISING

ADVERTISING

Advertising is the art of making whole lies out of half-truths.

Advertising makes you think you've longed all your life for something you've never even heard of before.

I saw a subliminal advert on TV for a deodorant – but it only keeps you dry for a second.

Advertising certainly brings quick results. Last week I advertised for a night-watchman, and that same night my safe was robbed.

An optimist says: "The glass is half-full." A pessimist says: "The glass is half-empty." A marketing consultant says: "Your glass needs re-sizing."

How can a product be "new and improved"? If it's new, there has never been anything before it; if it's an improvement, there must have been something before it!

ADVICE

When someone hits you in the face, turn the other cheek. That way the swelling is even.

If you're riding ahead of the herd, take a look back every now and then just to make sure the herd is still there.

I'm a bomb technician. If you see me running, try to keep up.

Don't sweat the petty things and don't pet the sweaty things.

Smile – it makes people wonder what you're thinking.

If Plan A doesn't work, the alphabet has 25 more letters, so keep calm.

Never test the depth of the water with both feet.

Don't judge someone until you have walked a mile in their shoes. Then they are a mile away and you have their shoes.

Never argue with a spouse who is packing your parachute.

Get the facts first – you can distort them later.

Don't hate yourself in the morning – sleep till noon.

Plan to be more spontaneous.

No problem is so big and complicated that you can't run away from it.

Never get stuck behind the Devil in a Post Office queue, for the Devil can take many forms.

Always remember to pillage *before* you burn.

Don't waste money on expensive binoculars. Simply stand closer to what you want to see.

Eat, drink and be merry, for tomorrow they may cancel your credit card.

Take an interest in your husband's activities: hire a detective.

When in doubt, mumble; when in trouble, delegate.

Never ask a two-year-old to hold a tomato.

There are two things you should avoid approaching from the rear – horses and restaurants.

If you can't convince them, confuse them.

If you're moving house, first put your goldfish and its bowl in the freezer to avoid transport spillage.

Advice is free; the right answer will cost plenty.

Don't ignore the tramp who asks you for 20 pence for a cup of tea. Give it to him, then follow him and find out where he gets a cup of tea for 20 pence.

See no evil, hear no evil, date no evil.

Take my advice; I don't use it anyway.

When embarking on an Amazon expedition, choose your companions carefully – you may have to eat them.

If you can't dazzle them with brilliance, baffle them with bullshit.

Take everything in moderation, including moderation.

Never underestimate the power of stupid people in large groups.

When you do a good deed, get a receipt – in case Heaven is like the tax office.

Keep a firm grip on reality so you can strangle it at any time.

Always speak well of your enemies – after all, you made them.

Dig where the gold is, unless you need the exercise.

He who lives in a glass house shouldn't invite him who is without sin over for dinner.

Always go the extra mile – especially if what you want is a mile away.

If you are asked to join a parade, don't march behind the elephants.

Don't justify sin. Just defy sin.

Always keep your words soft and sweet in case you have to eat them.

If you start up a summer camp to help Jewish kids with Attention Deficit Disorder, don't call it Concentration Camp.

Don't bite your nails, especially if you're a carpenter.

Never moon a werewolf.

Don't trust abductees. They get carried away sometimes.

If flattery gets you nowhere, try bribery.

Don't do anything that you're not prepared to explain to a paramedic.

My wife gives sound advice, although most of it tends to be sound rather than advice.

My granddad gave me some sound advice on his deathbed. "It's worth spending money on good speakers," he told me.

When tempted to fight fire with fire, bear in mind that the Fire Department usually uses water.

Never get in line at the bank behind someone wearing a ski mask.

Look out for number one, and don't step in number two.

Rely on the rabbit's foot if you must, but remember – it didn't work for the rabbit.

Drink till she's cute, but stop before the wedding.

Don't dye your hair if you want to trace your roots.

Be careful of your thoughts: they may become words at any moment.

Don't kick a man when he's down unless you're absolutely certain he won't get back up.

Never buy a DVD in the street from someone who is out of breath.

Be careful – the toes you step on today may be connected to the ass you have to kiss tomorrow.

Never knock on Death's door. Ring the doorbell and run – he hates that.

If you can't beat them, arrange to have them beaten.

Never hit a man with glasses – hit him with a baseball bat.

Sometimes the best helping hand you can give is a good, firm push.

Don't get into a pissing contest with a skunk.

Whatever you do, always give 100 per cent – unless you're donating blood.

AGILITY

Why did the arthritic contortionist claim state benefits?
Because he could no longer make ends meet.

I asked the gym instructor to teach me to do the splits. He said: "How flexible are you?" I said: "I can't do Tuesdays." *Tim Vine*

I'd give my right arm to be ambidextrous.

My mother obviously thought I was a contortionist because she used to say to me: "Look at the dirt on the back of your neck!"

My friend's a professional contortionist who got kicked out of his apartment for not paying his rent. He's been living out of a suitcase ever since.

Even before his accident, Captain Hook was all fingers and thumbs.

I was delighted to get a job as a circus acrobat. I really landed on my feet.

Acrobats don't like winter pepper; they prefer summer salt.

I didn't know my wife was a gymnast until she flipped when she caught me with her sister.

Is it easy to get a job as a contortionist?
No, you have to bend over backwards.

AIRPLANES

I wanted to sue the airline over the damage to my luggage, but my lawyer said I didn't have much of a case.

Passenger: "Do these types of plane crash often?"
Flight attendant: "No, only once."

Why did kamikaze pilots wear helmets?

If you board a plane and see a friend of yours named Jack, whatever you do, don't call out: "Hi, Jack."

Pilot: "Give me a rough time-check."
Tower: "It's Tuesday, sir."

Pilot: "Please call me a fuel truck."
Tower: "You are a fuel truck."

Tower: "Please state your height and position."
Pilot: "Six-foot-one and sitting."

Ground control: "Bear to the left, disabled aircraft on the right."
Pilot: "I see the disabled aircraft, but I can't see the bear."

A friend of mine is a pilot. Every time he gets in his car, he waits 45 minutes before pulling out of his driveway. *Steven Wright*

Female radar controller: "Can I turn you on at seven miles?"
Pilot: "Madam, you can try."

Passenger: "How high will you get?"
Pilot: "I don't do drugs, Madam."

I don't want to fly Virgin. Who'd want to fly an airline that doesn't go all the way?

Old lady: "I've never flown before. You will bring me down safely, won't you?"
Pilot: "All I can say, ma'am, is that I've never left anyone up there yet."

I remember when I joined the Mile High Club. I was flying solo at the time, but I think it still counts.

You know you're flying with a bad airline when the plane has an outside toilet.

You know you're flying with a bad airline when before take-off the passengers get together and elect a pilot.

You know you're flying with a bad airline when before take-off the flight attendant asks you to fasten your Velcro.

You know you're flying with a bad airline when there's a resident chaplain on board.

What's the purpose of an airplane propeller?
To keep the pilot cool; if you don't believe me, watch him sweat when it stops!

What's the definition of skyjacking?
A hand job at 35,000 feet.

Why do they sell luggage in shops at airports? Who the hell forgets their suitcase?!

Stewardess: "In the event of a water landing, your seat cushion may be used as a flotation device."
Passenger: "If the plane can't fly, why should I believe the seat can float?"

I always sit in the tail end of a plane, because you never hear of a plane backing into a mountain. *Tommy Cooper*

During his air test, a young pilot flew through a rainbow. He passed with flying colours.

Did you hear about the man who got air-sick just from licking an air-mail stamp?

The boss of Ryanair walks into a bar and sees a sign: "Guinness, $2 a pint." Thinking this is cheap, he asks for a pint, and the bartender says wryly: "Would you like a glass with that?"

A vulture gets on a plane, carrying two dead raccoons. The flight attendant says: "Sorry, sir, only one carrion allowed per passenger."

One good thing about airline food: at least they're considerate enough to give you only small portions.

I worry about mid-air collisions, especially when I realize the movie I'm watching is on another plane.

Mike: "I'd hate to be up there in a plane."
Marty: "I'd hate to be up there without one."

What did the kamikaze pilot instructor say to his students?
"Watch closely. I'm only going to do this once."

Pilots are people who talk about women when they're flying, and about flying when they're with women.

I want to make a complaint about the sushi bar at Gatwick Airport. The portions on the conveyor belt are too big and they taste very luggagey.
Milton Jones

What did Geronimo yell when he jumped out of the airplane?
"Meeeeee!"

If a stealth bomber crashes in a forest, does it make a sound?

A light airplane pilot and co-pilot are attempting their first loop-the-loop. One says: "Do you think we'll fall out?" "Of course not," says the other. "We've been friends for years."

Passenger: "This flight sure is bumpy."
Flight attendant: "Sir, we haven't left the runway yet!"

How do you know when you're halfway through a date with a pilot?
When he says: "That's enough about flying. Let's talk about me."

Small boy: "Wow! You're a pilot? That must be exciting!"
Pilot: "Not if I do it right."

A husband suspects his wife is having an affair with a pilot. She repeatedly denies it, saying: "I've told you once, I've told you twice, I've told you a thousand times, negative on the affair."

You know you're flying a Cessna when you have a bird strike – from behind.

The airlines are getting really security-conscious. You can still fly, but they won't tell you where you're going. *Bob Hope*

I'm not afraid of flying. I am, however, afraid of being 35,000 feet in the air and suddenly *not* flying.

What is the ideal flight-deck complement for a modern airplane?
A captain, a co-pilot and a dog. The dog is there to bite the captain if he tries to touch the controls, and the co-pilot is there to feed the dog.

If flying is so safe, why do they call the airport the terminal?

Any landing you can walk away from is a good one.

ALCOHOL

Alcohol is not the answer – it just makes you forget the question.

A new club has opened offering as much as you can drink all night for just under $20. So tonight I'm going to party like it's $19.99.

Whisky is a great drink. It makes you see double and feel single.

Why did God invent alcohol?
So fat chicks can get laid too.

Many things can be preserved in alcohol. Dignity is not one of them.

Ever have trouble opening a bottle of champagne? My advice: hit it with a ship. I've seen people do that. It works. ***Russell Kane***

Scientists have located the gene for alcoholism. They found it at a party, talking way too loud.

I don't have a drinking addiction: I have a drinking dedication.

Alcoholism is the only disease that tries to convince you that you don't have it.

Why is it called Alcoholics Anonymous when the first thing you do is stand up and announce your name?

I never drink unless I'm alone or with somebody.

Personal ad: "Alcoholic man seeks similar woman for a drink or two, maybe more."

It's easy to quit booze: I've done it dozens of times.

Alcohol is a perfect solvent. It dissolves marriages, families and careers.

I asked my girlfriend what she'd like to drink. She said: "I guess I'll have champagne." I said: "Guess again."

I'm not a hard drinker – I actually find it very easy.

I've been on that new whisky diet. I lost three days last week.

Alcohol *does* make you more attractive to the opposite sex – after they've drunk enough of it.

I'm the only one in my family who drinks, which is great because to me they're all potential liver donors.

There's a new club called the AA-AA. It's for people who are being driven to drink.

Dear Alcohol, we had a deal where you would make me funnier, smarter and a better dancer. I saw the video. We need to talk.

I asked my girlfriend if she fancied drinking a yard of vodka. I knew it was a long shot . . .

Alcohol may be slow poison, but who's in a hurry?

WARNING: The consumption of alcohol may cause you to think you can sing.

WARNING: The consumption of alcohol may cause you to roll over in the morning and see something really scary.

WARNING: The consumption of alcohol may make you think you're whispering when you're not.

WARNING: The consumption of alcohol may lead you to believe that ex-lovers are keen to hear from you at three o'clock in the morning.

WARNING: The consumption of alcohol may make you think you can converse with members of the opposite sex without spitting.

WARNING: The consumption of alcohol may cause you to tell your friends over and over again that you love them.

WARNING: The consumption of alcohol may lead you to believe that people are laughing *with* you.

I like a drink as much as the next man – unless the next man's Charlie Sheen.

The only time I ever said no to a drink was when I misunderstood the question.

We call my granddad the exorcist, because every time he visits he rids the house of spirits.

I just drank some WKD with ice in it. It was wicked.

I just rang Alcohol Concern. I told them I was worried I didn't have enough beer in the fridge. They're quite rude, aren't they?

AMBITION

Ambition is a poor excuse for not having enough sense to be lazy.

I yearn for a better tomorrow where chickens can cross the road without being questioned about their motives.

I'd kill for a Nobel Peace Prize.

Someone once said to me: 'You'll never make it as an astronaut." I told him to watch this space.

My ambition is to go to the four corners of the earth planting horse chestnuts. It's my plan to conker the world.

I'll tell you what's holding me back – my spine.

My burning ambition is to be an arsonist.

My ambition is to marry a rich girl who is too proud to let her husband work.

AMERICAN FOOTBALL

Why did the useless American football team change their name to the Opossums?
Because they play dead at home and get killed on the road.

American football is a lot like the average American – it's a great achievement to move 10 yards forward.

I would have played football, but I have an intestinal problem – no guts.

As the football coach was walking on the field alongside the band, a majorette threw her baton in the air and dropped it. A fan yelled: "I see you coach the band, too."

How is the Florida State football team like a Florida State cheerleader?
They both suck for four quarters.

American football is a game where 22 players run around for two hours while 50,000 people who really need the exercise sit in the stands and watch them.

You know that your job as coach is in trouble when at half-time the marching band lines up in the shape of a noose.

American football is rugby after a visit from a Health and Safety inspector.

Why did God invent football?
So that married men could have some form of physical contact in their lives.

Shoulder pads are designed to make footballers look as fearsome as female executives.

Girl: "What position does your brother play in the school football team?"
Boy: "I think he's one of the drawbacks."

Why does the running back run forward?

Did you hear about the fan who lost $50 on a TV football play? He lost another $50 on the instant replay.

How could you tell that the footballer was on steroids?
His IQ and neck size were the same number.

We play in a dome stadium. We prefer to kick with the air-conditioning at our backs.

What's the most brutal thing about American football?
The price of the tickets.

After missing his attempt at a field goal, the place kicker was so angry he could have kicked himself – but he'd probably have missed that, too.

Why do Montana football stadiums have Astroturf?
To stop the cheerleaders grazing.

Husband to wife: "Hey, honey, do you have anything you want to say before the football season starts?"

AMISH

What do you call an Amish guy with his hand up a horse's butt?
A mechanic.

What goes Clip, Clop, Clip, Clop, Bang, Bang, Clip, Clop, Clip, Clop?
An Amish drive-by shooting.

What does a rebellious Amish teenager say?
"Talk to the hand 'cos the beard ain't listening."

What do they say at an Amish celebration?
"Tonight we're going to party like it's 1699."

Sign behind an Amish carriage: "Energy-efficient vehicle. Runs on grass and oats. CAUTION! Avoid exhaust."

You know your Amish child is going off the rails when he sometimes stays in bed until after 5 a.m.

You know your Amish child is going off the rails when you find his secret stash of coloured socks.

You know your Amish child is going off the rails when his name is Jebediah, but he goes by the name "Jeb Daddy".

You know your Amish child is going off the rails when in his drawer you find pictures of women without bonnets.

You know your Amish child is going off the rails when, in response, to criticism, he yells: "Thou sucketh!"

You know your Amish child is going off the rails when he starts wearing his big black hat backwards.

AMUSEMENT PARKS

What adults like most about roller coasters is being able to sit down for two minutes after standing in line for two hours.

The key to having fun at an amusement park is to bet whether the kids will get sick on the rides or on the food.

Another way to have fun is to bring nuts and bolts with you and then show them to the person sitting next to you once the ride has begun.

I was on this fairground ride, and one minute I was laughing and the next I was crying. It was an emotional roller coaster. *Tim Vine*

While doing community service at a funfair, I stole one of those distorted mirrors. I hope it doesn't reflect badly on me.

I had a go on one of those fairground stalls where you shoot ducks over and win a prize. I found that if you point the gun at the guy who's running the stall, you get all the prizes.

I went to an invisible fairground last week, but I didn't think it was very good. I couldn't see the attraction.

ANGER

My window cleaner was banging on my window shouting and swearing. I thought to myself: He's lost his rag.

Never go to bed angry. Stay awake and plot your revenge.

If your dad is angry with you and asks, "Do I look stupid?" don't answer him.

Did you hear about the new designer drug that makes you angry? It's all the rage.

Jackie: "I never get angry with my husband. Instead I clean the toilet bowl."
Jill: "How does that help?"
Jackie: "I use his toothbrush."

ANIMALS

Apparently animals make different sounds in different languages. For example, in Korea a dog makes a sizzling sound.

What should you do if you see an endangered animal eating an endangered plant?

What did the polar bears say when they saw tourists in sleeping bags?
"Mmmm, sandwiches!"

What's a zebra?
26 sizes larger than an A bra.

Two cows in a field – which one's on holiday?
The one with the wee calf.

What do you get virgin wool from?
Ugly sheep.

I phoned the spiritual leader of Tibet, and he sent me a kind of goat with a long neck. It turned out I'd phoned dial a llama. *Milton Jones*

What did the doe say as she came running out of the trees?
"That's the last time I do that for two bucks."

What does a moose take for indigestion?
Elkaseltzer.

So it turns out that if you bang two halves of a horse together, it doesn't make the sound of a coconut.

Why did the hedgehog cross the road?
To see his flat mate.

Why did the hedgehog cross the road a second time?
To pick up his squash partner.

Why did the hedgehog cross the road a third time?
To show his wife he had guts.

What are two hedgehogs called?
A prickly pair.

What do you get if you insert human DNA into a goat?
Banned from the petting zoo.

What do you call the king of the jungle in a designer outfit?
A dandy lion.

What does a lion say before going out hunting with the other lions?
"Let us prey."

LIZARD . . . lizard . . . liz . . . Is there a gecko in here? – *Tim Vine*

What four animals does a woman like to have in her house?
A tiger in bed, a mink in her closet, a jaguar in her garage, and a jackass to pay for it all.

What do you get if you cross a pig with a dinosaur?
Jurassic Pork.

Squirrels: nature's speed bumps.

I call my horse Treacle because he's got golden stirrups.

What's the dumbest animal in the jungle?
The polar bear.

What did the mouse say as he screwed the female elephant?
"Suffer, bitch!"

Why do tigers have stripes?
So they won't be spotted.

How do you make a walrus commit suicide?
Point at its chest and say, "What's that?"

How do you stop a bull from charging?
Take away his credit card.

What do you get if you cross a hedgehog with a giraffe?
A 10-foot-tall toothbrush.

If the world were a logical place, men would be the ones who ride horses sidesaddle.

Two cows in a field. One says: "Aren't you worried about mad-cow disease?" The other replies: "Not me. I'm a rabbit."

What's a zebra?
A horse behind bars.

What is a Mole?
A Vole on crutches.

How do you tell a male rhino from a female rhino?
The male's the one with the remote.

If a donkey is an ass and a sheep is a ram, how come a ram in the ass is a goose?

How does a pig write home?
With a pig pen.

I'm passionate about preserving endangered animals. You should taste my panda jam.

Why are lemmings often wrong?
Because they are always jumping to conclusions.

Why did the mother kangaroo jump up and down in pain?
She caught the kids smoking in bed.

Hedgehogs: why can't they just share the hedge? *Dan Antopolski*

Do sheep count people when they go to sleep?

How do you count a herd of cattle?
With a cowculator.

A female rabbit was irritable after being bullied by some of the field's larger residents. "Don't worry about her," said one male rabbit to another. "She's just having a bad hare day."

What do you get if you cross a motorway with a flock of sheep?
A flock of dead sheep.

I've just bought a shire horse – as if my other horse wasn't shy enough.

What do you get when three giraffes collide?
A giraffic jam.

How do you get five donkeys on a fire engine?
Two in the front, two in the back, and one on the roof going "Ee-aw-ee-aw-ee-aw . . ."

How do you circumcise a whale?
Send in four skin divers.

Two moles are mating underground. Afterwards, the male says to the female: "Well, did the earth move for you?"

Why do mother kangaroos hate rainy days?
Because then the kids have to play inside.

What do you call a pig with three eyes?
A piiig.

Did you hear about the hyena that jumped into a pot of boiling water with some onions and made a laughing stock of himself?

Does distressed leather come from very tense cows?

Zebra: "Let's swap roles for a while." Lion: "OK. I'm game."

What does a bull do to stay warm on a cold day?
He goes into the barn and slips into a Jersey.

Why did the World Wildlife Fund choose the giant panda as their symbol?
Because they didn't have a colour printer.

People can't work out why giant panda couples only have sex once a year. It's because they're married. *Frank Skinner*

What have twelve legs, six eyes, three tails and can't see?
Three blind mice.

First rhinoceros: "Hi, my name's Neil."
Second rhinoceros: "Not the rhino Neil?!"

Do pigs have pen pals?

How do you save a drowning mouse?
Give it mouse-to-mouse resuscitation.

What do you get if you sit under a cow?
A pat on the head.

How do you hire a horse?
Stand it on four bricks.

What do you get when you cross an alligator and a railroad track?
Three pieces of alligator.

Rhino poaching is a real problem, which is why I prefer mine grilled.

What animal has four wooden legs?
A timber wolf.

I saw a chameleon today, so I guess it's safe to say it wasn't a very good chameleon.

Did you hear about the cannibal lion? He had to swallow his pride.

I think unicorns are just horses that are not very adept at eating ice cream cones.

What do you call a sheep with no legs?
A cloud.

I went to the office of an animal welfare charity. It was tiny. You couldn't swing a cat in there. *Tim Vine*

What has horns and walks through walls?
Casper the friendly goat.

Some crocodiles can grow up to 14 feet, but usually they only have four.

What would you get if you crossed a mole with a porcupine?
A tunnel that leaks.

I've got pony spittle all down my left arm – and that's straight from the horse's mouth!

What happens to cows during earthquakes?
They give milk shakes.

What do you call a cow with two legs?
Lean beef.

What do you call a cow with no legs?
Ground beef.

Did you hear about the exhausted kangaroo? He was out of bounds.

Why are giraffes slow to apologize?
Because it takes them a long time to swallow their pride.

As a donkey leaves his stable, he trips over a fallen tree branch. Another donkey laughs: "Hee haw hee haw he always does that!"

How do you make a tortoise fast?
Don't feed him.

I love defenceless animals, especially in gravy.

One rat says to another rat: "I've got this psychologist well trained. Every time I ring this bell, he brings me food."

What do you get if you cross a Frisbee with a cow?
Skimmed milk.

How do you know that milking a cow is easy?
Because any jerk can do it.

Why is a giraffe's neck so long?
Because its feet smell.

What did one horse say to the other?
"Any friend of yours is a palomino."

An iguana can stay under water for 28 minutes. Or longer, if you don't mind it dying. *Jimmy Carr*

What do you call a donkey with three legs?
A wonkey.

What do you call a donkey with three legs and one eye?
A winky wonkey.

What do you call a donkey with three legs and one eye who can play the piano?
A honky tonky winky wonkey.

What has two humps and is found at the South Pole?
A camel with a faulty GPS.

Cows would live longer if they weren't made of steak and leather jackets.

What's the worst thing that can happen to a sleeping bat?
Diarrhoea.

Do pigs use soap or is that just hogwash?

I don't know why pandas have such difficulty mating. It's all in front of them in black and white.

A young camel walks into his parents' room at 3 a.m. and asks for a glass of water. "Another one?" says his father. "That's the second glass this month!"

What's the difference between a buffalo and a bison?
You can't wash your hands in a buffalo.

What do you call a deer with no eyes?
No eye deer.

What do you call a deer with no eyes and no legs?
Still no eye deer.

What do you call a deer with 20/20 vision?
Good eye deer.

Is a distorted tortoise just an oise?

What did all the other animals say when wildebeest became extinct?
"That is the end of the gnus."

Why don't sheep shrink when it rains?

Two male camels watch a female camel walk past. "Look at her!" says one. "Do you think she's had her humps enhanced?"

What animals can't you trust?
Hippocrites.

Do you know how long cows should be milked?
The same as short ones.

What's a bear's favourite pasta?
Tagliateddy.

A pig is an amazing animal. Feed it an apple and it makes bacon. *Jim Gaffigan*

Why don't giraffes do drugs?
Because they're naturally high.

Two cows are standing in a field. One goes, "Mooooo." "Damn!" says the other. "I was going to say that!"

What's the only animal with an asshole in the middle of its back?
A police horse.

Two giraffes were in a race: it was neck and neck.

What did the father buffalo say when he left the baby buffalo? "Bison."

ARCHAEOLOGY

How do you annoy a female archaeologist?
Give her a used tampon and ask her what period it came from.

Why was the archaeologist depressed?
His career was in ruins.

Archaeologists have discovered a toilet which they think was constructed between 500 and 400 BC. Even back then plumbers took their time.

Archaeology is the science that proves you can't keep a good man down.

Ever since my smart-ass brother got his archaeology degree, all he's done is have a dig.

Why aren't archaeologists choosy about who they ask out?
Because they will date anything.

ARGUMENTS

I had a row with my girlfriend last night, and she accused me of being childish. What does she know? She's just a stinky poo face!

In an argument, the woman always has the last word. Anything a man says after that is the beginning of a new argument.

For my birthday, my wife let me do something I'd always dreamt of doing – she let me win an argument.

What did Eve say to Adam during their first argument?
"Tell me straight, Adam, is there another woman?"

My wife kept going on and on about what she should use the empty drawer for. Eventually I told her to put a sock in it.

My wife and I were fighting like hammer and tongs. She won. She had the hammer.

Following a row with his wife, a husband tried to make the peace. He suggested: "Why don't you meet me halfway on this? I'll admit you're wrong if you admit I'm right."

I had an argument with my wife, which ended with me pouring a Knickerbocker Glory over her. Sweet revenge.

My wife and I had words, but I didn't get to use mine.

An argument is a discussion where two people try to get the last word in first.

I tried to compliment my wife but it ended in an argument. How was I to know she wasn't celebrating Movember?

There are two theories about arguing with a woman. Neither works.

My wife started going on about the fillings of duvets and pillows. I said: "I've told you before, don't talk down to me."

In all the years we've been married, my wife and I have never had an argument serious enough to consider divorce; murder, yes, but divorce, never.

Marriage counsellor: "Why did you hit your wife with a chair?"
Husband: "I couldn't lift the table."

My friend spent a week away on an anger management course. Actually the course only lasted two days, but he spent the rest of the time arguing with them about the fee.

Did you hear about the row between two topless models? It was a storm in a D-cup.

I never argue with my wife. I might win, and then there'd be a proper row.

Any argument which begins with "What do you mean by that?" will not end with "Now I know what you mean by that".

I got into an argument with an agoraphobic. I said: "Do you want to take this outside?"

"I don't want to talk about it" is woman code for "I want to argue about this for a week".

I was teasing my wife about her terrible knitting when she suddenly stabbed me in the foot. I didn't expect her to get the needle.

Never argue with a woman who's tired – or rested.

The worst moment in a heated argument is when you announce triumphantly, "And another thing" . . . and then your mind goes blank.

We've been married 14 years and we've only had one quarrel. It started on our wedding day, and hasn't ended yet.

Mike: "Why do you and your wife fight all the time?"
Marty: "I don't know. She never tells me."

My girlfriend said we would have less arguments if I wasn't so pedantic. I said: "Fewer arguments . . ."

ARMY

I used to be in the army, and one day the sergeant said to me: "What does 'surrender' mean?" I said: "I give up!"

Join the army, meet interesting people, kill them.

Why are soldiers so tired on 1 April?
Because they just had a 31-day March.

Remember: mines are equal opportunity weapons.

During the war, my nan was an army midwife. She was in C-section.

Never trust a private with a loaded weapon or an officer with a map.

Never share a fox hole with anyone braver than you.

In the pub I met a former soldier who has a steel plate in his head and a prosthetic leg made from aluminium and titanium. He has become both a friend and an alloy.

Without the firing pin, the grenade is not your friend.

Did you hear about the British World War Two soldier in France who thought a bidet was two days before D-Day?

Why did the soldier faint?
It was his passing-out parade.

An officer asks: "Who likes music?" Two soldiers step forward. "Very well," says the officer. "I've bought a piano. Take it to my apartment on the fifth floor."

Why was the bullying sergeant kicked out of the Marines?
Because he was rotten to the corps.

My cousin William didn't want to join the army because he'd heard that the enemy would often fire at will.

Sergeant: "You, you and you, panic. The rest of you, come with me."

I joined the Foreign Legion to forget my wife. Unfortunately the sergeant-major looked just like her.

The sergeant-major yelled: "Private Philpott, I didn't see you at camouflage training this morning!" Philpott replied: "Thank you, sir."

The army made a man out of my neighbour. They paid for the operation and everything.

What do you get if you cross a soldier and a chilli?
A pepperarmy.

A new recruit waits for his food in the battalion dining room. He asks a sergeant: "Is there a choice?" "Sure," says the sergeant. "You can eat it or not."

Army food is very tasty. I got out of the army 15 years ago and I can still taste it.

How long was I in the army?
Five foot eleven. *Spike Milligan*

What has an IQ of 42?
40 Marines plus their lieutenant.

How are military smells graded?
According to rank.

I signed up to a training programme that promised to turn me into a soldier. I ended up with egg on my face.

A knight walked into a blacksmith's shop. The blacksmith said: "You've got mail."

When a knight in armour was killed in battle, what words did they put on his gravestone?
Rust in peace.

Why is being in the army like having sex?
The closer you get to discharge, the better you feel.

Did you hear about the army pastry chef who desserted?

Did you hear about the military artist? He kept drawing enemy fire.

ART

I've finally decided to retire after a long career as a graffiti artist. To be honest, the writing's been on the wall for some time.

I visited the Louvre last week as a tourist. I asked, "Is it OK to take a picture?" "Yes," they said, so I did – and I must say the *Mona Lisa* looks pretty impressive on my living-room wall.

What's the title of the wooden sculpture of the Chinese Emperor Chung?
Chung in Teak.

An artist and his model are kissing on the sofa when he hears the front door open. "Oh, no, it's my wife!" he exclaims. "Quick! Get your clothes off!"

Van Gogh was notoriously vague. Whatever you said to him went in one ear and out the same ear.

Rembrandt painted 700 pictures and Americans have all 7,000 of them.

A modern artist is one who throws paint on a canvas, wipes it off with a cloth and sells the cloth.

They couldn't find the artist so they hung the picture.

Son: "What do you think about my plan to become a professional artist?"
Father: "Well, it looks good on paper."

Did you hear about the two small boys who found themselves in a modern-art gallery? "Quick!" said one. "Run, before they say we did it!"

I painted my wife in oils. Now she looks like a sardine.

Why did the artist stick a stamp on his forehead?
He was a post-impressionist.

As a painter, I'm proud to say that some of my work is on show in the National Gallery. I did the skirting boards.

What's the difference between art and pornography?
An Arts Council grant.

Why was the art dealer broke?
He didn't have any Monet.

Did you hear about the man who hanged himself in a modern-art gallery? It was three weeks before anyone noticed.

Modern art is like trying to follow the plot in a bowl of alphabet soup.

There's a simple rule with modern art. If it hangs on the wall, it must be a painting; if you can walk around it, it must be a sculpture.

The best way to tell if a modern painting is completed is to touch it. If the paint is dry, it's finished.

The Mona Lisa: not exactly an oil painting, is she?

A foolproof method of sculpting an elephant: you get a huge block of marble, then you chip away everything that doesn't look like an elephant.

My girlfriend is like a fine impressionist painting – best appreciated at a distance.

He was such a lousy artist it was a wonder he could draw breath.

Salvador Dalí for Coca-Cola: it's surreal thing.

You must be an artist if the highlights in your hair are from your palette, not Clairol.

You must be an artist if the only piece of new furniture in your home is a $2,000 easel.

You must be an artist if you butter your toast with your fingers just to feel its texture.

You must be an artist if you are more concerned about the colour of your car than its fuel consumption.

You must be an artist if you can't find a nice outfit for your date because everything has paint smears on.

You must be an artist if you do judge a book by its cover.

You must be an artist if you buy expensive brushes, but have nothing to do your hair with.

You must be an artist if your family takes out a life insurance plan on you for less than $5,000.

You must be an artist if there are Prussian Blue fingerprints on your phone.

You must be an artist if you know what shade of green the lichen on the trees is.

Mother: "The picture of the horse is good, but where's the wagon?"
Child: "Oh, the horse will draw that."

AUCTION

An auction is a place where, if you aren't careful, you'll get something for nodding.

Auctioneers are proof that white guys could rap if they tried hard enough.

An auctioneer has no friends, only nodding acquaintances.

I'm currently at auction bidding for a house with a lengthy corridor. I'm in it for the long hall.

AUSTRALIANS

An Australian gentleman is someone who offers to light his girlfriend's farts before lighting his own.

An Australian gentleman is someone who gets out of the bath to pee in the sink.

What does an Australian say by way of foreplay?
"Brace yourself, Sheila!"

Why do so many Australian men suffer from premature ejaculation?
Because they have to rush back to the pub to tell their mates what happened.

Why do Australian men wear shorts?
To keep a cool mind.

An increased terrorism threat has forced Australia to raise its security level from "No worries, mate" to "We may need to cancel the barbie".

An Englishman wants to emigrate to Australia. The emigration official asks: "Do you have a criminal record?" "No," says the Englishman. "Do I need one?"

The boomerang is Australia's biggest export . . . and then import.

Australian man: "Wanna fuck?"
Australian woman: "Looks like you talked me into it, you sweet-talking bastard!"

When Australia got their first female Prime Minister, many experts were predicting that their economy would crash . . . into the back of another economy.

What's the definition of an Australian aristocrat?
Someone who can trace his ancestry back to his father.

Did you hear about the gay Australian? He left his wife and went to Sydney.

AUTOMOBILES

Women drivers – the reason people look both ways when crossing a one-way street.

Do women shake the petrol pump after filling up their car or is it just a man thing?

What did the motorist say to the one-legged hitchhiker?
"Hop in."

Multi-storey car parks: they work on so many levels.

Did you hear about the guy who had a personalized number plate BAA BAA? He had a black jeep.

I hate getting into the car after my wife has used it because I have to put everything back where it was before – like the mirror, the seat, the airbag . . .

You never really learn to swear until you learn to drive.

What should you do if a bird shits on your car?
Don't ask her out again.

I was stopped for doing 53 in a 35 m.p.h. zone. I told the police I had dyslexia.

Drive carefully – it's not only cars that can be recalled by their maker.

Why don't they teach driver's education and sex education on the same day in Arab countries?
They don't want to wear out the camel.

I bought a new Japanese car. I turned on the radio, but I didn't understand a word they were saying. ***Rodney Dangerfield***

Have you noticed, no matter how loud car alarms are, they never seem to wake up?

My driving instructor said I just wasn't getting any better at tackling roundabouts. He said it felt like we were going round in circles.

The other day I got pulled over for speeding. Apparently "Because you were chasing me" isn't a valid reason.

Did you hear about the guy who passed a Ferrari? He couldn't get the toilet seat down for weeks.

I always keep emergency flares in my car. You never know when you're going to be invited to a seventies disco.

My friend gets the shakes whenever he tries to park his car. I think he could be suffering from parking zones disease.

When two cars are double-parked, how can you tell which one was parked by a woman?
Hers is the one on top.

I locked my coat hanger in the car. Good thing I had a key.

Three weeks ago, my wife learnt how to drive. Last week she learnt how to aim it.

How did the driver get a puncture?
He didn't see the fork in the road.

My old car was such a wreck that it was only the Garfield on the side window that was holding it together.

How do we know you can fit 12 people into a Honda car?
Because in the Bible it says all the disciples were in one Accord.

I recently designed a new car without a steering wheel. Quite straight forward really.

Did you hear about the wooden car that had wooden wheels and a wooden engine? It wooden start.

My wife is a very careful driver. She always slows down when passing a red light.

I've figured how to avoid getting parking tickets. I've taken the windshield wipers off my car.

I pulled my wife bleeding from the wrecked car as she screamed and pleaded for me to let her have one more shot at parking it.

The garage said they couldn't repair my brakes, so they just made the horn louder.

I finally confused my GPS lady. She said: "In 200 yards stop and ask for directions."

I failed my driving test. The examiner asked: "What do you do at a red light?" I said: "I usually check my emails."

My wife's parking is unparalleled.

Husband: "Could you step out and tell me if my indicator light is working?"
Wife: "OK. Yes . . . no . . . yes . . . no . . . yes . . . no . . ."

As I left for work this morning, I was annoyed to find my car being boxed in. I had to admire the guy's carpentry skills though.

For my daughter's first day at school, I took her in our old banger. It looks as if I was lucky to avoid the hazardous off-road terrain the other parents obviously had to cross in their vehicles.

Somebody complimented me on my driving today. They left a note on the windscreen. It said: "Parking Fine". **Tommy Cooper**

Traffic cop: "I'm going to have to report you, sir. You were doing 85 m.p.h."
Motorist: "Nonsense. I've only been in the car 10 minutes."

Did you hear about the device that makes cars go 90 per cent quieter? It fits right over her mouth.

If you don't like the way women drive, get off the pavement!

The first time my nephew rode in a limousine, he got a bit silly and started mooning out of the window. Thankfully he stopped when he was told he was upsetting the other mourners.

Driving along a flooded road, a woman spots a man's head sticking out of a vast puddle. "Would you like a lift?" she asks. "No, it's OK," he replies. "I'm on my bike."

I'd describe my style of driving as "slap-dash", which I think sounds nicer than "hit-and-run".

My sister has a lifesaving tool in her car. It's designed to cut through a seat belt if she gets trapped in the car. She keeps it in the trunk.

I've got a stereo system in my car – my wife at the front and her mother at the back.

Traffic cop: "Didn't you see the 30 m.p.h. sign?"
Driver: "No, officer, I was going too fast to see it."

I bought a Swiss car. It runs like clockwork, but I can't figure how to get it out of neutral.

If you lined up all the cars in the world end-to-end, some idiot would still try to pass them.

Husband: "Why are there so many dents on the driver's side of your car?"
Wife: "I think the brakes must be bad on that side."

I call my car "Flattery" because it gets me nowhere.

What is a pedestrian?
A motorist with two or more children of driving age.

The great thing about parallel parking is that the worse you are at it, the more people you have rooting for you.

I picked up a hitchhiker. You've got to when you hit them. *Emo Philips*

Did you hear about the driver with piles who suffered from 'roid rage?

Why is the time of day with the slowest traffic called rush hour?

My driving instructor told me: "Never brake if there's an animal in the road." How was I to know the rule didn't apply to mounted policemen?

What's the smoothest thing about a used car?
The salesman.

Traffic cop: "When I saw you driving down the road I thought 60 at least."
Woman driver: "You're wrong, officer. It's only my hat that makes me look that old."

My new car has something that will last a lifetime – monthly payments.

I bought a car from a little old lady who only drove it on Sundays . . . when she took it drag racing.

If you smuggle cars into the country, are you trafficking?

Traffic cop: "Is this car licensed?"
Driver: "Yes."
Cop: "Great, I'll have a beer then, please."

Doctor: "Have you ever fallen asleep while driving?"
Patient: "Not that I remember, but I have woken up driving several times."

Jackie: "The thing I hate most about parking is all the twisting and turning."
Jill: "What I hate most about parking is that crunching of metal at the end."

After a woman parks her car, she has only a short walk to the pavement.

I want to start a car repair shop. I've already got the air for the tyres.

My wife took me out for a drive in the country. Suddenly she said: "Why don't we do something we've never done in the car before?" "Go on then," I said, "put it into fourth gear."

Driving on so many turnpikes was taking its toll.

My wife said the car wasn't running well, there was water in the carburettor. I asked where the car was. She said: "In the lake."

I was getting into my car, and this man said to me: "Can you give me a lift?" I said: "Sure, you look great, the world's your oyster. Go for it." *Tim Vine*

I've just spent ages waxing my car. I'm still not sure how it gets that hairy.

What is car sickness?
The feeling you get when your monthly car payment is due.

Every time my car passes a scrapyard it gets homesick.

I found a way of making my wife drive more carefully. I told her that if she was ever involved in an accident, the newspapers would print her real age.

Why do they rarely sell car boots at car boot sales?

Traffic cop: "Why didn't you check your speedometer?"
Motorist: "It broke when I hit 100."

My wife said building a spaghetti car was impossible. You should have seen her face when I drove pasta.

I took my car for a service last week. It was a real struggle getting it into the church.

How can you tell when an auto mechanic just had sex?
One of his fingers is clean.

Apparently 95 per cent of French-made cars sold in 2008 are still on the road. The other 5 per cent made it back to their driveways.

If your wife wants to learn to drive, don't stand in her way.

A traffic cop stops a speeding car, only to find that the driver is the local mayor. "What's the problem, officer?" asks the mayor. "Well," splutters the cop, "I just wanted to warn you about driving too fast in the next town."

A hermit was arrested for doing 100 m.p.h.? The charge was recluse driving.

I came home, and the car was in the dining room. I said to my wife: "How did you get the car in here?" "Easy," she said. "I took a left at the kitchen." *Henny Youngman*

I saw a woman break down in her car last night – tears, tantrums, throwing things . . .

How can you be sure that the car you've bought is genuinely new?
When it's recalled by the factory.

What happened when the government cut 1p from petrol?
They called it etrol.

I bought a second-hand car. It gets me from A to B, which would be fine except I live in Kew.

Husband: "You just backed the car over my bike!"
Wife: "Well, you shouldn't have left it on the lawn."

A careful driver is one who has just spotted a speed camera.

A police patrolman pulls over a car and whips out the breathalyzer. "What makes you think I've been drinking?" asks the male driver. The officer says: "You've got a fat chick in the passenger seat."

I bought an electric car but could only go 200 yards in it. That was as far as the cord would reach.

Never buy a car you can't push.

You can tell a lot about a person by their car. For example: if it's in a ditch, the driver's a woman.

Why is it that when you're driving and looking for an address, you turn down the volume on the radio?

What happened to the man who drove his expensive car into a tree?
He found out how his Mercedes bends.

I bought one of those new cars that talk – but during the warranty period it will only talk if its attorney is present.

What do you call a country where all the cars are pink?
A pink carnation.

Patrol cop: "Why were you speeding?"
Motorist: "I was trying to get home before I ran out of gas."

Rule of the road: anyone driving faster than you is an idiot and anyone driving slower than you is a moron.

What's the most dangerous part of a car?
The nut behind the wheel.

When I'm bored, I like to drive into town, find a good parking spot, then sit in my car and count how many people ask me if I'm leaving.

I'm one of those people who give BMW drivers a bad name. I indicate.

Why did the American call his Volkswagen Beetle "Elephant"?
Because it had the trunk in front.

Traffic cop: "Your eyes are red. Have you been drinking?"
Driver: "Your eyes are glazed. Have you been eating doughnuts?"

I replaced the headlights on my car with strobe lights. Now it looks like I'm the only one moving.

What do you call a man with a car on his head?
An ambulance.

How do we know the world's first car had a noisy exhaust?
Because in the Bible it says that David's Triumph was heard throughout the land.

I was sitting in traffic the other day, which was probably why I got run over.

Customer: "You told me this car was rust-free!"
Car salesman: "Well, we didn't charge you extra for the rust, did we?"

My doctor told me I'd be lucky to reach 50. That's the last time I give him a lift in my Robin Reliant.

Patrol cop: "Have you seen the state of your rear lights?"
Driver: "Never mind my rear lights, where the hell's my caravan?"

Why did the leper crash his car?
He left his foot on the accelerator.

My wife had her driving test the other day. She got 8 out of 10. The other two guys jumped clear. *Rodney Dangerfield*

What do you call a Yugo with a sun roof?
A dumpster.

How do you double the value of a Yugo?
Put a gallon of gas in it.

Why does a Yugo have a rear window defroster?
To keep your hands warm while you're pushing it.

What comes with every Yugo user's manual?
The bus timetable.

What do you call the shock absorbers inside a Yugo?
The passengers.

What do you call a Yugo with twin exhausts?
A wheelbarrow.

What do you call a Yugo driver who says he's had a speeding ticket?
A fantasist.

How can you get a Yugo to do 60 m.p.h.?
Push it off a cliff.

What's the difference between a Yugo and a golf ball?
You can drive a golf ball more than 200 yards.

What happens if you apply rust remover to a Yugo?
It disappears.

What do you call a Yugo at the top of a hill?
A miracle.

What do you call a Yugo with a flat tyre?
A write-off.

What's the difference between a Yugo and the flu?
You can get rid of the flu.

Why don't Yugos sustain much damage in a front-end collision?
The tow truck takes the impact.

What do you call a Yugo with a long radio aerial?
A bumper car.

What's the difference between a Jehovah's Witness and a Yugo?
You can shut the door on a Jehovah's Witness.

Why do Yugos need two spare wheels?
So you can cycle home.

A young woman was having a driving lesson. Partway through, the instructor told her: "You're in the wrong gear." "Oh," she said. "What should I have worn?"

My car has a gas-saving feature for winter driving – it won't start.

I got really emotional this morning at the petrol station. Don't know why, I just started filling up.

My neighbour's battery went in his Smart car this morning. I had to give him a jump start from my iPod.

BABIES

Did you hear about the guy whose wife asked him to go into town and buy a baby monitor? He couldn't find one anywhere, so he bought her an iguana instead.

If you add water to baby powder, why don't you get a baby?

Woman: "Should I have another baby after 35?"
Doctor: "No, 35 children is enough."

I was so surprised at being born I couldn't talk for 15 months.

Man: "Our baby was born last week. When will my wife start to feel and act normal again?"
Doctor: "When the kids leave home."

A baby is something that gets you down in the daytime and up at night.

Women are often pressured into naming their babies too soon. I think that was probably the case with my sister's daughter Epidural.

My doctor asked if I'd ever been present at a child's birth and what it was like. I said it was dark, then very bright. *Tim Vine*

I was such a big baby that when I was born my parents didn't know whether to buy a crib or a cage.

A maternity ward is the only place in the world where there isn't a chance of dodging the issue.

Did you hear about the couple who called their baby Coffee because he kept them awake all night?

A baby is nine months' interest on a small deposit.

They said the baby looked like me. Then they turned him the right way up.

Why do we dress baby girls in pink and baby boys in blue?
Because they can't dress themselves.

Did you hear about the baby born in a hi-tech delivery room?
It was cordless.

Friends of mine decided to flip a coin to choose a name for their new son. So now he's called Tails.

Mike: "You're going to be a father? That's great! So why are you looking so worried?"
Marty: "My wife doesn't know about it yet."

When my daughter was born, she had jaundice. She was all round and yellow. We called her Melanie. *Milton Jones*

My wife decided on an underwater birth. The leisure centre manager was furious.

If they squeeze olives to get olive oil, how do they get baby oil?

I was a premature baby. My father wasn't expecting me.

My friend's just become a dad. He says he'd do anything to stop someone hurting his child, and would even take a bullet for his boy. I said: "Why are so many people trying to assassinate your baby?"

The joy of having a baby today can only be expressed in two words: tax deduction.

Children may be deductible, but they're still taxing.

Who is the best babysitter in the Bible?
David. He rocked Goliath to sleep.

We have two boys. We named them Jackson and Grant. We figured, "What the heck? They're going to fight anyway." *Henry Cho*

I was a man trapped in a woman's body. Then I was born.

What did the mother name her identical twin sons?
Pete and Repete.

My wife says there's nothing more painful than giving birth, but I think that's only because she's never trodden on an upturned electric plug in the middle of the night.

I was a war baby. My parents took one look at me and started fighting.

After giving birth to sextuplets, a woman berated her husband: "I warned you what would happen if we did it doggie-style!"

Husband to wife: "The baby's swallowed a pin. But don't worry, it was a safety pin."

If your partner is giving birth, and the midwife doesn't turn up on time, is it a midwife crisis?

People who say they sleep like a baby usually don't have one.

What did the mama tyre and the papa tyre name their baby girl tyre?
Michelle Lynn.

I find breastfeeding in public offensive. What particularly annoys me is when they turn away so you can't see. **Sean Lock**

My wife asked me to change our daughter, but I quite liked the old one.

Anyone who says it's as easy as taking candy from a baby has never tried it.

My sister-in-law was cradling her newborn baby boy. "Would you like to wind him?" she asked. I thought it was a bit harsh, so I gave him a dead leg instead.

BANKERS AND BANKING

What's the difference between a tragedy and a catastrophe?
A tragedy is a ship full of bankers going down in a storm; a catastrophe is when they can all swim.

What do a banker and a slinky have in common?
They're both fun to watch tumble down the stairs.

What's the difference between a banker and a trampoline?
You take off your boots to jump on a trampoline.

I went to my bank to discuss a loan. The bank manager said: "Certainly, sir. How much can you lend us?"

What's the difference between a no-claims bonus and a banker's bonus?
You lose your no-claims bonus after a crash.

What's the difference between a banker and a haddock?
One's cold and slimy, the other's a fish.

How do you stop a banker from drowning?
Shoot him before he hits the water.

A man went into a bank and said to the cashier: "Will you check my balance?" So she pushed him.

What's the difference between a banker and an onion?
You cry when you cut up an onion.

What's the difference between a bank and a rowing boat?
When you bail out a rowing boat, it stops sinking lower.

What do you have if three bankers are buried up to their necks in sand?
Not enough sand.

What does a banker use for birth control?
His personality.

A small boy asks a banker: "What does two and two make?" The banker says: "Are you buying or selling?"

Customer: "I'd like to speak to Mr Fisher who I believe is a tried and trusted employee of yours."
Bank manager: "Yes, he certainly was trusted, and he'll be tried as soon as we catch him."

Why didn't the banker have many friends?
Because he was a loaner.

Give a man a gun and he can rob a bank; give a man a bank and he can rob the world.

I used to have a lot of arguments with my bank manager, but then I decided to consolidate all my rants into one simple monthly outburst.

Did you hear that the Isle of Dogs bank has collapsed? They've called in the retrievers.

A banker, a politician and a nurse are at a conference. On the table is a plate with ten biscuits, of which the banker eats nine. The banker then whispers to the politician: "That nurse is after your biscuit."

My bank sent back a cheque with a note saying "Insufficient Funds'. Them or me?

I saw a bank that offered 24-hour banking. But I didn't go in because I didn't have that much time.

If bankers can count, how come they have eight windows and only two tellers?

My bank usually has two windows open, except at busy times when they have one.

What's the difference between a banker and a sperm?
A sperm has a one-in-a-million chance of turning into a human being.

What's the difference between a dead snake in the road and a dead banker in the road?
There are skid marks in front of the snake.

Why did the Post Office have to recall its series of stamps depicting famous bankers?
People were confused about which side to spit on.

If a banker and a lawyer were both drowning and you could only save one, would you go to lunch or read the paper?

A woman bemuses the bank staff by walking in with $50 in her right ear and $50 in her left ear. "Oh, don't worry about her," says the manager. "She's $100 in arrears."

BARBIE

If Barbie is so popular, why do you have to buy her friends?

How can you tell when Barbie has her period?
Your Tic Tacs are missing.

Did you hear about the new Divorce Barbie? It comes with all Ken's stuff.

Did you hear about the new Lion Tamer Barbie? Lion is included, Barbie's head is not.

Did you hear about the new East German athlete Barbie? It's Barbie's head on Ken's body.

BARS AND PUBS

What does a skeleton order when he goes into a bar?
A beer and a mop.

Charles Dickens walks into a bar. The bartender says: "Olive or twist?"

A termite walks into a bar and says: "Is the bar tender here?"

A seal pup walks into a bar, and the bartender asks him what he wants to drink. The baby seal says: "Anything but a Canadian Club."

A mushroom walks into a bar and makes a move on a pretty woman. She turns him down, but he pleads: "Come on, lady, I'm a fun guy!"

Two sewing machines are in a bar. One says: "What do you do?" The other sewing machine replies: "I'm a Singer."

Bartender: "Do you always drink your whisky neat?"
Customer: "No, sometimes my shirt's hanging out."

William Shakespeare walked into a bar and asked for a beer. The bartender said: "I can't serve you – you're bard."

A goldfish flops into a bar. The bartender says: "What can I get you?" The goldfish gasps: "Water."

Customer: "Do you serve women in this bar?" Bartender: "No, sir, you have to bring your own."

A religious woman got a job in my local pub – she's the best bar nun.

An Englishman, an Irishman and a Scotsman walk into a bar. The bartender says: "What is this – some kind of joke?"

A Scotsman, an Irishman and an Englishman walk into a bar. The bartender says: "You're out of order!"

I got chatting to a lumberjack in a pub. He seemed like a decent feller.

Descartes walks into a bar. The bartender says: "Would you like a drink?" Descartes replies: "I think not," and disappears.

A brain walks into a bar and orders a beer. The bartender says: "I'm not serving you: you're out of your skull."

An amnesiac walks into a bar and says: "Do I come here often?"

The Beach Boys walk into a bar, and in well-rehearsed harmony say: "Round? Round? Get a round! I'll get a round."

Customer: "Why do those cashews keep saying nice things about my hair?"
Bartender: "They're the complimentary nuts."

The barman said: "How would you like to buy a vodka drink for two cents?"
I said: "That's a cheap shot and you know it." *Tim Vine*

Why did the bartender say when he spilt a drink down his shirt?
"This one's on me."

A compulsive liar walked into a bar. Well, that's where he said he was.

A man walks into a bar and says: "I'd like something tall, icy and full of vodka." The bartender shouts into the kitchen: "Hey, Miranda! Someone to see you."

A cowboy hedgehog walks into a bar and says: "Gimme a slug of whisky."

A bacterium walks into a bar, but the bartender says: "Sorry, we don't serve bacteria." The bacterium says: "But I work here. I'm staph."

A man saw Van Gogh in a pub and said; "Vince, can I get you a drink?" "No, you're OK," said Van Gogh. "I've got one 'ere."

A man walked into a bar, and all the customers patted him on the backside. "What sort of bar is this?" he yelled. The bartender replied: "It's a tapas bar."

A one-inch metal pin and a two-inch metal pin walked into a bar. It was a nail bar.

Two fonts walk into a bar. The bartender says: "Sorry, we don't want your type in here."

Two jump leads walk into a bar. The bartender says: "I'll serve you, but don't start anything."

A little pig goes into a bar and orders nine drinks. After the last one, the bartender asks: "Do you need to know where the toilet is?" "No," says the little pig. "I'm the one that goes wee, wee, wee, wee all the way home."

A man walks into a bar and starts chatting up a cheetah. The bartender says: "Don't try to pull a fast one."

A bear walks into a bar and says: "I'd like a whisky and . . . . . . a packet of peanuts." The bartender says: "Why the big pause?"

A man walks into a bar. Ouch! It was an iron bar.

A horse walks into a bar. The bartender says: "Why the long face?"

A horse walks into a bar. The bartender says: "Why the long face?" The horse replies: "Because you tell that same bloody joke every time I come in here!"

A grasshopper walks into a bar. The bartender says: "We've got a drink named after you." "Really?" says the grasshopper. "You've got a drink named Kevin?"

A friend of mine walked into a bar with a fish on his head. It was positioned high on his head with its broad tail hanging down the back of his neck. I said: "Hi, Dave. Nice mullet."

I walked into a bar and asked for a double. The bartender brought out a guy who looked exactly like me.

A snake slithers into a bar, but the bartender refuses to serve him. "Why?" asks the snake. The bartender says: "Because you can't hold your drink."

A neutron walks into a bar and asks how much a beer is. The bartender says: "For you, no charge."

A nose walks into a bar and demands a drink. "No way," says the bartender. "You're off your face."

David Hasselhoff walks into a bar, orders a drink and says to the bartender: "I want you to call me David Hoff." "Sure," says the bartender. "No hassle."

A broken bottle walks into a bar and demands a beer. "I'm not serving you," says the bartender. "You're already smashed."

A man sees a beautiful girl in a bar, walks over to her and gushes: "Where have you been all my life?" "Well," she says, "for the first half of it, I wasn't even born!"

A man walks into a bar wearing a tie fastener. The bartender says: "We don't want your tie-pin here."

A pirate walks into a bar and orders a drink. Glancing down, the bartender says: "Do you know you've got a steering wheel in your pants?" "Aye," says the pirate. "It's driving me nuts."

A limbo dancer walked into a bar. He came sixth.

I'm watching my drinking, so now I only visit bars that have mirrors on the walls.

A penguin walks into a bar and asks the bartender: "Have you seen my brother?" "I don't know," says the bartender. "What does he look like?"

A man walks into a bar with a piece of tarmac over his shoulder and says to the bartender: "I'll have a pint of beer, and one for the road."

The other day I went into a bar called The Moon. The beer was OK, but there was no atmosphere.

Have you heard about the pub called The Fiddle? It really is a vile inn.

A man goes into a bar where all the customers have nasty skin rashes and blisters. "What kind of place is this?" he asks. The bartender replies: "It's a shingles bar."

The man who goes into a bar very optimistically usually leaves it very misty optically.

A racehorse walks into a bar with two men. The bartender tells the horse: "You can't come in here, not with those trainers."

Two dragons walk into a bar. One says: "It's hot in here." The other says: "Shut your mouth!"

Did you hear about the bailiff who moonlighted as a bartender? He served subpoena coladas.

A man walks into a bar with a pelican on his head. The bartender says: "Where did you get that?" The pelican replies: "I won him in a poker game."

Two men walk into a bar. One says: "Your round." The other says: "So are you, you fat bastard!"

Two oranges walk into a bar. One says: "Your round." "Thank you," says the other.

Bar owner: "You can't stand here. You're blocking the fire exit."
Customer: "Don't worry. If there's a fire, I won't be standing here!"

A man walks into a bar and orders a beer and a packet of helicopter crisps. The bartender says: "Sorry, we haven't got any helicopter crisps, we've only got plane."

A woman walks into a bar and asks for a double entendre. So the bartender gives her one.

A man wanks into a bar. The bartender says: "Sorry, we don't serve your typo in here."

The bartender says: "We don't serve time travellers in here." A time traveller walks into a bar.

BASEBALL

Why are there so many baseball autobiographies?
Because every pitcher tells a story.

Why is baseball all wrong?
Because a man with four balls can't walk.

A coach raged: "Listen, Tommy, you know the Little League doesn't allow temper tantrums or swearing at the umpire. So will you please explain that to your mother?!"

Where is the first baseball game in the Bible?
In the big inning, Eve stole first, Adam stole second, Cain struck out Abel, and the Prodigal Son came home.

I'm not saying his batting style was bad, but I've seen better swings on a condemned playground.

My team lost 20 games in a row. One day they had a rain out and threw a victory party.

The team was so bad that when the National Anthem was played, the flag was at half-mast.

The team was so bad that the guy who handled their side of the scoreboard was sick for three weeks and nobody noticed.

I once made a presentation to do a baseball team's PR. I didn't get the contract – they said my pitch wasn't very good.

Baseball is three minutes of action crammed into three hours.

Why didn't the coach bother with winter flu jabs for the team?
Because they couldn't catch anything.

A Little League coach consoled his beaten team: "Boys, you did your best and it's no disgrace to lose heavily. Anyway those girls were good!"

What's the difference between a New York Yankees fan and a dentist?
One roots for the yanks, the other yanks for the roots.

Why couldn't the violent baseball umpire have his little boy sitting on his lap?
Because the son never sits on the brutish umpire.

BASKETBALL

Why was the basketball court wet?
Because the players kept dribbling.

When NBA players win the championship, do they feel 10 foot tall?

The team had so many injuries they started hiring nurses as cheerleaders.

They had so many injuries the team photo was an X-ray.

What do you call two Mexicans playing basketball?
Juan on Juan.

I play in the over-40 basketball league. We don't have jump balls. The ref just puts the ball on the floor and whoever can bend down to pick it up gets possession.

What do you call a man with no arms and no legs playing basketball?
Magic Johnson.

He's an extremely versatile player. He can do anything wrong.

Did you hear about the basketball player who later took up boxing? He ended up with a cauliflower navel.

I did a slam dunk this morning. Tea everywhere.

BEAUTY

Bikini waxing: is it just a rip-off?

Some wives get their good looks from their mothers. Mine gets hers from the pharmacy.

Beauty is in the eye of the beer-holder.

Mike: "What do you first notice in a woman?"
Marty: "It depends which way she's facing."

Why is it called lipstick if you can still move your lips?

Some women bleach the hairs on their upper lip to make themselves look more beautiful, but does anyone actually find a blonde moustache on a woman attractive?

My wife was at the beauty parlour for five hours yesterday – and that was just for the estimate.

Nobody's ugly after 2 a.m.

My girlfriend has a complexion like a peach – all yellow and fuzzy.

Pretty women don't bother me. I wish they would.

I was going to buy my wife some lipstick, but then I realized I don't know the size of her mouth.

Wife: "What has she got that I haven't?"
Husband: "Shall I give it to you alphabetically?"

Beauty comes from within – within jars, tubes, bottles . . .

A wife comes out of a beauty salon and asks her husband: "How do I look?" He says: "Well, at least you tried."

Milihelen: the amount of beauty required to launch one ship.

I told my girlfriend she'd drawn her eyebrows on too high. She looked surprised.

Every night my wife puts a mudpack on her face and slices of cucumber over her eyes. It doesn't work though. I can still tell it's her.

A woman is as old as she looks before breakfast.

Why do women wear lipstick?
So short-sighted men have a target to aim at.

The first time I saw my wife I thought she was drop-dead gorgeous. In fact I said: "You're gorgeous", and she replied: "Drop dead!"

The girl at the bus stop looked so intriguing, sitting there with her cute hairdo, her little dangly earrings, and her can of Mace.

Beauty is only skin deep; ugly goes right to the bone.

Woman in cosmetics store: "Do you have a product that will bring out my eyes?"
Sales assistant: "Have you tried meat hooks?"

Wife: "I just got back from the beauty salon."
Husband: "What happened? Was it closed?"

Sometimes a woman's best beauty aid is a short-sighted man.

If a man tells a woman she's beautiful, she'll overlook most of his other lies.

The Miss Universe pageant is fixed. The winner is always from earth.

Mike: "Why doesn't your wife wear lipstick?"
Marty: "Because her mouth is never still long enough for her to put it on."

The mudpack definitely improved my wife's looks – but then it fell off.

Everyone is beautiful if you squint a little.

I married my wife for her looks, but not the ones she's been giving me lately.

BEER

A beer in the hand is worth two in the fridge.

What do American beer and a rowing-boat have in common?
They're both close to water.

Scientists have revealed that beer contains small traces of female hormones. To prove their theory, they gave 50 men 10 pints of beer and observed that 100 per cent of them started talking nonsense and couldn't drive.

Beer: helping ugly people have sex since 3,000 BC.

I was at a bar nursing a beer. My nipple was getting quite soggy.

Why did God make beer?
So that the Irish wouldn't take over the world.

My dad used to collect empty beer bottles, which is a nice way of saying he was an alcoholic. – *Stewart Francis*

Why does beer go through your system so fast?
It doesn't have to stop to change colour.

Jackie: "My first husband drowned in a vat of beer."

Jill: "Was it quick?"
Jackie: "No, he got out three times to go to the bathroom."

Beer doesn't make you look fat: it makes you lean. Lean against bars, walls, other drinkers . . .

As I opened my beer, I heard a voice say: "Hi, how are you?" I thought it was probably just the drink talking.

The beer I had last night was so weak it needed to be on life support.

Why does Guinness have a white head?
So that drunks know which end to start from.

I tried to get a job as a beer taster, but in the end I bottled it.

Draft beer, not people.

Who says beer won't make you smarter? It made Bud wiser.

Mike: "Would you care for a beer?"
Marty: "Like it was my own mother."

Save water: drink beer.

To some, it's a six-pack; to me, it's a support group.

I drank so much beer that when I ate peanuts you could hear them splash.

Beer: it's not just for breakfast any more.

How many men does it take to open a beer?
None. It should be opened by the time she brings it to the couch.

My mates said I was tight-fisted, so I bought them a beer. It turns out they wanted one each.

BICYCLES

I took lessons in riding a bicycle, but I could only afford half of them. So now I ride a unicycle.

A couple on a tandem struggled to the top of a steep hill. "I didn't think we'd make it," said the man. "Nor did I," said the woman. "It's a good thing I kept the brakes on or we'd have slid all the way back down."

What happened when the bicycle salesman broke his ankle?
He was unable to peddle his wares.

I've started cycling to work to try to get fit, but some people say it makes me look gay. So for a more macho look, I've painted some racing stripes on my basket.

Mike: "My dog chases everyone on a bicycle. What can I do?"
Marty: "Take his bike away."

Why couldn't the bicycle stand up for itself?
It was two-tyred.

Teacher: "Lie on your backs and circle your feet in the air as if you were riding your bikes. Johnny, why aren't your legs moving?"
Little Johnny: "I'm freewheeling."

Why did the lazy boy take his bicycle to bed with him?
He didn't want to walk in his sleep.

A young cyclist hit an old lady in the street. "Don't you know how to ride a bike?" she snapped. "Yes," he said, "but I don't know how to ring the bell yet."

"We're becoming increasingly concerned about the theft of bicycles," said a spokesman.

A policeman stops a man on a tandem. "You may not be aware, sir, that your wife fell off your bike half a mile back." "Thank goodness," says the man. "I thought I'd gone deaf."

BIRDS

Two male rooks are sitting in a bar. One says to the other: "Bred any good rooks lately?"

If the dove is the bird of peace, what is the bird of true love?
The swallow.

Why do seagulls have wings?
So that they can beat tramps to the dumpster.

Did you hear about the hungry crow? He was ravenous.

How can you spot a bald eagle?
Its feathers are combed to one side.

Why do birds fly south in the winter?
Because it's too far to walk.

What do you call a bird that's been dead for a week?
A hummingbird.

Every day the hummingbird eats its own weight in food – by eating another hummingbird. *Steven Wright*

Where do crows go for a drink?
To a crowbar.

Did Noah have woodpeckers on the Ark? If so, where did he keep them?

What kept the seabirds entertained?
A funny tern.

What's the difference between a seagull and a baby?
A seagull flits along the shore . . .

What bird goes well with a kebab?
A skua.

Why don't penguins fly?
They're not tall enough to be pilots.

What do you get if you cross a pelican and a zebra?
Two streets further away.

What owl is common in people's homes?
The teat owl.

Why does a flamingo lift up one leg?
Because if it lifted up both legs, it would fall over.

What do you call a bird that digs for coal?
A mynah bird.

I planted some bird seed. A bird came up. Now I don't know what to feed it.

How did the cockatoo feel after its head plumage had moulted?
It was crestfallen.

What do you call dyslexic owls?
Slow.

Why do seagulls fly over the sea?
Because if they flew over the bay, they'd be bagels.

Why do penguins carry fish in their beaks?
Because they haven't got any pockets.

I wonder what kind of bird Humpty Dumpty would have hatched out as? *Harry Hill*

Aren't birds amazing? I sometimes watch them soaring through the clear blue sky and I think to myself: "If I could fly like a bird, who would I shit on?"

Why don't owls mate when it's raining?
Because it's too wet to woo.

What do you get if you cross a woodpecker with a carrier pigeon?
A bird that knocks before it delivers a message.

What did Frank Sinatra say when he was asked if he had ever kept wading birds as pets?
"Egrets, I've had a few . . ."

BIRTHDAYS

I got my wife a vibrator for her birthday. She's done nothing but moan ever since.

I bought my wife a power fan for her birthday. She was blown away.

I bought my wife a pair of boxing gloves for her birthday. She was knocked out.

Birthday candles are for people who want to make light of their age.

I got my wife a bag and a belt for her birthday. She wasn't happy, but at least the Hoover works fine now.

I got my wife a special limited-edition kite for her birthday. I had to pull some strings.

What did Quasimodo's wife get him for his birthday?
A wok. She thought it would help her iron his shirts.

For her birthday, my wife told me to get something that would make her look sexy. So I got drunk.

I bought my blind friend a cheese grater for his birthday. He says it's the most violent book he's ever read.

I bought my five-year-old a torch for his birthday. You should have seen his face light up.

When a man has a birthday he takes a day off. When a woman has a birthday she takes a year off.

Jackie: "What is your husband getting for his fiftieth birthday?"
Jill: "Bald and fat."

For her birthday, my wife said she wanted me to take her somewhere expensive. So I dropped her off at the gas station.

My wife said: "Get me something from The Body Shop." So I bought her a pancreas.

The most effective way to remember your wife's birthday is to forget it once.

The best birthday gift I ever received was a kitchen herb. There's no present like the thyme.

For her birthday, I want to get my wife something she needs, but it's not easy wrapping a bath.

Why do men always remember their partner's age but forget their birthday?

Wife: "Why did you buy me such a small diamond?"
Husband: "I didn't want the glare to hurt your eyes."

I said to my sister: "It's my birthday next week. Do you know what I need? Yes," she said, "but how do you wrap a life?"

My wife said what would really be a nice birthday surprise was if I got her something to run around in. So I bought her a tracksuit.

For her birthday, my wife said she wanted something with fur. It took me ages to find an old kettle.

It's a terrible thing to grow old alone. My wife hasn't had a birthday for six years.

I asked my wife what she wanted for her birthday. She said: "Nothing would make me happier than a 24-carat gold ring." So that's what I got her – nothing.

Jackie: "What did your husband give you for your birthday?"
Jill: "A skirt and sex. Both were too short."

I've just had a sneaky look at my birthday presents. One is a bag of rice. I think it's from Uncle Ben.

For my wife's birthday, I bought her a small bottle of exclusive perfume called ample. I just hope she doesn't notice where I scraped off the "S".

When I was a boy, my birthday present one year was an empty box. My parents told me it was an Action Man deserter.

I never forget my wife's birthday. It's the day after she reminds me about it.

My wife said she wanted something black and lacy for her birthday, so I bought her a pair of football boots.

What did the birthday balloon say to the pin?
"Hi, Buster."

Mike: "I forgot my wife's birthday last month."
Marty: "What did she say?"
Mike: "Nothing, yet."

The only time a man listens to a woman is when she insists she doesn't want anything expensive for her birthday.

At first my wife thought a split tube of superglue was a lousy birthday present, but over the months she's become quite attached to it.

My son wanted to go places, so for his sixteenth birthday I bought him a chemistry set.

What's the best birthday present for a child?
A drum takes a lot of beating.

I got my son a flat piece of cardboard for his birthday, although why he wants an ex-box I'll never know.

I bought my wife a mood ring for her birthday. When she's in a good mood, it turns green; when she's in a bad mood, it leaves a red mark on my forehead.

Husband to wife: "But you still haven't used the birthday present I bought you last year – that plot in the cemetery."

I bought my wife a kite as a surprise birthday gift. She said: "I bet there are strings attached."

It's my birthday today, and my wife says she's going to make it my most fantastic birthday ever. I wonder where she's going?

Birthdays are good for you. The more you have, the longer you live.

For her birthday my wife said she wanted something with diamonds. So I bought her a pack of playing cards.

Wife: "I'm looking forward to my fortieth birthday."
Husband: "Yes, but you're looking in the wrong direction."

My wife asked me for something that does 0–60 in five seconds for her birthday. So I bought her a set of bathroom scales.

BLONDES

Did you hear about the blonde at a funeral? She tried to catch the wreath.

What's the definition of paralysis?
Four blondes at a crossroads.

How do a blonde's brain cells die?
Alone.

What do you call a blonde with two brain cells?
Pregnant.

What do you call 20 blondes sitting in a circle?
A dope ring.

How did the blonde try to kill her pet goldfish?
By drowning it.

Why does it take longer to build a blond snowman?
Because you have to hollow out the head.

How do you change a blonde's mind?
By blowing in her ear.

Why was the blonde talking into an envelope?
She was sending a voicemail.

How can you tell which tricycle belongs to the blonde?
It's the one with the kickstand.

Did you hear about the guy who asked his blonde girlfriend to put his laptop in hibernate mode? Six weeks later he's still getting twigs and leaves out.

What did the blonde call her pet zebra?
Spot.

What do you call a blonde between two brunettes?
A mental block.

What do you call a brunette between two blondes?
An interpreter.

What's a blonde's idea of natural childbirth?
No make-up.

How did the blonde die raking leaves?
She fell out of the tree.

I told my blonde girlfriend I wanted to go to a place that served all-day breakfast, but she said: "I could never eat that much breakfast."

Two blondes walk into a bar. You'd have thought that one of them would have seen it.

Did you hear about the power cut at the shopping mall that left two blondes stranded on an escalator for four hours?

I said to the blonde stuck on the escalator: "Why didn't you walk down?"
She said: "Because I was going up."

Why did the blonde weigh her watch?
To see if it was gaining time.

When blondes have more fun, do they know it?

Did you hear about the blonde who decided to bake a birthday cake?
The candles melted in the oven.

Why did the blonde go outside with her purse open?
She had heard there was going to be some change in the weather.

How can you keep a blonde occupied for hours?
Give her a piece of paper with "PTO" on both sides.

A blonde wife went to the doctor for some cream because she was
worried about the seven-year itch.

Why did the blonde try to squeeze the cans of grapefruit in the
supermarket?
To see if they were ripe.

What did the blonde say when she received a book for her birthday?
"Thanks, but I've got one already."

What did the blonde say when she received a second book for her
birthday?
"Thanks, but I haven't finished colouring in the first one yet."

Did you hear about the blonde who couldn't understand why whenever
she washed ice cubes in hot water, she couldn't find them?

Why did the blonde give away the scarf that a friend had bought her for
Christmas?
She said it was too tight.

Why don't blondes eat bananas?
They can't find the zippers.

Why is a blonde's brain the size of a pea in the morning?
It swells at night.

A man finds his blonde wife propping up their washing machine on
one side with two bricks. "What are you doing?" he asks. She says: "The
washing at 30 degrees."

What did the blonde get on her IQ test?
Nail varnish.

Did you hear about the blonde stripper who wanted iron breast implants so she could show her mettle?

What did the blonde do when she missed the number 42 bus?
She caught the number 21 twice.

Blonde to friend: "If you can guess how many candies are in my hand, I'll give you both."

Why didn't the blonde go waterskiing?
She couldn't find a lake with a slope.

What can strike a blonde without her even knowing it?
A thought.

Why do blondes always smile during lightning storms?
They think their picture is being taken.

A blonde driver is stopped by a police officer who asks to see her licence. "I wish you cops would get your act together," she grumbles. "Yesterday you take my licence away, and today you expect me to show it to you!"

Did you hear about the blonde who thought the world's most prolific inventor was an Irishman named Pat Pending?

How do you keep a blonde at home?
Build a circular driveway.

Did you hear about the blonde who almost killed her toy poodle? She tried to insert batteries.

How can you tell which blonde is the waitress?
She's the one with the tampon behind her ear, wondering what she did with her pencil.

How do you make a blonde's eyes light up?
Shine a torch into her ear.

Why did the blonde get fired from the banana plantation?
She threw out all the bent ones.

What happened to the blonde who went to a movie theatre where the poster said: "Under-16 not admitted"?
She went home and phoned 15 friends.

Why do blondes wear pony tails?
To hide the air valve.

What is it called when a blonde dyes her hair brown?
Artificial intelligence.

How do you make a blonde laugh on Monday morning?
Tell her a joke on Friday night.

Doctor: "Have you ever been incontinent?"
Blonde: "Yes, I've been to Europe twice."

What do blondes and beer bottles have in common?
Both are empty from the neck up.

Why couldn't the blonde call 911?
Because there's no 11 on the phone.

Two blondes are having an intellectual discussion about geography. Eventually one says to the other: "What's the correct way of saying it, Iraq or Iran?"

Did you hear about the blonde who thought Doris Day was a national holiday?

How do you get a blonde to burn her ear?
Phone her while she's ironing.

How do you get a blonde to burn her ear twice?
Phone her again while she's ironing.

A survey shows that blondes do have more fun – they just don't remember who with.

Two blondes are walking along an Australian beach at night. One says: "Which do you think is nearer, the moon or New York?" The other blonde says: "Hellooooo! Can you see New York?"

Did you hear about the blonde who lost her Internet connection? She put a notice up in the newsagent's window.

What did the blonde driver say when she ran out of gas?
"Will it hurt the car if I drive with an empty tank?"

How can you steal a blonde's seat near the front of a plane?
Tell her that only the rear half of the plane is going to Los Angeles.

Did you hear about the blonde who thought Meow Mix was a CD for cats?

Why did the blonde put her finger over the nail while she was hammering?
The noise gave her a headache.

How do you know when a blonde has been on a computer?
There's Wite-Out all over the screen.

After buying a Christmas tree, a blonde found it was too big to fit in her car. "You'll have to cut the top off," said the shopkeeper. "That's a good idea," said the blonde, "and I've always wanted a convertible."

What do you see when you look into a blonde's eyes?
The back of her head.

Why did the blonde throw breadcrumbs in the toilet?
To feed the toilet duck.

Did you hear about the blonde who was found frozen to death in her car at a drive-in movie theatre? She had gone to see *Closed For Winter*.

A brunette, a blonde and a redhead are all in third grade. Who has the biggest boobs?
The blonde, because she's 18.

Did you hear about the blonde who thought Eartha Kitt was a set of garden tools?

Postcard from a blonde: "Having a wonderful time. Where am I?"

I said to my blonde girlfriend: "What would you say to a nice glass of wine?" She giggled: "Hello, nice glass of wine."

Why do blondes wear earmuffs?
To avoid the draught.

Going into a bank to cash a cheque from her husband, a blonde was asked to endorse it. So she wrote on the back: "My husband is a wonderful man."

Why were there bullet holes in the mirror?
The blonde had tried to shoot herself.

Why did the blonde secretary chop off her fingers?
So she could write short hand.

How many blondes does it take to play hide and seek?
One.

A man says to his blonde girlfriend: "Look, a dead bird." The blonde looks up to the sky and says: "Where?"

What do you call a blonde with half a brain?
Gifted.

My blonde friend texted me saying, "What does 'idk' stand for?" I texted back, "I don't know", and she replied, "OMG, no one does!"

Radio quiz DJ: "What's the capital of Wisconsin?"
Blonde: "Oh, that's easy. W."

The blonde was puzzled because whenever she asked what time it was, she got a different answer.

Why do blondes take the pill?
So they know what day of the week it is.

What do you call a blonde in a black leather jacket?
A rebel without a clue.

Did you hear about the blonde who gave birth to twins? Her blond husband is out looking for the other man.

Did you hear about the blonde secretary who always filed her nails . . . under N?

How can you tell if a blonde has been using your lawnmower?
The green "Welcome" mat is ripped to shreds.

Why did the blonde have a hysterectomy?
She wanted to stop having grandchildren.

Why did the blonde bury her driving licence?
Because she was told it had expired.

Did you hear about the blonde who went to hospital to give blood and was asked what type she was? She told them she was an outgoing cat-lover.

Why don't blondes like M&Ms?
They're too hard to peel.

Why did the blonde get fired from the M&M factory?
For throwing out all the Ws.

What job function does a blonde have in an M&M factory?
Proofreading.

How do you know when a blonde has been making chocolate chip cookies?
There are M&M shells all over the floor.

Why don't blondes have elevator jobs?
They can't remember the route.

Why did God create blondes?
Because sheep can't fetch beer from the fridge.

One blonde says to the other: "It's a shame you've spoiled your lovely blonde hair by dying the roots black."

Why was the blonde looking for the reverse button on her computer?
She'd been told to back up at the end of each day.

I told my blonde girlfriend I was going skeet shooting. She said she didn't know how to cook them.

Why did the blonde have sex in the microwave?
She wanted to have a baby in nine minutes.

Why did the blonde tiptoe past the medicine cabinet?
She didn't want to wake the sleeping pills.

A blonde orders a pizza. The clerk asks: "Do you want it cut into six pieces or twelve?" "Six, please," replies the blonde. "I could never eat twelve."

Why did the blonde go to the dentist?
She wanted him to put in a wisdom tooth.

Why did the blonde move to LA?
It was easier to spell.

Two blondes are walking down the street. The first blonde says: "Look at that dog with no eyes." The second blonde says: "How am I supposed to see it?"

Why did the blonde keep grabbing at air?
She was collecting her thoughts.

Blonde: "I get a terrible pain in my eye whenever I drink a cup of coffee."
Doctor: "Try taking the spoon out."

Why didn't the blonde want a window seat on the plane?
She didn't want her hair to get blown about.

What did the blonde say when she dropped the priceless Ming vase?
"It's OK, Daddy. I'm not hurt."

Did you hear about the blonde who got locked in the bathroom? She was in there so long, she peed her pants.

Last week I got chatting to a blonde in a cemetery. She said: "Would you like to go somewhere quieter?"

My blonde girlfriend said: "I think the man who invented the clock was a genius. I mean, how did he know what time it was?"

How do you get a blonde to marry you?
Tell her she's pregnant.

Why did the blonde keep running around the bed?
She was trying to catch up with her sleep.

Why did the blonde have a sore belly button?
Because her boyfriend was blond too.

A blonde is stopped by a police officer and asked to identify herself. She pulls a mirror from her purse, looks in it and says: "Yes, officer, it's definitely me."

What do you call a smart blonde?
A golden retriever.

What do you get if you offer a blonde a penny for her thoughts?
Change.

Did you hear about the blonde who put lipstick on her forehead because she wanted to make up her mind?

A blonde went alligator hunting to get a pair of alligator shoes. After catching her third alligator, she groaned: "Damn! This one's barefoot, too!"

Why did the blonde get excited at finishing her jigsaw puzzle in nine months?
Because on the box it said 2–4 years.

A blonde sees a waitress with a name tag on her shirt. "Gee, that's nice," says the blonde. "What did you name the other one?"

Why do employers give blondes only half an hour for lunch?
Any longer and they'd have to retrain them.

What do you do when a blonde throws a pin at you?
Run like hell, she's got a grenade in her mouth.

Why do blondes wear their hair up?
To catch everything that goes over their heads.

What's the difference between a blonde and a supermarket trolley?
A supermarket trolley has a mind of its own.

Why did the blonde Disney fan try to make her Internet password "MickeyMinnie DonaldPlutoGoofy"?
Because she read it had to have at least five characters.

Why don't blondes use vibrators?
They chip their teeth.

What's a blonde's idea of safe sex?
A padded dashboard.

Why do blondes drive cars with sunroofs?
More leg room.

What's the mating call of a blonde?
"I'm soooo drunk!"

What do a blonde and a turtle have in common?
When they're on their back, they're fucked.

Brunette: "My husband had really bad dandruff, so I gave him Head and Shoulders."
Blonde: "How do you give shoulders?"

What's the difference between a blonde and the Grand Old Duke of York?
The Grand Old Duke of York only had 10,000 men.

What's the first thing a blonde learns when she takes driving lessons?
You can sit upright in a car.

What did the doctor say to the blonde?
"Stay out of bed for two days."

Why do blondes wear hoop ear-rings?
So they have somewhere to rest their ankles.

Why do blondes have orgasms?
So they know when to stop having sex.

What's the difference between a blonde and a brick?
When you lay a brick, it doesn't follow you around.

How did the blonde know she'd been sleepwalking?
She kept waking up in her own bed.

What do blondes put behind their ears to attract men?
Their legs.

How can you tell when a blonde is dating?
By the buckle print on her forehead.

What does a blonde use for protection during sex?
A bus shelter.

Why did the blonde fail her driving test?
Every time the car stopped, she jumped into the back seat.

What do bottle blondes and 747s have in common?
Black boxes.

What's blonde, brunette, blonde, brunette . . .?
A blonde doing cartwheels.

A stunning blonde started at our office, and I heard she wanted to give me one. Unfortunately it was out of 10.

Doctor: "Are you sexually active?"
Blonde: "No, I usually just lie there."

Why do blondes wear underwear?
To keep their ankles warm.

What's the difference between a blonde and a bowling ball?
You can only put three fingers in a bowling ball.

What's the difference between a blonde and the *Titanic*?
They know how many men went down on the *Titanic*.

What's the difference between a blonde and an ironing board?
It's hard to get an ironing board's legs open.

What did the blonde's right leg say to the left leg?
Nothing, they've never met.

Did you hear about the blonde who thought "love handles" referred to her ears?

Why don't blondes like pickles?
They keep getting their head stuck in the jar.

What does a blonde say after having sex for the first time?
"So you guys are all on the same team?"

How can you tell when a blonde reaches orgasm?
She drops her nail file.

What's the first thing a blonde does in the morning?
Puts on her clothes and goes home.

A blonde goes to the doctor complaining of morning sickness. "Congratulations!" says the doctor. "Do you know who the father is?" The blonde replies: "If you ate a tin of beans, would you know which one made you fart?"

BODY

I had my neck removed two years ago, and I haven't looked back since.

If your feet smell and your nose runs, you're built upside down.

Why is the space between a woman's breasts and her hips called a waist?
Because you could fit another pair of breasts in there.

Gargling is a good way to see if your throat leaks.

Is my wife dissatisfied with my body? A small part of me says yes.
Stewart Francis

My figure used to be my fame. Now my fame has spread.

What did one saggy boob say to the other saggy boob?
We'd better get some support or people will think we're nuts.

A woman's cleavage is something you can both approve of and look down on.

I've just plucked my eyebrows. I think they're out of tune.

I don't have a beer gut. I have a protective covering for my rock-hard abs.

If God had meant us to touch our toes, he would have put them further up our body.

What did the right testicle say to the left testicle?
"The guy in the middle thinks he's so hard!"

I owe my athletic physique to my wife and clean living. "Clean the car . . . clean the attic . . . clean the garage."

My brother has no hands. I feel for him.

Did you hear about the tattoo artist who had designs on his clients?

What do toy train sets and women's breasts have in common?
They're both intended for children, but it's the dads who play with them.

I used to be a big fan of *Robocop*, and now I've been fitted with a robotic leg. Oh, the iron knee!

What are the small bumps around women's nipples?
It's Braille for "suck here".

My girlfriend says I have the body of a man half my age, which would be a nice compliment if I wasn't 22.

Did you hear about the two podiatrists who opened offices on the same street? They were arch enemies.

I'll tell you what I'd really grown attached to: my umbilical cord.

I don't like my hands. I always keep them at arm's length. ***Tim Vine***

My friend's nose is so big you could go bowling with his boogers.

I was born with a deformed penis. As soon as sex is mentioned it rears its ugly head.

My brother made fun of the hard skin on my foot. I told him not to be so callous.

Admiring his body in the mirror, a man says: "Look at that, 13 stone of pure dynamite." His wife sneers: "Shame about the two-inch fuse."

How did the blind woman pierce her ear?
By answering the stapler.

Castration: that's a eunuch experience.

When he was a slim young man, my dad had a tattoo of a cheetah on his chest, but now he's 75 it's a giraffe.

I'll show you my tattoo of a rose, but not outside. I'm constantly bothered by bees.

Tattoos are great for preserving memories – otherwise I would have totally forgotten about that anchor.

One more wrinkle and she could pass for a prune.

I would help but my hands are tied – five digits all.

What's the most commonly misspelled blood group?
Typo.

Pretty girl to teenage boy in blue swimming trunks: "Hey, did you know your eyes match your trunks?"
Boy: "Why? Are my eyes bulging?"

If the palm of your hand itches, you're going to get something. If your head itches, you've already got it.

My grandma says she has eyes in the back of her head. I hope it's not hereditary.

I once met a girl who had trouble written all over her. It wasn't the most artistic of tattoos.

It's tough having a big nose. I can't swim backstroke in the sea without someone shouting, "Shark!"

When a clown gets an erection, does he call it his funny bone?

If a man doesn't have any fingers, can he be counted on?

How can you make five pounds of fat look good?
Put a nipple on it.

One-armed butlers: they can take it, but they can't dish it out. *Tim Vine*

Other people's tattoos are like other people's children. Only you can see how bad they are.

Why does a penis have a hole in the end?
So men can be open-minded.

Wife: "Jean says I've got the skin of a 19-year-old."
Husband: "Well, give it back. You're getting it all wrinkled."

It's not how you pick your nose but where you put the booger.

Did you hear about the man who used to pick fluff out of his belly button but gave it up for lint?

Women's breasts are like the sun: you can look, but it's dangerous to stare.

I'll tell you what's close to my heart: my left lung.

Mike: "Hey, what's that in your ear? Since when have you worn an earring?"
Marty: "Since my wife found it in our bed."

What's the best way to get a youthful figure?
Ask a woman her age.

I got up this morning and thought it looked nice out, so I left it out.

Did you hear about the man who was illiterate and ambidextrous?
He was unable to write, with both hands.

My feet are killing me. Every night they grab me around the throat. –
Tommy Cooper

My wife used to have an hour-glass figure, but the sand shifted.

I've got a 12-inch penis, but I don't use it as a rule.

I love my six-pack so much I protect it with a thick layer of fat.

What is it that even the most careful person overlooks?
His nose.

I mixed up my anti-perspirant with my anti-depressant last night, and now my arms won't go back down.

The last time my wife gave me a foot massage, my back ended up smelling funny.

Transsexuals just aren't what they used to be.

Wife: "Come on then, sexy. What would you most like to do with my body?"
Husband: "Identify it."

What's the least sensitive part of the penis?
The man attached to it.

My wife walked into the room and said: "Have you seen my flip-flops?" I said: "I've seen them before. Now put your bra back on!"

My son was born with only two toes, which at least makes bedtime easier. "This little piggy went to market, this little piggy stayed at home . . . Goodnight."

BOOKS

I went to our local bookshop to buy a book about conspiracies. There were none there. Coincidence?

Do gun manuals have a trouble-shooting section?

Which book teaches animals how to mate?
The Llama Sutra.

I want to write a mystery novel, or do I? ***Stewart Francis***

I'm reading a book about superglue – I couldn't put it down.

Last year I wrote a book about poltergeists – it flew off the shelves.

I went to a bookshop and asked the saleswoman where the self-help section was. She said if she told me it would defeat the purpose.

An autobiography is a book which reveals that the only thing wrong with the author is his memory.

You know how tough it is in children's book publishing: it's bunny-eat-bunny.

I once read a book about the digestive system. The ending was crap.

Never read a pop-up book about giraffes. ***Sean Lock***

Is a book on voyeurism a peeping tome?

Mike: "Have you ever read Shakespeare?"
Marty: "No. Who wrote it?"

I tried to read a book today on the history of Sellotape, but I couldn't find the beginning.

A woman goes into a library and says: "I'm looking for the title *The Perfect Man*." The female librarian replies: "Comics are in the children's section."

I bought a book about witches, but it wasn't very good. The author clearly hadn't run a spell check.

When I read a book, I always underline the bits I don't understand. That way, if I ever lend it to someone, they'll think I'm really clever. ***Adam Bloom***

People often ask me how I got my job as a book editor. Well, to cut a long story short . . .

I lost my job in the bookstore for putting "Signed by Author" stickers on the Bible.

Did you hear about the girl who went to the library and ordered a book called *How to Hug*? It turned out to be volume seven of an encyclopedia.

I've written a book on how to chop onions. Read it and weep.

Which John Milton novel is about why he can't play Monopoly any more?
Pair o' Dice Lost.

I've upgraded my dictionary to high-definition.

A dwarf walked into a library and asked for a book on irony. The librarian said: "Yes, it's on the top shelf."

I see the new book *CPR for Dummies* has been a big hit with ventriloquists.

Have you read that book about a Spanish mule called Hote? I believe it's called *Donkey Hote.*

I once tried reading a book upside down, but I had a hard time keeping my legs up in the air.

There's a new book by Amber Greene called *Traffic Light Sequences*. Have you read Amber Greene?

Did you read that new novel about a destructive tornado? There's a real twist at the end.

I was 41 when I finished my first novel. I guess I'm just a slow reader.

Jackie: "So have you sold anything since you took up writing full-time?"
Jill: "Yes. My car, the TV, a couple of items of jewellery . . ."

If a book about failures doesn't sell, is it a success?

My granddad's got a book coming out next week. He shouldn't really have eaten it.

I went to the book shop today because it was a third off all titles. I bought *The Lion, The Witch* . . . *Jimmy Carr*

Did you hear about the guy who loved Roman poetry? He was an Ovid reader.

Why does Harry Potter sometimes get confused between his cooking pot and his best friend?
They're both cauld-ron.

Why did the woman slip on the library floor?
She was in the non-friction section.

I don't know to speed-read. Instead I listen to audio books on fast-forward.

Why did the man have his nose in a book all day?
He'd lost his bookmark.

Who attacks customers with an ancient sword while lending books?
Conan the Librarian.

I'm reading a very unusual murder mystery. It seems like the victim was shot by a man from another book.

My nan just accused me of stealing her copies of *The Mirror Crack'd* and *The Body in the Library*. I think she's lost her marples.

A man walked into a library and said: "I hope you don't have a book on reverse psychology."

For sale: full set of encyclopedias. No longer needed. Got married last week. Wife knows everything.

Did you hear about the author who was so shy, he didn't even mention himself in his autobiography?

A man went into a bookshop and bought a book on suffocation. The sales clerk said: "Would you like a bag with it?"

My girlfriend got me this book on feng shui, but I didn't know where in my home to put it. **Irwin Barker**

I went to a crime writers' dinner once. Everyone was scared to taste the soup.

A woman walked into a library and asked for a book on innuendo. So the librarian took her up the rear aisle and let her have it.

Every time I lend my neighbour a book, he keeps it. Then I discovered he's a professional bookkeeper.

Always read a book that will make you look good if you die in the middle of it.

I went into a library and asked for a book on suicide. "No way," said the librarian. "You won't bring it back."

It looks like the council is going to build a new library between the tram tracks . . . well, reading between the lines.

Was there a first draft of *Gone with the Wind*?

The editor denied leaving his work in the kitchen, but the proof was in the pudding.

Have you tried the *Where's Wally* audio book? It goes, "Not Wally, Not Wally, Not Wally, Not Wally, Not Wally, Not Wally . . ."

I got into bed, and a book fell on my head. I've only got my shelf to blame.

I didn't mind when he kept borrowing my books, but I drew the line when he asked to borrow my bookcase.

There's a new book out today – *The Korean Canine Training Manual: 50 Ways To Wok Your Dog*.

Did you hear about the carpenter-turned-author from Salt Lake City? Morman Nailer.

I've just taken up speed reading. Last night I did *War and Peace* in 20 seconds. I know it's only three words, but it's a start.

There's a new book about a couple who have sex in unusual places. It's on the shelves Monday, hanging from a chandelier Tuesday . . . **Rob Brydon**

My parents got me a really cheap dictionary for my birthday. I couldn't find the words to thank them.

BORES AND BOREDOM

When I'm bored I like to play a game with my deaf wife while she is Hoovering. I unplug it and time how long it takes her to notice.

Sometimes when I'm bored I like to fill my bath up with water and turn on the shower so that I can pretend I'm in a submarine that just got hit.

He's the kind of bore who's here today and here tomorrow.

I'm not saying my uncle is boring, but he has the knack of staying longer in a couple of hours than most people do in a couple of weeks.

He's so dull that it took him 25 years of marriage to get the seven-year-itch.

Bores are interesting to a point – the point when they start talking.

He is so insignificant you could lose him in a crowd of two.

He can bore more than the average termite.

A bore is someone who, generally speaking, is generally speaking.

He's the kind of guy who can brighten a room just by leaving it.

I have seen people in comas with livelier personalities than him.

A bore deprives you of solitude without providing you with company.

His wife encouraged him to take up rifle shooting because he's a small bore.

He's so boring that when he watches a movie, the actors fall asleep.

He's so boring that when he throws a boomerang it doesn't come back.

He is so boring his idea of a night on the tiles actually involves grouting.

A friend of mine was boared to death: he was killed by a wild pig.

BOWLING

My brother goes bowling once every three years to make sure he still hates it.

If you can't hear a pin drop, there's something wrong with your bowling.

William Tell and his family were reputed to be keen bowlers, but all the Swiss league records were destroyed in a fire. So we'll never know for whom the Tells bowled.

Did you hear about the bowler who fell upon hard times? He was found in the gutter.

When I go bowling, I like to make my name "2 Dicks". So when I'm bowling well, the screen will say: "Congratulations 2 Dicks! You have a spare!"

BOXING

A boxer complains to his doctor about insomnia. "Have you tried counting sheep?" asks the doctor. "Yes," says the boxer, "but whenever I get to nine, I stand up."

Women's boxing will never catch on. Most women wouldn't dream of putting on gloves without a handbag and shoes to match.

He boxed as Kid Candle. One blow and he was out.

He fought under the name of Kid Cousteau because he took so many dives.

He boxed as Kid Picasso because he spent so much time on the canvas.

He was a colourful boxer – black and blue all over.

Boxer: "Just think. Tonight I'll be fighting on TV in front of millions of people!"
Manager: "And they'll all know the result at least 10 seconds before you do."

Why does everyone hate boxer Audley Harrison? He never hurt anyone!

What does Audley Harrison have in common with a five-year-old schoolboy?
They both need picking up 'round 3.

Every morning I shadow box. Sometimes I even win.

Did you hear about the boxer who didn't know the meaning of defeat? So his manager bought him a dictionary.

After battering an opponent to defeat, the boxer said he didn't want a rematch because he didn't think his hands could stand the punishment.

When I was a fighter I kept my head. I lost my teeth but I kept my head.

Why are short people so good at boxing?
To beat them you really need to knuckle down.

A boxer is a man who makes money hand over fist.

What was the difference between Evander Holyfield and Mike Tyson?
Holyfield was champing at the bit, Tyson was biting at the champ.

It's easy to download the Tyson–Holyfield fight off the Internet. It doesn't take much memory – just two bytes.

Who was the last person to box Joe Louis?
His undertaker.

What did the boxer have written on his gravestone?
"You can stop counting. I'm not getting up."

When the fight ended he was handed a cup – to keep his teeth in.

A boxer was taking a terrible beating. At the end of the round, his coach said: "Let him hit you with his left for a while. Your face is crooked."

Manager: "How would you like to fight for the crown?"
Boxer: "Great. I think I can take the Queen in about five rounds."

BUSES

I was drinking in town last week, so I took a bus home. It might not sound a big deal to you, but I've never driven a bus before.

A man goes for an interview as a bus driver. The interviewer says: "You're 30 minutes late! The job's yours."

I only became a bus driver so I could tell people where to get off.

A bus is a vehicle that travels twice as fast when you are running after it as it does when you're on it.

Why did gangsters shoot the information officer at the bus station?
He knew too much.

Mike: "Isn't it disgusting the way those men are staring at that girl getting on the bus?"
Marty: "What bus?"

Passenger: "Driver, do you stop at the Savoy Hotel?"
Driver: "Not on my salary."

Never give up your seat for a lady. That's how I lost my job as a bus driver. *Milton Jones*

I wish the bus company would tell me when times have changed. I felt really silly standing at the bus stop in my flares, cheesecloth shirt and gold medallion.

How do you know when a bachelor offers you his seat on the bus?
Because he leaves the seat up.

Why did the bus stop?
Because it saw the zebra crossing.

A man was sitting on a bus chewing gum and staring into space. The old woman sitting opposite him said: "It's no good you talking to me, young man, I'm stone deaf!"

Let buses pull out – and reduce the minibus population.

A man with no arms and no legs is waiting at a bus stop. The bus driver pulls up and shouts: "How you getting on, Jim?"

BUSINESS

My sign shop is running low on stock. I can't see a Way Out.

I've founded a company fixing car ignitions. It's a start-up business.

Did you hear about the man who went into business prospecting for gold? It didn't pan out.

I started up a business manufacturing tabletops for shops, but it was counterproductive.

My accountant told me the only reason my business is looking up is because it's flat on its back.

How do you start a small business?
Buy a big one and wait.

Why did the shareholders of a compass manufacturing firm call an emergency meeting?
They were worried that the company wasn't heading in the right direction.

I set up a business building submarines, but it went under.

Did you hear that Xerox and Wurlitzer are merging to make reproductive organs?

I wanted to start a bakery business, but I couldn't raise the dough.

Chairman to directors: "Three weeks ago we were teetering on the edge of a precipice. Today we are going to take a giant step forward."

Things weren't going well in my trapeze business and I was looking for an excuse to sack my assistant. In the end, I just let her go.

What happened to the man who tried to start a hot-air balloon business?
He couldn't get it off the ground.

I set up a sauna business, but eventually we ran out of steam.

I once employed a really emotional delivery driver. He used to take everything the wrong way.

The secret of personal growth is to wear shoes with lifts.

I've moved my tomato ketchup company from England to India. It's called outsaucing.

I'm delighted when people stick their noses in my business – my company makes paper tissues.

Clearasil soon regretted moving their factory to London when Hackney disappeared overnight.

My business making Polos without the hole in the middle is really doing well. I'm making an absolute mint.

Did you hear about the self-employed security guard who minded his own business?

My brother and I have had to close down our archery business – we didn't hit any of our targets in the first 12 months.

Then I opened an army surplus store, but nobody wanted to buy a surplus army.

I told my friend I made $600 a month selling dog poop. He said: "That's gross!" I said: "No, that's net."

Did you hear about the guy who had a great business plan – he was going to build bungalows for dwarfs? There was just one tiny flaw . . .

I'm designing a new line of straitjackets for prisoners and the criminally insane. I'm aiming at a captive market.

I used to have two employees in my fart cushion business, but I had to let one go.

CALIFORNIA

How do you know when a relationship gets serious in California?
They take you to meet their Tarot Card reader.

California is wonderful. On a clear day when the fog lifts, you can see the smog.

When the smog lifts in Los Angeles, U C L A.

What's the difference between Los Angeles and yoghurt?
Yoghurt has real culture.

If you drive at less than 50 m.p.h. in California, they consider you double-parked.

A new car has been designed specifically for the Los Angeles rush hour. It's called a stationary wagon.

I went to San Francisco. I found someone's heart. Now what?

Did you hear about the Californian who has invented a robotic parking attendant? He's calling it the Silicon Valet.

It was so quiet in the Hollywood Starbucks this morning you could hear a name drop.

You're from California if you've been to a baby shower for an infant who has two mothers and a sperm donor.

You're from California if your pet has its own psychiatrist.

You're from California if your family of four owns six vehicles.

You're from California if your co-worker says she has 10 body piercings . . . and none are visible.

You're from California if you go to a tanning salon before going to the beach.

You're from California if you spend more on facelifts than on groceries.

You're from California if you drive to a store across the street.

You're from California if your pizza delivery guy is also on contract with Warner Bros.

You're from California if you see 20 lawyers chasing an ambulance.

You're from California if gym membership is mandatory.

You're from California if you don't exterminate your cockroaches, you smoke them.

You're from California if a really great parking space can move you to tears.

You're from California if your best friend named her twins after her life coach and her personal shopper.

You're from California if you'd kill your parents to be in movies.

You're from California if you have killed your parents to be in movies.

CAMPING

Campers: nature's way of feeding mosquitoes.

When using a public campground, a tuba placed on your picnic table will keep the pitches on either side vacant.

When smoking a fish, never inhale.

Whenever I go camping, I always remember to take a compass with me – because you never know when you might suddenly need to draw a circle.

A potato baked in coals for an hour makes a good meal; one baked for three hours makes a good hockey puck.

When camping, always wear a long-sleeved shirt. It gives you something to wipe your nose on.

Any stone in a hiking boot migrates to the point of maximum pressure.

The distance to a campsite remains constant as twilight approaches.

Your side of the tent is always the side that leaks.

The probability of diarrhoea increases in proportion to the number of thistles in the vicinity.

Given a chance, matches will find a way to get wet.

You can duplicate the warmth of a down-filled bedroll by climbing into a garbage bag with half a dozen geese.

Bear bells are a good way of avoiding contact with grizzlies. Of course, the hardest part is fitting them on the bear.

Camper: "I thought you said this camp had no mosquitoes?"
Campsite manager: "That's right. These mosquitoes come from the camp down the road."

How is it that one careless match can start a forest fire, but it takes a whole box to start a campfire?

When I was in the scouts, the leader told me to pitch a tent. I couldn't find any pitch, so I used creosote. *Tommy Cooper*

Acupuncture was invented by a camper who found a porcupine in his sleeping bag.

In an emergency, a drawstring from a parka hood can be used to strangle a snoring tent mate.

The best way to make a fire by rubbing two sticks together is to make sure one of them is a match.

The tent was small, but I had no room to complain.

CANADA

What do you call a Canadian who moves to the US and becomes famous?
An American.

Canada is so boring, even their transvestites are women.

In Canada there are only two seasons – six months of winter and six months of poor snowmobiling.

Why did the Canadian cross the road?
To get to the middle.

In what way is America better than Canada?
America has nicer neighbours.

Canadians are more polite when they're being rude than many New Yorkers are when they're being friendly.

What are the four seasons in Canada?
Almost winter, winter, still winter, and road construction.

Did you hear about the visitor to Canada who was delighted to be given a room with running water as he had always wanted to meet a Red Indian?

Why don't Canadians have group sex?
Too many thank-you letters to write afterwards.

You're Canadian if you know more than three guys named Gordon.

You're Canadian if you can eat more than one maple sugar candy without feeling nauseous.

You're Canadian if you think minus 10°C is mild weather.

You're Canadian if you substitute beer for water when cooking.

You're Canadian if your snow blower has done more mileage than your car.

You're Canadian if you have sex doggie-style so you can both watch hockey on TV.

You're Canadian if you have 10 favourite recipes for moose meat.

You're Canadian if you think driving is better in winter because the potholes are filled with snow.

You're Canadian if you know which leaves make good toilet paper.

You're Canadian if the trunk of your car doubles as a freezer.

You're Canadian if when someone steps on your foot, you apologize.

You're Canadian if you've ever had your tongue frozen to something.

CANNIBALS

A cannibal is a man who sometimes has his friends for dinner.

What does a cannibal do after dumping his girlfriend?
He wipes his ass.

Why did the cannibal eat a tightrope walker?
He wanted a balanced meal.

Did you hear about the cannibal who had a wife and ate kids?

What did the cannibal get when he was late for dinner?
The cold shoulder.

Why do cannibals like Jehovah's Witnesses?
They're free delivery.

What's a cannibal's favourite game?
Swallow the leader.

First cannibal: "Who was that lady I saw you with last night?"
Second cannibal: "That was no lady, that was my supper."

Why did the cannibal become a police officer?
So he could grill suspects.

What's a cannibal's favourite type of buffet?
A finger buffet.

When do cannibals leave the table?
When everyone's eaten.

What did the cannibal say when he was full up?
"I couldn't eat another mortal."

The cannibals' cookbook: *How To Better Serve Your Fellow Man.*

A cannibal came home from holiday on crutches with only one leg. He said: "That's the last time I go self-catering."

Did you hear about the cannibal who was expelled from school for buttering up his teacher?

What do cannibals do at a wedding?
They toast the bride and groom.

Did you hear about the cannibal who loved fast food?
He ordered a pizza with everybody on it.

A cannibal is someone who goes into a restaurant and orders the waiter.

Two cannibals are eating dinner. One says: "Your wife makes a great roast." "I know," says the other. "I'm going to miss her."

Definition of a cannibal: someone who is fed up with people.

What happened when the cannibal ate a missionary?
He got a taste of religion.

Why did the cannibal decide to become a missionary?
If you can't eat them, join them.

Did you hear about the cannibal who converted to Catholicism? Now he only eats fishermen on Fridays.

What did the cannibal cook say when a visitor told him the soup was the best he'd ever tasted?
"It's all relatives."

What happened when the cannibal turned vegetarian?
He only ate swedes.

Did you hear about the cannibal who passed his cousin in the woods?

A vegetarian, a meat eater and a cannibal walk into a bar. The vegetarian orders a salad and the meat-eater orders a burger. "Anything for you?" asks the bartender. "No, thanks," says the cannibal, "I'll wait till they're done."

Have you heard about the cannibal restaurant where dinner costs an arm and a leg?

Why was the cannibal sick after eating his mother-in-law?
Because she still didn't agree with him.

A cannibal arrives home to find his wife chopping up a cobra and a small man. "Oh, no," he groans, "not snake and pygmy pie again!"

Father and son cannibals spot a beautiful girl showering naked in a waterfall. The son asks: "Shall we take her home and eat her?" "No," says the father cannibal. "We'll take her home and eat your mother."

When their numbers dwindled from fifty down to eight, the remaining dwarfs began to suspect Hungry.

CATS

I like cats, too. Let's exchange recipes.

How do you know if your cat has eaten a duckling?
It has that "down-in-the-mouth" look.

Do radioactive cats have 18 half-lives?

How did a cat take first prize at the bird show?
By reaching into the cage.

Mother: "Stop pulling the cat's tail!"
Boy: "I'm not. I'm just holding the tail. The cat's doing the pulling."

When is it a bad time to cross a black cat?
When you're a mouse.

Why do you always find the cat in the last place you look?
Because you stop looking after you find it.

What did the cat do after eating cheese?
He waited by a mouse hole with baited breath.

What do you get if you cross a cat with a gorilla?
An animal that puts *you* out at night.

Cats took thousands of years to domesticate humans.

How do we know cats are smarter than dogs?
You can't get eight cats to pull a sled through snow.

At the cat Oscars, Tiddles won nine Lifetime Achievement Awards.

Apparently nine out of ten single women who sit at home and have conversations with their cats are mentally disturbed. My dog's full of useful information like that.

Cats may think they're clean, but really they're just covered in cat spit.

Why did the cat take up golf?
He liked to chase birdies.

Why did the litter of Republican kittens become Democrats?
Because they finally opened their eyes.

I thought about buying a cat, but then I realized that buying a cat isn't going to make me any less lonely. It's just going to give my loneliness a mascot. *Simon Amstell*

What was the cat's golf handicap?
Scratch.

Police suspected that a Manx cat was responsible for a series of break-ins at a hen house, so they put a tail on him.

Anything not nailed down is a cat toy.

How do you know when your cat's finished cleaning himself?
He's smoking a cigarette.

Wife: "Did you put the cat out?"
Husband: "I didn't even know it was on fire."

My cat can talk. I asked her what four minus four was, and she said nothing.

What's the difference between a cat and a comma?
One has the paws before the claws, and the other has the clause before the pause.

Never try to out-stubborn a cat.

You know when people see a cat litter box in your home, they always say: "Oh, have you got a cat?" Just once I want to say: "No, it's for visitors."

What happened to the cat that ate a ball of wool?
She had mittens.

What's the difference between cats and dogs?
Dogs have owners, cats have staff.

If you tied toast butter side up to the back of a cat and dropped it from a height, what would happen?

Letting the cat out of the bag is a whole lot easier than putting it back in.

I was really shocked when my sister told me her beloved cat had died and they were going to bury it in quick-drying cement. It still hasn't sunk in.

Did you hear about the cat that hijacked a plane and said: "Take me to the canaries"?

I'm getting fed up with the cat's constant scratching. I wish I'd never taught it to DJ. *Tony Cowards*

You know your cat is overweight when it needs a ramp to get into its cat litter box.

You know your cat is overweight when you apply wax to its belly to polish the floor.

You know your cat is overweight when it has a hula hoop for a collar.

You know your cat is overweight when it lands on its belly before it lands on its feet.

You know your cat is overweight when you can drill three holes in it and use it for a bowling ball.

You're a cat lover if your cat sleeps in your bed more often than your spouse.

You're a cat lover if you sleep in the oddest positions just to accommodate your cat.

You're a cat lover if you get a fish tank and fish as pets for your cat.

You're a cat lover if you know all the ingredients in Meow Mix by heart.

You're a cat lover if you have more cat toys than clothes.

You're a cat lover if when you wear black, people think you're shedding.

You're a cat lover if you cough up hairballs daily, too.

A tomcat purrs into a female cat's ear: "I'd die for you." She says: "How many times?"

CELEBRITIES

How do you find Will Smith in the snow?
Follow the fresh prints.

Celine Dion walked into a bar. The bartender said: "Why the long face?"

Michelle Pfeiffer has a silent P. But when she has a dump you can hear it downstairs.

Why is David Beckham like Ferrero Rocher?
They both come in a posh box.

It's people like Bob Geldof and Jamie Oliver who give kids a bad name.

Piers Morgan boasts that he and Manchester United footballer Wayne Rooney have a combined Twitter following of 3,000,000. That's amazing! Who would have thought Wayne Rooney would have 2,999,999 Twitter followers?

How did Bill Gates accumulate all his wealth?
By never spending more than $3 on a haircut.

A tan can look nice but Katie Price has gone way too far. She's now the colour of a hangover piss. *Sean Lock*

Police found a chocolate bar up George Michael's ass. It must have been a careless Wispa.

George Clooney taught me never to be a name-dropper.

When Joan Rivers has her make-up confiscated by airport security, the terrorists will realize they've gone too far.

I bought a 2011 Brigitte Bardot calendar. We've both seen better days.

Did you hear about the reality TV star whose career nose-dived so much that she was dropped from switching on the Christmas lights in her own home?

Why does Shane Warne never go to bed late?
So he can get up Hurley.

Paris Hilton had a nightmare. She was being chaste.

Kim Kardashian was apparently the most Googled celebrity last year – no doubt due to people Googling, "Who the hell is Kim Kardashian?"

Did you hear about the big argument that Madonna, Cher and Rihanna had? Apparently they're no longer on first-name terms.

What was Dolly Parton voted in school?
Most likely to breast-feed Africa.

Sean Connery has found his niche. She was in his back garden chatting to his nephew.

Why is Paul McCartney glum about his new wife?
He's buying twice the amount of shoes.

Rod Stewart is a man of principle. He absolutely will not go out with a woman with brown hair. *David Walliams*

Arnold Schwarzenegger was asked if he wanted to upgrade to Windows 7? He replied: "I still love Vista, baby."

CENTIPEDES

Do ten millipedes equal one centipede?

What has 50 legs but can't walk?
Half a centipede.

What do you get if you cross a centipede and a chicken?
Enough drumsticks to feed an army.

What lies on the ground 100 feet in the air?
A dead centipede.

My pet centipede just died. I'm not too surprised: it was on its last legs.

What's worse than a giraffe with a sore neck?
A centipede with athlete's foot.

What did the boy centipede say to the girl centipede?
"Wow! What a nice pair of legs, pair of legs, pair of legs . . ."

CHAVS

What do you say to a chav in a uniform?
"Big Mac and fries, please."

What do you call a chav in a suit?
The accused.

What do you call a chav at university?
The cleaner.

Did you hear about the chav who got into university?
Someone left the window open.

What do you call a chavette in a white tracksuit?
The bride.

What do you call a chav in a box?
Innit.

What do you call an Eskimo chav?
Inuinnit.

What do you call a chav in a four-bedroom house?
A burglar.

People say chavs contribute nothing to the economy, but they've done wonders for the paternity test industry.

I saw a chavette giving her chav boyfriend a really hard time. I thought, I can see who wears the tracksuit bottoms in that relationship.

What do you call a 30-year-old chavette?
Granny.

What is a belly button for?
It gives a chavette a place to park her gum on the way down.

What's the most confusing day of the year for a chav?
Father's Day.

What's the first question at a chav quiz night?
"What you lookin' at?"

What do you call a chav in a filing cabinet?
Sorted.

Why do 18-year-old chavs take sex education courses?
To find out what they've been doing wrong for the past five years.

What do you do if you see a chav riding a bike?
Chase after him; it's probably yours.

Did you hear about the chav who sued a baker for forging his signature on a hot cross bun?

What do you do if you run over a chav?
Reverse, just to make sure.

Why doesn't Viagra work on chavs?
Because they only get hard when they've got 10 mates behind them.

Chav proverb: necessity is the mother of invention, but nobody knows who the father is.

What's a chav's favourite car?
One without an alarm.

How do you know if a chav is a bad father?
He lets his 13-year-old daughter smoke in front of her kids.

What's the difference between Americans and chavs?
Americans have forefathers; chavs have four fathers.

CHICKENS

Who was the first person to say: "See that chicken? I'm going to eat the next thing that comes out of its butt."

Yesterday I told a chicken to cross the road. It said: "What for?"

Why did the chicken commit suicide?
To get to the other side.

Why did the rubber chicken cross the road?
To stretch her legs.

Why did the chicken go halfway across the road?
Because it wanted to lay it on the line.

Why doesn't a chicken wear pants?
Because his pecker is on his head.

Why did the chicken run on to the soccer pitch?
Because the referee blew for a fowl.

What do you get if you cross a chicken and a sergeant-major?
A pecking order.

What goes cluck, cluck, boom?
A chicken in a minefield.

Did you hear about the chicken that got sick with people pox?

How do we know that woodpeckers are smarter than chickens?
Ever heard of Kentucky Fried Woodpecker?

How are chickens like humans?
The rooster crows, but the hen delivers the goods.

A chicken laid an orange instead of an egg. One of her chicks said excitedly: "Look at the orange Mama laid."

On which side do chickens have the most feathers?
On the outside.

Do chickens think rubber humans are funny?

Did you hear about the habitual thief who had a pet chicken? He made a run for it.

What do you get when you cross a rooster with an owl?
A cock that stays up all night.

I used to run a dating agency for chickens, but I was struggling to make hens meet.

What bird lays electric eggs?
A battery hen.

What did the chicken say when it went to borrow three items from the library?
"Book, book, book."

Why did the starstruck chicken cross the road?
To see Gregory Peck.

What do you call a chicken in a shell suit?
An egg.

What do you call a chicken on a skateboard?
Poultry in motion.

How can you keep a rooster from crowing on Monday morning?
Eat him for Sunday lunch.

What do you get if you cross a cement mixer with a chicken?
A bricklayer.

A chicken and an egg were lying in bed together after a hot sex session. The chicken turned to the egg and said: "Well, that settles that old question."

CHILDHOOD

Childhood is like being drunk. Everyone remembers what you did, except you.

When I was a child, my mother told me I could be anyone I wanted to be. Turns out the police call this "identity theft".

I remember the time I was kidnapped and they sent a piece of my finger to my father. He said he wanted more proof. ***Rodney Dangerfield***

When I was in the Boy Scouts, I slipped on some ice and hurt my ankle. A little old lady had to help me across the street.

As I boy I ran away with the circus, but the police made me take it back.

I was such a beautiful child that my parents used to have me kidnapped just so they could see my picture in the papers.

When I was a kid, people used to cover me with cream and put cherries on my head. Yes, it was tough growing up in the gâteau.

I asked my mother if I was a gifted child. She said she certainly wouldn't have paid for me.

I never saw my granddad while I was growing up because he was excellent at hiding. *Harry Hill*

As a boy I always had my nose in a book. My parents couldn't afford Kleenex.

When I was a kid my parents moved a lot but I always found them.

I remember my aunt buying me a walkie-talkie for my sixth birthday. She said if I was good, she'd give me the other one for my seventh birthday.

When I was young, I had everything handed to me on a plate. Soup was a nightmare.

The older a man gets, the farther he had to walk to school as a boy.

I was the type of kid my mother told me not to play with.

When I was a kid I never went to Disneyland. My father told me Mickey Mouse died in a cancer experiment. *Rodney Dangerfield*

When I was a kid, I used to play the piano, and our dog used to howl along. Eventually my dad got fed up with this and yelled: "For God's sake, play something the dog doesn't know!"

When I was young, everyone said I had my mother's eyes. So I had to give them back to her.

CHILDREN

My wife and I decided we don't want children. If someone wants them, we'll drop them off tomorrow. *Stewart Francis*

My wife just had a real go at me for throwing a snowball at our son. To top it off, I've been banned from the maternity ward.

Boy to mother: "I'm glad you named me Ben because everybody calls me that."

Be nice to your children – they choose your nursing home.

A child's greatest period of growth is the month after you've bought new school uniforms.

Pride is what you feel when your kids net $180 from a garage sale. Panic is when you realize your car is missing.

My wife's carrying our first child. I told her: "He's nine; he should be walking by now."

Watching a vicar perform a baptism, a little girl turned to her father and said: "Why is he brainwashing that baby?"

Having one child makes you a parent; having two makes you a referee.

Children seldom misquote you. In fact, they usually repeat word for word what you shouldn't have said.

I wanted to name our son after my father, but my wife didn't think Dad was a good name for a boy.

What's the way to stop your children being spoiled?
Keep them in the fridge.

Boy: "Dad, can I have another glass of water?"
Dad: "But I've given you 10 already!" Boy: **"I know, but my bedroom's still on fire."**

At the age of six I was left an orphan. What kind of idiot gives an orphan to a six-year-old?

Adults are always asking children what they want to be when they grow up because they are looking for ideas.

Never put a child wearing Superman pyjamas on the top bunk.

I take my kids everywhere, but they keep finding their way back.

Family planning means having all your children while their grandparents are still young enough to be babysitters.

Child: "Please can I wear a bra, Mum? I'm 14 now."
Mother: "For the last time: no, Jonathan."

Every relationship needs children. Who else is going to teach us how to program the DVD player?

We bought our young son a jigsaw to keep him occupied while we were out. We came back to find he had cut his fingers off.

Children certainly brighten up a home – they never turn the lights off.

My son asked me where the most dangerous place in the world is. I'm stuck between Iraq/Kandahar place.

I've got two wonderful children – and two out of five isn't bad.

The cheeky children next door challenged me to a water fight. I said: "OK, I'll be five minutes – as soon as the kettle's boiled."

I want to have a kid the way other people want to own stock in Google: I don't want to be responsible for it; I just want to go to parties and talk about how well it's doing.

How did the blind boy's parents punish him?
They rearranged the furniture.

A small boy came home from school carrying a sofa on his back and an armchair under each arm. His father raged: "How many times have I told you about accepting suites from strangers?"

My kids are seven and five. We couldn't think of better names.

Which sexual position produces the ugliest children?
Ask your mother.

If you wonder where your child left his roller skates, try walking around the house in the dark.

Son: "Dad, what's a hermaphrodite?"
Father: "I don't know, son, but ask your mother – he'll know."

Children are like farts – your own are just about tolerable but everyone else's are horrendous.

I learnt today that the world is a dangerous place – I tripped over my son's globe.

Why did the couple call their son Isaiah?
Because on his face one eye's 'igher than the other.

Father: "And what will you do when you grow up to be as big as me?"
Son: "Diet."

My wife and I already have five kids, but we're going to keep on trying until we get one we like.

Boy to friend: "I know the name of my next brother: Quits. Because I heard my dad say, 'After this one, we're going to call it Quits.'"

My young son is being referred to a child psychologist. We'd rather he saw an adult, but they're so expensive.

Teach a child to be polite and courteous, and when he grows up he'll never be able to edge his car on to a freeway.

Mother: "Why did you swallow those coins I gave you?"
Boy: "You said it was my lunch money."

Most children eat broccoli so they'll grow up big and strong enough to refuse it.

A mother kept telling her child not to swing from the tree branch, but he ignored her. Exasperated, she said: "Well, if you break your leg, don't come running to me."

I want to have three kids and name them Ctrl, Alt and Delete. Then if they mess up, I will just hit them all at once.

Son: "Dad, what's the difference between confident and confidential?"
Father: "Well, you are my son. Of that I am confident. Your friend James is also my son. That is confidential."

A small boy arrives home from school and wails: "Mom, everyone says I'm too hairy." The mother yells to her husband: "Honey, the dog is talking!"

Young girl to friend: "I'm never having kids. I hear they take nine months to download."

There are three ways to get something done: do it yourself, pay someone to do it, or tell your kids *not* to do it.

We have learnt to space our children. Ten feet apart is about right.

When you give a child a hammer, everything becomes a nail.

It's amazing how time flies. It's my daughter's seventh birthday today, and it seems like only yesterday that she was six.

I sat down with my nine-year-old son today. We had the "birds and bees" chat. I learnt a lot.

When she was at school my daughter always said she wanted to work with animals. Yet she wasn't the least bit grateful when I got her a job in an abattoir.

Parents are the one thing that children wear out faster than shoes.

How do you get a child to stop wetting the bed?
Give him an electric blanket.

Two children were deciding what game to play. "Let's play doctor," said one. "Good idea," said the other. "You operate and I'll sue."

Boy to mother: "I broke a vase in Charlie's house, but you don't have to worry about buying another one. Charlie's mother said it was irreplaceable."

It doesn't matter what you buy children for Christmas, they always prefer the box it came out of . . . which, ironically, is exactly how I feel about kids.

Mother: "Why did you kick your brother in the stomach?"
Boy: "Because he turned around."

A scoutmaster asked his troop to name a good deed they had done that day. One boy put his hand up and said: "Mom only had one dose of castor oil left, so I let my baby brother have it."

What do you get when you cross LSD with a birth control pill?
A trip without the kids.

You're a mother if you count the number of sprinkles on each kid's cupcake to make sure they are equal.

You're a mother if you hide in the bathroom to be alone.

You're a mother if your child throws up and you catch it.

You're a mother if you find yourself cutting your husband's sandwiches into unusual shapes.

You're a mother if you only have time to shave one leg at a time.

You're a mother if you consider finger paint to be a controlled substance.

You're a mother if you fast-forward through the scene where the hunter shoots Bambi's mother.

I've just found out I've got a three-year-old daughter. My wife says I need to be a bit more attentive around the house.

CHINA

Why is there no Disneyland in China?
No one's tall enough to go on the good rides.

What do people in China call their good plates?

A Chinese couple are in bed. The husband says: "I want a 69." The wife replies: "You want beef with broccoli at this time of night?"

What has two wings and a halo?
A Chinese telephone.

A man orders soup in a Chinese restaurant. When the waitress brings it, the man is looking out of the window. "Looks like rain," he says. The waitress says: "Yeah, but it's soup!"

Do Chinese people get English sayings tattooed on their bodies?

The lights were too bright at the Chinese restaurant, so the manager decided to dim sum.

Chopsticks are one of the reasons the Chinese never invented custard.
Spike Milligan

It must be really difficult telling someone a secret in China.

A customer in a Chinese restaurant says: "Waiter! This chicken is rubbery." "Thank you," says the waiter.

There's a new Chinese diet. You can eat whatever you want, but you only have one chopstick.

A friend of mine said he wanted to contact the Chinese Mafia. I said: "Triads?" He said: "I hadn't thought of that."

My barometer is made in China. It tells me when it's raining in Shanghai.

Last week there was a lookalike contest in China. Everybody won.

CHRISTMAS

I discovered Santa wasn't real when my plan to drug him and rob his sleigh put my dad in ER having his stomach pumped.

Why is Santa always so jolly?
He knows where all the bad girls live.

I bought myself a barge pole for Christmas. Thought I'd push the boat out. *Tony Cowards*

I got a herbal belt for Christmas – complete waist of thyme.

He knows when you're awake. He knows what you look like. He knows what you've been doing all year round. Sounds like Santa has Facebook.

Why is Santa's sack so big?
He only comes once a year.

I bought my daughter a neurotic doll for Christmas – it was wound up already.

What did Adam say on 24 December?
"It's Christmas, Eve."

Last year for Christmas, I got a humidifier and a dehumidifier. I thought I'd put them in the same room and let them fight it out. *Steven Wright*

My donkey ate our Christmas tree . . . which was a pine in the ass.

What do you get if you eat all the Christmas decorations?
Tinselitis.

The run-up to Christmas is the one time of year that you can slam your laptop shut when your girlfriend walks into the room and not get disgusted looks.

Which playwright was terrified of Christmas?
Noël Coward.

I'm doing my bit to help the homeless this Christmas. I've got stacks of cardboard boxes to give away.

Father: "Did you see Santa this year, son?"
Boy: "No, it was too dark. But I heard what he said when he stubbed his toe on my bed."

What did Santa's wife say during a thunderstorm?
"Come and look at the rain, dear."

If you work from home, you can save a fortune on Christmas presents. Just wait for the postman to deliver your neighbours' parcels to you when they're out.

Is it just me, or does people moaning about Christmas beginning earlier every year begin earlier every year? *Gary Delaney*

I've just bought some Emo Christmas lights. They're great: they hang themselves.

It was so cold last Christmas that Mum served pigs in electric blankets.

At Christmas, nothing says "I couldn't give a damn about you" quite like an e-card.

I bought my wife a wooden leg for Christmas. It's not her main present – it's just a stocking filler.

I've found that the best place to hide Christmas presents is in the mouth of a gift horse.

What did Santa call the reindeer with an injured leg?
Dinner.

New regulations say Santa's helpers must wear a seatbelt at all times when they're on the sleigh. It's elfin safety gone mad.

On the first day of Christmas my true love gave to me a partridge in a pear tree. I got her socks.

What did the fireman's wife get for Christmas?
A ladder in her stocking.

The quietest Christmas I remember was when my mum accidentally put temazepam on the cake. *Milton Jones*

Our town's Christmas lights used energy-saving bulbs for the first time. After the big switch-on, we only had to wait two hours to see how pretty it was.

Remember: a puppy isn't just for Christmas. With any luck there'll be some left over to eat on Boxing Day as well.

I like to decorate the tree with the kids, but now they're getting older it's harder to find branches that will support their weight.

Apparently turkeys did actually vote for Christmas, but afterwards many complained that they found the ballot papers confusing.

My brother's a keen scuba diver, so one Christmas I bought him a mask and a pair of flippers, which was awkward because we always wear our new presents when we visit our mother on Boxing Day.

He got his own back on me the following year by buying me ten pairs of underpants.

What do you call Santa's helpers?
Subordinate clauses.

I come from a very traditional family. One Christmas Eve my uncle hanged himself, and we didn't take his body down till 6 January.

Due to a typo, this year the local school is putting on a "Naivety Play", in which Joseph and Mary make all kinds of silly assumptions.

I've finally found the true meaning of Xmas. It's for people who can't spell Christmas.

They say get your Christmas shopping done early to avoid the rush but this year I did mine a whole 12 months early and the shops were as busy as ever.

Why is Christmas just like a day at the office?
Because you do all the work and the fat guy in the suit gets all the credit.

I love to give homemade gifts. Which one of my kids do you want?

Last Christmas someone stole my present. I've spent this year living in the past. *Terry Alderton*

I got a sweater for Christmas. But really I wanted a screamer or a moaner.

Did you know Santa has a tenth reindeer, Olive? She's mentioned in Rudolph's song: "Olive the other reindeer . . ."

Santa goes to a psychiatrist and says: "Doc, I just don't believe in myself."

Father Christmas. Wears red. Good at breaking into houses. Has loads of electrical goods that nobody can trace. Drives an unlicensed vehicle. Works only one day a year. He's not from Lapland, he's a Scouser!

CHUCK NORRIS

Chuck Norris does not wear a condom because there's no such thing as protection from Chuck Norris.

Some people wear Superman pyjamas. Superman wears Chuck Norris pyjamas.

They once made Chuck Norris toilet paper, but it wouldn't take shit from anybody.

Chuck Norris doesn't worry about changing his clocks twice a year for Daylight Saving Time. The sun rises and sets when Chuck tells it to.

Chuck Norris will never have a heart attack because his heart isn't foolish enough to attack him.

Chuck Norris is the reason why Waldo is hiding.

When Chuck Norris does a push-up he isn't lifting himself up, he's pushing the Earth down.

There used to be a street named after Chuck Norris, but it was changed because nobody crosses Chuck Norris and lives.

Aliens do exist. They're just waiting for Chuck Norris to die before they attack.

Chuck Norris's tears cure cancer. Too bad he has never cried.

Chuck Norris has a grizzly-bear carpet in his room. The bear isn't dead: it's just afraid to move.

There's no such thing as a tornado. Chuck Norris just hates trailer parks.

Chuck Norris doesn't flush the toilet. He scares the shit out of it.

When Alexander Bell invented the telephone, he found he had three missed calls from Chuck Norris.

Chuck Norris once kicked the Earth. It hasn't stopped spinning since.

When the bogeyman goes to sleep, he checks under the bed for Chuck Norris.

CLOTHES

The chief stealer of T-shirts in order of size is still at large.

I saw this gorgeous girl in a nightclub wearing a chess-patterned top. So I made a move on her.

Husband: "What do you mean, you need a new dress? What's wrong with the one you've got?"
Wife: "It's too long, and the veil keeps getting in my eyes."

Wear short sleeves – support your right to bare arms.

Did you hear about the fashion designer who combined the national dress of India with the carefree styling of Polynesia? He called it his "Sari, Sarong number".

I went into the changing room several times, but it was still the same.

People wear designer clothes to show that they can afford to. They should just wear a T-shirt with a photocopy of their most recent bank statement on it. *Michael McIntyre*

The designers of jeans are always looking at the bottom line.

Mike: "What do you think of my new suit?"
Marty: "Very nice. Were you there for the fitting?"

Did you hear about the man who bought his wife a hamster fur coat? He took her to Blackpool for the day and she spent six hours on the big wheel.

Her dress looked good considering the shape it was on.

I knew I could count on my wife – she always wears beads.

Panties: not the best thing on earth, but next to the best thing on earth.

Wife to husband: "Do you remember that backless, frontless, bottomless, topless evening gown I bought? I just found out it's a belt."

I bought some jeans marked "50 per cent off". They only had one leg.

The state of Georgia is banning the wearing of low-slung pants. Police refuse to comment on the crackdown.

What's another name for the zip on men's jeans?
A penis fly trap.

A man says to his friend: "My wife has only two complaints: nothing to wear and not enough closet space."

Why are the short corsets kept apart from all the other items of underwear in Victoria's Secret?
The manager's a basque separatist.

His suit was so loud he had to buy a muffler to wear with it.

My wife was looking through a fashion magazine, and she saw a fur coat. She said: "I want that." So I cut it out and gave it to her. *Tommy Cooper*

I thought my wife was happy to repair my jeans fully – or at least sew its seams.

Mike: "Is that an Italian suit you're wearing?"
Marty: "Yes, can't you see the spaghetti Bolognese stains down the front?"

I went into this place and an Asian girl started stroking my neckwear. Turned out it was a tie massage parlour.

Did you hear about the woman who got so fed up with putting name tags on her son's school shirts that she changed his name by deed poll to Machine Washable?

Why did the idiot buy his girlfriend fishnet stockings?
She told him she had crabs.

My sister likes to dress provocatively in case she has a stalker. She says she doesn't want to be a disappointment to anyone.

Why did the belt go to jail?
Because it held up a pair of pants.

My wife was trying on different things yesterday and asked me what would make her new dress look sexier. I said: "Give it to your sister."

I used to be a member of the Robust Neckwear Society. I still have strong ties with them.

Why are there many more organizations against fur clothing than against leather clothing?
Because it is easier to harass rich women than bikers.

I've decided to paint all my clothes. I've just finished the second coat.

How many fish in a pair of tights?
Five. Two eels, two soles, and a little wet plaice.

Short skirts make men polite. Have you ever seen a man get on a bus ahead of one?

I went out with a girl last week, and she wore a real slinky number. She looked great going down the stairs. *Milton Jones*

I saw a woman wearing a T-shirt with "Guess" on it. I said: "Implants?"

Autumn is the season when your wife buys new winter clothes so she will have something to wear when she goes out shopping for spring outfits.

I used to dress off the peg, but now my neighbours take their washing in at night.

Before mini-skirts became popular, you had to listen if you wanted to know if a girl was knock-kneed.

I'm done with tucking in shirts – too many people complaining that I'm invading their "personal space".

Husband to wife: "Whatever kind of look you were aiming at, you missed."

Jackie: "Whenever I'm down in the dumps I buy myself a dress."
Jill: "I've always wondered where you got them."

Did you hear about the guy who left his Viagra tablet in his shirt pocket when he sent it to the laundry? Now the shirt is too stiff to wear.

I said to my girlfriend: "You look really awful in those jeans." She said: "That's below the belt."

The best way to remove red wine stains from a white blouse is with a pair of scissors.

Did you hear about the man who bought his wife a pair of fur panties because he wanted something that would tickle her fancy?

Some bikinis are smaller than their price tag.

Bikinis today are really something – if you can call nothing something.

A girl in a swimsuit wears nothing to speak of, but plenty to talk about.

I hate turtlenecks. Wearing a turtleneck is like being strangled by a really weak guy – all day. **Mitch Hedberg**

Why is it that when you hang something in your closet for a few months, it automatically shrinks two sizes?

What did the tie say to the hat?
"You go on ahead and I'll hang around."

What did the bra say to the sock?
"I'll cover these two. You go on foot."

Mike: "Why are you wearing loud socks?"
Marty: "So my feet don't fall asleep."

My wife is very big in fashion – she's a size 22.

Did you hear about those new reversible jackets? It will be interesting to see how they turn out.

On a crazy impulse, I decided to throw out all my socks. But at the last minute I got cold feet.

Our next-door neighbours had a huge row, which ended with the wife throwing her husband's clothes out of the window. Unfortunately he was wearing them at the time.

Never trust a man with a tassel on his loafer. Did his foot just graduate?

I bought a suit made from cactus. I looked pretty sharp in it.

So it's perfectly acceptable for me to come home to find my wife wandering around the house in a pair of my shorts and a T-shirt, but as soon as it's the other way round, suddenly "We need to talk." **Sean Lock**

Wear black: all the non-conformists are doing it.

They should put expiry dates on clothes, so we men know when they go out of fashion.

How can you tell if a woman is wearing pantyhose?
Her ankles swell when she farts.

The definition of irony: size 20 skinny jeans.

Those push-up bras don't work. I bought one for my girlfriend, but she can still only do 10 or so before her arms get tired.

The one thing you can be sure about a well-dressed man is that his wife chooses his clothes.

How can you get four suits for $2?
Buy a pack of cards.

Did you hear about the man who bought a jacket from a charity shop?
The only thing wrong with it was that one sleeve was slightly longer than the other two.

I went to buy some camouflage trousers the other day, but I couldn't find any.

COLLECTIVE NOUNS

An aarmory of aardvarks

An absence of waiters

An ambush of widows

An annoyance of mobile phones

An assemblage of jigsaw puzzlers

A barren of mules

A bevy of alcoholics

A billow of smokers

A bloat of hippopotami

A blur of cyclists

A boast of egotists

A bodge of DIY-ers

A body of pathologists

A bond of secret agents

A brace of orthodontists

A bunch of florists

A cast of orthopaedists

A chapter of authors

A clutch of auto mechanics

A complex of psychiatrists

A confusion of traffic cones

A decanter of publicans

A deck of sailors

A dilation of pupils

A dose of doctors

A drove of cabbies

An embarrassment of parents

An exaggeration of fishermen

An expectation of midwives

A fidget of suspects

A flash of paparazzi

A flood of plumbers

A flunk of students

A flutter of cardiologists

A formation of geologists

A fright of ghosts

A galaxy of chocoholics

A giggle of schoolgirls

A gossip of relatives

A greed of lawyers

A gross of farts

A gush of sycophants

A hack of journalists

A hail of taxi drivers

A hamper of helpers

A hoard of misers

A hover of hummingbirds

A hoy of sailors

A huff of people who write letters to the editor

An immersion of Baptists

An imposition of in-laws

An incision of surgeons

An indifference of supermarket checkout girls

A jam of tarts

A karen of carpenters

A knot of shoelaces

A lechery of priests

A lie of politicians

A lot of car dealers

A magnum of hitmen

A mass of Catholics

A maul of bears

A murder of crime writers

A nucleus of physicists

A pack of holidaymakers

A plump of weightwatchers

A pod of vegetarians

A prevarication of consultants

A pride of actors

A reflection of narcissists

A set of ladies' hairdressers

A shortage of dwarves

A slice of circumcisions

A sloth of mailmen

A snatch of muggers

A spread of nymphomaniacs

A stretch of giraffes

A sulk of teenagers

A tenet of palindromes

A tyranny of dictators

A wiggle of Marilyn Monroe impersonators

COMMUNICATION

Wrestlers don't like to be put on hold.

Somebody sent me "gabn" in a text message last week. I think that's bang out of order.

A man texts his wife: "Honey, I'm just having one more beer in the pub and then I'm coming home. If I'm not back in 30 minutes, just read this text again."

It's always difficult texting someone to tell them one of their loved ones has passed away, especially when your name is Lol.

My wife sent me a blank text. When I asked why, she texted back: "Because I'm not talking to you."

I received a massive phone bill today. I've no idea why they've started using A1 paper.

Instead of her usual two hours, my wife was on the phone for only 25 minutes last night. I said: "Wow! That was short! What happened?" She said: "It was a wrong number."

What do you get if you iron a call centre worker?
A smooth operator.

I phoned the bondage helpline, but all the operators were tied up.

Mike: "Can you telephone from an airplane?"
Marty: "Sure, anyone can tell a phone from an airplane."

I think I may be a talented photographer. I took just one picture with my camera phone and it asked me if I wanted to open a gallery.

Whoever said talk is cheap hasn't seen our phone bill.

With mobiles, Apple and BlackBerry are rivals. But in a crumble, they're harmony. *Sean Lock*

Why are there so many Smiths in the phone book?
Because they all have phones.

My girlfriend said I spend far too much time texting. I just tilted my head sideways and smiled at her.

I cancelled my mobile phone contract. I was offered 500 texts a month for $20, but it's been six months now and I haven't received a single text.

I just got a new mobile phone but I can only use it in church. I think it must be "pray as you go".

Mobile phones are the only things where men boast about who's got the smallest.

The mobile phone, the fax machine, email: call me old-fashioned, but what's wrong with a chain of beacons? *Harry Hill*

A self-addressed envelope would be addressed "Envelope".

People usually get what's coming to them – unless it was mailed.

An old lady takes a package to the Post Office to be weighed. "It's too heavy," says the clerk. "You'll need to put more stamps on it." "Oh," says the old lady. "Will that make it lighter?"

Another old lady takes a letter to the Post Office. The clerk says: "You put too much postage on this letter." "Oh, dear," she says. "It won't go too far, will it?"

A letter landed on my doormat with "Do not bend" on it. I thought: How am I going to pick it up?

Important letters that contain no errors will develop errors in the mail.

Mailman: "Is this letter for you? The name is smudged."
Man: "No, it can't be for me. My name is Jones."

I got a letter offering me a heavy duty protective metal vest for half price. Bloody chain mail!

I like to annoy my Israeli flatmate by giving him any mail addressed to "The Occupier".

Never answer an anonymous letter.

I phoned a company and asked to speak to Dave. They said: "Dave's on vacation. Would you like to hold?"

When my answering machine broke, my neighbour who is a DJ offered to fix it. But now I'm getting mixed messages.

Telegram company boss: "This telegram doesn't make sense, boy. What on earth have you done?"
Employee: "But, sir, you told me to pull out all the stops."

What's worse than your girlfriend sending you a text to break up?
Another text saying, "Sorry that wasn't for you."

Captain Hook is better at text messaging than my brother.

Is an insulting telegram a barbed wire?

How does a cheerleader answer the phone?
"H-E-L-L-O."

I rang a call centre, and the automated voice said: "All our advisers are engaged." Congratulations to them all. Now answer the damn phone!

Why is it that whenever you call a wrong number, someone always answers?

Answering machine message: "Hi, I'm probably home. I'm just avoiding someone I don't like. Leave a message and if I don't call back, it's you."

Answering machine message: "Hi, John's answering machine is broken. This is his refrigerator. Please speak very slowly and I'll stick your message to myself with one of these magnets."

Answering machine message: "My wife and I can't come to the phone right now, but if you leave your name and number we'll get back to you as soon as we're finished."

Answering machine message: "Hi, I'm John's answering machine. What are you?"

Is being a telephone operator a job or a profession?
Actually it's more like a calling.

Some days I have to take three or four baths to make the phone ring.

When is the cheapest time to call your friends long distance?
When they're not at home.

Having a mobile phone is the technological equivalent of lying on the bed with your legs wide open all the time.

My wife said we needed to communicate more. I knew she was right, so I gave her my email address.

I rang the phone company to report a nuisance caller. They said: "Oh, no. Not you again!" *Tim Vine*

I just typed "married" and it came out "martyred". Damn' smart phone is becoming self-aware.

I sent a text to my granddad using my dead nan's phone. I'm sure he'll see the funny side, once he recovers from his heart attack.

COMPUTERS

How can you tell when your computer's starting to get old?
It loses its memory.

How can you stop your husband reading your email?
Rename the email folder "Instruction Manual".

What happened when the boy computer mouse met the girl computer mouse?
They clicked straight away.

A clean house is the sign of a broken computer.

My laptop keeps playing "Someone Like You" over and over again. Probably because it's a Dell.

A TV can insult your intelligence, but nothing rubs it in like a computer.

I can hear music coming from my printer. I think the paper's jamming again.

Why did the idiot take his computer to the shoe shop?
Because he had been told to re-boot it.

My spell czech is still broken.

When Tim Cook took charge of Apple, I was expecting the headlines to say: "Cook promises to improve Apple turnover".

What is a cursor?
Someone who is having problems with his computer.

Teacher: "Why do you want me to email your exam results to your parents? They don't have a computer."
Pupil: "Exactly!"

Computers are almost human – except they don't blame their mistakes on other computers.

I got a good deal on a new computer, and they threw in the operating system to boot.

Your ideal computer comes on the market about two days after you bought some other computer.

Did you hear about the man who thought it would be funny to choose "Mydick" as his computer password? A message came back: "Not long enough".

My son broke his Apple computer and had the cheek to ask me for a new one. I told him: "Apples don't grow on trees, you know!"

People who plug their computer keyboards into their hi-fi systems aren't idiots. That would be stereotyping.

Doesanyoneknowwhatthebaronthebottomofthekeyboardisfor?

A woman was having problems with her computer, so she rang tech support. The guy asked: "Do you have any windows open right now?" She said: "Are you crazy? It's the middle of winter!"

There are only two kinds of computer: the latest model and the obsolete.

I tried my hand at computer hacking, but I think I need a larger machete.

You can guarantee that your computer will always crash one second before you remember to save.

I'm all for computer dating, but I wouldn't want one to marry my sister.

If Bill Gates had a penny for every time I had to re-boot my computer . . . Oh, wait. He does.

Computers will never replace books. You can't stand on a floppy disk to reach the top shelf.

Did you hear about the husband and wife computer programmers who made a fortune? He wrote viruses, she wrote anti-viruses.

For sale: one computer, slightly used. Bullet hole in screen.

If I leave my computer idle for 10 minutes, an image of Jesus pops up. It's my screen saviour.

Did you hear about the man who took his laptop for a run so he could jog his memory?

If a "fatal" error is made with an email you've sent, does it mean you've killed somebody?

"Knock knock." "Who's there?" Very long pause. "Java."

A printer consists of three main parts: the case, the jammed paper tray and the blinking red light.

I recently realized that the letters T and G are far too close together on a keyboard. This is why I'll never again be ending a works email with "Regards". *Stewart Francis*

Who is General Failure, and why is he reading my hard disk?

What goes choo choo choo while online?
Thomas the search engine.

Do computer files get embarrassed when they're unzipped?

Did you hear about the man who dropped a computer on his toes? He had megahertz.

Our computers went down at work, so we had to do everything manually. It took me 20 minutes to shuffle the cards for solitaire.

There's only one satisfying way to boot a computer.

I found a spider living in my keyboard. It's OK, it's under Ctrl.

Why was the computer tired when it got home?
Because it had a hard drive.

Jackie: "So what makes you think you've been spending too much time on the computer?"
Jill: "Yesterday I tried to enter my password on the microwave."

Why are computers like air conditioners?
They work fine until you start opening Windows.

I can't see an end. I have no control and I don't think there's any escape – I don't even have a home any more. Definitely time for a new keyboard.

CONFUCIUS, HE SAY . . .

Woman who sleep with judge get honourable discharge.

Man who go to bed with hard problem wake up with solution in hand.

Man who eat crackers in bed wake up feeling crummy.

Woman who stay on bedspring too long get offspring.

Man who run behind car get exhausted.

Man who sink into woman's arms soon have arms in woman's sink.

Man who leap off cliff jump to conclusion.

Man with hand in pocket always on the ball.

Man who throw dirt will lose ground.

Man who put head in fruit drink get punch in nose.

Man who fight with wife all day get no piece at night.

Wise man never play leapfrog with unicorn.

Man who sit on tack get point in the end.

Good for girl to meet boy in park, but better for boy to park meat in girl.

Man who cut self while shaving lose face.

Foolish man give wife grand piano, wise man give wife upright organ.

Man who smoke pot choke on handle.

Chemist who fall in acid get absorbed in work.

Man have more hair on chest than woman, but on whole woman have more.

Man who kiss girl on hill not on level.

Man who jump off Paris bridge in Seine.

With great power come huge electricity bill.

Man who confuse food processor with word processor end up mincing words.

Man who drive like hell bound to get there.

Woman who spend too much time on bed spring should get off spring.

Man who eat prunes get good run for money.

Crowded elevator smell different to midget.

Man who put head on railroad track to listen for train likely to end up with splitting headache.

Man who stand on toilet is high on pot.

Man who eat photo of father soon spitting image of father.

Man who handle privates all day not necessarily sergeant.

Man who put cream in tart not necessarily baker.

Woman's charms like spider's web – lead to flies undoing.

CONSCIENCE

A clear conscience is usually the sign of a bad memory.

A conscience does not prevent sin. It merely prevents you enjoying it.

Why does a man have a clear conscience?
Because it's unused.

COOKING

I'm the kind of guy who stops the microwave at one second just to feel like a bomb defuser.

Wife: "The two things I cook best are meatloaf and apple pie."
Husband: "And which is this?"

His first wife could cook but wouldn't. His second wife can't cook but does.

My wife's cooking is like a good man – hard to keep down.

I often experiment with recipes by adding German white wine. This is nothing formal, just an add hock approach.

Wife: "So, darling, what will I get if I cook a dinner like that every day?"
Husband: "My life insurance."

Home cooking is where many a man thinks his wife is.

Wife: "I've made the chicken soup."
Husband: "Oh, good. I was worried it was for us."

I miss my wife's cooking – as often as I can. *Henny Youngman*

Woman to dinner party host: "You must give me the recipe – so you can't cook it again."

What is a wok used for?
Throwing at wabbits.

Wife: "I've baked two kinds of cookies today. Would you like to take your pick?"
Husband: "No, I'll just use the hammer as usual."

A Tibetan housewife walks into her smoke-filled kitchen and groans: "Oh, my baking yak!"

My wife must worship me: she puts burnt offerings in front of me every day.

Mike: "Hey, Marty, what should I do? Before she left for work, my wife told me to put the casserole in at 220, but I don't get in till a quarter-to-four."

I read recipes the way I read science fiction. I get to the end and think, "Well, that's not going to happen."

Husband: "Honey, what's this on the plate in case I have to describe it to my doctor?"

She's such a lousy cook, she uses the smoke alarm as a timer.

She's such a lousy cook, her cat has only three lives left.

She's such a lousy cook, even the cockroaches eat out.

She's such a lousy cook, even Oliver Twist declined seconds.

She's such a lousy cook, her microwave displays "Help!"

She's such a lousy cook, the only thing you get for dessert is indigestion.

How can you tell when a turkey is done?
~~It flushes the toilet.~~

Jackie: "Why don't you cook?"
Jill: "I can't be good in every room of the house!"

Wife: "Quick! There's a burglar in the kitchen eating my homemade steak pie."
Husband: "Who shall I call, police or ambulance?"

I'm dreading the weekend. I've got to go to my mother's cremation – or Sunday lunch as she calls it.

My wife's cooking leaves me speechless, because most of it is still stuck to my teeth.

Husband: "OK, honey, have we got everything we need to accompany your dish – salt, pepper, stomach pump?"

What happened when the chef got his hand caught in the dishwasher?
They both got fired.

I've just spent $350 on a set of top-quality chef's knives, but I'm not sure which one I'm supposed to use for piercing the film on my microwavable meal.

The German meal my wife cooked was so authentic, I feel ready to invade Poland.

Husband: "Hi, honey, are we eating out tonight? I can't smell anything burning."

Wife: "I'm sorry the cat ate your dinner."
Husband: "Don't worry. We'll get another cat."

COWBOYS

Why do cowboys wear two spurs? If one side of the horse goes, surely the other side goes, too.

Did you hear about the cowboy who dressed from head to toe in brown paper? He was wanted for rustling.

A lot of conflict in the old Wild West could have been avoided if nineteenth-century architects had made their towns big enough for more than one person.

How did the sheriff capture the chocolate-loving cowboy?
There was a Bounty on his head.

What did the cowboy say when he walked into the German car showroom?
"Audi!"

Why are cowgirls bowlegged?
Because cowboys like to eat with their hats on.

What do you call a dinosaur that wears a cowboy hat and boots?
Tyrannosaurus Tex.

Cowboys never saw the irony of transporting liquor on the wagon.

Why can't the bankrupt cowboy complain?
He has got no beef.

Did you hear about the cowboy who bought himself a dachshund . . . because everyone kept telling him to get a long, little doggie?

Two cowboys are in the kitchen. Which is the real cowboy?
The one on the range.

Cowboy wisdom: don't squat with your spurs on.

A cowboy takes his new wife to a hotel and asks for a room. The receptionist says: "Do you want the bridal?" The cowboy replies: "No, I'll just hold on to her ears till she gets used to it."

CRICKET

An American watching cricket says: "Hey, that bowler is awesome! He hits that bat right in the middle every goddamn time!"

"You need glasses," said the dismissed batsman as he passed the man in the white coat. "So do you, mate," said the man. "I'm not the umpire, I'm selling ice cream!"

Why couldn't Robin play cricket?
He'd lost his bat, man.

Bowler: "I had three catches dropped today."
Captain: "Yes, but they were all dropped by spectators in the stand!"

Greek spectator to his brother: "I don't know what you think of this cricket game, but it's all English to me!"

Watching cricket, I told my wife I wanted a divorce. She said: "Can't we talk this over?" I said: "You'll have to be quick. There are only two balls left."

CRIME

Did you hear about the woman who was sexually assaulted by a gang of mime artists? They performed unspeakable acts on her.

Why has the thief who stole items of ladies' underwear not been caught yet?
He gave police the slip.

Following the theft of a dozen boxes of wigs and hair extensions from a store in Essex, police are reported to be combing the area.

Did you hear about the limbo dancer who had his pockets picked? How could anyone stoop so low?

Did you hear about the thief who stole a calendar? He got 12 months.

Did you hear about the woman at the flower shop who was robbed at knifepoint? She was a petrified florist.

What goes 99 thump?
An ice cream man being mugged.

Barrister: "Madam, can you explain to the court how you came to stab your husband 125 times?"
Defendant: "I couldn't turn off the electric knife."

What would happen if you hired two private investigators to follow each other?

I've had a lot of stuff go missing since that keyhole surgeon moved in next door. Mostly small things, mind you. *Sean Lock*

Why did the robber have a bath?
He wanted to make a clean getaway.

Did you hear about the woman who was mugged by an acupuncturist? She was stabbed 128 times but the next morning she felt great.

Does shoplifting from the Apple store only count as scrumping?

If you watch an Apple store getting robbed, are you an iWitness?

These days, gangs just go around shooting each other and driving off. At least back in the old days, like in *West Side Story*, they used to dance with each other first.

Which American duo were famous horse thieves?
Bonnie and Clydesdale.

Did you hear about the barber who was arrested for running a clip joint?

What happened after a ladder was stolen from the hardware store?
The manager said steps will be taken.

My mood ring was stolen last night. I'm not sure how I feel about it.

A quantity of silk was stolen from a fabric factory, but the robbery was seen by a roll of cotton. It was held as a material witness.

A man suspected of chopping people's fingers off with a machete was released today because nobody could point him out in a line-up.

Police are on the lookout for a cross-eyed burglar. They have told members of the public: "If you see him peering in your front window, please warn your next-door neighbour."

A thief stole 500 bottles of Viagra from a local pharmacy. Police say they are looking for a hardened criminal.

In another raid, a drugstore was broken into and all the Viagra tablets were taken. Police later arrested two men for being in possession of swollen goods.

The police have announced that criminals who steal Viagra will face stiff penalties.

Hot-air-balloon theft: it's on the rise.

Say what you like about burglars, but at least they still make house calls.

I believe in justice – ever since the guy stealing my tyres was run over by the man stealing my car.

Why was the unit of electricity convicted of murder?
He was a kilowatt.

I paid $75 for a correspondence course on mail fraud. It never arrived.

Did you hear about the boy who killed his parents and then begged the court for mercy because he was an orphan?

Crime figures show that your car is most likely to be stolen when it's parked outside your house. That's why I now park outside my neighbour's house.

If you trade in stolen garden panels, does that make you a fence?

A man has stabbed several people in the buttocks with knitting needles. Police believe the attacker could be following some kind of pattern.

The Scotch factory was robbed last night. The police will know more when they've checked the tape.

Why did the Mafia boss cross the road?
Revenge. The road had crossed him earlier.

Is murdering a vicar classed as a white-collar crime?

Police arrested two children yesterday. One was drinking battery acid, the other was eating fireworks. They charged one and let the other one off. *Tommy Cooper*

The Serial Killers' Association of America recently announced its annual dismembership drive.

Police officer: "Can you describe the missing cashier?"
Bank manager: "He's five foot nine tall and $6,000 short."

Police are looking for a robber with honey, walnuts and filo pastry smeared on his face. A witness said he was wearing a baklava.

Did you hear about the three-fingered thief? He only steals bowling balls.

I was attacked by a deaf, dumb, blind and armless man with no nose. It was a senseless crime.

A thief wearing gloves makes a stainless steal.

Whenever I go out lately, I'm followed by a bird with long legs. I think I'm being storked.

An inflatable man was suspected of stealing two inflatable dolls, but the police couldn't pin anything on him.

To stop lead being stolen from the roof, six of my mother's sisters spent all night outside our local church holding candles. The police didn't welcome the presence of the vigil aunties.

A basketball player and a jockey robbed a store last night. The police are looking high and low.

I'd like to say to the man wearing camouflage gear and using crutches who stole my wallet at the weekend: "You can hide, but you can't run."
Milton Jones

Dr Watson: "Holmes, I've just seen a mysterious creature, only 12 inches long!"
Sherlock Holmes: "Something's afoot, Watson."

Shoplifters have the gift of the grab.

A guy in a pub tried to sell me a brake light and a tailboard. I said: "No way! I bet they've fallen off the back of a lorry."

Don't steal. That's the government's job.

What were the Chicago mobster's last words?
"Who put that violin in my violin case?"

Did you hear about the armed robber who mistakenly picked up his knife by the blade as he threatened bank staff? He was caught red-handed.

Two dozen items of police dog equipment were stolen last week. The police are appealing for new leads.

Did you hear about the guy who was jailed just because he made big money – about an inch too big?

What did the thief call out after breaking into Elton John's house?
"Hey, Elton, I've got all your records."

How did the police find a suspect standing on a set of bathroom scales?
He gave himself a weigh.

Did you hear about the guy who stole dozens of swimming inflatables? He thought he'd better lilo.

And the thief who stole 50 cans of prunes and 50 cans of rhubarb is still on the loose.

I was walking home last night when someone drew a knife on me. He used permanent marker, so it took ages to wash off.

How can you tell who has been caught stealing in the Middle East?
Ask for a show of hands.

Police are searching for a robber who threatens his victims with a lit match. They want to catch him before he strikes again.

Hands up if you've ever been robbed at gunpoint.

Why did the private investigator always have a lump of earth strapped to the side of his head?
He liked to keep his ear to the ground.

If you are under house arrest but live in a mobile home, can you still go wherever you want?

A window of opportunity for me usually involves a rock. *Jay London*

A man was found face down today in his bathtub, which was filled with milk, cornflakes and sugar. The police say they're dealing with a cereal killer.

Did you hear about the men who were arrested for throwing bombs from a boat? They dropped the charges.

I was mugged by a gang of 15 Santas last week. I tell you, I saw red.

Did you hear about the music store that was robbed? The thief ran off with the lute.

Jigsaw murderer falls to pieces at trial and gets sentenced to four years and over.

I've been charged with murder for killing a man with sandpaper. To be honest, I only intended to rough him up a bit.

A man ran out of a supermarket with a joint of beef under his arm. The security guard shouted: "What are you doing with that?" The thief replied: "Yorkshire pudding, carrots and gravy."

I looked out of the window this morning and saw a guy stealing my gate. I didn't say anything in case he took a fence.

I probably should have walked home from the pub last night, especially as I walked there in the first place.

I've just been robbed by a Teenage Mutant Ninja Turtle – although ironically because he wasn't wearing a mask, I have no idea which one it was.

What do you call a Belgian detective with an air conditioner on his head?
Air Cool.

A man tried to hijack a busload of Japanese tourists. Luckily the police had 500 photos of the suspect.

I told the police: "My house has been broken into but the only things taken were two canaries, a goldfish and a pot of cream." The officer replied: "Sounds like that cat burglar we've been after."

I took some chocolate from some chocolatiers. They were reduced to tears.

A large town in West Yorkshire was stolen last night. Police are looking for Leeds.

Did you hear about the woman who was seen on a dimly lit street carrying a file full of house deeds and wills? She was arrested for soliciting.

My mate Sid was a victim of ID theft recently. Now he's just called S.

CRISIS

He who smiles in a crisis has found someone to blame.

There is no problem that can't be solved by a good miracle.

Remember the kettle. Even though it's up to its neck in hot water, it continues to sing.

Whenever I fill out an application, in the part that says, "If an emergency, notify:", I put "Doctor". What's my mother going to do?

CROSSWORDS

Apparently a really difficult crossword clue prevents depression. It stops you getting two down.

I met the man who invented crosswords. I can't remember his name; it's P something T something R. *Tim Vine*

Mike: "Can you help me with this crossword clue? 'To egg on'."
Marty: "Toast?"

Two idiots are doing a crossword. One asks: "How do you spell paint?"
The other says: "What colour?"

After reading the crossword clue "Physically aggressive behaviour (8)",
I've realized that violence *is* the answer.

Did you hear about the crossword puzzle fanatic who died? They buried
him six down and three across.

CURSES

May all your teeth fall out except the one that aches!

May your liposuction oversuck!

May your in-laws be many and vocal!

May your daughter's hair grow thick and abundant, all over her face!

May your reflection disown you!

May your flyaway hair fly away!

May an old egg and a fresh skunk be your constant companions!

May a thousand fleas infest your groin and may your arms be too short
to scratch!

May your DVD recorder suddenly revert to the Julian calendar!

As you slide down the banister of life, may the splinters always point
the wrong way!

May your clients' ideas be precise and their descriptions vague!

May your life coach commit suicide!

May your accountant be honest!

May your son marry his anime pillow!

DAFFYNITIONS

Aardvark: the honest way to make money
Abash: a high school graduation party
Abdicate: to give up all hope of having a flat stomach
Abominable: an explosive device concealed in a male bovine
Absentee: a missing golf peg
Absolute zero: the lowest mark you can get on a test
Abundance: a baker's ball
Accord: a thick piece of string
Ache: joint concern
Acoustic: the thing used to hit the balls in snooker, pool or billiards
Acquire: a group of singers in a church
Adorn: what comes after the darkest hour
Afterbirth: when the hard part begins
Alarms: what an octopus is
Alibi: to purchase a back street
Allegro: one leg becoming longer than the other
Alphabet: the first step in a gambling career
Annex: a former partner
Aromatic: an automatic crossbow
Arthritis: twinges in the hinges
Aspersion: an Iranian donkey
Assassinate: a hired killer finished lunch
Asymmetry: where you bury dead people
Auto-erotic: lusting after a Ferrari
Bacteria: back door to the cafeteria
Balderdash: a rapidly receding hairline
Baloney: place to where some hemlines fall
Barbecue: a line of people waiting for a haircut
Barium: what doctors do when the treatment fails
Bigamy: a large pygmy
Billow: what you sleep on when you have a bad cold
Bitch: a female of a dog or vice versa
Broadband: an all-girl musical group
Buoyant: a male insect
Camelot: where humped beasts are parked
Cantaloupe: a melon that is unable to run off and get married
Castanet: basic fishing method

Castrate: hotel room price for actors
Catacomb: a feline grooming device
Catalyst: several cows' names written alphabetically
Cauterize: made eye contact with her
Cellulite: what a power company does
Circumspection: an inspection after the circumcision
Cistern: opposite of brethren
Climate: what you do with a ladder
Cobra: a bra for Siamese twins
Cochineal: to bash a small, narrow fish
Coffee: a person who is coughed upon
Coincide: the murder of a Jew
Condominium: birth control for dwarfs
Counterfeiters: workers who assemble kitchen units
Crick: the sound made by a Japanese camera
Damage: how old a beaver's house is
Damnation: any country you don't approve of
Decadent: a person with 10 teeth
Deliberate: take back to prison
Dictum: Harry's two companions
Diphthong: to wash skimpy underwear
Dulcet: boring tennis
Dynamite: take a flea out to dinner
Elixir: what a dog does to his owner when she gives him a bone
Emulate: a large, dead bird
Endorse: the last runner in the Derby
Esplanade: to attempt an explanation while drunk
Exorbitant: a costly satellite that has fallen out of the sky
Eyebrows: what I do when I go shopping
Falsehood: a wig
Farcical: a long bike ride
Faucet: what you do when the tap won't turn on
Fibula: a small lie
Fjord: a Norwegian car
Flabbergasted: appalled by discovering how much weight one has gained
Flamenco: a big pink dancing bird
Flatulence: emergency vehicle that picks up someone who has been run over by a steamroller
Flatulent: an apartment where you allowed your friends to stay while you were away

Footstool: a personal best on the toilet
Forfeit: what most animals stand on
Fulgent: a man following a large dinner
Fundamental: to give money to a mad person
Gables: homosexual cattle
Gastric: a whoopee cushion
Genealogy: adverse medical reaction to inhabitants of magic lamps
Gneiss: compliment paid to metamorphic rocks
Handkerchief: cold storage
Heroes: what a guy in a boat does
Hootananny: a big-breasted au pair
Hormone: a complaint from a hooker
Humdrum: what a percussionist does when he forgets his sticks
Hundred: what Attila induced
Impeccable: immune to woodpeckers
Impolite: a burning elf
Impunity: agreement among elves
Information: how geese fly
Inkling: a baby fountain pen
Irrepressible: hopelessly wrinkled
Isolate: the White Rabbit's exclamation from *Alice in Wonderland*
Jargon: a missing glass container
Juicing: Rabbi karaoke
Kangaroo: spiritual adviser for metal food containers
Khaki: a device for starting a vehicle
Kidney: the midpoint of a child's leg
Kindred: fear of relatives
Lobster: a tennis champion
Lymph: walks with a lisp
Mandolin: a musical citrus fruit
Marigold: find a rich spouse
Matricide: killing oneself on a bed
Metronome: a subway pixie
Microfiche: sardines
Migraine: possessive farmer talking about his wheat
Morbid: a higher offer
Negligent: absent-mindedly answering the door while wearing only a
  nightgown
Nitrate: rate of pay lower than day rate
Node: was aware of

Notwithstanding: how to win a sitting contest
Octopus: an eight-sided cat
Ostracized: having the same dimensions as an ostrich
Outpatient: a patient who has fainted
Oyster: a large crane
Paradox: two physicians
Parasites: what can be seen from the Eiffel Tower
Pasteurize: too far to see
Pharmacist: someone who helps around the farm
Polarize: what penguins see with
Porcupine: a craving for bacon
Posse: a Wild West cat
Potash: all that's left after you smoke a joint
Propaganda: a gentlemanly goose
Protein: in favour of youth
Ptarmigan: a pbird
Quadruplets: four crying out loud!
Rambling: jewellery for sheep
Relief: what trees do in spring
Rheumatic: storage area at the top of a house
Rubberneck: what you do to relax your wife
Seamstress: 250 pounds in a size six
Shebang: a girl who can't say no
Squalid: hat worn by Native American Indian woman
Stalemate: an old spouse
Stampede: a mad rush to the Post Office
Staple: Irish church tower
Subdued: a cool guy who works on a submarine
Syntax: a way by which you pay for your misdmeanours
Taciturn: a very quiet vase
Tantamount: riding a French aunt
Tapestry: where Spanish appetizers grow
Tea: break fluid
Testicle: a funny exam question
Thesaurus: a dinosaur with a wide vocabulary
Ukraine: a female sheep-lifting device
Vanish: kind of like a van
Ventilation: the joy of turning on a fan
Vertigo: how Germans ask for directions
Viper: what you find on the windshield of a German car

Wholesale: where a gopher goes to buy a home
Willy-nilly: impotent
Yearning: a Texan's current salary
Zit: command given to a spotted dog

DANCING

It's one of life's ironies that people with club feet generally aren't very good at dancing.

I've started taking ballet lessons – well, it keeps me on my toes.

A sex-starved guy travelled all the way to the Arctic because he'd heard so much about Lapp dancing.

Who invented break dancing?
A guy trying to steal the hubcaps off a moving car.

What do you call the costume of a one-legged ballerina?
A one-one.

Since Viagra came on to the market, pole dancers say they receive a lot more standing ovations.

The music was so bad at the social club dance that when the fire alarm sounded everyone took to the floor.

I arrived suitably dressed for the "lap dancing" club. But I felt such a fool when I realized some vandal had removed the crossbar on the letter T.

I wanted to dance at the metric party, but I have two left 0.305 metres.

Did you hear about the man who became addicted to line dancing? It got so bad he had to enter a two-step programme.

Did you hear about the guy who was new to line dancing? He got run over by a train.

My dad was kicked to death in the pub last night. He tripped over while leading the conga.

Why do Morris Dancers wear bells?
So they can annoy blind people as well.

Dancing is the art of pulling your feet away faster than your partner can step on them.

I've got two left feet, and it's not easy finding a girl with two right ones.

Man: "I have dancing in my blood."
Woman: "Well, you must have poor circulation because it hasn't got to your feet yet."

Don't drink and dance. Always have a designated dancer.

What happened when Ginger Rogers spilled ice cream sundae over Fred Astaire?
He got pudding on his top hat, pudding on his white tie and pudding on his tails.

I went to the ballet once. I couldn't even tell who won.

My daughter asked me to make her a ballerina's costume. I had no idea where to start, but then I put tu and tu together.

How do you make a tissue dance?
Put a little boogie in it.

My wife says I dance like a coma victim being stood up and zapped with a cattle prod.

Sometimes I think I'll never learn how to waltz properly. It's just two steps forward, one step back.

You know what they say about French dance teachers: those who can cancan do; those who can't cancan teach.

I come from a long line of conga dancers.

My sister took a degree in ballet. She got a 2:2.

How do you know when a man is a really bad dancer?
He can step on Dolly Parton's toes.

What's the best thing about line dancing?
One grenade gets them all.

DATING

I've started dating Little Red Hiding Hood's gran. She's an animal in bed.

I'm currently dating a couple of anorexics. Two birds, one stone. **David Gibson**

I recently dated a recluse, but I had to end it. I just couldn't see us going anywhere.

I've just finished with my cross-eyed girlfriend. She was seeing someone else.

Did you hear about the couple who met in a revolving door? They're still going around together.

I usually spend first dates asking the girl about the street she grew up on and the name of her first pet so I'll at least have access to her passwords.

I always like to impress girls by telling them I once had a flat on Park Lane. I tend to leave out the "on my mountain bike" bit.

I once went out with a Cyclops, but we didn't see eye to eye.

The seven qualities for the perfect girlfriend are beautiful, intelligent, gentle, thoughtful, innocent, trustworthy and sensible – or, in short, B.I.G.T.I.T.S.

I once went out with a girl who had fiery red hair and a pale thin body. I met her on Match.com.

What did Jack the Ripper's mother say to him?
"How come you never go out with the same girl twice?"

I used to see this girl across the road from me, but she closes her curtains now.

I'm going on a blind date tonight. I hope our dogs get on.

I've been with my girlfriend for 11 months now, although the first three months she didn't know it.

A girl phoned me the other day. She said: "Come on over, there's nobody home." I went over. Nobody was home. **Rodney Dangerfield**

Jackie: "What happened to that handsome man who sent you flowers every week?"
Jill: "He married the girl who sold him the flowers."

My girlfriend said I was a real catch – but only because I had a face like a cod.

My girlfriend came round last night. I didn't even know she'd been in a coma.

A blind date is when you expect to meet a vision and she turns out to be a sight.

I asked my girlfriend to tell me something that would make me happy and sad at the same time. She said: "You've got a bigger dick than your dad."

Did you hear about the girl who went out with a postman? At the end of the date, he dropped her off at the wrong house.

I made myself a girlfriend out of plastic food wrap, but she's a bit clingy.

My girlfriend's a wonder: every time I see her, I wonder why I'm going out with her.

I could tell my last date didn't really like me. There was something about the way she asked for the money.

Why did the girl in a wheelchair end up back in hospital?
Her date stood her up.

I used to go out with an anaesthetist – she was a local girl. *Tim Vine*

A female gondolier asked me out last week. I said: "You must be joking. I wouldn't touch you with a barge-pole."

My girlfriend said I should be more affectionate. So I got two girlfriends.

Did you hear about the matchmaking agency that caters exclusively for Siamese twins? It's called Connect 4.

I used to go out with a stage hand from the local theatre company. But I called it off because every time we went out she made a scene.

I've got a new anorexic girlfriend, but it's not going too well. I'm seeing less and less of her.

I once went out with identical twins called Earth and Water. I soon found out their names were mud around here.

I'm dating a girl who works at Marks & Spencer. That way I can exchange her if I don't like her.

I used to go out with a Welsh girl who had 36DDs. She had a ridiculously long name.

What's the best thing about dating a homeless woman? **You can drop her off anywhere.**

I once dated a supermarket cashier because she was always checking me out.

All the women on the 55 Internet dating sites I've joined seem so sad and desperate.

A young couple park up in a lovers' lane at night. The girl says: "It's so peaceful. Just listen to the crickets." The boy replies: "They're not crickets, they're zippers."

I was engaged once to a girl with a wooden leg, but she broke it off.

I met a chick in Kiev. *Milton Jones*

Chatting up a girl in a bar, I said: "What part of my body is as long as your thigh, contains over 120 muscles and is an anagram of " 'pensi'?" It was only when she pulled my pants down at her apartment a few minutes later that I told her the answer was "spine".

I don't trust my imaginary girlfriend. I think someone else is seeing her.

Did you hear about the couple who met at a summer fair? Fête brought them together.

Everything my girlfriend does is magic, so I had her burnt at the stake.

My girlfriend dated a clown before we got together. So I've got some pretty big shoes to fill!

I said to my sister: "Why do you still go out with that sadist?" "I don't know," she said. "Beats me."

I once dated a girl who wore an eye patch. She said she wanted to stop seeing me, so I poked her in her good eye.

I've been dating a homeless woman recently, and it's getting serious. She's asked me to move out with her.

My sister has been stood up more times than a bowling pin.

My new girlfriend really takes my breath away. She's inflatable.

I met a girl in a club, and she said she'd show me a good time. So we went outside, and she ran the 100 metres in 10.74 seconds.

My girlfriend sent me a "Get Better Soon" card. I'm not ill, just not very good at sex.

A man on a date wonders if he'll get lucky. The woman already knows.

I once went out with this wild girl. She made French toast and got her tongue caught in the toaster. **Rodney Dangerfield**

My girlfriend said to me: "Why don't you slip into something more comfortable . . . like a coma?"

I was on a date with this gorgeous girl. Well, when I say it was a date, we just ate dinner and saw a movie. Then the plane landed.

My last girlfriend looked like Elle Macpherson, only shorter and Filipino.

Few things are more expensive than a girl who is free for the evening.

I went on a date with a bionic girl. Afterwards she said: "Part of me would like to see you again . . ."

I get very nervous on a first date, which is surprising as they are the only kind I have.

I met this girl who asked me to paint the town with her. It turned out it was part of her community service.

I said to my girlfriend: "For you I would climb the highest mountain, swim the deepest ocean and cross the hottest desert. So I'll see you tomorrow . . . provided it's not raining."

With girls, I don't think right. I had a date with one girl, she had mirrors all over her bedroom. She told me to come over and bring a bottle. I got Windex. **Rodney Dangerfield**

I tried Internet dating, but I quickly realized it wasn't for me when they matched me up with my wife.

My girlfriend thinks I'm a stalker. Well, she's not actually my girlfriend yet.

My new girlfriend has been around the block a few times. Like most women, she's lousy at parking.

A girl rushed home to tell her mother: "I've found a man just like Dad!" The mother said: "What do you want from me? Sympathy?"

I got told off for not opening the door for my girlfriend on a date. Instead I just swam to the surface.

I went out with a promiscuous impressionist. She did everybody. *Jay London*

I'll never forget winning my girlfriend's heart – what a hospital raffle that was!

I asked a girl if I could see her home, so she got out a photograph.

I used to date a girl called Helvetica, but it didn't work out. I guess she just wasn't my type.

I'm seeing this girl with eczema. She's got a cracking body.

DEATH

The man who invented the taser died suddenly last night. His relatives said they were stunned.

My wife's in a bit of a pickle. From what I understand, it's the best way to preserve her.

He who dies with the most toys is nonetheless dead.

A bitter husband says to his wife: "On your gravestone, I'll put COLD AS EVER." The wife replies: "On yours, I'll put STIFF AT LAST."

What happens if you get scared half to death twice?

Did you hear about the man who died in a bowl of muesli? He was pulled under by a strong currant.

Glass coffins, will they be a success? Remains to be seen.

An angel in Heaven was welcoming a new arrival. "How did you get here?" he asked. The new angel replied: "Flu."

Why did the wife shoot her husband with a bow and arrow? **She didn't want to wake the children.**

Health freaks are going to feel stupid someday, lying in hospital dying of nothing.

My granddad would never throw anything away. He was killed by a grenade. *Milton Jones*.

If you choke a Smurf, what colour does it turn?

I said to my elderly mother: "Do you want to be buried or cremated?" "Oh, I don't know," she replied. "Surprise me."

Say what you like about hangmen, but at least they always keep their customers in the loop.

Mike: "I was sorry to hear you buried your mother last week." **Marty: "We had to. She was dead."**

I hope that after I die, people will say of me: "That guy sure owed me a lot of money."

Nobody expected our window cleaner to kick the bucket.

A stranger in town asked an old man: "What's the death rate around here?" "Same as everywhere else," replied the old man. "One per person."

The man who invented Chinese Whispers has died. Pass it on.

My uncle knew the exact day and time he was going to die. The judge told him.

I want to die peacefully in my sleep like my grandfather – not screaming and yelling like the passengers in the car he was driving.

The Incredible Hulk has died. RIP.

A husband suddenly turned to his wife and said: "I never want to live in a vegetative state dependent on some machine and fluids from a bottle. If that ever happens, just pull the plug." So his wife got up, unplugged the TV and threw out his beer.

If you die in an elevator, be sure to press the "Up" button.

I've just read a list of the top 100 things to do before you die. I'm surprised "Yell for help" wasn't one of them.

The man who wrote the song "The Hokey Cokey" was buried yesterday, but the undertakers had trouble keeping his body in the coffin. They'd put his left leg in . . .

Lou Gehrig died of Lou Gehrig's disease. You'd think he'd have seen it coming.

Police found a criminal who had been shot dead with exit wounds but no entry wounds. They think it was an inside job.

My grandfather's death was ironic. He died in his living room.

My Korean friend died last week. So Yung . . .

Did you hear about the twin campanologists who died? They were dead ringers.

After my friend died, we got him a wreath in the shape of a lifebelt. It's what he would have wanted. *Gary Delaney*

Did you hear about the ice-cream seller who was found dead in his van covered in hundreds and thousands? The police say he topped himself.

I spent some time by the wife's grave today. She doesn't know; she thinks I'm digging a pond.

How did they know the man eaten by a shark had dandruff? **They found his head and shoulders on the beach.**

I'll tell you what's making a comeback: reincarnation.

Did you hear about the man who was such a firm believer in reincarnation that in his will he left everything to himself?

Humpty Dumpty has been found dead. Next of Kinder have been informed.

Did you hear about the man in the electric chair who asked the executioner to reverse the charges?

It's not the bullet that kills you, it's the hole.

I said to my wife: "When I die, I'm going to leave everything to you." She said: "You do anyway, you lazy sod!"

Did you hear about the cartoonist who was found dead in his home? Details are sketchy.

Death is God's way of saying, "You're not alive any more."

When my uncle was dying, his wife Tina and his sister Marge were grieving at his bedside. He turned to them and whispered: "Don't cry for me, Marge and Tina."

First ghoul: "You don't look too well today."
Second ghoul: "No, I'm dead on my feet."

How did the bearded lady and the three-legged dwarf die?
In a freak accident.

The National Rifle Association says, "Guns don't kill people. People do." But I think the gun helps. *Eddie Izzard*

An eccentric bachelor died and left a nephew nothing but a collection of 360 clocks. The nephew is now busy winding up the estate.

I'll never forget my father's last words. "Son, you're standing on my oxygen tube!"

How many mimes must have died because nobody believed they were choking?

Death is nature's way of saying "slow down".

Did you hear about the optimist who drowned in a bath half full?

My nan died on her ninety-second birthday. It was really sad. We were only halfway through giving her the bumps at the time.

Where do they put the toetag on a murder victim if his toes have been hacked off?

The President of the Glaucoma Sufferers' Association died recently. There were a lot of misty eyes at the funeral.

A solicitor is reading out his client's will. "And to my grasping nephew Alvin: I always said I'd mention you in my will, so . . . Hi, Alvin."

Did you hear about the man who overdosed on Viagra? They couldn't get the coffin lid shut.

It's not the fall that kills you. It's the sudden stop at the end.

Teacher: "I'm sorry to hear about your Uncle Tom. What did he die of?"
Boy: "I don't know, but apparently it wasn't anything serious."

I don't mind dying. The trouble is you feel so stiff the next day.

Did you hear about the man who drowned in a vat of varnish? A terrible end, but a lovely finish.

When my grandfather died, we didn't get the chance to say goodbye. It was made even more poignant by the fact that he drowned in a bowl of Cheerios. *Milton Jones*

Did you hear about the guy who was chopping carrots with the Grim Reaper? He was dicing with death.

The man who created the design for deckchairs died last week. It took five attempts before they got him in the coffin.

DENTISTS

My cavity wasn't fixed by my regular dentist but by a guy who was filling in.

What does the dentist of the year get?
A little plaque.

I went to the dentist today and sat in the waiting room flicking through the magazines. Isn't it terrible John Lennon's dead?

Patient: "What should I do with all the gold and silver in my mouth?"
Dentist: "Don't smile in a bad neighbourhood."

What was the name of the Scottish dentist?
Phil McCavity.

Patient: "Can you recommend anything for yellow teeth?"
Dentist: "Yes. A brown tie."

I didn't know my uncle had a false tooth until it came out in conversation.

Her teeth have so many cavities, she talks with an echo.

Why did the Buddhist refuse Novocaine when having root canal surgery?
He wanted to transcend dental medication.

The dentist went to great pains to fix my teeth.

Did you hear about the dentist who was a keen photographer? He had film on his teeth.

The dentist told me: "Your teeth are fine, but your gums will have to come out."

If you have toothache, hit your thumb hard with a hammer. Then you'll forget about the toothache.

Be good to your teeth, or they will be false to you.

I told my dentist that $90 was a lot of money for pulling a tooth – just five seconds' work. So he pulled it slowly.

What's red and bad for your teeth?
A brick.

What did the dentist say to the tooth?
"You look so cute I'd like to take you out."

Why are dentists always broke?
Because they live from hand to mouth.

I used some of that striped toothpaste, and now I've got striped teeth.

Why did the jacket potato go to the dentist?
He had to have some fillings.

I went to the dentist. He said: "Say 'Aaah'." I said: "Why?" He said: "My dog died." *Tommy Cooper*

He has teeth like the Ten Commandments – all broken.

People with big teeth are popular at parties – until someone finds the bottle opener.

I've been to the dentist several times, so I know the drill.

Patient: "I'm very nervous. This is my first extraction."
Young dentist: "Don't worry. It's my first extraction, too."

Nurse: "Why did you hit the dentist?"
Patient: "He got on my nerves."

My wife has had so much bridge work, every time I kiss her I have to pay a toll.

You should be nicer to dentists – they have fillings too.

My dentist makes the best false teeth. They're so lifelike, they even ache.

A husband gets home from a visit to the dentist. His wife asks in concern: "Does your tooth still hurt?" "I don't know," says the husband. "He kept it."

Why did the king go to the dentist?
To get his teeth crowned.

Dentist: "OK, Mrs Grimshaw, there's no need to open your mouth any wider. When I pull your tooth, I expect to stand outside."

Did you hear about the dentist who went out with a manicurist? They used to fight tooth and nail.

DEPRESSION

My cross-eyed friend has just been diagnosed with depression. I'm not surprised – he never looks forward to anything.

Depression is merely anger without enthusiasm.

My girlfriend suffers from depression brought on by anorexia. I told her she should lighten up.

Whenever I feel blue, I start breathing again.

After Monday and Tuesday, even the week says WTF.

When I feel depressed, I like to cut myself . . . another piece of cake.

Yesterday I took laxatives in addition to my regular Prozac. I can't get off the toilet, but I'm happy about it.

If you ever feel sad, remember there's a number you can call and a pizza will be with you in 30 minutes.

DIPLOMACY

Diplomacy is making your guests feel like they're at home, even if you wish they were.

Diplomacy is the ability to tell someone to "go to hell" in such a way that they look forward to the trip.

Discretion is being able to raise your eyebrow instead of your voice.

DISLIKES

You know what I hate most? Rhetorical questions.

I absolutely hate being schizophrenic. Best thing in the world.

My friend Max hates going up steep hills. He's always been a bit of an anti-climb Max.

Don't you hate it when the gas people ring up asking if you want cheap gas? "Not really. It's quality I'm looking for when it comes to my gas."
Jack Dee

The last thing I want to do is insult you, but it is on the list.

Teacher: "Tell me, what's your pet hate?"
Little Johnny: "Me pulling his fur."

"It's not you, it's me." I hate sorting through photos with my twin brother.

I hate street performers. Then again, I'm a mime artist, so I can't really talk.

DIVORCE

I asked my wife what she wanted for her birthday, and she said: "A divorce." I said: "I wasn't thinking of spending that much."

My brother and his wife divorced over religious differences. He thought he was God, and she didn't.

Divorce is the screwing you get for the screwing you got.

Did you hear about the guy who found himself in a really strange place after his divorce? It was called the kitchen.

I still miss my ex-wife, but my aim is improving.

Woman: "My husband has flat feet. Is that grounds for divorce?"
Lawyer: "Not unless his feet visit the wrong flat."

Jackie: "What did your husband do before you divorced him?"
Jill: "A lot of things I didn't know about."

A lawyer is never entirely comfortable with a friendly divorce, any more than a mortician wants to finish his job and then have the patient sit up on the table.

A faithful husband is one whose alimony cheque is always on time.

Did you hear about the leper whose wife left him? He was in pieces.

Lawyer: "You want a divorce because your husband is careless about his appearance?"
Woman: "Yes, he hasn't showed up in 18 months."

I should have known it would never have worked out with my ex-wife. After all, I'm an Aquarius and she's a bitch.

My uncle has had so many wives, he can't remember their names. So to keep things simple, he just calls them "plaintiff".

Jackie: "Doesn't it upset you to see your ex with someone else?"
Jill: "No, I was always taught to recycle my old trash."

If I don't pay alimony this month, can my wife repossess me?

My divorce has taught me that poker isn't the only game that starts with holding hands and ends with a big financial loss.

My first wife was a very good housekeeper, and sure enough when we got divorced she kept the house.

Alimony is what a woman charges for name-dropping.

What should a woman do if she sees her ex-husband rolling around on the ground in pain?
Shoot him again.

Mickey and Minnie Mouse were in the divorce court. The judge told Mickey: "You say here that your wife is crazy." "No," replied Mickey, "I didn't say she was crazy – I said she was fucking Goofy."

Alimony means having an ex-husband you can bank on.

Lawyer: "Why do you want a divorce?"
Woman: "Every time I sit on my husband's lap, he starts dictating."

My wife and I got remarried. Our divorce didn't work out.

Since his divorce three months ago, my friend has put on six stone. His doctor says he's got to stop celebrating.

Love is grand. Divorce is 15 grand.

Jackie to Jill: "I've got a real dilemma. I'll give my husband his divorce, but only when I've figured out a way of doing it without making him a happy man."

Lawyer: "You say you're divorcing your husband for health reasons?"
Woman: "Yes, I'm sick of him."

Why is divorce so expensive?
Because it's worth it.

The difference between divorce and legal separation is that a legal separation gives a husband time to hide his money.

Alimony is a man's cash surrender value.

A friend of mine just got divorced. He and his ex-wife split the house. He got the outside.

Lawyer: "Why do you want to divorce such a beautiful wife?"
Man: "Look at my shoe. It's beautiful, too, but only I know how much it pinches!"

What is the main cause of divorce?
Marriage.

Jackie: "Are you upset about your divorce?"
Jill: "No, I'm only upset that I'm not a widow."

Divorce court judge: "Mr Kelly, I've decided to give your wife $700 a week."
Mr Kelly: "That's very generous, Your Honour, and every now and then I'll try to send her a few bucks myself."

Why do divorced men get married again?
Bad memory.

Alimony is when a bride continues to get wedding gifts after the divorce.

How is an ex-husband like an inflamed appendix?
It caused you a lot of pain and after it was removed, you found out you didn't need it anyway.

DOCTORS

A man went to the doctor and said: "Do you treat alcoholics?" "Yes," said the doctor. "Oh, good," said the man, "get your coat on, I'm skint."

A man had trouble with his hand and wanted to show it to the doctor. Three fingers were willing to co-operate but the thumb and forefinger were opposed.

Why did the doctor carry out blood tests on secretarial candidates?
So that he could eliminate type-Os.

Doctor: "Do you drink to excess?"
Patient: "I'll drink to anything."

Holding a stethoscope to a young female patient, the doctor says: "Big breaths." "Yeth," replies the girl, "and I'm thtill only thixteen."

Never trust a doctor whose office plants have all died.

My doctor charges so much, when he gets sick he can't afford himself.

Patient: "My daughter believes in preventative medicine, Doctor. She tries to prevent me from making her take it."

A doctor gave a man six months to live. The patient couldn't pay his bill, so the doctor gave him another six months.

Patient: "What's wrong with me, doc?"
Doctor: "Well, I think it could be pneumo-bacterisilimicroscopioniasis, but it's hard to say."

A paper bag tells the doctor: "I've got a terrible disease." The doctor says solemnly: "I'm afraid it's hereditary. Your mother may have been a carrier."

Doctor: "You'll live to be 70." Patient: "I am 70!" Doctor: "See, what did I tell you?"

The doctor told me I'd got just four minutes to live. I said: "Is there anything you can give me?" He said: "A boiled egg."

Woman: "You say you're a naval surgeon? My, how you doctors specialize!"

Doctor: "I can't be sure what's wrong with you. I think it's due to drinking."
Patient: "In that case, I'll come back when you're sober."

I went to the doctor. I said: "I'm frightened of lapels." He said: "You've got cholera." *Tim Vine*

Dermatologists often make rash statements.

How did the doctor get into dermatology?
He had to start from scratch.

What's the difference between a haematologist and a urologist?
The haematologist pricks your finger.

What does a gynaecologist do when he feels sentimental?
He looks up an old girlfriend.

How is a gynaecologist like a pizza delivery man?
Both get to smell the goods, but neither one can eat it.

What do puppies and near-sighted gynaecologists have in common?
Wet noses.

Gynaecologist: "Relax, Madam. Haven't you ever been examined like this before?"
Patient: "Yes, but not by a doctor."

Did you hear about the gynaecologist who papered the hall through the letterbox?

What's the difference between a genealogist and a gynaecologist?
A genealogist looks up your family tree, and a gynaecologist looks up your family bush.

Why do women prefer elderly gynaecologists?
They have shaky hands.

If tennis players get tennis elbow and squash players get squash knees, do gynaecologists get tunnel vision?

The doctor says I can have up to 20 units a week. I'm not sure I want to eat my kitchen. *Milton Jones*

Did you hear about the proctologist who uses ferns to clean out your system? His motto is: "With fronds like these, who needs enemas?"

Why is it that you wait six weeks for a doctor's appointment and then he says: "I wish you'd come to me sooner"?

Doctor: "Did you follow my advice and drink carrot juice after the hot bath?"
Patient: "No, I haven't finished drinking the bath yet."

My wife was running a temperature so I phoned the doctor. He asked: "Is she hot?" I said: "Well, with a little make-up and a short skirt . . ."

Patient: "I have spent 80 per cent of my life savings on doctors."
Doctor: "Why didn't you come to me earlier?"

What did the doctor prescribe for the patient with swine flu?
Oinkment.

Doctor: "I haven't seen you for a long time, Mrs Johnson."
Patient: "I know, doctor, I've been ill."

A man walked into a doctor's office with a lettuce leaf sticking out of his ear. The doctor said: "That's strange." The man said: "That's just the tip of the iceberg."

The doctor said: "I want you to lie on the couch." I said: "What for?" He said: "I need to sweep the floor." *Tommy Cooper*

Doctor: "Why are you jumping up and down?"
Patient: "I've just taken that new medicine you prescribed, but I forgot to shake the bottle."

You should go and see my doctor – you won't live to regret it.

Doctor: "You seem to be in excellent health. Your pulse is as regular as clockwork." Patient: "That's because you've got your hand on my watch."

Patient: "What should I do if my temperature goes up seven more?"
Doctor: "Sell!"

Why did the doctor ask the patient to stand by the window and stick his tongue out?
He didn't like the doctor across the street.

Doctor: "The best time to take a bath is just before retiring."
Patient: "You mean I don't need to take another bath till I'm 65?"

Doctor: "Have you ever given yourself a prostate examination?"
Man: "Not deliberately, but my wife sometimes buys cheap toilet paper."

My doctor said he would have me on my feet in three weeks. He was right. I had to sell my car to pay his bill.

Ward sister: "The patient doesn't seem to be doing very well with this new drip."
Nurse: "No, I think he'd be better off with his old doctor."

Why do doctors leave the room when you change? They're going to see you naked anyway.

Patient: "Well, doctor, how do I stand?"
Doctor: "I don't know. It's a miracle."

Doctor: "Madam, your cheque came back."
Woman: "So did my arthritis."

Why did the doctor make a lousy kidnapper?
Nobody could read his ransom notes.

What did the doctor say when he found a suppository in his breast pocket?
"Some bum's got my pen!"

Doctors write prescriptions illegibly so you can't read that it says: "This one has insurance. Don't kill him."

Patient: "Tell me straight, doc. Is it bad?"
Doctor: "Put it this way: I wouldn't start reading a long book."

I've just got a job as a doctor for the World Health Organization. I didn't want the job; I just thought I was auditioning for *Doctor Who*. **Milton Jones**

My doctor cancelled me as a patient. He said I'd gone too long without having anything expensive.

My doctor said: "Do you know your sperm count?" I said: "I didn't know they were that clever."

Doctor: "So you swallowed a clock two months ago? Why didn't you come to me sooner?"
Patient: "I didn't want to alarm you."

"Doctor, doctor, I only have 59 seconds to live."
"Wait a minute, will you?"

"Doctor, doctor, I keep thinking I'm a pair of curtains."
"Pull yourself together, man."

"Doctor, doctor, I'm having trouble with my breathing."
"I'll give you something that will soon put a stop to that."

"Doctor, doctor, my leg hurts. What can I do?"
"Limp."

"Doctor, doctor, I feel like a pack of cards."
"I'll deal with you later."

"Doctor, doctor, I keep thinking I'm a tennis racket."
"Don't worry, you're just highly strung."

"Doctor, doctor, I was attacked last night by a giant beetle with an axe."
"Yes, there's a nasty bug going around."

"Doctor, doctor, I've swallowed my camera film."
"Well, let's hope nothing develops."

"Doctor, doctor, my wife has lost her voice. How can I help her get it back?"
"Try coming home at three o'clock in the morning."

"Doctor, doctor, I keep thinking I'm an elevator."
"You may be coming down with something."

"Doctor, doctor, I'm addicted to Twitter."
"Sorry, I don't follow you."

"Doctor, doctor, I've got water on the knee, water on the elbow and water on the brain."
"Have you tried getting out of the shower?"

"Doctor, doctor, my daughter eats only yeast and car wax, and refuses to get out of bed."
"Don't worry. Eventually she'll rise and shine."

"Doctor, doctor, I keep thinking I'm a clock."
"Try not to get wound up."

"Doctor, doctor, I'm on a diet and it's making me irritable. Yesterday I bit my friend's ear off."
"Oh dear. That's a lot of calories."

"Doctor, doctor, I keep seeing hearts, spades, clubs and diamonds, and then rabbits, doves and silk scarves."
"Don't worry, it's just your eyes playing tricks."

"Doctor, doctor, I keep thinking I'm a packet of savoury biscuits."
"You must be crackers!"

"Doctor, doctor, I've hurt my arm in several places."
"Well, don't go there any more."

"Doctor, doctor, I can't stop stealing things."
"Take these pills for a week and if they don't work, get me a 42-inch flat-screen TV."

"Doctor, doctor, I'm a kleptomaniac. Do you have anything I can take?"
"Yes, but it will hurt, so you'll have to steel yourself."

"Doctor, doctor, I keep thinking I'm a caterpillar."
"Don't worry. You'll soon change."

"Doctor, doctor, my son has swallowed my pen. What should I do?"
"Use a pencil till I get there."

"Doctor, doctor, I think I'm shrinking."
"You'll have to be a little patient."

"Doctor, doctor, I think I'm becoming a nymphomaniac."
"Why don't you lie down and tell me about it?"

"Doctor, doctor, I feel bad because I've been having an affair with a meteorologist."
"You're just a bit under the weather."

"Doctor, doctor, I feel like I'm part of the Internet."
"Well, you do look a site!"

"Doctor, doctor, my right ear is warmer than my left ear."
"You need to adjust your toupee."

"Doctor, doctor, I can't pronounce my Fs, Ts or Hs."
"Well, you can't say fairer than that."

"Doctor, doctor, there's a strawberry growing out of the top of my head."
"Don't worry. I'll give you some cream to put on it."

"Doctor, doctor, I'm convinced I'm a wheelbarrow."
"You shouldn't let people push you around."

"Doctor, doctor, I think I'm a racehorse."
"Nonsense! Just take one of these pills every five furlongs."

"Doctor, doctor, I keep seeing images of Mickey Mouse and Donald Duck."
"Right. How long have you been having these Disney spells?"

"Doctor, doctor, I think I'm a moth."
"Get out of the way, you're in my light."

"Doctor, doctor, I've got a pen wedged up my butt."
"Sit down and write your name."

"Doctor, doctor, look, I've got grass, a tree and a picnic table growing on my face."
"Don't worry. It's only a beauty spot."

"Doctor, doctor, I think I'm suffering from déjà vu."
"Didn't I see you yesterday?"

"Doctor, doctor, last night I dreamt I was a wigwam, and the night before I dreamed I was a teepee."
"Just relax – you're two tents."

"Doctor, doctor, the letters A, E, I, O and U really annoy me. What's my problem?"
"You have irritable vowel syndrome."

"Doctor, doctor, I keep thinking I'm a spoon."
"Sit there, and don't stir."

"Doctor, doctor, my baby's swallowed a bullet."
"Well, don't point him at anyone until I get there."

"Doctor, doctor, my ear is ringing."
"Well, hurry up and answer it."

"Doctor, doctor, I feel like a window."
"Tell me where the pane is."

"Doctor, doctor, I get heartburn every time I eat birthday cake."
"Next time take off the candles."

"Doctor, doctor, when I get up in the morning, I always feel dizzy for an hour."
"Try getting up an hour later."

"Doctor, doctor, every bone in my body aches."
"Just be thankful you're not a herring!"

"Doctor, doctor, I keep thinking I'm an apple."
"Hmmm. We must get to the core of this."

"Doctor, doctor, I've got warts and I hate them."
"Don't worry, they'll grow on you."

"Doctor, doctor, what's good for excessive wind?"
"A kite."

"Doctor, doctor, that medicine you prescribed makes me walk like a crab."
"Ah, yes, those will be the side effects."

"Doctor, doctor, I feel like I'm at death's door."
"Don't worry, I'll pull you through."

"Doctor, doctor, when I press with my finger here, it hurts . . . and here . . . and here. What do you think is wrong with me?"
"You have a broken finger."

"Doctor, doctor, I'm worried that people keep ignoring me."
"Next!"

"Doctor Doctor, don't you get fed up with having the same surname as your profession?

DOGS

If you think you're a person of influence, try ordering somebody else's dog around.

I bought a new dog yesterday. I've called him Rolex. He's a watchdog.

In the winter my dog wears his coat, but in the summer he wears his coat and pants.

My dog Minton swallowed a shuttlecock. Bad Minton.

I bought my grandmother a guide dog, but he's a little sadistic. He does impressions of cars screeching to a halt.

What goes "Mark!"?
A dog with a hare lip.

Never stand between a dog and a hydrant.

Did you hear about the dog that ate nothing but garlic? His bark was much worse than his bite.

What do you call a dog that's been run over by a steamroller?
Spot.

What do you call a dog that has four-inch legs and six-inch steel balls?
Sparky.

My sister had a dog with no back legs. She called him Cigarette because every night she'd take him out for a quick drag.

My talking dog gave me a stick the other day and told me he found it 600 miles away. That's a bit far-fetched. *Tim Vine*

Why do dogs wag their tails?
Because no one else will do it for them.

Where does a dog go when it loses its tail?
To a retail outlet.

If a bulldog mated with a shih tzu, would it create a bullshit?

I was once bitten on the butt by a German shepherd. But then he apologized and introduced me to his dog.

Why does my wife kiss our dog on the lips, yet she won't drink from my glass?

The veterinary said: "I'm afraid I'm going to have to put your dog down." I said: "Why?" He said: "He's just too heavy."

What has four legs and one arm?
A pit bull leaving a playground.

What's the difference between a poodle humping your leg and a pit bull humping your leg?
You let the pit bull finish.

What do you do when a pit bull is humping your leg?
Fake an orgasm.

There's a new breed of dog – a pit bull crossed with a collie. It bites your leg off, then goes for help.

I had a dog that was half poodle, half pit bull. Not much of a guard dog, but a vicious gossip.

If you blow in a dog's face, he gets mad at you. But if you take him on a car ride, he sticks his head out of the window!

Why did the police dog have rough, matted fur and a scruffy tail?
He was working undercover.

Jackie: "Why does your dog sit and watch me eat?"
Jill: "Probably because you have the plate he usually eats from."

What did the Dalmatian say after enjoying a hearty meal?
"That hit the spots."

What happened to the man whose dog gave birth to puppies by the side of the road?
He was cited for littering.

Sniffer dogs do indeed smell nice.

How do you stop a dog smelling?
Put a clothes peg on its nose.

Why did the dog cross the street to sniff the fire hydrant?
He was checking his messages.

I've trained my dog to bring me a glass of red wine. He's a Bordeaux collie.

What breed of dog would you want on an American football team?
A golden receiver.

I bought a Dalmatian puppy, and I found that if you join all the dots together with a marker pen . . . it doesn't wash off.

Mike: "Our Great Dane is just like one of the family."
Marty: "Oh, which one?"

My dog is afraid of burglars. I had to put a dog alarm in his dog house.

Why is a dog like a baseball player?
He runs for home when he sees the catcher coming.

Every time the doorbell rings, my dog goes and sits in the corner. He's a boxer.

My dog barks all night. I'm thinking of buying him a burglar.

What do you get if you cross a Rottweiler and a hyena?
I don't know, but join in if it laughs.

Mike: "Our dog doesn't eat meat."
Marty: "Why not?"
Mike: "We don't give him any."

I've got a dog called Curiosity . . .

What's the difference between a barrow-boy and a dachshund?
One bawls out his wares on the pavement . . .

My German shepherd landed a job with a police dog display team. He had to jump through hoops to get it.

What do they say at a dog wedding?
"You may sniff the bride."

We bought a dachshund so all the kids could pet him at once.

They say that the dog is man's best friend, but is that really true? How many of your friends have you had neutered?

My dog was barking at everyone the other day. Still, what can you expect from a cross-breed?

An appeals court has upheld a ban on pit bulls. That's another victory in the war on terrier.

I bought a dog whistle, but it's not very good. Whenever I put it in his mouth he just starts dribbling.

When I woke up this morning, I could feel Tension mounting. Tension is my dog. *Tom Cotter*

How do you stop a dog howling in the back of a car?
Put him in the front.

People say our dog is vicious but he loves children . . . especially with a nice side salad.

How can you tell if your dogs like kinky sex?
They mate in the missionary position.

Man: "Hey, lady, that's a nice bulldog you've got!"
Woman: "He's not a bulldog. He was chasing a cat and ran into a wall."

My dog works for the fire department. He helps locate hydrants.

A three-legged dog walked into a Wyoming bar and said: "I'm looking for the man who shot my paw."

When dogs watch orchestra conductors, do they think: "Just throw the bloody thing"?

Apparently most dogs in Korea are inbred . . . like in a sandwich or something.

My dog's so lazy. When I'm watering the garden he never lifts a leg to help.

My dog's so lazy that he can't be bothered to bark. He just waits for another dog to bark, then nods.

I taught my dog to beg. Today he came back with $12.50.

Two dogs walked over to a parking meter. One said to the other: "How do you like that? Pay toilets!"

I watched my dog chase his tail in circles for 10 minutes, thinking how stupid and easily entertained he was. Then I realized I had just watched my dog chase his tail for 10 minutes.

Why did the dachshund bite the woman's ankle?
Because he couldn't reach any higher.

When I get a dog, I'm going to call him "Stay" just to confuse him. "Come here. Stay. Come here. Stay." *Steven Wright*

Mike: "Have you tried putting a message on the Internet for your missing dog?"
Marty: "There's no point. He never reads his emails."

Why are dogs lousy poker players?
Because when they get a good hand they wag their tail.

I call my dog Handyman, because he's always doing odd jobs around the house.

My dog always barks when there's someone at the door. I don't know why, it's never for him.

Why aren't dogs good dancers?
Because they've got two left feet.

First dog: "My name's Goldie. What's yours?"
Second dog: "I'm not sure, but I think it could be Down Boy."

I've never liked dogs since I went to a fancy-dress party as a lamp-post.

What do you get if you cross a dog with a sheep?
A sheep that rounds itself up.

I bought a robot puppy. Dogmatic.

What guard dog lets anyone in?
A UK border collie.

Where do you find a dog with no legs?
The same place you left him.

What do you call a dog with no legs?
It doesn't matter, he won't come anyway.

My dog is a blacksmith. Every time I open the front door, he makes a bolt for it.

A man was reported to animal welfare authorities for feeding Viagra to his pet labrador. The man is now banned from keeping any pets – and the labrador is now a pointer.

Did you hear about the dog that went to the flea circus? He stole the show.

I lost my dog, so I put an advert in the newspaper saying, "Here, boy!"

DREAMS

Did you hear about the guy who dreamt he wrote *The Lord of the Rings*? He was Tolkien in his sleep.

Follow your dreams, except for that one where you're naked at work.

I had a recurring dream once.

I have friends who swear they dream in colour. I say it's just a pigment of their imagination.

This morning I dreamed someone was shouting: "On your marks, get set, go!" I woke up with a start.

Light night I dreamt I ate a giant marshmallow. When I woke up this morning the pillow was gone.

Last night I dreamt about replacing our house's guttering for under $50. I think it was just a pipe dream.

I sometimes go into my own little world, but it's OK. they know me there.

Wife: "Why are you wearing your glasses in bed?"
Husband: "I want to get a better look at the girls I dreamt about last night."

I had a nightmare that I was in Panama during a snowstorm. I was dreaming of a white isthmus.

I tried to daydream but my mind kept wandering.

Last night I had a fantastic dream about Cameron Diaz, Megan Fox and Katy Perry. I beat them all at Monopoly.

I had a crazy dream that I weighed less than a thousandth of a gram. I was like, 0mg!

I had a terrible dream that there was a horse in my bed. It was a nightmare.

I have a recurring nightmare where me and two friends get a restaurant bill for $25 and have to split it three ways. That's 8.33333333333 . . .

Show me a man who has both feet on the ground, and I'll show you a man who can't put on his trousers.

Last night I dreamt I was flying. Row 25, Seat C.

Did you hear about the man who kept dreaming about sadism, necrophilia and bestiality? His doctor said: "Forget it, you're flogging a dead horse."

Keep the dream alive: hit the snooze button.

I dream of a better tomorrow, where chickens can cross the road without being questioned about their motives.

DRUGS

I tried sniffing Coke once, but the ice cubes got stuck up my nose.

I'm not addicted to cocaine. I just like the way it smells.

Cocaine is never a solution. Unless, of course, you dissolve it in water.

A police officer with a sniffer dog came up to me and said: "This dog tells me you're on drugs." I said: "You reckon I'm on drugs? You're the one who thinks his dog talks to him!"

Drugs may lead to nowhere, but at least it's the scenic route.

I used to do drugs. I still do but I used to, too. **Steven Wright**

It's OK to smoke weed in the rain, but don't in hail.

Drugs don't ruin your career. Drug tests do.

How can you buy marijuana over the phone?
Press the hash key.

I think my wife is selling drugs. Yesterday I was running late for work and the phone rang. I answered it but before I could say anything, a male voice on the line said: "Hey, honey, is that dope gone yet?"

Did you hear about the drug dealer who held a January cocaine sale? Selected lines only.

How do you get a drug addict into bed?
With e's.

My younger brother's an example of what can happen to people who get involved with drugs: his own house and a Porsche at the age of 23.

Blow your mind – smoke gunpowder.

Did you hear about the man who supplied drugs to seabirds? He left no tern unstoned.

I don't do drugs. If I want a rush, I get out of the chair when I'm not expecting it. **Dylan Moran**

I said "no" to drugs, but they wouldn't listen.

A chemist walks into a pharmacy and says: "Do you have any acetylsalicylic acid?" The pharmacist says: "You mean aspirin?" "That's it," says the chemist. "I can never remember the word."

People who think it's OK to give drugs to animals need to get off their high horse.

Who was the first drug addict in the Bible?
Nebuchadnezzar. He was on grass for seven years.

I hate people who think it's cool to take drugs. Like customs officers.

Don't pay through the nose for cocaine.

Boy: "Have you seen my pills? They're labelled LSD."
Grandmother: "Never mind about your pills! Have you seen the dragon in the kitchen?"

Whether or not sex is better than pot depends on the pusher.

I tell you who I blame for all the drugs in schools – the supply teachers.

How do we know Humpty Dumpty took drugs?
Because he died a crack head.

DRUNKS

I got home and my wife said: "How many drinks have you had?" I said: "I don't know – I'm an alcoholic, not an accountant."

A drunk goes to court. The judge says: "You've been brought here for drinking." "Great," says the drunk. "Let's get started."

My wife hates the sight of me when I'm drunk, and I hate the sight of her when I'm sober.

Two drunks are walking home along a railway track. One says: "There are a lot of steps here." The other says: "And this handrail is so low!"

A weekend wasted isn't a wasted weekend.

I'm in trouble with my wife. She came to the pub looking for me, and I asked her for her number.

A drunk boards a bus, prompting a Bible thumper to exclaim: "You're going straight to hell!" "Damn!" says the drunk. "I'm on the wrong bus."

Spotting a nun outside a bar, a drunk punches and kicks her repeatedly before sneering: "Not so tough tonight, are you, Batman?"

You're not drunk if you can lie on the floor without holding on.

Never get drunk when you're wearing a hooded sweatshirt, because eventually you'll think there's someone right behind you. *Dave Attell*

I was so drunk when I got home last night that I picked a fight with a mop. Wiped the floor with him, I did!

I can tell when my wife drinks. Her face gets blurred.

A drunk falls into a fountain in Trafalgar Square and starts floundering around. Looking up, he sees Nelson standing on top of the column. "Don't jump!" yells the drunk. "This is the shallow end!"

When a paraplegic gets drunk, do you still call him legless?

Cop: "Can you explain why you're out on the street at four in the morning?"
Drunk: "If I could, I'd be home by now."

My drinking's getting out of hand. I dropped three pints last night.

Man in lake: "Help! I can't swim!"
Drunk on park bench: "So what? I can't play the piano, but I'm not shouting about it."

Last night I was way too drunk to drive home, so I drove to another party.

Wife: "This is the last time I tell you about coming home drunk."
Husband: "Good, because I'm sick of hearing it."

What device tells you that you've drunk too much?
A karaoke machine.

Two guys are drinking at a bar when one falls off his stool and slumps motionless to the floor. The other guy says to the bartender: "I'll say this for Kev, he knows when to stop."

Wife: "What's the idea coming home half drunk?"
Husband: "Sorry, I ran out of money."

I wouldn't call him a steady drinker – his hands shake too much.

A drunk goes up to a parking meter, puts in a quarter, and the dial goes to 60. "Huh!" he says. "I lost 100 pounds."

My usually teetotal uncle once got so drunk that he slid off the chair while we were saying our pre-dinner prayers. It was a real fall from grace.

I can't think of anything worse after a night of drinking than waking up next to someone and not being able to remember their name, or how you met, or why they're dead. *Laura Kightlinger*

A drunk was staggering home through the park when he saw a man doing push-ups. He yelled: "I think you should know, pal – your girlfriend has gone home!"

Dr Watson was in a bar. It was past closing time and he was a bit drunk. "Come on," said the barman. "Haven't you got Holmes to go to?"

Did you hear about the drunk who was taking a shortcut home across a cow field when he dropped his hat? He had to try on 30 others before he found it again.

A drunk staggers into an Alcoholics Anonymous meeting. A member asks: "Are you here to join?" "No," says the drunk, "I've come to resign."

Mike: "My wife drives me to drink."
Marty: "You're lucky. I had to walk."

A man arrives home so drunk that his wife attacks him with a broom. He turns to her and asks: "Are you cleaning, or were you flying somewhere?"

What's the difference between a drunk and an alcoholic?
Drunks don't have to go to the meetings.

I got so drunk last night I found myself dancing in a cheesy bar . . . or as most people call it, a delicatessen. *Sean Hughes*

Don't drink and drive. You might have a bump and spill your drink.

A drunk driver was pulled over by a traffic cop. Smelling his breath, the cop said: "You're drunk!" "Thank God for that," said the drunk. "I thought the steering had gone."

Why did the drunk come home and leave his clothes on the floor?
He was still in them.

Policeman: "I'd like you to accompany me to the station." Drunk: "Sorry, officer, I've left my piano at home."

Last Christmas I got drunk on advocaat, and then things just snowballed.

A man was trying to repair his broken-down car when a drunk came over to see what was going on. "Piston broke," said the man. "Me, too," replied the drunk.

Sometimes too much to drink isn't enough.

A drunk vomits on a dog. The dog runs away yelping. The drunk says: "I don't remember eating that."

Man to police officer: "I swear to drunk I'm not God!"

With a beer bottle in his back pocket, a drunk fell over on the way home. As he staggered to his feet, he felt something running down his leg. "Please God," he implored. "Let it be blood!"

When deaf people get drunk, do they slur their hands?

Did you hear about the guy who got drunk and collapsed in a heap next to the bar? It caused a major delay in the gymnastics competition.

A traffic cop pulls over a guy who has been driving erratically. He walks over to the driver's window and asks: "You drinkin'?" The driver replies: "You buyin'?"

I once got drunk and passed out on someone's satellite dish. My dreams were broadcast across the whole world. *Steven Wright*

You know you're drunk when you feel sophisticated but can't pronounce it.

You know you're drunk when there are traces of blood in your alcohol stream.

You know you're drunk when you get out of bed and miss the floor.

You know you're drunk when you can't find the way out of a bus shelter.

You know you're drunk when mosquitoes get a buzz after biting you.

You know you're drunk when you wake up dressed as a woman and think, "Hey, I look all right."

You know you're drunk when the parking lot seems to have moved while you were in the bar.

A drunk is staggering along the street with one foot on the kerb and the other in the gutter. A police officer stops him and says: "You're drunk!" "Thank God!" says the drunk. "I thought I was crippled."

DUCKS

Two ducks are walking down a Belfast street. One goes "quack". The other goes, "I'm going as quack as I can."

How do you turn a duck into a soul singer?
Put it in a microwave until its bill withers.

I find that ducks' opinion of me is greatly influenced by whether or not I have bread. *Mitch Hedberg*

A duck walks into a pharmacy and says: "Gimme some chapstick and put it on my bill."

A chicken walks up to a duck standing at the side of the road and says: "Don't do it, mate, you'll never hear the end of it!"

DYSLEXIA

The chairman of the Dyslexic Society has been given an OBE. He said: "What's the point? I can't even play the bloody thing."

If you're cross-eyed and dyslexic, can you see perfectly?

My girlfriend left me a note which said: "I'm leaving you because you're stupid and bigoted." Well, I'm not stupid, I'm dyslexic; and I can't help it if I have big toes.

How would a dyslexic person dance the YMCA?

Dyslexic homosexuality: the love that cannot spell its name.

What do you get if you cross an insomniac, an agnostic and a dyslexic?
Someone who's up all night wondering if there is a dog.

I was moved to tears when my dyslexic son made a sign for my vegetable patch. Mentallot.

Dyslexic IT technicians wait ages for a USB, then three come along at once.

A dyslexic was found dead in bed. He had choked on his own vimto.

What's yellow and stinks of pee?
The "To Let" sign outside my dyslexic neighbour's house.

Is "vice-versa" a pointless expression to a dyslexic?

Did you hear about the guy who thought DNA was the National Dyslexics Association?

Did you hear about the dyslexic angler? He landed a giant crap.

Did you hear about the dyslexic guy who went to a toga party dressed as a goat?

Did you hear about the dyslexic lawyer? He studied all year for the bra exam.

Did you hear about the dyslexic Satanist? He sold his soul to Santa.

Did you hear about the dyslexic pimp who bought a warehouse?

Did you hear about the dyslexic pervert who went into an S&M shop and came out with a nice cardigan?

Did you hear about the paranoid dyslexic? He was convinced he was following someone.

Grab your taco. You've pulled a dyslexic Mexican.

Two dyslexics are in a kitchen. One asks: "Can you smell gas?" The other says: "I can't even smell my own name."

I asked my dyslexic friend, "Which American rock band split up in 2011?" He said: "Erm . . ."

Why did the dyslexic send his girlfriend a small rodent for Valentine's Day? He wanted to show his vole for her.

My dyslexic friend's a heron addict.

When life gives you melons, you know you're dyslexic.

How do you recognize a dyslexic Yorkshireman?
He's the one wearing a cat flap on his head.

EARTHQUAKES

Did you hear about the earthquake near the Galaxy chocolate factory? It sent ripples through the whole building.

What did one tectonic plate say when it bumped into another? **"Sorry, my fault."**

Why did the geologist look embarrassed? **Because he realized his theory about earthquakes was on shaky ground.**

Did you know James Bond once slept through an earthquake? He was shaken, not stirred.

ECONOMY

Inflation is cutting money in half without damaging the paper.

Petrol is so expensive these days that the last time I went dogging I had to ask my mum to give me a lift.

The economy is so bad that the pen on the counter is now more valuable than the bank.

The economy is so bad that I got a pre-declined credit card in the mail.

The economy is so bad that last week I saw a Mormon with only one wife.

The economy is so bad that CEOs are now playing miniature golf.

The economy is so bad that Jewish women are starting to marry for love.

The economy is so bad that the Mafia is starting to lay off judges.

The economy is so bad that I put my wife back on Match.com just so she could get free dinners.

The economy is so bad that wives are having sex with their husbands because they can no longer afford batteries.

The economy is so bad that when Bill and Hillary Clinton travel together, they have to share a room.

The economy is so bad that a picture is now worth only 200 words.

The world's economies are not just flirting with disaster, they've reached the heavy petting stage.

The Allied Irish Bank has issued a credit warning about Kellogg's. It's worried about the Harvest Crunch.

If financial planners made toasters, the bread would pop up and down, but would turn out just fine in 5–10 years.

With rising prices, I changed my gas supplier today – to Heinz.

Things were so bad last year that the Eurozone changed its Facebook currency status from "single" to "it's complicated".

A recession is a period when you have to tighten your belt; a depression is when you have no belt to tighten.

I'm 500 per cent against inflation.

The Greeks have stopped making hummus and taramasalata – it's a double-dip recession.

Due to the economic crisis, to save on energy costs the light at the end of the tunnel will be switched off.
God.

EGOTISM

What three words are guaranteed to wreck a man's ego?
"Is it in?"

When two egotists meet, it's an I for an I.

What's the height of conceit?
Calling out your own name during sex.

He's such an egotist he joined the navy so that the world could see him.

A lot of people say I'm egocentric, but enough about them.

My wife is the most wonderful woman in the world, and that's not just my opinion – it's hers.

He never needs to go on vacation, because he's always on an ego trip.

People who are wrapped up in themselves are overdressed.

At the feast of ego, everyone leaves hungry.

How can you spot an egotist at a party?
He is me-deep in conversation.

Has anyone else noticed that mirrors look really sexy?

If the world really did revolve around you, you'd get terribly dizzy.

He's so far up himself, he's in danger of turning inside out.

What's the kindest thing you can say about egotists?
At least they don't talk about other people.

I don't have a big ego. I'm way too cool for that.

ELEPHANTS

What did Tarzan say when he saw 500 elephants coming over the hill?
"Look, there's 500 elephants coming over the hill."

What did Tarzan say when he saw 500 elephants in sunglasses coming over the hill?
Nothing; he didn't recognize them.

Why is it difficult for an elephant to ride a bicycle?
He doesn't have a thumb to ring the bell.

What has two grey legs and two brown legs?
An elephant with diarrhoea.

What do you give an elephant with diarrhoea?
Plenty of room.

Why are elephants wrinkled?
Have you ever tried to iron one?

What's the red stuff between an elephant's toes?
Slow pygmies.

What do you call two elephants on a bicycle?
Optimistic.

What is grey, has large ears, a trunk, and squeaks?
An elephant wearing new shoes.

How do you know there's an elephant in your bed?
By the "E" on his pyjamas.

What do elephants have for lunch?
An hour, like everyone else.

How can you tell that an elephant has been in your fridge?
By the footprints in the butter.

What do you get if you take an elephant into work?
Sole use of the elevator.

How do you know if there's an elephant in the pub?
Its bicycle is outside.

How do you know if there are two elephants in the pub?
There is a dent in the handlebars.

What do you get when you cross an elephant with a skin doctor?
A pachydermatologist.

How can you tell if an elephant is sitting behind you in the bathtub?
You can smell the peanuts on his breath.

What's grey, has a wand, big ears, big wings and gives money to
young elephants?
The tusk fairy.

What do elephants use as tampons?
~~**Sheep.**~~

What was the elephant doing on the motorway?
About 5 m.p.h.

A male elephant saw a beautiful female elephant stroll over to the
watering hole. "Wow!" he exclaimed to the other males. "Look at that
figure: 3,600, 2,400, 3,600."

How do you get down off an elephant?
You don't. You get down off a duck.

Elephants are overprotected. Then again, that's easy for me to say from my ivory tower. **Milton Jones**

What's grey, beautiful and wears glass slippers?
Cinderelephant.

How much did the psychiatrist charge the elephant?
$500: $100 for the visit, and $400 for the couch.

What do you get when you cross an elephant with a hooker?
A two-ton pick-up.

What weighs four tons and is bright red?
An elephant holding its breath.

What is more difficult than getting an elephant in the back seat of your car?
Getting a pregnant elephant in the back seat of your car.

What is more difficult than getting a pregnant elephant in the back seat of your car?
Getting an elephant pregnant in the back seat of your car.

First elephant: "I hear you've been trying to trace your ancestors on the internet."
Second elephant: "Yes, and it's a mammoth task."

An elephant robbed a bank. The police officer asked the witness: "Would you recognize him again?" "No," said the witness, "he was wearing a stocking over his head."

Why does an elephant have four feet?
Because he'd look silly with only six inches.

I was playing the piano when an elephant suddenly burst into tears. I said: "Do you recognize the tune?" He said: "No, I recognize the ivory."

Two elephants walk off a cliff . . . boom boom!

ENGLAND AND THE ENGLISH

England is the only country that runs more efficiently through a world war than a snow storm.

Why did the English aristocrat eat starch every day?
To keep a stiff upper lip.

An Englishman was being shown Niagara Falls for the first time. "Isn't it something!" said his American host. "I suppose it runs all night, too," grumbled the Englishman.

A woman went into a Newcastle hairdresser's and asked for a perm. The Geordie stylist said: "I wandered lonely as a cloud . . ."

What's the difference between a kangaroo and a kangaroot?
One's a marsupial, the other's a Geordie stuck in a lift.

Is the Isle of Dogs the Isle of Man's best friend?

In north London, they erect blue signs to say, "A famous person lived here"; in south London, they erect yellow signs to say, "Did you see this murder?"

I met a transvestite from Greater Manchester yesterday. He had a Wigan address.

Did you hear about the Manchester advent calendar? The windows were all boarded up and someone had stolen the chocolates.

Why does the River Mersey run through Liverpool?
Because if it walked, it would get mugged.

In Liverpool your wallet gets off the bus one stop before you do.

Why do Scousers have two left feet?
Because Liverpool shoe shops won't put the right ones on display.

I just saw a Scouse security guard, or as his mates call him, "the inside man".

Part of Liverpool was closed last week after a suspicious object was seen in a car. On closer inspection, the police identified it as a tax disc.

Why did audiences scream so loudly at Beatles concerts?
It was the shock of seeing four Scousers working.

Have you heard about the Scouse version of *Silence of the Lambs*? It's called *Shurrup Ewes*.

How does a Yorkshireman say: "It isn't in the tin"?
"Tin tin tin."

Did you hear about the Brummie who fought in Vietnam and kept getting flashbacks to being in Birmingham? *Milton Jones*

What's the popular form of greeting in Norfolk?
High sixes.

People don't think there's a time difference in the UK but there is. If you go to Norfolk, it's still 1973.

You're English if you complain when the weather's too cold.

You're English if you complain when the weather's too hot.

You're English if you're still mentally at war with Germany, France, Scotland, Ireland, the American colonies and the Vikings.

You're English if you understand the rules of cricket.

You're English if you rarely leave home without an umbrella.

You're English if you think dried pig's blood is a delicacy.

You're English if first you learnt to talk, then you learnt to walk, then you learnt to queue.

You're English if you know that an inch of snow will bring the entire country to a standstill.

You're English if you have a proverb to cover any eventuality.

You're English if you think Marty Wilde was just as good as Elvis.

You're English if you mention the weather at least half a dozen times a day.

ENVIRONMENT

Wind turbines: I'm a big fan.

I don't see how these new light bulbs save energy. I still have to get up and switch them on.

I just bought a low-energy light bulb. The sales assistant said: "Will you be putting it up yourself?" I said: "No, it's going in the lounge."

My wife left me because of my views on the environment. I'd tried saving water by showering with the woman next door.

I went to a wind farm. The little baby breezes were cute, but I decided not to keep one because when they get bigger and stronger they can become destructive.

In an underdeveloped country, don't drink the water; in a developed country, don't breathe the air.

Air pollution is when your city is hit by a blizzard, and three weeks later the snow still hasn't fallen to the ground.

You'll know global warming is real when you see Scottish people with suntans.

Environmentalists tell us that every day an area of rainforest the size of Wales is destroyed. Why is it never Wales? *Jimmy Carr*

Climate-change zealots say that in 20 years the only place we'll be able to see polar bears is in a zoo. So what's new?

Asked to illustrate the dangers of oil pollution, a boy said: "When my mom opened a tin of sardines last night, it was full of oil and all the sardines were dead."

Environmentalists now warn that worms are about to take over the world. So watch out for advice on the threat of global worming.

Fly tipping is so wrong – unless they have given really good service.

I'm not saying my wife's old, but the candles on her last birthday cake contributed to global warming.

The environmentalist warned: "If we don't conserve water, we could go from one ex-stream to another."

Save the earth! It's the only planet with chocolate.

Did you hear about the environmentalist who tried to save water by diluting it?

A man bursts into a bank, waving a can of aerosol. "Quick! Hand over the money!" he yells. "Or the ozone layer gets it!"

Climate is what you expect; weather is what you get.

I don't have a carbon footprint . . . because I drive everywhere.

ESKIMO/INUIT

An Eskimo girl spent the night with her boyfriend and next morning found that she was six months pregnant.

Why don't Eskimos get married?
Cold feet.

What do Eskimos get from sitting on the ice too long?
Polaroids.

An Eskimo was arrested on suspicion of burgling a neighbour's igloo. Police want to know what he was doing on the night between September and March.

Have you ever played the Eskimo lottery?
You have to be Inuit to win it.

Two Eskimos sitting in a kayak were chilly, so they lit a fire in the craft. But it sank, proving once again that you can't have your kayak and heat it too.

Why do Eskimos eat whale meat and blubber?
You'd blubber too if you had to eat whale meat!

Why do Eskimos have so many words for snow?
Because otherwise a game of "I Spy" would be rubbish.

Why did the Eskimo wash his clothes in Tide?
Because it was too cold outtide.

What's the difference between a eunuch and an Eskimo?
A eunuch is a massive vassal with a passive tassel, while an Eskimo is a rigid midget with a frigid digit.

EXERCISE

What do aerobics instructors and people who process bacon have in common?
They both tear hams into shreds.

Why did the aerobics instructor cross the road?
Because someone on the other side could still walk.

I joined a health club last month. It cost me $500, but I haven't lost a pound. Apparently you have to go there.

Exercise is such a dirty word that I have to wash my mouth out with chocolate.

I jogged backwards last week and put on five pounds.

I've just been to the gym, and they've got a new machine. I only used it for about an hour because it started to make me feel sick, but it's great. It's got Kit Kats, Mars Bars, crisps . . . everything you could want.

Mike: "Why do you roll your own cigarettes?"
Marty: "My doctor said I needed the exercise."

Did you hear about the overweight woman who gave up jogging for her health? Her thighs kept rubbing together and setting her pantyhose on fire.

I exercise religiously. I do one sit-up and say, "Amen!"

A man asked the gym trainer: "I want to impress that beautiful girl. Which machine should I use?" He said: "Try the ATM."

My doctor advised me to start running. I wasn't ill, but he'd just caught me in bed with his wife.

Everywhere is walking distance if you have the time.

I read that exercise kills germs, but it's so difficult getting them to exercise.

Did you hear about the guy who was banned from the gym for throwing his weight around?

When I was younger, I looked forward to getting up early to exercise. Now getting out of bed in the morning is my exercise.

How can anyone believe in survival of the fittest when you see some of the people running around in jogging shorts?

My doctor told me I needed to get in shape. I pointed out to him that round *is* a shape.

I just want to thank the girl with no sports bra who ran with me through the last few miles of yesterday's marathon. Your lack of support got me through.

I really need to exercise. I get exhausted just winding my watch.

Why did the bald man take up jogging?
To get some fresh 'air.

When you stop and think about them, treadmills are really dangerous.

I got a jump rope, but it's just a rope. Turns out you have to do the jumping part.

My girlfriend helps me to keep fit. Every time she mentions marriage, I run a mile.

Some people claim to enjoy exercise, but then some people claim to have been abducted by aliens, too.

I'm not really the athletic type. I once sprained my wrist while reading *Sports Illustrated*.

The advantage of exercising every day is you die healthier.

If you had an affair with your yoga teacher, would it put you in a difficult position?

I get enough exercise just by pushing my luck.

Did you hear about the jogger who overslept? He was running late.

I hope that rapidly clicking this arrow on Google Street View counts as jogging.

Exercise must be good for you. My wife's tongue has never been sick a day in her life.

My granddad's joined a rambling group. It takes them ages to finish a story.

I asked the gym instructor what I could do for my body. He said: "Schedule it for demolition."

The trouble with jogging is that by the time you realize you're not in shape for it, it's too far to walk back.

I read an advert saying I could have the body of an 18-year-old. But where would I keep it?

What's the definition of macho?
Jogging home from your own vasectomy.

I have to exercise early in the morning before my brain figures out what I'm doing.

My idea of exercise is to sit in the bath tub, pull the plug and fight the current.

I do 10 sit-ups every morning. It might not sound much, but there are only so many times you can hit the snooze button.

How do you get a man to exercise?
Tie the TV remote to his shoelaces.

How do men exercise on the beach?
By sucking in their stomach every time they see a bikini.

My wife's yoga pants have come to terms with the fact that they are really just "sit on the couch and watch movies" pants.

I never thought I'd be the type to get up early in the morning to exercise. And I was right.

The only yoga stretch I've perfected is the yawn.

What's the difference between an aerobics instructor and a dentist?
A dentist lets you sit down while he hurts you.

I signed up for an exercise class and was told to wear loose-fitting clothes. I said: "If I had any loose fitting clothes, I wouldn't have needed to join."

Doctor: "Does your husband exercise?"
Wife: "Yes, doctor. Last week he was out four nights running."

I had to quit my aerobics class because I broke a toe. Unfortunately it wasn't mine.

I'm on a strict running programme. I started yesterday. I've only missed one day so far.

Don't forget, your brain needs exercise, too. So spend plenty of time thinking up excuses for not working out.

My girlfriend bought a training bra. Now her breasts have learnt to sit up and beg to be played with.

FACES

How do you stop your mouth from freezing in winter?
Grit your teeth.

A face can say so many things – especially the mouth part.

Girl: "Where did you get all those freckles?"
Boy: "I fell asleep next to a screen door."

Do you know what really makes me smile?
Facial muscles.

Wife: "I'll have you know, I've got the face of a teenager."
Husband: "Well, give it back. You're wearing it out."

He's got a smile like a crocodile with wind.

I don't know where you got that face from but I hope you kept the receipt.

He was so pale the only way he could get any colour in his face was to stick his tongue out.

Husband: "Honey, there's something different about your face. What is it?"
Wife: "I'm wearing a gas mask!"

His face looked like the south end of a northbound donkey.

How can you tell when you've got a serious acne problem?
Blind people start reading your face.

If you get a tattoo on your face you can pretty much guarantee you are no longer anyone's emergency contact.

He had a mobile face – that is, he always took it with him. *Spike Milligan*

Why was the man with the crooked nose and mouth always laughing?
He couldn't keep a straight face.

He has the perfect face for radio.

She had a face that could launch a thousand ships – it certainly looked as if it had been smashed repeatedly on the side of a liner.

If my nose were 12 inches long, would it be a foot?

What do you find in a clean nose?
Fingerprints.

Jackie: "Be honest. Do you think my skin is starting to show its age?"
Jill: "I can't tell. There are too many wrinkles."

What do you call a pimple on each cheek?
Oppozits.

What did one eye say to the other eye?
"Between you and me something smells."

FACTS

The only time the world beats a path to your door is if you're in the bathroom.

An escalator can never break – it can only become stairs.

Whatever hits the fan will not be evenly distributed.

Rummaging in an old garden will always turn up an old ball.

Two needles of different length will never see eye to eye.

The easiest way to find something lost around the house is to buy a replacement.

People who don't drive always slam car doors too hard.

Those who live by the sword get shot by those who don't.

Taller people sleep longer in bed.

You always feel a bit scared when stroking horses.

There will always be empty beer cans rolling on the floor of your car when your boss asks for a lift.

Any tool dropped while repairing a car will roll to the exact centre.

Those who get too big for their britches will be exposed in the end.

If you're one in a million, there are still more than 7,000 of you.

No one knows the origins of their metal coat hangers.

The severity of the itch is directly proportional to the reach.

Paper is always strongest at the perforation.

A flying particle will seek the nearest eye.

Gossip is like an apple. In order to be really good, it has to be juicy.

The only difference between a rut and a grave is the depth.

The authority of a person is inversely proportional to the number of pens that person is carrying.

Trying to squash a rumour is like trying to unring a bell.

At the end of every party there is always a girl crying.

Opportunities always look bigger going than coming.

A signature always reveals a man's character, and sometimes even his name. *Spike Milligan*

You can't respect a man who carries a dog.

Some of us learn from the mistakes of others; the rest of us have to be the others.

People will believe anything if you whisper it.

It used to be that only death and taxes were inevitable. Now, of course, there's shipping and handling, too.

Despite the number you find, nobody ever recalls losing their plaster at swimming baths.

Silence is golden but duct tape is silver.

The advantages of easy origami are two-fold.

The only thing you ever get free of charge is a dead battery.

If it weren't for the last minute, nothing would get done.

The longer the title, the less important the job.

You don't have to swim faster than the shark, just faster than the guy next to you.

All inanimate objects can move just enough to get in your way.

If something is confidential, it will be left in the photocopier.

Some people would not recognize subtlety if it hit them on the head.

Whenever you cut your fingernails, you find a need for them an hour later.

Every snowflake in an avalanche pleads not guilty.

One of the most awkward things that can happen in a pub is when your drink-to-toilet cycle gets synchronized with a complete stranger.

An expert is a man who knows 62 ways of making love, but doesn't know any women.

When it's you against the world, I'd bet on the world.

Indecision is the key to flexibility.

Any wire cut to length will be too short.

Parallel lines have so much in common, it's a shame they'll never meet.

The file you are looking for is always at the bottom of the largest pile.

Those who know the least will always know it the loudest.

If you have always done it that way, it is probably wrong.

The trouble with bucket seats is that not everybody has the same-size bucket.

In every plate of fries, there is a bad fry.

The most important item in an order will no longer be available.

It's impossible to describe the smell of a wet cat.

Reality is for people who can't handle science fiction.

The shopping bag that breaks is the one with the eggs.

Even at a Mensa convention, someone is the dumbest person in the room.

The more crap you put up with, the more crap you are going to get.

If you wear a blindfold at the rifle range, you don't know what you're missing.

Just when you think you've reached rock bottom, someone hands you a shovel.

Nothing in the known universe travels faster than a bad cheque.

The necessity of the quietness of your footsteps lies in direct proportion to the number of objects you'll bump into.

Nothing is impossible for the man who doesn't have to do it himself.

Prodding a fire with a stick makes you feel manly.

It's easier to fight for principles than to live up to them.

Hindsight shows you how a mistake looks from the rear.

A gossip is someone with a great sense of rumour.

When a broken appliance is demonstrated for the repairman, it will work perfectly.

Good news rarely comes in a brown envelope.

Experience is that wonderful thing that enables you to recognize a mistake when you make it again.

Only the young die good.

The best photos are generally attempted through the lens cap.

The more an item costs, the farther you have to send it for repairs.

Behind every little problem there's a larger problem, just waiting for the little problem to get out of the way.

Everything unusual tastes more or less like chicken.

The easiest time to add insult to injury is when you're signing somebody's plaster cast.

In any hierarchy, each individual rises to his own level of incompetence and then remains there.

If you stand in one place long enough, you make a line.

If you step out of a short line for a second, it becomes a long line.

Any item you put in a safe place will never be seen again.

You never know when you've run out of invisible ink.

The person ahead of you in the queue will have the most complex transaction possible.

A person with two first names cannot be trusted.

Everything can be filed under "miscellaneous".

Great ideas are never remembered and dumb statements are never forgotten.

The last person who quit or was fired will be held responsible for all mistakes.

Criticism is not nearly as effective as sabotage.

The explanation of a disaster will be made by a stand-in.

There's no panic like the panic you momentarily feel when you've got a part of your body stuck in something.

Snowmen fall from Heaven unassembled.

The light you can see at the end of the tunnel is probably an oncoming train.

The greater the value of the rug, the greater the probability that the cat will throw up on it.

All things are possible, except skiing through a revolving door.

The more important it is to get to a website, the more likely the server is down.

Any repairman will never have seen a model like yours before.

A Smith & Wesson beats four aces.

Promises are like babies – fun to make but hell to deliver.

No postage stamp sticks better than one on an envelope with the wrong address.

Anything not nailed down is mine. Anything I can prise loose is not nailed down.

Home is where you can say whatever you like because nobody listens to you anyway.

A rumour is something that goes in one ear and in another.

Unless you're the lead dog, the view never changes.

Most rules of thumb suck.

If a thing's worth doing, it would have been done already.

Some mistakes are too much fun to make only once.

Everything takes longer than it should except sex.

Most of us know a good thing as soon as someone else sees it.

Despite constant warning, you have never met anybody who has had their arm broken by a swan.

Only dead fish go with the flow.

Opportunity knocks only once, but temptation bangs on your door for years.

If the grass is greener on the other side of the fence, you can be sure the water bill is higher.

A paint drip will always find the hole in the newspaper and land on the carpet underneath – and will not be discovered until it has dried.

Triangular sandwiches taste better than square ones.

Few things can match the satisfaction of high-fiving someone who is trying to give you the "Talk to the hand" gesture.

The trouble with being a good sport is that you have to lose to prove it.

Queue jumping: it's the way forward.

A rumour is like a used car. To find out how far it will go, first you have to get it started.

It doesn't matter whether you win or lose until you lose.

You never leave a parking space without someone in an adjacent space leaving at the same time.

The cost of the hairdo is directly related to the strength of the wind.

You've turned into your dad the day you put aside a thin piece of wood specifically to stir paint with.

Remember, no one is listening until you fart.

FAILURE

Failure is not an option. It comes bundled with the software.

Some people leave a mark on this world. I'll probably leave a stain.

My family branded me a failure, but then I invented an invisibility cloak. If only they could see me now . . .

Failure is not falling down: it's not getting up again.

My life goals were all offside.

I got this letter, and when I opened it, it said: "You may already be a loser." **Rodney Dangerfield**

Failure is the only thing I've ever been a success at.

A born loser is a man who calls the number scrawled in lipstick on the phone booth wall – and his wife answers.

My great-grandfather was a total failure. He once came third in a duel.

FAMILIES

I decided to trace my family tree, because I'm not very good at drawing.

Why are families like a box of chocolates?
They're mostly sweet, with a few nuts.

Why did the Siamese twins leave England for the US?
So the other one could have a chance to drive.

I come from a family of crack-shot police marksmen. This stems from my grandfather being an armed robber. He died recently . . . surrounded by his family. **Milton Jones**

Any of your friends can become an enemy, but a relative is one from the start.

My elderly aunts used to come up to me at weddings, prod me in the ribs and say, "You're next!" They stopped after I started doing the same to them at funerals.

I have two brothers – well, three actually, but one has learning difficulties so he doesn't count.

What's the best way to get in touch with your long-lost relatives?
Win the lottery.

My uncle's a man's man – which is a description he prefers to "gay".

My brother once drew on his face with green permanent marker pen. We never did get it off, so now he's known as the Indelible Hulk.

My big sister was always pulling my leg. That's why one is six inches longer than the other.

I call my sister Pilot Light because she never goes out.

The family that sticks together should bathe more often.

They had four sons. The first was a banker, the second was also in jail. The third was a college graduate and the fourth couldn't get a job either.

Child: "Am I descended from a monkey?"
Mother: "I don't know. I never met your father's family."

My brother picks up new things very quickly – and now he's doing 18 months for it.

I looked up my family tree, and found that some of my relatives are still climbing around in it.

I come from a broken home, although it was just a hairline crack before I came along.

I hurt my back the other day. I was playing piggy-back with my six-year-old nephew and I fell off. *Tommy Cooper*

When the landlord had to evict his relative again, he referred to him as his cousin, twice removed.

Did you hear about the guy who thought there was nothing wrong with incest as long as you keep it in the family?

Teacher: "Do you have any brothers?"
Boy: "No. but my sister does."

Did you hear about the Siamese twins?
Everything goes in one ear and out the brother.

My parents asked me to hand out invitations for my brother's surprise birthday party. That's when I realized he was the favourite twin.

My sister gives me the creeps – all her old boyfriends. *Terri Kelly*

Husband: "I wear the pants in my family – right under my apron."

I remember the same year that my uncle went to prison for forgery was when I stopped getting a birthday card from Pamela Anderson.

FARMING

Which farmer sits on his tractor, shouting: "The end is nigh, the end is nigh"?
Farmer Geddon.

Did you hear about the farmer who called his pig Ink because it was always running out of the pen?

Did you hear about the novice farmer who bought a patch of land five miles long and two feet wide? He wanted to grow spaghetti.

Why was the farmer hopping mad?
Because someone stepped on his corn.

Why did the farmer plough his field with a steamroller?
He wanted to grow mashed potatoes.

Did you hear about the farmer who couldn't keep his hands off his young wife? So he fired them.

I know a farmer who has 200 head of cattle. He thought there only 196 until he rounded them up.

Why did the woman lose her job as a cattle herder?
She couldn't keep her calves together.

Agriculture student: "Your methods are too old-fashioned. I wouldn't be surprised if this tree gives you less than 20 pounds of apples."
Farmer: "I wouldn't be surprised either. It's an orange tree."

How did the farmer win an award?
He was outstanding in his field.

Mike: "So you want to become a farmer? You'll need sheep, chickens . . . herd of cows?"
Marty: "Of course I've heard of cows!"

A rustler raided our farm last week. Really got my goat.

What's the difference between a dressmaker and a farmer?
A dressmaker sews what she gathers, and a farmer gathers what he sows.

Why don't shepherds have to pay much for their equipment?
They get staff discounts.

Did you hear about the shepherd who drove his flock through town, but got a ticket for making a ewe turn?

What happened when the farmer tried to cross a lion with a goat?
He had to get a new goat.

What breed of Scottish cattle are renowned for their waterproof coats?
Gaberdine Angus.

The local farmer almost gave me a job looking after his wheat fields. I could've been a corn tender.

Why did the farmer bury dollar bills in his field?
He wanted the soil to be rich.

Man: "Do you think I can catch the 5 o'clock train if I take a short cut through that field?"
Farmer: "Sure – and if the bull sees you, you might catch the four o'clock."

What did the farmer say to the barren nanny goat?
"You must be kidding."

Did you hear about the farmer who had two windmills on his land but knocked one down because he didn't think there was enough wind to operate two?

What do you call a person who used to like tractors?
An extractor fan.

Why do they bury farmers only three feet deep?
So they can still get a hand out.

Did you hear about the farmer who found dozens of phallic-shaped toadstools growing on his land? Unfortunately he's now having trouble with squatters.

What did the farmer say when he lost his tractor?
"Where's my tractor?"

A farmer spots a naked lamb in the field. "How have you lost all your wool?" he booms. "I hope you haven't been gambolling again!"

Why did the farmer feed his pigs sugar and vinegar?
He wanted sweet and sour pork.

Did you hear about the farmer who tried fish farming, but gave it up when his tractor kept getting stuck in the lake?

On my first day working on the farm, a threshing machine ripped both my legs off. Still, it's early days, and I'm sure I'll soon find my feet.

FEAR

I've been diagnosed with a chronic fear of giants – feefiphobia.

I discovered I scream the same way whether I'm about to be devoured by a great white shark or if a piece of seaweed touches my foot. *Kevin James*

Bad news for agoraphobics: a cure is just around the corner.

What phobia is the fear of being asked, "Who goes there"?
Friendorphobia.

I have a raging fear of commitment – I don't even like to write in pen.

Aibophobia – the fear of palindromes

As a child, I had a scary experience with a portrait photographer. I still have flashbacks.

I'm afraid of heights. Whenever I fly, I ask the pilot to stay on the runway as long as possible.

Anarachnophobia: the fear of spiders wearing waterproof jackets.

Iraqnophobia: the fear of spiders in Baghdad.

I won Agoraphobic of the Year. Sadly I wasn't able to collect my award.
Milton Jones

I'm not homophobic – I'm not afraid of my home.

There's no scarier feeling than the millisecond you think you're going to die when you lean your chair back just a little too far.

Fear is a little dark room where negatives are developed.

Just before you get nervous, do you experience caterpillars in the stomach?

Afrophobia: the fear of the return of 1970s hairstyles.

If Spider-Man became arachnophobic, would he be scared of himself?

What is the fear of meeting a fat man in a red suit in a confined space?
Santaclaustrophobia.

Is there such a thing as a closet claustrophobic?

Hypocoindria: the fear of not having the correct change.

I'm not afraid of heights, only widths. **Steven Wright**

I was going to buy a book on phobias, but I was afraid it wouldn't help me.

I live with fear every day, but sometimes she lets me go to the pub.

A friend of mine suffers from claustrophobia and agoraphobia. He spends most of his time standing in doorways.

Fobia: the fear of misspelled words.

I used to have a fear of hurdles, but I got over it.

Did you hear about the paranoid with low self-esteem? He thought that nobody important was out to get him.

Why did the paranoid always take the elevator up to his first-floor apartment?
He couldn't cope with the stares.

Anyone who isn't paranoid simply isn't paying attention.

My doctor said my heavy drinking was making me paranoid. He said: "When did you have your last drink?" I said: "What do you mean, last?"

If you want to know more about paranoids, try following them around.

I wanted to go to the Paranoids Anonymous meeting, but they wouldn't tell me where it was.

I'm kind of paranoid. I often think the car in front of me is following me the long way around. **Dennis Miller**

Did you hear about the paranoid comedian? He walked off-stage because people were laughing at him.

My doctor thinks I'm paranoid. He didn't say it, but I know he's thinking it.

FIRE

There was a fire at the Viagra factory last night. It went up in no time.

I just burned my fingers in boiling oil and screamed, "Ooh, aah, aah", like a monkey. It was a chip pan, see.

If there's H_2O on the inside of a fire hydrant, what is on the outside? **K9P.**

Why did the man join the Fire Department?
His girlfriend had told him to go to blazes.

Did you hear about the two Mexican firefighters – José and Hose B?

I saw a poster outside a shop saying "Fire Sale." I thought: Who would want to buy fire, and anyway how would they wrap it?

A good way to start a fire is to rub two Boy Scouts together.

Suspecting his crew of deliberately starting fires, the chief warned: "There's too much arson about in this station."

A shoe factory burned down last week. Ninety soles were lost.

Did you hear about the fire at the circus? The heat was intense.

An arsonist is someone who sets the world on fire, at least in a small way.

Sitting in front of a roaring fire, I thought to myself: Lions don't burn as well as logs.

If an indoor shooting range is ablaze, what do you shout to alert them?

Crime is rife among dyslexic arsonists.

Did you hear about the candle shop that burned down? Everyone stood around singing "Happy Birthday".

FISH AND FISHING

Two goldfish were swimming around in their bowl. One said to the other: "If there's no God, who changes our water every week?"

I bought a goldfish the other day, but it turns out it was epileptic. The weird thing was, as long as I left it in the bowl it was fine.

Sardines are fish that crawl into a tin, lock themselves up, and leave the key outside.

Two fish in a tank. One says to the other: "Do you know how to drive one of these things?"

A boy deep-sea fish asks a girl fish out on a date. "I can't," she says. "I'm not from around here." "Huh!" he moans. "I knew you were out of my league."

How do you communicate with a fish?
Drop it a line.

Why won't sardines travel on the London Underground?
They don't want to be squashed together like people.

What fish goes up the river at 100 m.p.h.?
A motor pike.

I went fly fishing the other day. All I caught was a two-pound blue bottle.

A husband takes his wife ice fishing. After four hours in the cold, she says: "Tell me again how much fun we're having – I keep forgetting."

Nothing makes a fish bigger than almost being caught.

Why are some fish at the bottom of the ocean?
Because they dropped out of school.

I went on a fishing trip but only caught three fish. I reckon they cost me about $400 each. It's a good job I didn't catch more – I couldn't have afforded them.

Did you hear about the lucky fisherman? He married a girl with worms.

Sharks are stupid. Why don't they just swim a few feet lower on approach? When will they realize that the fin is tipping everyone off?

How do you make a goldfish age?
Take away the G.

I wonder how much deeper the ocean would be without sponges.
Steven Wright

What fish do roadworkers use?
Pneumatic krill.

Fisherman: "You've been watching me for three hours. Why don't you try fishing yourself?"
Passer-by: "No, I haven't got the patience."

I've booked my wife and her mother in for a fish pedicure at the weekend – in a shark cage off the coast of South Africa.

One person can keep a fishing line clear, but it takes two to tangle.

Give a man a fish and he will eat for a day. Teach him how to fish, and he will sit in a boat and drink beer all day.

Fish wouldn't get into trouble if they learnt to keep their mouth shut.

Mike: "What's the biggest fish you've ever caught?"
Marty: "You've seen *Jaws*? Well, it was about the same size as the box the DVD comes in."

Why is cod hard to catch?
Because cod moves in mysterious ways.

Sharks don't deserve such bad press. If a stranger entered my house wearing only Speedos, I'd probably attack him, too.

Which fish performs operations to make other fish look pretty?
A cosmetic sturgeon.

First fish: "One of our shoal keeps trying to preach Communist doctrine to us."
Second fish: "Ah, that must be Erik, the famous red herring."

A short-armed fisherman isn't as big a liar as one with long arms.

Why couldn't the fish take the call?
He was on the other line.

Noah built arks for all God's creatures, including a split-level model for all the fish. He called it his multi-storey carp ark.

Why couldn't Noah catch many fish?
Because he only had two worms.

Dean Martin was singing to a group of deep-sea divers: "When an eel bites your boot, and draws blood from your foot, that's a moray . . ."

Did you hear about the haddock that ended up on the fishmonger's slab? It was gutted.

If smoking is so bad for you, how come it can cure dead salmon?

When you catch a fish and throw it back, does it tell its friends that it was abducted by aliens?

A fish grows fastest between the time it is caught and when a fisherman describes it to his friends.

Baby shark: "Why do we circle people in the water with our fins showing before we eat them? Why don't we just attack?"
Father shark: "They taste better without the shit inside them."

I'm afraid of sharks, but only in a water situation. *Demetri Martin*

How did the fisherman fare when he used liquorice as bait?
He caught all sorts.

A thoughtful wife is one who has the pork chops ready when her husband comes home from a fishing trip.

In France, one man's fish is another man's *poisson*.

Did you hear about the girl who went fishing for the weekend with six male friends? She came home with a red snapper.

What did the fish say when it swam into the wall?
"Dam!"

Woman: "Are you fishing?"
Fisherman: "No, just drowning worms."

Why are fishermen never happy on their wedding day?
They keep thinking about the ones that got away.

Why don't prawns give to charity?
They're shellfish.

Mother: "Did you put fresh water into the goldfish bowl?"
Boy: "No, they haven't finished the old water yet."

What do you give a deaf fish?
A herring aid.

There are two kinds of fishermen: those who fish for sport and those who catch something.

What's an eel's favourite dance?
The conger.

In the ocean, how come it's always the starfish that gets to be the sheriff?

What can you do in radiation-contaminated rivers?
Nuclear fission.

A man took his granddaughter fishing. After a while he asked: "Any luck?" "No," she replied. "I don't think my worm is really trying."

FOOD AND DRINK

Have you ever had a beaver curry? It's like a normal curry but a little otter.

Tofu is over-rated . . . it's just a curd to me.

Why did the tofu cross the road?
To prove it wasn't chicken.

Last week I entered a competition and won a year's supply of Marmite – one jar.

Pheasant and plum jam: the preserve of the upper classes.

What food do you get if you smear a goat with a member of the onion family?
Garlic butter.

Revels: a game of Russian roulette if you've got a nut allergy. *Milton Jones*

Who was the leading ice-cream manufacturer in Biblical times?
Walls of Jericho.

What's the best way to stop milk from turning sour?
Leave it in the cow.

A man went into a butcher's shop and asked: "Do you keep dripping?" "Yes, I do," said the butcher, "and it's very embarrassing."

Why did the orange stop in the middle of the street?
It ran out of juice.

Wife: "You left the fridge door open, you idiot, and now everything's gone off! What am I supposed to do with all this food?"
Husband: "OK, don't make a meal out of it."

I've just been offered eight legs of venison for $100. Is that two deer?

Is it me, or do Buffalo wings taste like chicken?

Why did the raisin go out with the prune?
Because he couldn't find a date.

If we're not supposed to have midnight snacks, why is there a light in the fridge?

Practise safe eating: always use condiments.

Why is parsley like public hair?
You push it aside and keep eating.

Two biscuits are crossing a street when one is crushed by a passing car. The other says: "Crumbs!"

Why is there no such organization as Chocoholics Anonymous?
Because nobody wants to quit.

I've just been enjoying a really hot curry while watching the cricket. The runs are flowing.

Try eating with a tuning fork. It does nothing for the taste of the food, but it sounds great.

How did the butcher introduce his wife?
"Meat Patty."

I have no problem with genetically modified food. I had a lovely leg of salmon the other day.

Two sausages are sizzling in a pan. One turns to the other and says: "It's hot in here." The other says: "Blimey! A talking sausage!"

Did you hear about the guy who was reluctant to enter the ammunition-eating competition? But in the end he had to bite the bullet.

I bought a waffle iron because I hate creased waffles.

Why is there an expiration date on sour cream?

I bought some cookies last week. On the packet, it said: "Store in a cool place." So I mailed them to Samuel L. Jackson's house.

I went to the pub and had a ploughman's lunch. He wasn't very happy.

How do you start a pudding race?
Sago.

If you can smell smörgås, call the smörgåsbord.

They demolished my local Domino's Pizza today, and all the other shops in the street fell down. ***Boothby Graffoe***

What's the fastest cake in the world?
Scone.

If white wine goes with fish, do white grapes go with sushi?

They say cheese gives you nightmares, but how many people are scared of cheese?

Last weekend I attended an animal-rights barbecue.

Why did the baker stop making doughnuts?
He got tired of the hole thing.

What do you get if you cross a door knocker with some courgettes, tomatoes and onions?
Rat-a-tat-a-touille.

I've just eaten brunch, but I've made sure to leave room for linner.

I used to eat a lot of natural foods until I learnt that most people die of natural causes.

Did you hear about the Frenchman who created a 20-foot-high dessert of fruit, jelly and sponge? He called it the Trifle Tower.

What did the grape say to the raisin?
"Why are you looking so worried?"

My wife can't stop eating chips, which makes her a liability at the casino.

How do bakers trade recipes?
On a knead-to-know basis.

Have you ever started to eat a horse and then realized you weren't that hungry after all? *Tim Vine*

My wife said: "I want you to toast some bread for me." So I raised my wine glass and said: "To bread!"

The lollipop industry is making suckers of us all.

What did the green grape say to the purple grape?
"Breathe! Breathe!"

Woman at food fair: "Why is this cake more expensive than your other cakes?"
Stallholder: "That's Madeira cake."

Why do people constantly return to the refrigerator in the hope that something new to eat will have materialized?

I'm on a seafood diet. Every time I see food, I eat it.

How do you make an apple puff?
Chase it round the garden.

What's the most fattening thing you can put in a banana split?
A spoon.

Oysters are supposed to be good aphrodisiacs, but I tried a dozen the other day and only six of them worked.

How does Good King Wenceslas like his pizzas?
Deep pan, crisp and even.

Raw toast is an ideal bread substitute.

If you ate pasta and antipasta, would you still be hungry?

How do you make a hot dog stand?
Take away its chair.

Shortbread: they're not making it any longer.

What do you call someone with jelly in one ear and custard in the other?
A trifle deaf.

A tomato family are walking down the street when the little boy tomato falls behind. The father tomato turns around and shouts: "Ketchup!"

Cow tongue is supposed to be a delicacy, but I don't like the thought of tasting something that is tasting me back.

Two packets of potato crisps are strolling along the road. A driver calls out: "Do you want a lift?" "No, thanks," say the crisps. "We're Walkers."

I got food poisoning today. Don't know when I'll use it though. *Steven Wright*

Did you hear about the new factory that Kraft Foods is building in Israel? It's called Cheeses of Nazareth.

What do you call cheese that is not yours?
Nacho cheese.

How do you approach an angry Welsh cheese?
Caerphilly.

What cheese do you use to lure a bear down a mountain?
Camembert.

What cheese would you use for hiding small horses?
Mascarpone.

Now you can buy Armageddon Cheese. On the pack it says: "Best Before End."

What do you call a gingerbread man with one leg?
Limp Bizkit.

What's the difference between beer nuts and deer nuts?
Beer nuts are $1.90, and deer nuts are just under a buck.

Rare, medium, well done: I've got all three types of burns on my hands from barbecuing this weekend.

Pot Noodle: for best results, put back on the shelf. **Andy Parsons**

What did the grape say when it was trodden on?
Nothing. It just let out a little wine.

Why did the man buy fish cakes?
It was his fish's birthday.

Why did the biscuit cry?
Because his dad had been a wafer so long.

If you think Special K is boring, wait till you try Normal K.

A boiled egg in the morning is hard to beat.

My wife eats like a horse, so I bought her a nosebag.

I was walking home last night when someone threw grated cheese all over me. Very mature, I thought.

When cheese gets its picture taken, what does it say?

Did you hear about the man who bought a plate with four corners so he could enjoy a square meal?

What do you say to a beefburger?
"How now, ground cow?"

I always get my naan bread from the supermarket. I don't know why; she's been dead for 12 years.

My traditional German Christmas cake has gone missing. I've reported it as stollen.

Corn-fed, free-range, farm-reared chicken: I don't want to know its life story, I just want to eat it.

When you eat a lot of spicy food, you can lose your taste. Last summer in India I listened to a lot of Michael Bolton. **Jimmy Carr**

Do bakers with a sense of humour make wry bread?

I ask my wife to leave the foil on ready-made meals, because it's often the tastiest part.

Why did the baby strawberry cry?
Because his mother was in a jam.

Husband: "Why do you spend so much money on food?"
Wife: "Sorry, but you and the kids won't eat anything else."

I bought a box of Animal Crackers and it said on it: "Do not eat if seal is broken." So I opened it up and sure enough . . .

We live in a society where pizza gets to your house before the police.

Now that food has replaced sex in my life, I can't even get into my own pants!

A Zen master walks up to a hot-dog seller and says: "Make me one with everything."

I can't stand mustard – ever since he came at me with a candlestick in the billiard room.

I went to Korea, and ate dog. I hadn't intended to, but I swallowed a fly and things just escalated.

What's the difference between roast beef and pea soup?
Anyone can roast beef.

Who discovered that you could get milk from cows? And what did he think he was doing at the time?

Uncle Ben has died. No more Mr Rice Guy. *Tim Vine*

My friend's allergic to rice. He's basmatic.

What can you make from baked beans and an onion?
Tear gas.

Did you hear about the man who ate metal paper fastenings? It was his staple diet.

The hardness of the butter is directly proportional to the softness of the bread.

After being violently attacked by a cough sweet, the chocolate screamed: "Get him off me! He's bloody menthol!"

I'm not sure about tasting molasses. I think I'd rather try another part of the mole.

Two peanuts were walking down the road. One was assaulted.

I've just mixed grass, basil, pine nuts and olive oil, and . . . hay, pesto!

How fast do hotcakes sell?

If you cook alphabet soup on the stove and leave it unattended, it could spell disaster.

Did you know it takes 40 pigs to make 4,000 sausages? Isn't it amazing what you can teach them?

How do you make gold soup?
With 18 carrots.

What happened when the rhubarb was arrested?
It was kept in custardy.

The healthiest part of a doughnut is the hole. Unfortunately you have to eat through the rest of the doughnut to get there.

Why did the orange use suntan lotion?
It didn't want to peel.

My uncle owned a kebab shop, but he's dead now. He was buried with all his equipment. He'll be turning in his grave . . . ***Milton Jones***

What's smelly, round and laughs?
A tickled onion.

I've just made the world's biggest pizza base. I'd like to see someone top that!

Mushrooms: breakfast of champignons.

I just drew a smiley face with jam on my toast, but I still don't believe it is really happy.

What was the best thing before sliced bread?

I always mix up chutney and pickle. It makes me chuckle.

A man walks into a chip shop and says: "Fish and chips twice." The woman behind the counter says: "I heard you the first time."

What's 55 metres high and made of dough?
The Leaning Tower of Pizza.

Did you hear about the man who passed out after eating too much curry?
He ended up in a korma.

Rich foods are like destiny. They, too, shape our ends.

What do you get if you cross a kangaroo and a chicken?
Pouched eggs.

How do you stop sandwiches from curling?
Take away their brooms.

What did baby corn say to mama corn?
"Where's popcorn?"

When is soup musical?
When it's piping hot.

I'm a light eater. As soon as it's light, I start eating. *Henny Youngman*

Did you hear about the guy who was half-French, half-pygmy? He was a great cook, but he couldn't reach the grill.

Tea is for mugs, but coffee isn't my cup of tea either.

I was walking down the street when a man threw a glass of milk over me. I thought, How dairy!

What is Snow White's favourite drink?
7 Up.

A Pepsi executive was fired last week. He tested positive for Coke.

Whenever I take a sip of my Evian, it comes straight back up. It must be spring water.

Did you hear about the guy who drank boiling water because he wanted to be able to whistle?

Drink coffee. Do stupid things faster and with more energy.

I was making coffee today. I pushed down on the plunger and a café in the next street blew up.

You know you're drinking too much coffee when you haven't blinked since the last lunar eclipse.

You know you're drinking too much coffee when you ski uphill.

You know you're drinking too much coffee when you lick your coffee pot clean.

You know you're drinking too much coffee when you walk 18 miles on your treadmill before you realize it's not plugged in.

You know you're drinking too much coffee when instant coffee takes too long.

You know you're drinking too much coffee when you chew on other people's fingernails.

You know you're drinking too much coffee when you can jump-start your car without cables.

You know you're drinking too much coffee when there's a picture of your coffee mug on your coffee mug.

You know you're drinking too much coffee when people get dizzy just watching you.

You know you're drinking too much coffee when you can take a picture of yourself from 10 feet away without the timer.

You know you're drinking too much coffee when Starbucks owns the mortgage on your house.

You know you're drinking too much coffee when you get drunk just so you can sober up with coffee.

You know you're drinking too much coffee when you help your dog chase its tail.

You know you're drinking too much coffee when you soak your dentures in coffee overnight.

You know you're drinking too much coffee when you can only watch DVDs on fast-forward.

You know you're drinking too much coffee when you sleep with your eyes open.

You know you're drinking too much coffee when instead of sweating, you percolate.

You know you're drinking too much coffee when you want to be cremated just so you can spend the rest of eternity in a coffee tin.

Coffee is proof that God loves us and wants us to pay attention.

My wife said: "Shall I put the kettle on?" I said: "OK, but it won't go with that skirt."

FORGIVENESS

Forgive and forget, but keep a list of names just in case.

It is far easier to forgive an enemy after you've got even with him.

THE FRENCH

I'm absolutely knackered from my French self-defence class last night. I've never run so far in my entire life.

How do you stop a French army on horseback?
Turn off the carousel.

Why do the French have the onion and the Arabs have the oil?
Because the French had first pick.

My son is being forced to smoke by our French exchange student. That's Pierre pressure for you.

When French people swear, do they say: "Pardon my English"?

What do you call a pointless race that covers 2,200 miles throughout France?
The French. *Al Murray*

What do you call a Frenchman in sandals?
Philippe Philoppe.

What's the difference between Frenchmen and toast?
You can make soldiers out of toast.

Why do French tanks have rear-view mirrors?
So that they can watch the battle.

What do you call a Frenchman with a medal for bravery?
An eBay customer.

Did you hear about the new French tank? It has nine gears: eight reverse and one forward, in case the enemy attacks from behind.

For sale: French army rifle. Never fired, dropped once.

How can you recognize a French veteran?
Sunburnt armpits.

How can you stop a French tank?
Say, "Boo!"

Why does the French flag have Velcro?
So the blue and red sections can be easily removed in times of war.

Why don't they have fireworks at Euro Disney?
Because every time they set them off, the French try to surrender.

How many Frenchmen does it take to defend Paris?
Nobody knows: it's never been tried.

Raise your right hand if you like the French; raise both hands if you are French.

What did the Mayor of Paris say to the German army as they entered the city in World War II?
"Table for 100,000, monsieur?"

Twitter became popular in France when they knew they could retweet.

How can you destroy France's military capability?
Burn down the white-flag factory in Paris.

The French are pathetic. They've got a town called Brest, and none of them think it's funny. *Al Murray*

I once tried to buy a town in the South of France, but the locals were Avignon of it.

What do you call a Frenchman who pees on your bathroom floor?
Monsieur Toilet.

FRIENDS

My mate rang me and said: "What are you doing at the moment?" I said: "Probably failing my driving test."

I had lousy luck. My best friend ran away without my wife.

My friend can't take a joke. I put some superglue on his darts last week, and he still can't let it go.

Friendship is like incontinence: everyone can see it, but only you can feel its true warmth.

Friends help you move. Real friends help you move bodies.

Real friends are the ones who survive transitions between address books.

A real friend stabs you in the front.

Mike: "A friend like you is hard to find."
Marty: "I know – there are so many bars I could be in."

I had a serious talk with my friend about the past, the present and the future. It was tense.

If you help a friend in need, they will remember you the next time they are in need.

I was a bit jealous when I saw my mate holding hands with a giant lollipop and a big box of chocolates. Then I realized they were just arm candy.

Never forget a friend, especially if he owes you money.

I've got a friend named Jay. We call him J for short.

I said to my friend: "If I was half as happy as you . . . you'd be twice as happy as me."

There are two kinds of friends: those who are around when you need them, and those who are around when they need you.

Friends may come and go, but enemies accumulate.

A lifelong friend is one you haven't borrowed money from yet.

We ran into some friends yesterday. My wife was driving.

My friend Daniel wouldn't believe me when I told him his name was an anagram. He's in denial.

Mike: "Lend me 50 cents. I want to call a friend."
Marty: "Here's a dollar. Call both of them."

Everyone should have at least two friends – one to talk to, and one to talk about.

A friend in need is a pest.

FROGS

What do you call X-rated DVDs of amphibians mating?
Frogs' porn.

A man walks into a shop with a large bullfrog on his head. "Where the hell did you get that?" asks the shopkeeper. "You won't believe it," says the frog, "but it started out as a little wart on my butt."

What's invisible and smells of frogs?
Frog farts.

Did you hear about the frog that was illegally parked? He had to be toad away.

Is a detective tale about frogs a "croak and dagger" story?

What did the two lesbian frogs say to each other?
"We *do* taste like chicken!"

The frog at the bottom of the well thinks the sky is only as big as a bucket.

How do frogs make beer?
They start with some hops.

Father: "Why did you put a frog in your sister's bed?"
Son: "I couldn't find a spider."

After eating, do amphibians have to wait one hour before getting out of the water?

What is a frog's view on life?
Time's fun when you're having flies.

What did Kermit say when he got to the top of the hill?
"M'uppet."

FUNERALS

I hate going to funerals because I'm not a mourning person.

A man had his wife cremated. As smoke came out, he said to his brother: "That's the first time I ever saw her hot."

My uncle died of asbestosis. It took us three months to cremate him.

I've just been to my friend's funeral. He was killed after being hit on the head by a tennis ball. It was a lovely service.

I get so angry at funerals. Crematoriums really make my blood boil.

Should crematoriums give discounts for burns victims?

My uncle was crushed by a piano. His funeral was very low-key.
Stewart Francis

As the coffin was lowered into the ground at a traffic warden's funeral, a voice from inside yelled: "I'm not dead! I'm not dead!" To which the vicar shouted back: "Sorry, the paperwork has already been done."

I saw half a dozen men wandering around a cemetery carrying a coffin and looking confused. I thought to myself, They've lost the plot.

Undertakers are the last people who will let you down.

Did you hear about the cemetery that raised its burial costs? It blamed the cost of living.

I went to a funeral last week with my girlfriend. It was the first time I had met most of her family. What a miserable bunch!

How does a funeral director sign his correspondence?
Yours eventually.

Wife: "If I die first, I want you to promise to let my mother ride in the first car with you at the funeral procession."
Husband: "OK, but it will totally ruin my day."

Are undertakers encouraged to think outside the box?

One of the world's leading chefs was cremated yesterday. The service lasted for 35 minutes at gas mark 5.

Why is it considered necessary to nail down the lid of a coffin?

Show me where Stalin is buried and I'll show you a Communist plot.

Gravediggers: they're down-to-earth.

In her will, my grandmother stipulated that she wanted to be buried with all of her favourite possessions. Her cat was not happy. **Tom Cotter**

How many men do you need for a Mafia funeral?
Just one, to slam the car boot shut.

My granddad was given 24 hours to live, so he drank a bottle of vodka and ate three packets of fireworks. It didn't save his life, but it gave us one hell of a show at the cremation.

I have a hard time at funerals. I'm a necrophiliac.

FURNISHINGS

Me and my recliner – we go *way* back.

What would a chair look like if our knees bent the other way?

Why is a sofa like a roast chicken?
They're both full of stuffing.

Did you hear about the man who went into an antique shop and asked: "What's new?"

Occasional tables – what are they the rest of the time? **Harry Hill**

An antique is an object that has made a trip to the attic and back.

How does Frankenstein sit in his chair?
Bolt upright.

I bought a bureau last week, and when I opened it a dozen people fell out. It was a missing persons' bureau.

Why are old people's chairs really cool?
They rock.

Our furniture goes back to Louis XIV – unless we pay Louis before the fourteenth.

If it weren't for Venetian blinds it would be curtains for everyone.

Antiques are things that one generation buys, the next generation gets rid of, and the following generation buys again.

What nationality is Mr Sheen?
Polish.

I walked in the room and the curtains were drawn. But the rest of the furniture was real.

We have period furniture. We keep it for a period, then send it back.

If something's hard to dust, it's probably an antique.

I have a decaffeinated coffee table. You'd never know it to look at it.

Corduroy pillows: they're making headlines. *Tim Vine*

I bought a self-assembly desk, but when I took it out of the box it just sat there, doing nothing. In the end *I* had to build it.

GADGETS AND INVENTIONS

How do you know if someone has an iPhone?
They tell you.

To the people who've got iPhones: you just bought one, you didn't invent it.

How do Geordies listen to music?
On a WhyiPod.

Forget the iPad, have you heard about the gadget Apple is releasing exclusively for women later this year? It's called the iRon.

Why did the man stick a photograph of his face on the back of his iPad?
So his family wouldn't forget what he looked like.

iMac + iPad + iPhone + iPod = iBroke.

Did you hear about the new Apple gadget that promises a life of misery as soon as you sign the contract? It's called the iDo.

My wife has an electric toothbrush. I only have an acoustic toothbrush.
Mark Watson

Why does a solar-powered computer watch, which is programmed to tell the time and date for 125 years, come with an 18-month guarantee?

I got a calculator, and now I can't add without it; I got a spellchecker, and I can't write without it; I got a blow dryer, and now my hair won't dry on its own.

When the wheel was invented, it caused a revolution.

The man who invented the wheel wasn't that smart. It was the guy who invented the other three that was clever.

My best friend's dad invented the zorb. He's rolling in it now.

Who would have thought Velcro would catch on?

Granny knot, surgeon's knot, hangman's knot, reef knot: I can't do them, but my damn' headphones can!

Did you hear about the man who has invented a knife that cuts four loaves of bread simultaneously? He calls it a four-loaf cleaver.

My battery had an alkaline problem, so it went to AA meetings.

Don't forget: when scissors were invented they were considered cutting edge.

Since getting my new Kindle, I have absolutely no idea how to judge a book.

I've invented a motorized broom. It's sweeping the nation.

If you understand how something works, it is obsolete.

Someone stole the plug off the kettle at work today. I can see trouble brewing.

I've just invented a wireless, battery-free, hand-operated hair-dryer. I'm calling it a towel.

I have five years' full guarantee on my new phone – provided I don't use it.

A keyring is a handy little gadget that allows you to lose all your keys at once.

I'm baffled. Yesterday my calculator was working fine; today it isn't working at all. It just doesn't add up.

Do the manufacturers of foolproof items keep some fools on the payroll for product testing?

I bought the new weed whacker. It's cutting-hedge technology.

Any technology distinguishable from magic is insufficiently advanced.

I've invented an electric spoon. It's causing quite a stir.

I'm not interested in watching TV on my phone in the same way I don't want to take a shit in my oven. *Mark Watson*

I've just bought a 3-D Kindle – or a book as it's commonly known.

A man attending an inventors' convention walked up to one of the speakers and said: "Correct me if I'm wrong, but didn't you invent Wite-Out?"

Japanese scientists have created a camera with such a fast shutter speed that it can photograph a woman with her mouth shut.

What did people go back to before drawing boards were invented?

I bought a pack of those 3-D glasses. If I wear them at the same time, I can see things in 12-D.

I bought one of those new microwave fireplaces. I kept warm all night in 30 seconds.

If you make something idiot-proof, someone will make a better idiot.

GAMBLING

I no longer see my wife and kids, and it's all because of gambling. I won loads of money and moved to Spain.

I bet you $689.44 you can't guess how much I owe my bookie.

Did you hear about the guy who came up with a great way of not losing money in Las Vegas? He kept playing the change machine.

Poker players: lull your opponents into a false sense of security by shouting "Snap" on the first hand.

Have you ever played gay poker? Queens are wild and straights don't count.

Never do card tricks for the group you play poker with.

Did you hear about the leper who was playing poker? He threw his hand in.

I was playing poker with Tarot Cards. I got a full house, and four people died.

What's the difference between a prayer in a church and at the poker table?
At the poker table you really mean it.

As a guy lays down a winning poker hand, one of the other players jumps to his feet and yells: "He's cheating! He ain't playing the cards I dealt him!"

No one can read my poker face . . . since my stroke.

What is the only game in which the more you lose, the more you have to show for it?
Strip poker.

I went to the butcher's and bet him $100 that he couldn't reach the meat off the top shelf. "No," he said, "the steaks are too high."

Gambling is an excellent way of getting nothing for something.

Gamblers Anonymous: how do they know where to send your winnings? *Harry Hill*

My wife has just left me because I'm a compulsive gambler. I'd do anything to win her back.

Why is Las Vegas so crowded?
Nobody has the plane fare to leave.

Did you hear about the compulsive gambler who bet his girlfriend that she wouldn't marry him? She not only called his bet, she raised him five.

GAMES

I wondered why the Frisbee was getting bigger, and then it hit me.

I went to the park today and played Frisbee with my dog, but it wasn't much fun. I think I need a flatter dog.

I just found that my Wii remote doesn't work if you take it out of the sync region – much like my wife.

Playing video games all night made it hard for me to get up and go to work in the morning. So I quit my job.

From playing video games, I have learnt that there is no problem in the world that cannot be solved by violence.

From playing video games, I have learnt that if it moves, kill it!

From playing video games, I have learnt that if someone dies they disappear.

From playing video games, I have learnt that bad guys move in predictable patterns.

From playing video games, I have learnt that piloting any vehicle is easy and requires no training.

From playing video games, I have learnt that when racing vehicles, you shouldn't worry if your vehicle crashes or explodes. A new vehicle will appear in its place.

From playing video games, I have learnt that when evil fat men are about to die, they start flashing red or yellow.

From playing video games, I have learnt that you should always seize the day because you only have six lives.

I was playing chess with my friend and he said: "Let's make this interesting." So we stopped playing chess. *Matt Kirshen*

Last week I got eczema, diarrhoea and haemorrhoids – the first time I've ever won a game of Scrabble.

Scrabble: it's all harmless fun until someone loses an i.

I was playing Scrabble with my dad when he spelt the word "stneve". It was an unexpected turn of events.

Never play Scrabble with a beekeeper.

Old Macdonald had a really bad Scrabble hand: E-I-E-I-O.

I found a way of making the game Operation more realistic. I told my kids they'd got it for Christmas but I didn't let them have it till July.

I bought the Iraqi version of Cluedo, but it's not very good. You can't find the weapons.

The special Beatles version of Cluedo is really boring. It's always Lucy, in the sky, with diamonds.

I remember as a boy playing hide-and-seek in the oven. Through a steamed-up door I heard my mother say: "You're getting warmer."

How do you get a sweet little 80-year-old lady to say the F-word? Get another sweet little 80-year-old lady to yell, "Bingo!"

I like to play chess with bald men in the park, although it's hard to find 32 of them. *Emo Philips*

How many squares are there on a chess board?
Two plus the spectators.

A woman sees a man playing chess with a dog. "What a clever dog!" she says. "Not really," replies the man, "I'm beating him by four games to two."

Ah, the irony of playing a game of chess against your Czech mate . . .

Now that there are gay bishops in the church, the rules of chess are being changed. Bishops can still make the same moves, but now they can only be taken from behind.

I got arrested for playing chess in the street. I said: "It's because I'm black, isn't it?" *Milton Jones*

My friend asked if I wanted to play electric-shock Monopoly. I jumped at the Chance.

The former sailor preferred to forget the days he spent playing cards in submarines. He said it was all just bridge under the water.

The only time most husbands and wives get enjoyment out of holding hands is when they are playing bridge.

If looks could kill, a lot of people would die with bridge cards in their hands.

Husband: "Shall we have a friendly game of cards?"
Wife: "No, let's play bridge."

Noticing the patient's shins are covered in bruises, the doctor asks: "Do you happen to play rugby or soccer?" "No," he says, "but my wife and I play bridge."

My wife made me join a bridge club. I jump off next Tuesday. ***Rodney Dangerfield***

I won an innuendo contest last week. I had to beat off some stiff competition.

Charades is my favourite game. Our friends come over, and my wife and I pretend to be happily married.

GARDENING

The daffodils have come out – I didn't even know they were gay.

First union leader: "I see the daffodils are coming out."
Second union leader: "Does that mean we have to come out, too?"

If you water your lawn with beer, the grass will come up half-cut.

Did you hear about the man who dug a hole in his garden and filled it with water? I think he meant well.

Why is the Incredible Hulk such a good gardener?
Because he's got green fingers.

If you mix poison ivy with a four-leafed clover, will you have a rash of good luck?

Did you hear about the geriatric gardener who was so happy one sunny day that he wet his plants?

What runs around a garden but never moves?
A fence.

Before starting your lawn mower, always count your toes and choose the ones you'd most like to keep.

How do you stop moles digging in your garden?
Hide their shovels.

My neighbours don't like it when I talk to my plants. I use a megaphone.

To all those men who moan and whine about how difficult it is to cultivate apples, I say: "Grow a pear!"

Gardens need a lot of water – mostly sweat.

Seeing Buckingham Palace for the first time, a young girl says: "Our front garden is concreted over, too."

Instead of talking to your plants, if you yelled at them would they still grow, but only to be troubled and insecure?

My fake plants died because I forgot to pretend to water them.

Don't pay the earth for topsoil.

What did the flower arrangers' skydiving team shout when they jumped out of the plane?
"Geranium!"

I went online to search for "difficult garden plants". Nothing came up.

My biologist friend tells me that constantly developing new plant varieties can be a strain.

A garden plant is something that dies if you don't water it and rots if you do.

Did you hear about the bonsai tree grower who became so successful that he started looking for a house with a smaller garden?

If only I could grow green stuff in my garden like I can in my refrigerator.

In public gardens how do they get the "Keep Off the Grass" sign on the grass?

I used to wear a flower in my lapel but I stopped because the pot kept banging on my belt.

Did you hear about the novice gardener who planted a bulb because his wife wanted a bedside lamp?

How do gardeners learn their craft?
By trowel and error.

Why don't gardeners think about sex in winter?
Because summer is the time for bedding.

For the third night in a row, someone has been mysteriously adding soil to my vegetable patch. The plot thickens . . .

A friend of mine is so vain he goes into the garden so that the flowers can smell him.

I used to get paid $70 an hour just to clean up leaves from people's gardens. I was raking it in.

Why did the man only water half his lawn?
Because he heard there was a 50 per cent chance of rain.

Did you hear about the flower arranger's children? One is a budding genius but the other is a blooming idiot.

I've just found pebbles stuck in my pond filter. Fred and Wilma are going to be devastated.

What do you send to a sick florist?

A friend of mine has devised a new chemical spray that kills the greenfly on his rose bushes. His formula kills the roses and the greenfly starve to death.

I've named a new rose I've grown after my wife, not because it's pretty, delicate and sweetly scented but because it's prickly and good against a wall.

Did you hear about the gardener who crossed a dahlia with a fuchsia? He called it a failure because it no longer had any fuchsia.

GAY AND LESBIAN

I've got a big gay following – I told him to cut down on carbohydrates.

How can you tell if your young son is gay?
He tries to push the cylinder shape into the star-shaped hole.

What's the definition of tender love?
Two gays with haemorrhoids.

How do you get four gay men on a bar stool?
Turn it upside down.

My cousin is an agoraphobic homosexual, which makes it difficult for him to come out of the closet.

How did the gay guy break his leg at the golf course?
He fell off the ball washer.

My cousin is gay. I always tell him that in our family tree, he's in the fruit section. *Rodney Dangerfield*

If homosexuality is a disease, can I call into work gay?

I've got a lighter with a pink flame. I use it to start camp fires.

Did you hear about the gay truckers? They exchanged loads.

What rank did the gay sailor aspire to?
Rear Admiral.

Gay men love mobile phones. They're always comparing their ring-tones.

How do you give a blind gay man a thrill?
Leave the plunger in the toilet.

How can you tell if you're at a gay amusement park?
They issue gerbils at the tunnel of love.

How many gay men does it take to fit a light bulb?
Just one, but it takes an entire Emergency Room staff to get it out.

Did you hear about the two gay guys who went to London?
They were disappointed to find out that Big Ben was a clock.

What happened when three gay men attacked a woman?
Two held her down while the third did her hair.

Did you hear about the bisexual pride parade? It went both ways.

What's the difference between a heterosexual man and a homosexual?
About five beers.

Wife to husband: "I think the correct term is to say Colin's on a Gay Pride march rather than say he's away with the fairies."

How do you know if you've had gay burglars?
All your soft furnishings have been stolen and your furniture has been rearranged.

Why do gay men have moustaches?
To hide their stretch marks.

How do you know you've walked into a gay church service?
Only half the congregation is kneeling.

Did you hear about the sewage worker who said he'd turned gay after entering so many manholes?

I don't understand the fuss about same-sex marriages. I've been married to my wife for 40 years, and we always have the same sex.

What do you call a lesbian with long fingernails?
Single.

How many nails are used to make a lesbian's coffin?
None. It's all tongue and groove.

How can you tell a tough lesbian bar?
Even the pool table has no balls.

I took my blind lesbian friend out for her birthday treat. We went to an indoor fish market.

There's a new drug for depressed lesbians. It's called tridixagen.

A lesbian went for a smear test, and the doctor said: "Yours is the cleanest vagina I've ever seen." "Yes," she said, "I have a woman in twice a week."

What do lesbians have in common with mechanics?
Snap-on tools.

What do you call a lesbian dinosaur?
Lickalotopuss.

I don't mind lesbians actually. They're still women who won't sleep with me, but at least it's nothing personal.

What do you call a lesbian with fat fingers?
Well hung.

I live next door to two lesbians and they asked me what I wanted for my birthday. They got me a Rolex, but I don't think they quite understood when I said: "I wanna watch."

GERMANS

Why do Germans build such high-quality products?
So they won't have to go around being nice while they fix them.

How does a German eat mussels? Knock! Knock! Knock! *Aufmachen!*

What do you get if you cross an Irishman with a German?
A man who's too drunk to follow orders.

Why didn't Hitler drink vodka?
It made him mean.

A German tourist had to fill in a form before being allowed to enter France. Under "Occupation", he wrote: "No, just visiting."

The bigger the German, the smaller the bathing trunks.

Did you hear about the German who started writing poetry as soon as he got up in the morning? He went from bed to verse.

A German orders two Martinis. The bartender says: "Dry?" The German says: "*Nein. Zwei!*"

GHOSTS

Did you hear about the two gay ghosts?
They put the willies up each other.

We found out that our house was once the site of an exorcism. It's due to be repossessed next week.

Where do ghosts hang out on a Saturday night?
At all their old haunts.

Did you hear about the ghost that was expecting a baby? It was a phantom pregnancy.

Why was the ghost signed by the football club?
To boost team spirit.

My house is haunted by a ghostwriter. I came downstairs this morning and my autobiography had been written.

What do you call a ghost at a hotel?
An inn spectre.

How can you tell if a ghost is about to faint?
He goes as white as a sheet.

What did one ghost say to the other ghost?
"Do you believe in people?"

What happened when the ghosts went on strike?
A skeleton staff took over.

When do ghosts usually appear?
Just before someone screams.

Did you hear about the US TV host who has her own ghost? It's called the Phantom of the Oprah.

I saw a dead baby ghost by the road today, or maybe it was a handkerchief. *Milton Jones*

How do you get a ghost to lie perfectly flat?
Use a spirit level.

I just bought a boomerang from a poltergeist. That will come back to haunt me.

GOD

What does God say when an angel sneezes?

Can atheists get insurance for acts of God?

What's the biggest problem for an atheist?
No one to talk to during orgasm.

I was going to become an atheist, but then I thought: You don't get any holidays.

A man prays to God: "O, Lord, give me patience, but give it to me *right now!*"

God must be in prison because that's where everyone finds him. **Robert Hawkins**

And God said: "Let there be Martinis!" And he saw that it was good. Then he said: "Let there be light!" And then he said: "Whoa! Too much light!"

What movie do atheists watch at Christmas?
Coincidence on 34th Street.

Teacher: "No, Johnny, God's last name is not Dammit."

God intended all fruit to be round, but when he created the banana his mind was on something else.

A child's prayer: "Dear God, please send clothes for all those poor ladies on Granddad's computer."

God created Man, stepped back and said: "Perfect." Then God created Woman, stepped back and said: "Hmm, I think this will have to wear make-up."

In the beginning, God made Heaven and Earth. The rest was made in China.

True, God made Heaven and Earth. But what has he done recently?

When I was a child, I asked God for a bike, but then I realized that God, in his wisdom, didn't work that way. So I stole a bike and asked him for forgiveness. **Emo Philips**

If there is no God, who pops up the next Kleenex in the box?

God spent ages trying to think of a name for a 24-hour period, but in the end he decided to call it a day.

What will happen to men if God turns out to be a woman? Not only will they all go to Hell, but they'll never know why.

GOLF

Did you hear about the couple who met on a golf driving range? They hit it off straight away.

On his way home from drinks at the golf club, a man is stopped by a traffic cop who tells him he's too drunk to drive. "Too drunk to drive?" says the man. "I can barely putt!"

Golf scores are directly proportional to the number of witnesses.

The only reason I play golf is to annoy my wife. She thinks I'm having fun.

The golf pro approaches two women and asks: "Are you here to learn how to play golf?" One woman answers: "My friend is. I learnt yesterday."

My doctor told me to go out and play 36 holes a day, so I bought a harmonica.

When you look up, thereby causing a bad shot, you always look down again at the exact moment that you should be watching your ball if you ever want to see it again.

The position of your hands is very important when playing golf. I use mine to cover up my scorecard.

Why are golf balls like eggs?
They're white, they're sold by the dozen, and you need to buy fresh ones each week.

Golf is truly Scottish – a game invented by the same people who think music comes out of a bagpipe.

My golf is definitely improving. I'm missing the ball much closer than I used to.

Last week I missed a spectacular hole-in-one by only six strokes.

The other day I broke 70. That's a lot of clubs.

A man played golf with his boss. The boss hit his drive 80 yards, leaving him 280 yards from the hole. The putt was conceded.

It's amazing how a golfer who never helps around the house will replace his divots, repair his ball marks and rake his sand traps.

I know you're supposed to replace your divots, but mine are too heavy to carry back.

If your opponent has trouble remembering whether he shot a six or a seven, he probably shot an eight.

You can always spot an employee who's playing golf with his boss. He's the guy who gets a hole-in-one and says, "Oops!" **Bob Monkhouse**

I'm too fat to play golf. If I place the ball where I can hit it, I can't see it; if I place it where I can see it, I can't hit it.

In golf terms, what's an Adolf Hitler?
Two shots in the bunker.

In golf terms, what sort of putt is a Rock Hudson?
One that looked straight, but wasn't.

In golf terms, what sort of putt is a gynaecologist's assistant?
One that just shaves the hole.

In golf terms, what sort of putt is a Diego Maradona?
A nasty five-footer.

In golf terms, what sort of putt is a Salman Rushdie?
An impossible read.

In golf terms, what sort of shot is a Douglas Bader?
One that looked good in the air but didn't have the legs.

In golf terms, what sort of shot is a Glenn Miller?
One that kept low and didn't make it over the water.

In golf terms, what's a Rodney King?
Over-clubbed.

In golf terms, what's a Princess Grace?
Should have taken a driver.

In golf terms, what's a Princess Diana?
Shouldn't have taken a driver.

It takes a lot of balls to play golf the way I do.

Why was the golfer worried when he saw the IRA man disappear into the woods?
It was his provisional.

I played golf yesterday and didn't once manage to break par. However I did break my putter, my two-wood, my three-iron . . .

Golf is a test of your skill against your opponent's luck.

Wife: "You're so obsessed with golf you can't even remember when we got married!"
Husband: "That's not true. It was the day after I sank that 40-foot putt."

One of the biggest challenges for a golfer is how to find the ball that everyone saw go in the lake.

Your best golf shots always occur when playing alone.

Your worst golf shots always occur when playing with someone you are trying to impress.

Why do golfers wear two pairs of pants?
In case they get a hole in one.

I set out hoping to shoot my age, but I shot my weight instead.

He is such a bad golfer, he shouts "fore" when he putts.

New golfer: "I can't get the hang of this game. Where am I going wrong?"
Coach: "Your problem is you're standing too close to the ball – after you've hit it."

Do pediatricians play miniature golf?

In golf, if the ball goes right, it's a slice; if it goes left, it's a hook; if it goes straight, it's a miracle.

Golf used to be a rich man's game; now it has millions of poor players.

"Is my friend in the bunker, or is the bastard on the green?"

I could have been a professional sportsman. My problem in baseball was that I could never hit a curve ball; my problem in golf was that I always did.

A bride arrives in church to find the groom carrying his golf clubs. She bellows: "What are your golf clubs doing here?" He says: "Well, this isn't going to take all day, is it?"

The secret of good golf is to hit the ball hard, straight and not too often.

I had my first golf lesson last week and did really well. After just one lesson I could throw my clubs as well as guys who have been playing for years.

When I play golf, the only time I ever hit two good balls is when I step on a rake.

Mike: "Why do you play so much golf?"
Marty: "The doctor said I must take my iron every day."

It is surprisingly easy to hole a 40-foot putt – for a 10.

The nineteenth hole is the only one on which golfers don't complain about the number of shots they took.

Did you hear about the golfer who was so accustomed to shaving his score that when he got a hole-in-one he carded a zero?

He has a great short game – but unfortunately it's off the tee.

Nonchalant putts count the same as chalant putts.

I can make divots in which a small boy could get lost. *Lewis Grizzard*

Two men are standing at a golf club bar. One says: "I'm a country member." The other says: "Yes, I remember."

Golfer: "You've got to be the worst caddie in the world."
Caddie: "I don't think so. That would be too much of a coincidence."

Golfer: "This is the worst golf course I've ever played on."
Caddie: "This isn't the golf course. We left that an hour ago!"

Golfer: "I'm going to drown myself in the lake."
Caddie: "Do you think you can keep your head down that long?"

Golfer: "I don't know what's wrong. This is the worst I've ever played."
Caddie: "So you've played before, have you?"

Golfer: "If you were me, how would you have played that last shot?"
Caddie: "Under an assumed name."

Golfer: "Will you stop looking at your watch all the time? It's distracting me."
Caddie: "It's not a watch, it's a compass."

Golfer: "I'd move heaven and earth to break 100 on this course."
Caddie: "Try heaven. You've already moved most of the earth."

Golfer: "How do you like my game?"
Caddie: "Very good, but personally I prefer golf."

Golfer: "Do you think it's a sin to play on a Sunday?"
Caddie: "The way you play, it's a sin any day."

Golfer: "That can't be my ball. It looks far too old."
Caddie: "Well, it has been a long time since we started."

Golfer: "Do you think I can get there with a five-iron?"
Caddie: "Eventually."

A bad golfer hits the ball into a huge bunker. "What club shall I take?" he asks. "Never mind the club," replies the caddie. "Just take plenty of food and water."

GORILLAS

Why do gorillas have big nostrils?
Because they have big fingers.

Why did King Kong climb up the side of the skyscraper?
Because the elevator was broken.

What do you call a gorilla named Keith?
Keith.

What's the best thing to do if you find a gorilla in your bed?
Sleep somewhere else.

What do baby gorillas sleep in?
Apricots.

Why did the gorilla wear blue underpants?
Because his red ones were in the wash.

What do you call a gorilla with a banana in each ear?
Anything you like. He can't hear you.

GRAMMAR

It's not who you know, it's whom you know.

Teacher: "You, boy, give me two pronouns!"
Boy: "Who? Me?"

I thought there might be a medical reason why my use of punctuation is so bad. So the hospital gave me a semi-colonoscopy.

Son: "Can I go to the bathroom?"
Dad: "*May* I go to the bathroom?"
Son: "But I asked first!"

Did you hear about the well-spoken truck driver? He was articulate.

It's always i before e. Isn't that weird?

It's i before e except after "Old MacDonald had a farm".

Punctuation is the difference between "Helping your uncle, Jack, off his horse" and "Helping your uncle jack off his horse".

Mike: "A double negative forms a positive, but apparently there is no language where a double positive is a negative."
Marty: "Yeah, right."

I think we're in for a bad spell of wether.

Mix your metaphors. It's not rocket surgery.

A noun and a verb were dating, but they broke up because the noun was too possessive.

GRANDPARENTS

My granddad said he always used to leave his back door open in the old days, which was probably why his submarine sank. ***Milton Jones***

My nan finally found a way of stopping Granddad chasing other women. She let the air out of his wheelchair tyres.

My grandfather's hard of hearing so he has to read my lips. The only trouble is he insists on using a yellow highlighter.

My grandfather always said: "Don't watch your money: watch your health." So one day while I was watching my health, someone stole my money. It was my grandfather.

My grandfather was shrewd. People threw small mammals at him till he suffocated.

My granddad spent most of the war on the lookout for German bombers. He was a lifeguard at Berlin Swimming Baths.

The doctor refused to give my granddad Viagra. He said it would be like putting a new flagpole on a condemned building.

My granddad's got a plaque on his head in memory of a dead bench.

Boy: "Granddad, why are you sitting outside with no pants on?"
Grandfather: "Well, last week I sat out here with no shirt on and got a stiff neck. So this is your grandma's idea."

Grandparents are like a piece of string – handy to have around and easily wrapped around the fingers of grandchildren.

Grandparents are the people who think your children are wonderful even though they're sure you're not raising them right.

My grandfather can't do what he used to do, bless him. You know, bomb the Japanese. *Milton Jones*

I asked my old granddad: "If you could have any superpower in the world, what would you choose?" He said: "Russia."

My granddad sent his photo to a Lonely Hearts Club. They sent it back, saying they weren't that lonely.

Granddad: "Why do you want me to make a frog voice?"
Boy: "Because Dad says when you croak we can go to Disneyland."

My granddad woke up with a puzzled look on his face – he'd fallen asleep on his jigsaw.

No cowboy was ever faster on the draw than a grandparent pulling a baby picture out of a wallet.

Boy: "Dad, why is Grandma always reading the Bible at her age?"
Father: "Shhh, son, she's cramming for her finals."

My nan didn't believe in taking chances. She even used to look both ways before crossing her legs.

My grandmother has found that at her age going bra-less pulls all the wrinkles out of her face.

Boy: "Grandma, are you happy to be 93?"
Grandma: "You bet I am! If I wasn't 93, I'd be dead!"

Where are grandmas stored?
In a granary.

What's the worst thing about having to kiss your grandmother?
When the coffin lid falls and smacks you on the head.

Mother: "So Grandma fell down the stairs?" Child: "Yes, but it wasn't really a problem. She wanted to come down anyway."

My grandma has very old-fashioned values. That's why we were both delighted when I bought her house for $8,000.

Boy: "Mom! There's a man collecting for the old folk's home. Shall I give him Grandma?"

As I watched them lower my 92-year-old grandmother into the ground this morning, I couldn't help feeling she was too old to go pot-holing.
Boothby Graffoe

HAIR

I have to take my hat off to my barber – it makes it easier for him to cut my hair.

Scientists have revealed that sperm helps hair grow, which has got me wondering about my nan's moustache.

My wife is going to a fancy-dress party as a Rastafarian and she wants me to do her hair. I'm dreading it.

Mike: "Is it sexual harassment if you go up to a woman and tell her that her hair smells nice?"
Marty: "Only if you're a dwarf."

Whenever I see a man with beard, moustache and glasses, I think, There's someone who has taken every precaution to stop people doodling on photographs of him.

Can bald people get hairline fractures?

What's the difference between an astronaut and Donald Trump's hair? **One amazes mankind by defying the laws of gravity, and the other is a spaceman.**

How can you tell that Donald Trump's hair believes in God? **Because it's dyed and ascending to Heaven.**

Wife to husband: "I'd love to run my fingers through your hair. Can you remember where you left it?"

I don't like the way my barber talks behind my back.

Did you hear about the guy who was so bald, it looked like his neck was blowing a bubble?

What did the bald guy say when he was given a comb? **"I'll never part with it."**

My wife has lovely long hair all down her back. None on her head – just all down her back. *Tommy Cooper*

I tried some of that revitalizing shampoo. My hair was awake all night.

Why did the man comb his hair forward? **He'd heard there were fringe benefits.**

A man walks into a barber's shop and says: "Can I have a number two?" "OK," says the barber, "so long as you don't do it in the chair."

Today I was taking the rip out of a bloke with a ridiculous wig on. He had the last laugh, though. He sentenced me to five years.

What hair colour do they put on the drivers' licences of bald men?

Have you heard about the new shampoo for hobos? It's called Go and Wash.

Did you hear about the hair stylist who was fired for making waves?

Why are brunettes so proud of their hair? **It matches their moustache.**

Wife: "Darling, will you still love me when my hair turns grey?"
Husband: "Why not? I've stuck with you through the other six shades."

A balding man walks into the barber's shop and says: "I'd like a haircut, please." "Certainly," says the barber. "Which one?"

My toupee blew off in high winds yesterday. I'd say it flew about 30 feet . . . off the top of my head.

Why did the bald man have tattoos of rabbits on his head?
Because from a distance they looked like hares.

How do we know Moses wore a wig?
Sometimes he was with Aaron and sometimes he wasn't.

A lot of people think I'm bald, but I just happen to prefer a very wide centre parting.

My friend was so bald you could see what he was thinking.

He was so bald that when he wore a turtleneck he looked like a roll-on deodorant.

Mike to Marty: "Look at that bald guy over there. It's the first time I've seen a parting with ears."

I was going to buy a book on hair loss, but the pages kept falling out.
Jay London

Why did the barber charge the bald man $30 for a haircut?
$10 for the cut and $20 for the search fee.

Show me a man with a flat-top and I'll show you a level-headed guy.

I was thrown out of our pub quiz over the question: "Where do women mostly have curly hair?" Apparently the answer was Africa.

My hair isn't just thinning, it's positively anorexic.

I don't consider myself to be bald. I'm simply taller than my hair.

Barber: "Were you wearing a red scarf when you came in?"
Customer: "No."
Barber: "Oh, dear. I must have cut your throat."

Real men don't waste their hormones growing hair.

Jackie: "What happened to that dumb blonde your husband used to hang out with?"
Jill: "I dyed my hair."

My girlfriend did a 24-hour charity hairdressing marathon. By the end she was completely lacquered.

I usually find that women with long grey hair have 12 cats and a history of mental illness. *Frank Skinner*

When one barber cuts another barber's hair, which one does the talking?

Woman: "My husband gave me a permanent wave, and now he's gone for good."

Why did the bald man cut holes in his pockets?
So he could run his fingers through his hair.

In America, most people have the same haircut as George Wendt in *Cheers*. It's the norm.

Did you hear about the woman who dyed her hair so often, her passport had a colour wheel?

Mike: "How do you get your barber to cut your hair that way?"
Marty: "I insult him."

What should you buy if your hair falls out?
A good vacuum cleaner.

I went into a hairdresser's, and all I could see in the back room was a huge set of antlers. I said to the proprietor: "What's that?" She said: "Oh, that's the new styling moose."

Did you hear about the woman who got fired from a hot dog stand for putting her hair in a bun?

My brother just couldn't cut it as a barber.

Barber: "You say you've been here before? I don't remember your face."
Customer: "Well, it's healed now."

Customer: "Couldn't you see I was going bald?"

Barber: "No, I was blinded by the shine from your head."
How does a barber cut the moon's hair?
Eclipse it.

Believe me, baldness will catch on. When the aliens come, who do you think they're going to relate to?

I used to be a mobile hairdresser, but it didn't work out. Apparently not that many people have hairy phones. *Gary Delaney*

Customer: "Why did you take off so much hair?"
Barber: "I didn't. Nature beat me to it!"

Patient: "Doctor, my hair keeps falling out. Can you give me something to keep it in?"
Doctor: "Certainly. Here's a paper bag."

I got a pocket comb, but who wants to comb their pockets?

My girlfriend said she wanted a Brazilian "downstairs". So Pele is now lodging with us.

I asked my hairdresser if I could have highlights, so he showed me a video of past haircuts.

HALLOWE'EN

I bought my wife a pair of crotchless panties for Hallowe'en – not for sexual purposes, just to give her a better grip on her broomstick.

What did the incestuous family do on Hallowe'en?
Pump kin.

What do you get if you divide the circumference of a pumpkin by its diameter?
Pumpkin pi.

Husband to wife: "Don't look out the window! People will think it's Hallowe'en already."

I got so sick of trick-or-treaters that I turned the lights out and pretended I wasn't in. To hell with the ships, it's my lighthouse!

HANGOVERS

I'm a recovering alcoholic. Well, I say recovering; I have a hangover.

A hangover is the wrath of grapes.

How does Stephen Hawking recover from a hangover?
He presses F5.

I brought up a spaniel furball this morning. That's the last time I have a hair of the dog.

Prevent hangovers: stay drunk.

A hangover is something to occupy a head that wasn't used the night before.

You're hung over if you're convinced that chirping birds are Satan's pets.

You're hung over if you'd rather have a pencil jammed up your nose than be exposed to sunlight.

You're hung over if looking at yourself in the mirror produces the same reaction as drinking a glass of fresh paint.

You're hung over if you set aside an entire morning to spend some quality time with your toilet.

If beer is proof that God loves us, hangovers are proof that he has a sadistic sense of humour.

HEALTH

Drinking your own urine is supposed to be good for you. Rubbish! I put my back out.

I passed a guy in an RAC van sobbing uncontrollably. I thought, That man's heading for a breakdown.

I don't have OCD. I've read 8,649 books on it, so I'd know if I did!

I'm hoping to find a cure for my hiccups, but I'm not holding my breath.

Did you hear about the man who was kicked out of a Tourette's Society meeting for using good language?

Good health is merely the slowest possible rate at which one can die.

Here's hoping I never get any splinters. Touch wood. **Milton Jones**

With air-conditioning you don't have to wait for winter to catch a cold. You can have one all summer.

When is the worst time to have a heart attack?
During a game of Charades.

Have you heard about the disease that has been found in soft butter? Doctors say it spreads very easily.

If you are always straightening things, you have OCD. If you are always eating things, you have OBCD.

People who say they never fart are full of hot air.

Why do farts smell?
So that deaf people can appreciate them too.

Is anyone else tired, or is it just M.E.?

An asthmatic receives an obscene phone call halfway through an asthma attack. The caller pauses and asks: "Did I call you, or did you call me?"

Join the Hernia Society. It needs your support.

The best cure for a cough is to take a large dose of laxatives. Then you'll be afraid to cough.

I'm lactose-intolerant. I can't bear anything that doesn't have toes.

My nephew has HDADD. He has trouble focusing but when he does it's unbelievably clear. **Steven Wright**

My wife accused me of having OCD. I immediately put her in her place.

Two bottles of herbal remedy meet in the pharmacy. One says to the other: "Aloe, Vera."

I went to donate blood the other day but they wouldn't accept it. Apparently they need to know where it comes from.

Hypochondria is the one disease I haven't got.

Someone threw a bottle of Omega-3 pills at me. Luckily my injuries were only super-fish-oil.

I went to the pharmacy and asked: "Have you got a cure for head lice?" The pharmacist said: "It depends what's wrong with them."

Have you heard about the pill that is half aspirin and half glue? It's for splitting headaches.

What should you do if your wife has a fit in the bath?
Put the dishes in.

My wife's attached to a machine that keeps her alive – the refrigerator.

Acupuncture: a jab well done.

I drink way too much. When my doctor drew blood, he ran a tab.
Rodney Dangerfield

I was woken up last night by the bulimic in the apartment next door. I banged on the wall and said: "Keep it down, love!"

There was a problem with the catering at the Bulimia Sufferers' Annual Convention. I didn't want to bring it up . . .

A hypochondriac's life is a bed of neuroses.

My friend had a heart attack while on holiday in the Black Forest. He isn't out of the woods yet.

We've just discovered our daughter suffers from severe allergic reactions to wheat, soy, dairy, and eggs. So her birthday cake this year is just three candles.

TB or not TB? That is congestion.

Did you hear about the woodchopper who had a pain in the lumbar region?

I have liver disease caused by years of heavy drinking. My wife said I should go to BUPA, but I did the complete opposite. I went to APUB.

A man goes into a pharmacy and asks: "Have you got anything for laryngitis?" The pharmacist says: "Good morning, sir. What can I do for you?"

What's the first sign of madness?
Suggs coming up your driveway.

My sister suffers from hay fever, and last week she found out she's diabetic, too. So to cheer her up I bought her some flowers and a box of chocolates. **Milton Jones**

You're never alone with schizophrenia.

Did you hear about the schizophrenic who followed himself on Twitter?

Every two in one people are schizophrenic.

My ex-wife is spreading false rumours about me being schizophrenic. Well, three can play at that game.

A schizophrenic saw a poster advertising a new stage play. He thought to himself: I've half a mind to go to that.

I used to be schizophrenic, but we're OK now.

Never get into an argument with a schizophrenic and say: "Just who do you think you are?"

A man goes to the pharmacy to inquire about a Viagra pill. "Will I be able to get it over the counter?" he asks. "Possibly," replies the pharmacist, "but you might need two."

I took a Viagra pill but it stuck in my throat. Now I've got a stiff neck.

I had a really expensive enema last week. It cleaned me right out.

Can acupuncture do anything for pins and needles?

The Colour Blind Association are holding a social night next week – they're going to paint the town grey.

My uncle was thrown out of a mime show for having a seizure. They thought he was heckling. **Jeff Shaw**

Deafness is now getting to be a real problem for me. I never thought I'd hear myself say that.

Smoking makes a woman's voice go harsh. If you don't believe me, try flicking cigarette ash on her new carpet.

My doctor said I should give up smoking, so I tried gum instead. But I couldn't keep it lit.

I was going to start an Apathy Anonymous group, but then I thought: Why bother?

The survey of bulimics was very successful. There was plenty of feedback.

When you're run down, the best thing to take is the licence number.

My doctor told me to cut down on sodium, but I'm taking his advice with a pinch of salt.

My wife has terrible sinus trouble. It's "sinus a cheque for this, sinus a cheque for that . . ."

Why did the anorexic cross the road?
There was a sudden breeze.

I've got Parkinson's disease, and he's got mine.

Have you heard about the new pill that is part-aphrodisiac, part-laxative? It's called Easy Come, Easy Go.

I have CDO. It's like OCD, but the letters are in alphabetical order. *Like they're supposed to be.*

A lot of men don't understand the importance of a prostate exam, but usually they get it in the end.

I'm pretty sure I have an abnormal convex curvature of the upper spine. Call it a hunch . . .

My whole family is lactose-intolerant. When we take pictures, we can't say "Cheese". *Jay London*

How do deaf people tell the difference between a yawn and a scream?

My wife's eating for two. She's not pregnant, just schizophrenic.

I'm a schizophrenic Gemini, so if you cross me you'll have four people to deal with!

Sometimes I can't remember if I'm the good twin or the evil one.

I was diagnosed with antisocial behaviour disorder, so I joined a support group. We never meet . . .

You know you've got bipolar disorder if last night you understood the secrets to the universe, and this morning you are contemplating whether the jam goes on top of the peanut butter or under it.

I sneezed really hard, and while I didn't break any bones, there was some tissue damage.

In what direction does a sneeze travel?
Atchoo!

I phoned the Weak Bladder Helpline about my problem. It's 1p a minute.

My father is allergic to cotton. He has pills that he can take, but he can't get them out of the bottle.

My mother made us eat all sorts of vitamins and supplements, until one day I nearly choked on part of the *Sunday Times*. **Milton Jones**

Doctor: "Tell me, have you ever been troubled by diphtheria?"
Patient: "Only when I've tried to spell it."

I went for my routine check-up today and everything seemed to be going fine until he stuck his finger up my butt. I think it's time I changed dentists.

What's the best cure for water on the knee?
A tap on the ankle.

What did one virus say to the other?
"Don't get too close. I think I've got penicillin."

I've stopped smoking thanks to those patches you can buy. I stuck one over each eye, and now I can't find my cigarettes.

My aunt reckoned smoking would help her lose weight. It did – one lung at a time.

I thought about giving up smoking, but I decided not to. I'm not a quitter. **Ed Byrne**

My uncle found the best way to give up smoking was to pour a can of petrol over his head every morning.

Remember, smoking doesn't kill people. Those who are trying to *quit* smoking kill people.

There are so many disorders these days. When I was young we just had crazy people.

Doctor to patient: "I have good news and bad news. The good news is that you're not a hypochondriac."

I think my Tourette's Syndrome has finally been cured. Thank fuck for that!

HIGHWAYS

At what age do you think it's appropriate to tell a highway it's adopted?

What qualifications do you need to be a road sweeper?
None. You just pick it up as you go along.

I just failed my driving test theory. The question said: "What is a sign you may see on a motorway?" Apparently "Pick your own strawberries" isn't an acceptable answer.

How do they get a deer to cross at that yellow road sign?

If ever I got the chance to name a street, I'd call it Skin Street, just so I could laugh at the people at number 4.

I was hitch-hiking the other day and a hearse stopped. I said: "No, thanks. I'm not going that far."

Mike: "Do you know the Milwaukee turn-off?"
Marty: "Know her? I married her!"

What is Scotland's friendliest motorway?
M8.

If carrots are so good for the eyes, why are there so many dead rabbits on the highway?

I don't understand speed bumps. If anything they slow you down!

A grey piece of tarmac says to a black piece of tarmac: "I'm gonna kick the crap out of that skinny bit of red tarmac." "Careful," says the black tarmac. "He may be small, but I'll warn you: he's a cyclepath!"

HIPPIES

How do you get a hippie out of the bath?
Turn on the water.

How do you hide money from a hippie?
Put it under the soap.

Why couldn't the lifeguard save the hippie?
He was too far out, man.

What do you call a hippie's wife?
Mississippi.

How many hippies does it take to screw in a light bulb?
Hippies don't screw in light bulbs, they screw in dirty sleeping bags.

What do hippie horses eat?
Hay, man.

How do you know if a hippie's been staying at your house?
He's still there.

How do you get twenty hippies into a phone booth?
Throw in a joint.

Why are there no hippies on the Starship *Enterprise*?
Because hippies don't have jobs in the future either.

Why are hippies like bears?
They both hug, eat honey and shit in the woods.

At what temperature does a hippie like to eat his pizza?
Cool. Really cool.

What's red and orange and looks good on a hippie?
Fire.

What's dumber than a box of rocks?
The hippie that carries it across the country.

What kind of cigarettes do hippies smoke?
Yours.

I was walking down the street when a hippie suddenly shoved a joss stick up my butt. I was incensed.

How can you recognize a burned-out hippie?
He used to take acid; now he takes antacid.

You know you're a hippie if you carry a picture of Gandhi in your wallet.

You know you're a hippie if your child is named after a celestial object.

You know you're a hippie if, out of habit, you pass your cigarette to whoever's sitting next to you.

You know you're a hippie if your hair contains a fully functional eco-system.

You know you're a hippie if half your furniture is bean bags.

First hippie: "What would you do if you saw a spaceman?"
Second hippie: "Park my car in it, man."

What do you call a hippie with a haircut?
The defendant.

How do you know a hippie chick is on her period?
She has only one sock on.

Did you hear about the hippie ghost?
He was ghoul man, really ghoul.

HISTORY

Why does history keep repeating itself?
Because we weren't listening the first time.

What was the name of Anne Boleyn's brother?
Tenpin.

Why did Henry VIII have so many wives?
He liked to chop and change.

Galileo invented the telescope and then five minutes later he invented spying on his neighbours.

Why wasn't Marie Antoinette coherent after being guillotined?
Because her head was all over the place.

In 1932, Amelia Earhart flew across the Atlantic from Canada to Britain. In 1934, her luggage arrived.

Tanning salons first became popular during the Bronze Age.

Why did King Arthur have a round table?
So no one could corner him.

Who was the roundest knight at King Arthur's Round Table?
Sir Cumference.

Have you heard about the daredevil knight at Camelot? Medieval Knievel.

Who was Guinevere's favourite chef?
Sir Loin.

Why were the early days of history called the Dark Ages?
Because there were so many knights.

Why did the knight run around shouting for a tin opener?
He had a bee in his armour.

Which English king invented the fireplace?
Alfred the Grate.

Who led the Pedants' Revolt?
Which Tyler.

If Benjamin Franklin were alive today, what would he be most famous for?
Being 306 years old.

How did the *Mayflower* show that it liked America?
It hugged the shore.

Why did the Pilgrims' pants keep falling down?
Because they wore their belt buckles on their hats.

Why did the Pilgrims eat turkey on Thanksgiving?
They couldn't get the moose in the oven.

Why did Julius Caesar buy crayons?
He wanted to Mark Antony.

When Julius Caesar asked the Romans to lend him their ears, did the Romans ever get them back?

Oedipus was a nervous rex.

Which document did thirteenth-century nobles on a volcanic island force the king to sign in order to give them more rights?
The Magma Carta.

Long ago, when men cursed and beat the ground with sticks, it was called witchcraft. Today it's called golf.

Can you tell me where Napoleon came from?
Course I can.

Where did Napoleon keep his armies?
Up his sleevies.

Which Jew rampaged across Asia in the thirteenth century?
Genghis Cohen.

People keep asking me where I was when Kennedy was shot. OK, so I don't have an alibi . . .

What did Mason say to Dixon?
"We've got to draw the line here."

When Noah was asked about his life, the memories came flooding back.

Where was King Solomon's temple?
On his forehead.

What's the difference between Joan of Arc and a canoe?
One was Maid of Orleans, the other is made of wood.

John F. Kennedy, Indira Gandhi, John Lennon: if history teaches us anything, it's that if you don't want your child to be assassinated, don't name them after an airport.

HOCKEY

Why do ice hockey players have such big egos?
Because they can walk on water.

In hockey you take a stick and hit either the puck or anyone who has touched the puck.

Why was time out called at the leper hockey game?
There was a face-off in the corner.

Why can't women play ice hockey?
They have to change their pads after every period.

I think hockey is a great game. Then again, my son is a dentist.

Hockey is figure skating in a war zone.

Did you hear about the guy who went to watch a fight and a hockey game broke out?

Why did Jesus quit playing hockey?
Because he kept getting nailed to the boards.

Hockey is the only sport that has its own coroner.

Reporter: "Did you ever break your nose?"
Hockey player: "No, but 11 other players did."

Did you hear about the ice hockey team who drowned during spring training?

Why doesn't the world's fattest man become a hockey goalie?

Why do hockey players wear numbers?
Because you can't always identify the body from dental records.

What's the difference between a game of ice hockey and the Friends Reunited website?
Hockey has fast pucks . . .

HOME IMPROVEMENT

Did you hear about the new Emo wallpaper? It hangs itself.

I gave an odd-job man a list of 10 things to do around the house, but he only did numbers 1, 3, 5, 7 and 9.

I'm really into DIY. Whenever my wife asks me to fix something around the house, I say: "Do it yourself."

I cleaned the attic with my wife last week. Now I can't get the cobwebs out of her hair.

Power drills have been improved – bit by bit.

I went into a DIY store and asked for some nails. "How long do you want them?" the sales assistant asked. I said: "I was rather hoping to keep them."

Jackie to Jill: "My husband is absolutely hopeless at fixing things, so everything in our house works."

You need only two tools, WD-40 and duct tape. If it doesn't move and it should, use WD-40; if it moves and it shouldn't, use the duct tape.

Last week I replaced every window in my house. Then I realized I had a crack in my glasses.

I've discovered how to hammer nails without hitting my thumb. I let someone else hold the nail.

My wife can be so annoying. "When are you going to paint the lounge? When are you going to paint the lounge? When are you going to paint the lounge?" Three times I've asked her, and still she hasn't done it!

When I do DIY, it's like playing blackjack in a casino. The house always wins.

My wife arrived home to find me dozing on the sofa next to a bench tool stand. She immediately accused me of sleeping with a Workmate.

The guys delivering a load of sand to me say unfortunately it's been delayed. Oh, well, the best laid plans of my sand men. . .

HONEYMOON

What is a honeymoon?
That short period of time between "I do" and "You'd better".

What's the difference between your first honeymoon and your second?
The first, Niagara; the second, Viagra.

Jackie: "Does your husband snore in his sleep?"
Jill: "I don't know. We've only been married five days."

A honeymoon is a vacation a man takes before starting work under a new boss.

After my honeymoon, I felt like a new man. Unfortunately, so did my wife.

Did you hear about the prudish man who went alone on his honeymoon because he didn't believe in sleeping with a married woman?

A honeymoon is a short period of doting between dating and debting.

On the first morning of their honeymoon, the wife says to her husband: "You're a lousy lover." "That's not fair," he says. "How can you tell after only 30 seconds?"

They married so late in life that Medicare paid for the honeymoon.

A honeymoon should be like a table – four bare legs and no drawers.

It was a shame my wife couldn't come on our honeymoon, but she couldn't get the time off work.

The honeymoon period is over when the husband calls home to say he'll be late for dinner, and the answering machine says it's in the microwave.

The honeymoon period is over when you start going out with the boys on Thursday nights, and so does your wife.

HOOKERS

Did you hear about the blind prostitute? Well, you've gotta hand it to her . . .

It was my regular dominatrix's birthday last week. All of her clients had a whipround for her.

Did you hear about the hooker who had her appendix out? The doctor sewed up the wrong hole and now she's making money on the side.

I rang up an old girlfriend and asked if she was free Friday night. She said no, but her prices were reasonable.

What happened when the hookers went on strike?
They downed tools from midnight.

How is a hooker made redundant?
She gets laid off.

What do you call a hooker with her hand in her panties?
Self-employed.

Did you hear about the hooker who got arrested in the coal fields? She was charged with having sex with a miner.

What do hookers and peanut butter have in common?
Both spread for bread.

You know you live in a small town when before you have sex with the local hooker, you have to meet her parents.

What did the leper say to the hooker after sex?
"You can keep the tip."

Did you hear about the hooker who took up bondage? She was strapped for cash.

Sleeping with prostitutes is like making your cat dance with you on its hind legs. You know it's wrong, but you try to convince yourself that they're enjoying it as well. *Scott Capurro*

What's the difference between a hooker and a wife?
One is contract, the other is pay-as-you-go.

What do you call a ginger prostitute?
Orange pay-as-you-go.

I'll never forget the first time I had sex because I kept the receipt.

Did you hear about the Old Testament hooker who was arrested for trying to make a Prophet?

What did the sign say on the door of the whorehouse?
"Beat it. We're closed."

Did you hear about the hooker with a degree in psychology? She could blow your mind.

What's the difference between a cheap hooker and an elephant?
One rolls on its back for peanuts and the other lives in a zoo.

HORSE RACING

A man is standing at the side of the track when a stranger whispers: "Do you want the winner of the next race?" "No, thanks," says the man. "I don't think my garden's big enough."

Trainer: "I thought I told you to come with a rush at the finish."
Jockey: "I would have, but I didn't want to leave the horse behind."

It would have been a photo finish, but by the time my horse finished it was too dark to take a picture.

The horse was certainly well bred. After leaving the starting gate, he used to turn around to close it behind him.

My horse would have finished in the first three, but he kept looking back for his plough.

Did you hear about the guy who put a thousand pounds on a horse? The horse collapsed.

I said to my wife: "Let me bet on one more horse and it'll be the last." It was, by about 30 lengths.

My horse won at the races today. I've no idea how he managed to write the betting slip.

I could tell my horse wasn't fit to race: it had to have a pacemaker.

A jockey was hitting his horse during a race. Eventually the horse said: "Why are you hitting me? There's nobody behind us."

My granddad rode over fences until he was run down by a steamroller. Luckily he went on to become a successful flat jockey.

Why are there so many lady jockeys?
Because they like the thought of having 14 hands between their legs.

A racehorse is an animal that can take several thousand people for a ride at the same time.

One racehorse to another: "Your pace is familiar, but I don't remember the mane."

Mike: "Does that horse stay?"
Marty: "Definitely. It stays longer than the mother-in-law."

In every race, a jockey's main aim is to keep his horse between himself and the ground.

Do racehorses slow down if they see police horses standing by the side of the track?

The horse I backed came in so late he had to tiptoe into the stables so as not to wake the other horses.

My horse came in so late the jockey was wearing pyjamas.

The horse I backed was so slow it was arrested for loitering.

The trainer said my horse could cover a mile in a minute. I learnt afterwards that was in its horse box.

I had a bet on three horses today called Sunshine, Moonlight and Good Times. Not one of them won. I blame it on the bookie.

My wife and daughter are leaving me because of my obsession with horse racing. And they're off . . .

HOSPITALS

The nurse who can smile when things go wrong is probably going off duty.

Never lie to an X-ray technician. He will see right through you.

Mike: "I can't believe Ben's in hospital. Only yesterday I saw him with a gorgeous blonde."
Marty: "So did his wife."

Who is the coolest person in the hospital?
The ultrasound guy.

Who is the coolest person in the hospital when the ultrasound guy is off?
The hip replacement guy.

A man was given a pig's ear during a transplant operation. He went back to the hospital a month later to complain that he was getting a bit of crackling.

What's the difference between an oral and a rectal thermometer?
The taste.

Man: "What is the exact purpose of the prostate gland?"
Doctor: "It's main purpose, when patients pass middle age, is to make money for urologists like me."

What happened after the mix-up in the urology department?
Orange squash was taken off the hospital menu.

In hospitals it's nurses who call the shots.

I always knew I was destined to be an osteopath. I could feel it in my bones.

Did you hear about the nurse who died and went to hell? It was two weeks before she realized she wasn't at work any more.

Nurse: "The patient you just treated has collapsed on the front step. What should I do?"
Doctor: "Turn him around so it looks like he was just arriving."

Jackie: "I heard your husband is in hospital. What's the trouble?"
Jill: "It's his knee. I found a strange woman on it."

How is a hospital gown like insurance?
You're never covered as much as you think you are.

Our hospital is so outdated that when a nurse asked for a blood count, they sent for Dracula.

An official stopped me in the hospital car park to tell me: "You can't park here. It's badge holders only." I said: "But I have got a bad shoulder."

Why was the amorous male patient thrown out of hospital?
After three days he took a turn for the nurse.

Doctor: "Did you take the patient's temperature?"
Trainee nurse: "Why? Is it missing?"

Doctor: "No, no, nurse! I said prick his boil!"

In one hospital ward, I heard the patients reciting Scottish poetry. Apparently it was the Serious Burns Unit.

Woman: "What's the condition of the little boy who swallowed all those coins?"
Nurse: "No change yet."

The condition of the patient who complained about the hospital food, her bed, the ward and the nurses was described last night as "highly critical".

A man admitted to hospital after insisting to doctors that he was a soft cushion was described today as "comfortable".

A man was taken to hospital covered in wood and hay and with a horse inside him. His condition was described as "stable".

Did you hear about the woman who had to have a canister of perfume removed from her rectum? It was Chanel No. 2.

Did you hear about the man who collapsed at the top of the London Eye? Doctors say he's slowly coming round.

An old man was admitted to hospital. The elderly night nurse told the pretty young day nurse that the patient's private tattoo read "ADAM", but the young day nurse managed to read "AMSTERDAM".

Two competitors were rushed to hospital after an accident at the World Tag Championships. A hospital spokesman said it was touch and go for a while.

Woman: "Any news on Mr Brown the repairman who was admitted yesterday?"
Doctor: "He'll soon be on the mend."

Woman: "My husband was admitted yesterday. How is he? He thinks he's a torpedo."
Doctor: "We're hoping to discharge him tomorrow."

Nurse: "How did your break your nose?"
Patient: "See that pillar at the front entrance? I didn't!"

Female patient: "Give me a kiss, doctor."
Doctor: "Certainly not. In fact, I shouldn't even be in bed with you."

Jackie: "I read they're planning a new wing for the hospital."
Jill: "It'll never get off the ground."

You might be a nurse if you have the bladder capacity of five people.

You might be a nurse if you have your weekends off planned for a year in advance.

You might be a nurse if your finger has gone more places than you ever thought possible.

You might be a nurse if you can identify different types of diarrhoea by their smell.

You might be a nurse if you live by the motto: "To be right is only half the battle; to convince the doctor is more difficult."

You might be a nurse if your favourite sedative is exhaustion.

You might be a nurse if you think caffeine should be available in IV form.

You might be a nurse if every time someone asks you for a pen, you can find at least four on you.

You might be a nurse if a patient has ever said: "Honestly, I have no idea how that got stuck up there."

You might be a nurse if you've ever told a story at a restaurant and made someone at another table throw up.

You might be a nurse if you've ever said "Great veins" when introduced to a stranger.

HOTELS

A man asked the hotel receptionist for a wake-up call. Next morning, she rang and said: "What are you doing with your life?"

Guest: "Does the water always come through the roof like this?"
Proprietor: "No, sir, only when it rains."

The hotel advertised "Bed and Board". After trying out my room, I didn't know which was the bed and which was the board.

A hotel is a place where a guest often gives up good dollars for poor quarters.

How do you know you're in a really bad hotel? When you call the front desk to say "I've got a leak in my sink", and the reply is "Go ahead then."

I'm staying in a strange hotel. I called room service for a sandwich and they sent up two hookers. *Bill Maher*

I knew the hotel had only two stars, but I didn't expect to see them through the ceiling at night.

Why is a cheap hotel like a tight pair of pants?
No ball room.

Did you hear about the hotel that served a special honeymoon salad? Lettuce alone without dressing.

There was a girl knocking on my hotel room door all night. Finally I let her out.

Did you hear about the student hostel? It had running rot and mould in every room.

The hotel I stayed in last month was really sleazy. At midnight the manager banged on my door and asked if I'd got a girl in there. When I said no, he asked me if I wanted one.

A photon checks into a hotel and is asked if he needs any help with his luggage. "No, thanks," he says, "I'm travelling light."

We stayed at a really smart hotel last year. The towels were so thick and plush I could hardly get my suitcase shut.

A man went into a lodge at Yellowstone National Park and asked: "Can you give me a room and bath?" The clerk said: "I can give you a room, but I'm afraid you'll have to wash yourself."

I'm not saying the hotel service was slow, but they sent me a wake-up letter.

Room service: "I've brought up your breakfast, sir."
Guest, lifting lid: "Yes, it looks like you have."

There was so little to do in the hotel I rang down for another Bible.

Guest: "Room service? Can you send up a towel?"
Hotel clerk: "In a few minutes, sir; someone else is using it."

Guest: "What are your weekly rates?"
Hotel clerk: "I don't know. Nobody's ever stayed that long."

Guest: "You said I'd be able to see the sea from my room!"
Hotel clerk: "You can. That's why there's a high-powered telescope on your balcony."

Guest: "How far is to the bus station?"
Hotel clerk: "A five-minute walk if you run."

Hotel clerk: "Do you have reservations?"
Guest: "One or two, but we'll take a chance anyway and book a room for the night."

My wife and I went to a hotel where we got a waterbed. She called it the Dead Sea. *Henny Youngman*

Porter to guest: "I hope you've got a good memory for faces."
Guest: "Why?"
Porter: "There's no mirror in the bathroom."

What's the difference between a chambermaid in the daytime and at night?
In the day, she's fair and buxom.

A spa hotel is like a normal hotel, but in reception there's a picture of a pebble.

Business is so bad some hotels in town are stealing towels from the guests.

Proprietor: "The room is $50 for the night, but only $20 if you make your own bed."
Guest: "I'll make my own bed."
Proprietor: "Right. I'll get you some nails and wood."

HOUSES AND HOUSEWORK

I went house hunting at the weekend. I went to see a house that had mirrors all over the walls. I thought: I can see myself living here.

What was the worst thing about Robin Hood's house?
It had a little John.

Mike: "I think I've seen that door chime before."
Marty: "It certainly rings a bell."

What's the best way to stop water coming into your house?
Don't pay the water bill.

The walls in our apartment are so thin, when I peel onions the neighbours cry.

The walls in our apartment are so thin, when I ask my wife a question I get three different answers.

I had to ask my housemate Calvin to leave because he kept breaking the washing machine. Washing machines live longer with Cal gone.

Why do people run over a string a dozen times with their vacuum cleaner, then reach down, pick it up, examine it, then put it down again to give their vacuum one more chance?

How do you know when it's time to get a new dishwasher?
When the old one expects you to "do your share".

Mike: "Do these stairs take you to the second floor?"
Marty: "No, you'll have to walk."

A plane crashed into our neighbour's house. He'd left the landing light on.

There was trouble in our kitchen last week. The pot called the kettle black, and the kettle wanted to know whether the pot had a problem with that.

Why did the Seven Dwarfs use Daz?
They wanted their little things to come up snow white.

A friend of mine had a magnificent country house with two wings. The downside was that it took off one night in strong winds.

Mike: "I saw a big crowd in front of your house last night. What was up?"
Marty: "My window shade."

My aunt was so houseproud she used to put a sheet of newspaper under the cuckoo clock.

I've just had skylights fitted. The people in the apartment above me are livid.

It's a nice little apartment – overlooking the rent.

My wife asked me to do some jobs around the house. So I cut the neighbours' lawns and swept the road.

What's the best way of keeping flies out of your kitchen?
Keep a dead cat in the hall.

The plumber said reassuringly: "I've dealt with the problem in your kitchen, and as far as I'm concerned, it's water under the fridge."

I sold my last house on eBay. I wouldn't advise it though. Nearly all the money I made went on postage. *Tim Vine*

My wife hired an Eastern European cleaner, but it took her six hours to Hoover the house. Turns out she was a Slovak.

My wife seems infatuated with our new kitchen units, but I'm fairly sure it's just cupboard love.

I couldn't work out which items my wife wanted me to put in the washing machine, so eventually I just threw in the towel.

She criticized my apartment, so I knocked her flat.

A man's idea of helping with the housework is lifting his legs so his wife can Hoover.

Actually I enjoy Hoovering because it stops me hearing about all the other chores my wife wants me to do.

How can you recognize a bachelor pad?
All the house plants are dead, but there's something growing in the refrigerator.

Mike: "I passed your house yesterday."
Marty: "Thanks. I appreciate it."

The reason why so many buildings have lobbies is the influence of the lobby lobby.

Did you hear about the couple who lived in a lighthouse? Their marriage was soon on the rocks.

I can't stand people who bang on your door, saying you need to be "saved" or you'll "burn". But I suppose the firemen were only doing their job.

HUNTING

How did the man know he had arrived at a good hunting spot?
A sign said: "FINE FOR HUNTING".

Two men hunted duck for five hours without any luck. Finally one said: "Maybe we ought to throw the dogs a bit higher."

A moose is an animal that has a head and antlers at one end and a living room wall at the other.

I'm a hunt saboteur. I go out the night before and shoot the fox. *Tim Vine*

I once killed a bear with a single punch. That'll teach a koala to mess with me.

Mike: "Have you ever hunted bear?"
Marty: "No, but I've gone fishing in my shorts."

Butcher: "Sorry, sir, we have no duck today. How about some chicken?"
Hunter: "Don't be silly. I can't tell my wife I shot a chicken!"

Two men set off hunting. After five miles they saw a sign that said, "BEAR LEFT", so they went home.

HYGIENE

My kids get so dirty that before they take a bath we have to pre-soak them.

Where is cleanliness next to godliness?
In the Irish dictionary.

Why do people always assume that the goo in soap dispensers is soap? I like to fill mine with mustard, just to teach people a lesson in trust.

Did you hear about the man who only used deodorant under one arm so he could find out what he would have smelt like?

The only time he washes his ears is when he eats watermelon.

Personal hygiene tip: bad breath isn't nearly as noticeable once you stop using deodorant.

My favourite form of lying to myself is to choose a deodorant that has the word "Active" or "Sport" in its name.

Mother: "What makes you say God uses the bathroom?"
Son: "Because I heard Dad say this morning: 'Oh, God, are you still in there?'"

Just because I don't like soap there's no need to rub it in my face.

Boy: "Is that a new perfume I smell?"
Girl: "It is, and you do."

I saw this nature show where the male elk douses himself in urine to smell sweeter to the opposite sex. What a coincidence! *Jack Handey*

My grandfather takes a bath every month, whether he needs one or not.

A girl asked her young brother: "How did Mom know you hadn't had a bath?" He replied: "I forgot to dirty the towel, wet the soap and flood the bathroom."

Mother: "How did you get your hands so dirty?"
Boy: "From washing my face."

Why do men take showers instead of baths?
Because peeing in the bath is disgusting.

The Seven Dwarfs were sitting in a tub feeling Happy. So Happy got up and left.

My wife once bathed in a spring. I think it was the spring of 1978.

What good is a mouthwash that kills germs? Who wants a mouth full of dead germs?

There's a new genital deodorant for men called Umpire. It's for foul balls.

Did you hear about the man who spent years trying to find a cure for his halitosis only to find that people didn't like him anyway?

I bought a new deodorant stick today. The instructions said: "Remove the wrapper and push up bottom." I can hardly walk, but when I fart the room smells lovely.

Twelve days until I stop using aerosol deodorants. Roll on.

IMAGINATION

Sex therapist: "When you're making love to your husband, try using your imagination."
Wife: "You mean, try to imagine that it's good?"

Some people hear voices. Some see invisible people. Others have no imagination whatsoever.

Imagine how weird phones would look if your mouth was nowhere near your ears. *Steven Wright*

Have you ever imagined a world with no hypothetical situations?

Thirty years ago, there were no computers. Can you imagine your job without solitaire?

I can the buy the idea of a snowman coming to life, but I have a hard time buying the idea of him wearing a scarf to stay warm.

Imagine if the Earl of Kirkcudbright, Dumfries and Galloway had invented the sandwich . . .

IN-LAWS

I took my mother-in-law out last night. One punch. What a beauty!

What are the two worst things about a mother-in-law?
Her faces.

Mike: "Why do you want to be buried at sea?"
Marty: "My mother-in-law always says she is going to walk on my grave."

A mother-in-law is a woman who destroys her son-in-law's peace of mind by giving him a piece of hers.

Wife: "My mother said I should never have married you. She says you're effeminate."
Husband: "Everyone is, compared to her."

What's the best way to talk to your mother-in-law?
Through a medium.

My mother-in-law is a big woman. She got run over last week. The driver said he had enough room to get round her, but he didn't have enough petrol.

When my mother-in-law hangs her bra out to dry, we lose an hour of daylight.

I'd like to smother my mother-in-law in diamonds. Then again, there has to be a cheaper way of doing it.

What's the difference between in-laws and outlaws?
Outlaws are wanted.

I just found a Christmas present for my mother-in-law in the loft. I'll take it up to her later.

Lawyer: "I'm sorry to inform you that your mother-in-law has passed away. Shall we order burial, embalming or cremation?"
Man: "Take no chances. Order all three."

My wife was terribly upset, so I had to sort out the order for my mother-in-law's funeral. I couldn't decide which should come first – pass the parcel or musical chairs.

My mother-in-law came to stay. I said: "Treat the house as your own." She did. She sold it the next day.

I walked in to find my mother-in-law lying down. My wife wasn't best pleased when I said: "I think it's going to rain."

What's the definition of mixed emotions?
Seeing your mother-in-law driving over a cliff in your new car.

I went into town and ordered a mother-in-law sandwich – cold shoulder and tongue.

Husband: "No, I don't hate your relatives. In fact, I like your mother-in-law better than I like mine."

What's the penalty for bigamy?
Two mothers-in-law.

I took my wife's family out for tea and biscuits. They weren't too happy about having to give blood, though. *Les Dawson*

A police recruit was asked during his exam: "What would you do if you had to arrest your mother-in-law?" He answered: "Call for backup!"

My mother-in-law phoned today and said: "Come quick. I think I'm dying." I said: "Call me back when you're sure."

We've had some worrying news. Last week, my mother-in-law was dangerously ill. Now I hear she's dangerously well again.

My mother-in-law fell down a wishing well. I was amazed: I never knew they worked.

I saw six men kicking and punching my mother-in-law. My wife said: "Aren't you going to help?" I said: "No, six should be enough."

Mike: "Sorry to hear your mother-in-law died. What was the complaint?"
Marty: "I haven't heard any yet."

I just got back from a pleasure trip. I took my mother-in-law to the airport.

Woman: "So you want to become my son-in-law?"
Young man: "Not exactly. I just want to marry your daughter."

Marry an orphan: you'll never have to spend long, boring holidays with the in-laws.

My mother-in-law has been coming to our house for Christmas for the last 10 years. This year, we're finally going to let her in.

INSECTS

How did the firefly burn to death?
It tried to mate with a lighted cigarette.

Communism first took off in the insect world when a wary wasp joined the cagey bee.

Who was the first person who looked at a fiercely buzzing beehive and thought: Those bastards are hiding something delicious in there, I know it?

Two fleas leaving a cinema. One says to the other: "Do you want to walk or take the dog?"

Where did Noah keep his bees?
In archives.

What did the maggot say to the caterpillar?
"Who did you have to sleep with to get that fur coat?"

What's worse than finding a maggot in an apple?
Finding half a maggot.

Butterflies aren't what they used to be.

Did you hear about the fly that killed itself? It committed insecticide.

Even though ants are always at work, isn't it wonderful how they still find time to go to picnics?

It's only when you look at an ant through a magnifying glass on a sunny day that you realize how often they burst into flames. *Harry Hill*

Why did the bee cross his legs?
Because he couldn't find the BP station.

Two flies in a teapot. Which one's pregnant?
The one up the spout.

If a stick insect laid its eggs in a jar of Bovril, would it give birth to a litter of twiglets?

Why didn't Noah swat those two mosquitoes?

What happened to the two bedbugs who fell in love?
They got married in the spring.

Two flies in an airing cupboard. Which one is in the army?
The one on the tank.

What do you call a clumsy bee that drops things?
A fumble bee.

What do you call a fly with no wings?
A walk.

Two flies are feeding on a cow pat when one of them farts. "Do you mind?" says the other. "I'm eating!"

I went into a shop to buy a can of fly spray. I said: "Is this any good for flies?" The shopkeeper said: "Not really. It kills them."

Why do bees stay in their hives during winter?
Swarm.

What's the best part of a bee?
Its knees.

Do butterflies remember life as a caterpillar?

What's the difference between a mosquito and a fly?
Try sewing buttons on a mosquito!

Why did the fly fly?
Because the spider spied 'er.

How many ants do you need to fill an apartment?
Ten ants.

What's the last thing to go through a fly's brain when it hits your car windshield?
Its butt.

I just sprayed a mosquito with mosquito repellent. Now he'll never have any friends.

What did the worried fly do?
It paced the ceiling all night.

What's the difference between a sick horse and a dead bee?
One is a seedy beast, the other is a bee deceased.

Mothballs are a waste of time. I threw a whole box of them once and didn't hit a single moth.

What do you call a male ladybug?

Two cockroaches feasting in a garbage can. One says: "Last week I was in this spotless kitchen, all new clean, shiny surfaces." The other says: "Must you talk like that while I'm eating?"

What do you call a greenfly with no legs?
A bogey.

Why did the bees go on strike?
Because they wanted more honey and shorter working flowers.

Mother moth to young moth: "If you don't eat all that cashmere sweater, you'll get no silk tie for dessert."

A male fly sees a pretty female fly land on a dog poop. He buzzes down and says to her: "Excuse me, is this stool taken?"

INSURANCE

Why did the actuary say he expected low claims for a new "senility insurance"?
If you remember you have a policy, it's proof that you're not senile.

Did you hear about the man who called to find out whether he could get insurance if the nearby volcano erupted? They said he would be covered.

My wife and I took out life insurance on each other. So now it's just a waiting game.

A woman in a bar asks an actuary for his phone number. He says: "I've seen so many numbers today, I can't remember it exactly, but I can probably estimate it to within 10 per cent."

I bumped my head, and my insurance company paid me a lump sum.

A health insurance company is one that docks your pay to pay your doc.

What's the difference between a man and an insurance policy?
An insurance policy eventually matures.

Why don't cats take out life insurance?
Because they have to pay nine times more.

Life insurance keeps you poor all your life so you can die rich.

Life insurance salesman: "If your husband were to die, what would you get?"
Woman: "A parrot, I think. Then the house wouldn't seem so quiet."

In every insurance policy the big print giveth and the small print taketh away.

A limited warranty is one which covers all the parts that don't break down.

Last month I bought a retirement policy. If I keep up the payments for the next 20 years, my insurance salesman can retire.

Life insurance agent: "Don't let me frighten you into a decision. Sleep on it tonight, and if you wake up in the morning, let me know what you think."

According to actuarial tables, people who live the longest are rich relatives. ***Bob Monkhouse***

What's the definition of a computer?
An actuary with a heart.

An actuary is someone who takes a fake bomb on the plane because that decreases the chance that there will be another bomb on the plane.

An actuary is someone who'd rather be completely wrong than approximately right.

An actuary is someone who takes a cheap guess and calls it an expensive opinion.

An actuary quoted a low premium for an automobile "fire and theft" policy. Asked why it was so cheap, he said: "Who'd steal a burnt car?"

After collecting hundreds of obituaries, an actuary concludes that on any given day, people die in alphabetical order.

Actuaries love to have fun . . . so long as nobody is watching.

I'm not saying my life is heavily insured, but when I go the insurance company goes!

INTELLIGENCE

Did you hear about the guy who did a series of multiple-choice tests? He got all a's.

Light travels faster than sound, which is why some people appear bright until you hear them speak.

Intelligence is knowing that a tomato is a fruit; wisdom is not putting it in a fruit salad.

My girlfriend claimed she was as bright as the brightest star in the night sky. I said: "Are you Sirius?"

Some come to the fountain of knowledge to drink; others prefer just to gargle.

What's the difference between ignorance and apathy?
I don't know, and I don't care.

90 per cent of being smart is knowing what you're dumb at.

There are three kinds of people: the ones who learn by reading, the ones who learn by observation, and the rest who have to touch the fire to learn it's hot.

I may be 35, but I have the intelligence of a 36-year-old.

Brains are what a man looks for in a woman when he's looked at everything else.

Dolphins are so smart that within a few weeks of captivity they can train people to stand at the edge of the pool and feed them fish.

If dolphins are so clever, how come they're always getting caught in tuna nets?

For every person with a spark of genius, there are a hundred with ignition trouble.

A little knowledge can be a dangerous thing. I just tripped over a pocket encyclopedia.

INTERNET

The people who invented the Internet would never have got around to doing it if they'd had the Internet.

Did you hear about the *anti*-social networking site? It's called Shutyerfacebook.

And what about the website for drunks? Offyerfacebook.

It's not easy finding what you want on eBay. I was searching for cigarette lighters and found over 10,000 matches.

My wife said: "I keep getting emails offering me cans of processed meat." I said: "Don't worry, it's only spam."

On the website for the charity Shelter, they've got a home page. That's a bit insensitive, isn't it?

I love watching videos of rivers and lakes on the Internet – in fact, I'm watching a live stream right now.

Did you hear about the man who bought Viagra online? Now he has more pop-ups than ever.

My wife is leaving me because I believe everything I read on the Internet. I'll be fine, though, because apparently there are some sexy Russian girls living in my area.

I found lots of pictures of corpses on the Internet, but my girlfriend said that wasn't what she meant when she said: "Let's go body surfing."

What is the new O. J. Simpson website address?
Slash slash backslash escape.

When I told my wife I was looking for cheap flights on the internet, she got very excited, which was odd as she's never shown an interest in darts before.

The Internet: where men are men, women are women, and children are undercover police officers.

Apparently it takes men longer to shop on the Internet than at an actual store – but that's because there are no naked women at the store.

Some people change their profile pictures more often than I should change my underwear.

Mike: "You can learn anything on the Internet. It can even teach you to talk like an Indian."
Marty: "How?"
Mike: "See, it's working already."

The new website dedicated to hitchhikers has been getting the thumbs-up.

I loaded a video of me with the flu on to YouTube, and within a week the whole street had caught it. Apparently it had gone viral.

I love eBay. I sold my homing pigeon eight times last month.

I ordered a load of bubble wrap off eBay today – just to see what it gets delivered in. *Steven Wright*

I was shopping online and I saw a horse I rather liked. So I clicked, "Add to cart."

I found a website devoted solely to sticky paper. I couldn't tear myself away.

What do lumberjacks like most on the Internet?
Logging on and off.

I've just been banned from an online fashion forum. Apparently my threads weren't cool enough.

Facebook is the adult way of having imaginary friends.

What is Forrest Gump's Facebook password?
1Forrest1.

Did you hear about the idiot shoplifter who put items into his online shopping basket and then logged off without paying?

Boy, my new Nigerian girlfriend sure needs a lot of money wiring to her! Still I bet Sxbonjmo Qzwabjkxv will be worth it when I finally meet her in person.

The Lawn Tennis Association's website is down. Apparently they're having problems with their server.

I bought a self-help DVD online. It was called "How to Handle Disappointment". When I opened the box, it was empty.

Did you know Jesus is on Twitter? But he's only got 12 followers.

Why did the mummy stop using the Internet?
He was getting far too wrapped up in it.

In future I'm dating girls on Amazon, because they'll be sure to recommend other girls I might like.

Google celebrated its thirteenth birthday in 2011, which means for the next few years any searches will be met with "Do I *have* to?" or "It's just not fair!"

My friend's a tightrope walker and he loves the Internet. He's always online.

Why is Facebook like a refrigerator?
Because every few minutes you keep opening and closing it to see if there's anything good in it.

Why is Facebook like prison?
You have a profile picture, you sit around all day writing on walls, and you get poked by guys you don't really know.

X-rated websites have been given approval to have the .xxx domain name. Surely this will confuse Americans when they are shopping for clothes online.

I needed a password eight characters long, so I picked Snow White and the Seven Dwarfs. **Nick Helm**

I learned all about the trapeze online. I couldn't have done it without the net.

After I die, they will look through my tweets and see that my life was not wasted.

I'm so unlucky with women that when I go online, the adverts say: "There are no girls in your area for you."

Don't you hate it when the person you're Facebook-stalking never updates anything?

If you sent a cauliflower over the Internet, would it arrive as e.coli?

Arguing with autocorrect is the new yelling at the television.

"Just because we have the same last name doesn't mean we have to be Facebook friends, Dad."

I read about a new website www.needleinahaystack.com. It took me ages to find it.

I broke up with my girlfriend by email. I don't know what upset her most, the fact that I did it by email or the fact that I cc'd my new girlfriend who wanted proof.

Breaking Windows is no longer just for kids.

If your Facebook status says, "It's complicated", you might as well save time and just change it to "Single".

I went on a website about toasters. There were too many pop-ups.

I used to like to think of something really stupid to say but not actually say it. Then along came Twitter . . .

Watch what you say on Twitter. Remember: you are what you tweet.

Did you hear about the guy who bought a rug on eBay that was advertised as being "in mint condition"? When it arrived, there was a big hole in the middle.

Do you have osteoporosis? Click here.

Before the Internet, people probably spent a lot of time wondering what to do with photos of their cats.

Someone has started up a blotting paper website. I found it very absorbing.

I got an email today from a bored local housewife who said she was looking for some "hot action". So I sent her the ironing.

I bet Dracula does all his shopping online, just so he can keep clicking on "Your Account".

What do Yorkshiremen call eBay?
ebaygum.

Why did the paranoid guy quit Twitter?
He thought he was being followed.

Mike: "Have you been on www.busfull.com?"
Marty: "No, that one passed me by."

Facebook should have a limit on the number of times people can change their relationship status. After five it should default to "Unstable".

Welcome to the Alzheimer's information web page. Please enter your 18-digit password.

There's a new website that caters exclusively for women drivers. Unfortunately it keeps crashing.

What note did the Internet hacker pin to his door?
Gone phishing.

I was going to tweet about anti-climaxes, but in the end I didn't.

"The problem with quotes on the Internet is you can never tell if they're genuine" **Winston Churchill, 1944**

I got an email saying, "At Google Earth we can read maps backwards." I thought: That's just spam.

www.conjunctivitis.com – a site for sore eyes.

My girlfriend has got so fed up with me playing online poker that she issued me with an ultimatum: it's either poker or her. But I think she's bluffing.

You're an Internet addict if you email your husband upstairs to tell him dinner is ready.

You're an Internet addict if you've never actually met any of your friends.

You're an Internet addict if you refer to going to the bathroom as "downloading".

You're an Internet addict if your worst nightmare is switching on your computer and seeing the blue screen of death.

You're an Internet addict if you're amazed to learn spam is actually a food.

You're an Internet addict if your wife looks deep into your eyes and sees a screen saver.

You're an Internet addict if you can't talk to your mother because she's not on Skype.

You're an Internet addict if you have an identity crisis because someone is using a screen name similar to yours.

You're an Internet addict if, after brushing your teeth in the morning, the first thing you do is relay the news to your Twitter followers.

You're an Internet addict if you turn on your computer and turn off your spouse.

THE IRISH

Did you hear about the Irish cryptologist who cracked the Highway Code?

Did you hear about the Irish farmer who packed up and went to live in the city because he heard the country was at war?

Did you hear about the Irish sea scout? His tent sank.

Paddy: "Here, Mick, did you know Christmas Day falls on a Friday this year?"
Mick: "I hope it's not the thirteenth!"

What's the definition of an Irish cocktail?
A pint of Guinness with a potato in it.

Did you hear about the Irish money launderer who lost a fortune when the bills rotted in the washing machine?

How does an Irish farmer count his sheep?
He counts the legs and then divides by four.

Why did the Irishman add starch to his whiskey?
He needed a stiff drink.

Paddy: "I've bought a new clock. It goes eight days without winding."
Mick: "How long does it go if you do wind it?"

Did you hear about the Irishman who went tap dancing? He broke his ankle when he fell into the sink.

What's Irish and stays out all night?
Paddy O'Furniture.

Did you hear about the Irishman who tried to do Riverdance and drowned?

How do you confuse an Irishman?
Give him two spades and tell him to take his pick.

Paddy tells Mick he's thinking of buying a Labrador puppy. "Don't do it," says Mick. "Have you seen how many of their owners go blind?"

Did you hear about the new Irish doorman in a London tower block? He was OK with the PUSH and PULL signs, but he was last seen struggling with his fingers under a door marked LIFT.

What do you call a dead Irishman in a closet?
The 2011 National Hide and Seek champion.

An Irish glazier was examining a broken window. "It's worse than I thought," he said. "It's broken on both sides."

Did you hear about the Irish hitchhiker? He sets off early to avoid the traffic.

Wife: "Paddy! Paddy! My waters have broken!"
Paddy: "Don't worry yourself, my love. I'll call a plumber right away."

100 people died in a Dublin plane crash – 50 in the accident and another 50 in the reconstruction.

How do you sink an Irish submarine?
Knock on the hatch.

Did you hear about the Irish explorer who paid €10 for a sheet of sandpaper? He thought it was a map of the Sahara Desert.

Why did the Irishman ask his friends to save all their burned-out light bulbs? He was building a darkroom.

Did you hear about the Irishman who wanted to ride the surf but could never get his horse to fit on the board?

What's the difference between an Irish boomerang and a conventional boomerang?
An Irish boomerang doesn't come back, but it sings drunken, sentimental songs about how much it wants to.

Where did they find the Irish woodworm?
Dead, in a brick.

Have you seen the Irish jigsaw puzzle? One piece.

Why did the Irishman try to buy a potato clock?
"Because I start my new job at nine tomorrow, and so my wife said: 'You'd better get a potato clock.' "

What do you call an Irishman with an IQ of 130?
A village.

A major row broke out among the Irish synchronized swimming team when Paddy accused Mick of copying him.

What was the name of the bullet-proof Irishman?
Rick O'Shea.

Have you heard about the Irish tug-of-war team? They were disqualified for pushing.

Paddy and Mick saw a sign in the Job Centre saying: "Tree Fellers Wanted". "Shame there's not another one of us," said Mick. "We could have applied for that."

How can you spot the Irish Jew at the Wailing Wall? He's the one with the harpoon.

Why did the Irishman swallow razor blades?
To sharpen his appetite.

Did you hear about the Irish car pool? They all meet at work.

Why do Irishmen wear two condoms?
To be sure, to be sure.

Did you hear about the Irish wolfhound? It got stuck in a trap, chewed off three legs and was still stuck.

Did you hear about the Irish orphanage that held a parents' night?

Many people die of thirst, but the Irish are born with one. *Spike Milligan*

An Irishman is not drunk until he can't move.

An Irishman walks out of a bar . . . well, it could happen!

ITALIANS

What do you call it when an Italian has one arm shorter than the other?
A speech impediment.

What do you call an Italian with his hands in his pockets?
A mute.

What's the difference between an Italian grandmother and an elephant?
50 pounds and a black dress.

How do you sink an Italian battleship?
Put it in water.

Why does the new Italian Navy have glass-bottomed ships?
To see the old Italian Navy.

An increased threat of terrorism has forced the Italians to raise their alert level to "Shout excitedly and wave arms".

How do you brainwash an Italian?
Give him an enema.

How do you know if you're flying in an Alitalia plane?
By the hairs under the wings.

What's the name of the new Italian airline that flies out of Genoa?
Genitalia.

What did the barber say to the Italian boy?
"Do you want your hair cut or should I just change the oil?"

Why did the Italian boy want to grow a moustache?
So he could look like his mama.

What do you call Italian women in a sauna?
Gorillas in the Mist.

Why do Italians wear gold chains around their necks?
So they know when to stop shaving.

I spat right in the face of an Italian girl and she thanked me. Her moustache was on fire. *Jackie Martling*

What is different about the Italian version of Christmas?
One Mary, one Jesus and 33 wise guys.

How can you tell if the Mafia is involved in a cock fight?
When the duck wins.

What do you call an Italian man with a rubber toe?
Roberto.

What do you call an Italian medium?
Luigi Board.

I've just finished building my Lego model of Rome. It only took a day.

What does FIAT stand for?
Frenzied Italian At Traffic-lights.

Silvio Berlusconi angered Fiat workers in Italy by hinting that Ford makes better cars. He said he prefers to get into an Escort.

I bought my wife a little Italian car: a Mafia. It has a hood under the hood. *Henny Youngman*

Why don't Italians like Jehovah's Witnesses?
They don't like *any* witnesses.

On the other hand, Rome was burnt in a day.

JEHOVAH'S WITNESSES

What's the world's shortest Jehovah's Witness joke?
Knock, knock.

What do you get when you cross a Jehovah's Witness with an atheist?
Someone who knocks on your door for no apparent reason.

What do you get when you cross a Jehovah's Witness with a Hell's Angel?
Lots of converts.

Why did the householder have a spring in his step?
It was a launch pad for Jehovah's Witnesses.

Two guys knocked on my door and said: "We want to talk to you about Jesus." I said: "Oh, no. What's he done now?"

Jehovah's Witnesses won't participate in Hallowe'en trick-or-treating. Maybe it's against their religion, but they just don't seem to approve of strangers knocking on their door and disturbing them.

What do you get when you cross a skunk with a Jehovah's Witness?
A smell you can't get rid of.

Even Jehovah's Witnesses are moving with the times. Young Jehovah's Witnesses don't knock on your door, they call or text you to let you know they're outside.

Jehovah's Witness: "Tell me, sir. Do you believe in God? What are your convictions?"
Houseowner: "Well, I was fined once for doing 50 in a 40 m.p.h. zone."

Did you hear about the new gym for religious minorities? It's called Jehovah's Fitness.

Why are there no Jehovah's Witnesses in Heaven?
Because God and St Peter are behind the Pearly Gates saying: "Sssshhhh! Pretend we're not in."

JEWISH

Why do Jewish mothers make great parole officers?
They never let anyone finish a sentence.

Why don't Jewish mothers drink?
It interferes with their suffering.

How do you start a Jewish marathon?
Roll a penny down a hill.

What's the definition of a genius?
An average student with a Jewish mother.

Jewish mother to children: "If you two are going to kill each other, do it outside. I've just finished cleaning."

How is Christmas celebrated in a Jewish home?
They put a parking meter on the roof.

I was raised half-Catholic and half-Jewish. At confession, I'd say: "Bless me, Father, for I have sinned – and you know my lawyer, Mr Cohen." *Bill Maher*

What does the Jewish Santa say?
"Ho, ho, ho! Anybody want to buy some toys?"

Why are Jewish men the most optimistic in the world?
Because they have some cut off before they even know how big it will get.

What's the difference between an Italian mother and a Jewish mother?
One says: "If you don't eat, I'll kill you"; the other says: "If you don't eat, I'll kill myself."

Did you hear about the Jewish girl who went with two men in one night? She could hardly walk afterwards. Can you imagine? Two dinners!

Where does the Jewish husband hide his money from his wife?
Under the vacuum cleaner.

Have you seen the new Jewish American princess horror movie?
It's called *Debbie Does Dishes?*

What's a Jewish American princess's favourite position?
Facing Tiffany's.

How do you tickle a Jewish American princess?
Say "Gucci, Gucci, Gucci".

A little Jewish boy asks his father for seven dollars. "Six dollars!" exclaims the father. "What do you need five dollars for?"

In the Jewish doctrine, when does a foetus become a human?
When it graduates from medical school.

A Jew and a Scotsman go into a restaurant. The waiter hears the Scotsman say: "I'll pay for this meal." The next day's headline reads: "Jewish ventriloquist found dead in alley."

What's the definition of a Jewish pervert?
Someone who likes girls more than money.

Did you hear about the Jewish kamikaze pilot?
He crashed his plane into his uncle's scrap metal yard.

Jewish mother's motto: always wear clean underwear in case you're in an accident.

Jewish mother's motto: anything worth saying is worth repeating a thousand times.

Jewish mother's motto: always whisper the names of diseases.

Jewish mother's motto: if you're going to whisper in the movies, make sure it's loud enough for everyone to hear.

Jewish mother's motto: if you have to ask the price, you can't afford it. But if you can afford it, make sure you tell everyone what you paid.

Jew's motto in a restaurant: why spoil a good meal with a big tip?

How was copper wire invented?
Years ago, two Jews found the same penny.

Why is it so important for the groom at a Jewish wedding to stamp on a wine glass?
Because it's probably the last chance he'll get to put his foot down.

What did the rabbi say as he circumcised the little boy?
"It won't be long now."

Did you hear about the rabbi who was drunk on the job? He got the sack.

How do you know when a Jewish woman has had an orgasm?
She drops her nail file.

Did you hear about the Jewish Mother cash machine? When you take out money, it says: "What did you do with the last $50 I gave you?"

Jewish telegram: "Begin worrying. Details to follow."

Did you hear about the Jewish porn movie? It consists of 45 minutes of begging, 3 minutes of sex and 17 minutes of guilt.

Why do Jewish men like to watch porn movies backwards?
They like the part where the hooker gives the money back.

What's the most common disease transmitted by Jewish mothers?
Guilt.

I bought an Israeli-built car. It's great. Not only can it stop on a dime, it picks it up, too.

Two Jewish women in New York. One says: "Do you see what's going on in Israel?" The other says: "I live in the back. I don't see anything."

A Jewish mother's lament: "Is one Nobel Prize so much to ask from a child, after all I've done?"

If Jesus was a Jew, how come he has a Mexican first name? *Billy Connolly*

Why are so many Jewish girls single?
They're still waiting to meet Dr Right.

What did the Jewish mother say when her daughter told her she was having an affair?
"Who's doing the catering?"

What did the waiter ask the group of dining Jewish mothers?
"Is *anything* all right?"

What's the definition of a Jewish threesome?
Two headaches and an erection.

Two Jewish businessmen meet in the street. "Oy, Abraham," says one. "I'm sorry to hear about that fire at your warehouse." "Shhhh!" hisses the other. "It's not till next week."

Without Jewish mothers, who would need therapy?

A Jewish woman had two chickens. One got sick, so she made chicken soup out of the other one to help the sick one get well.

Have you heard about the new face lotion developed specifically for Jewish women? Oil of Oy Vay.

Why do Jews have big noses?
Because air is free.

A car hits a Jewish man. The paramedic says: "Are you comfortable?" The man says: "I make a good living."

Why did the Jews wander in the desert for 40 years?
Someone dropped a quarter.

Moses dragged the Jews through the desert for 40 years to take them to the one place in the Middle East where there was no oil.

What's the ultimate Jewish dilemma?
Pork on special offer.

What is Jewish Alzheimer's Disease?
Where you forget everything but the guilt.

What's the difference between a Rottweiler and a Jewish mother?
The Rottweiler eventually lets go.

Why do Jewish women go for circumcised men?
They can't resist anything with 10 per cent off.

What did the Jewish woman say when the flasher opened his coat and exposed himself to her?
"Nice lining."

What's the difference between a Catholic wife and a Jewish wife?
A Catholic wife has real orgasms and fake jewellery.

Refusing to believe her husband is dead, Mrs Goldberg feeds him chicken soup in the mortuary. The doctor asks what she's doing. "It might not help," she smiles, "but it can't hurt."

What's the definition of a Jewish nymphomaniac?
A woman who will have sex on the same day she has her hair done.

How did Israel manage to defeat Egypt in just six days in 1967?
Because the military equipment was rented.

JUDGES

If a judge loves the sound of his own voice, expect a long sentence.

What did the judge say to his dentist? "Pull my tooth, the whole tooth, and nothing but the tooth."

Did you hear about the two gay judges? They tried each other.

What do you call a judge with no thumbs? Justice Fingers.

When the judge gave the defendant a suspended sentence, he fainted because he thought it meant he was going to hang.

Did you hear about the judge who always delivered his sentences in rhyming verse? He was a firm believer in poetic justice.

Sentenced to 15 years in prison, an 80-year-old man told the judge: "I'll never live that long." The judge replied: "Well, do the best you can."

Why did the defendant have a bruise on his forehead? Because the judge threw the book at him.

Judge: "You have been found not guilty of robbery and are therefore free to leave this court without a stain on your character."
Defendant: "Great! Does that mean I can keep the money?"

Defendant: "I don't recognize this court!"
Judge: "Why not?"
Defendant: "Because you've had it decorated since I was last here."

Judge: "Do you wish to challenge any of the jurors?"
Defendant: "I think I can beat the little guy on the end."

Judge: "Is this the first time that you have been up before me?"
Defendant: "I don't know, Your Honour. What time do you get up?"

Judge: "Don't you know that crime doesn't pay?"
Defendant: "Yes, but the hours are good."

Judge: "Guilty. Seven days or $100?"
Defendant: "I'll take the $100, Your Honour."

Judge: "This is the sixth time you have appeared before me. I fine you $200."
Defendant: "Don't I get a discount for being a regular customer?"

Judge: "I thought I told you I never wanted to see you here again."
Defendant: "That's what I tried to tell the police, Your Honour, but they wouldn't listen."

Judge: "Are you showing contempt for this court?"
Defendant: "No, I'm doing my best to hide it."

Judge: "Order in court!"
Defendant: "Thank you, Your Honour. I'll have a cheeseburger and fries."

Judge: "Do you realize you are facing the electric chair?"
Defendant: "I don't mind facing it – it's sitting down in it that worries me."

Judge: "Have you anything to offer to this court before I pass sentence?"
Defendant: "No, Your Honour, my lawyer took every penny."

Judge: "You have been found not guilty of bigamy. You may go home."
Defendant: "Which one?"

Why should we feel sorry for judges?
Because every day is a trying day.

How did the defendant manage to jump out of the dock and then bound to freedom with one leap through a high, open window?
It was a kangaroo court.

A police officer mistakenly arrested a judge who had dressed as a convict for a fancy-dress party. The cop learnt never to book a judge by his cover.

KISSING

My girlfriend used to kiss me on the lips, but now it's all over.

Boy: "What would it take to get you to give me a kiss?"
Girl: "Anaesthetic."

A kiss is an application in the top floor for a job in the basement.

Boss: "Who said you can come and go as you please just because I kissed you last night?"
Secretary: "My lawyer."

I'll always remember her kisses – every time I open the refrigerator.

A kiss is two divided by nothing.

What's an Australian kiss?
It's like a French kiss, but given down under.

My girlfriend said: "I want to be kissed like I've never been kissed before." So I got our Great Dane to pucker up.

A survey found that 20 per cent of men kiss their wife goodbye when they leave the house, and 80 per cent kiss their house goodbye when they leave their wife.

A kiss is upper persuasion for lower invasion.

Have you heard about Belgian kissing? It's like French kissing, but more phlegmish.

LANGUAGES

What was the greatest accomplishment of the early Romans?
Speaking Latin.

"Latte" is Latin for "you paid too much for that coffee".

Veni, Vidi, Vice – I came, I saw, I partied.

Veni, Vidi, Visa – I came, I saw, I shopped.

Veni, Vipi, Vici – I came, I'm a very important person, I conquered.

Volvo, Video, Velcro – I came by car, I watched a film, I stuck around.

Posh Mortem – death styles of the rich and famous.

Ad Hoc – pawn shop advertisement.

Et Tu Brute – I like your aftershave.

Cogito Ergo Spud – I think therefore I yam.

Quip Pro Quo – a fast retort.

I'm really glad I studied Latin. It comes in handy if someone in the family gets possessed.

I used to think "in loco parentis" meant "My dad's an engine driver".

Using Latin phrases to sound smart is my modus operandi.

Harlez-vous Français? – Do you drive a French motorcycle?

Haste Cuisine – French fast food.

Le Roi Est Mort, Jive Le Roi – the king is dead, no kidding!

Zit alors! – my God, what a pimple!

Toot Ensemble – 40 cars waiting for a green light at a busy road junction during rush-hour.

Après Moe Le Deluge – Larry and Curly get wet.

Visa La France – don't leave your château without it.

Menage à Trois – I am three years old.

Mirage à Trois – act of having sex with two imaginary people.

Bone Voyage – an archaeological trip.

Répondez S'Il Vous Plaid – answer if you're Scottish.

Déjà Fu – the feeling that somehow, somewhere, you've been kicked in the head like this before.

Dijon Vu – the feeling you've experienced this mustard before.

What's Urdu?
What you get from a Liverpool barbershop.

I just can't seem to get a girlfriend even though I speak two languages fluently – English and Klingon.

Gott in Rimmel! – what the hell's happened to your make-up?

I don't speak much Italian: just enough to have my face slapped.

Que Sera Serf – life is feudal.

They call our language the mother tongue because the father rarely gets a chance to use it.

Idios Amigos – we're wild, crazy guys.

What speaks every language in the world?
An echo.

How do you say "energy-saving light bulb" in Chinese?
Ka Ching.

LAUGHTER

Laughter is the best medicine. Unless you're really sick. Then you should ring the emergency services.

If a cow laughed, would milk come out of her nose?

I tried to tell a girl a joke about a balaclava, but it went over her head.

Laughing a woman into bed and having a woman laugh at you in bed are two entirely different things.

Did you hear about the leper who laughed his head off?

My granny heard a joke that made her laugh so much she said she could feel the tears running down her legs.

Who was the greatest comedian in the Bible?
Samson. He brought the house down.

If laughter is the best medicine, how come someone died laughing?

He's a born comedian who loves the spotlight. Every time he opens the fridge door, he does two minutes.

I have a great joke about shoehorns. I just wish I knew how to get it into conversations.

They said being blind would hinder my chances of becoming a comedian. I don't see them laughing now.

Laughter is the best medicine, although if you're laughing for no reason, you probably need medicine.

I honestly thought my marriage would work because me and my wife did share a sense of humour. We had to really, because she didn't have one. *Frank Skinner*

Chicken-related humour is at a crossroads.

Comedy is in his blood. I just wish it was in his act.

How do you make an octopus laugh?
Ten-tickles.

Happiness is not a clown performing his circus routine with a bucket of water: happiness is when he stops.

He who laughs last thinks slowest.

My friend Ena is very giddy. Whenever we meet and I say: "Hi, Ena", she laughs her head off.

LAWYERS

Why do people take an instant dislike to lawyers?
It saves time.

What do you call 1,000 lawyers at the bottom of the sea?
A start.

What's the difference between a lawyer and a vampire?
A vampire only sucks blood at night.

What's the ideal weight of a lawyer?
About three pounds, including the urn.

What's black and white and looks great wrapped around a lawyer's neck?
A pit bull terrier.

Why do bankruptcy lawyers expect to be paid?

What's the difference between a lawyer and a leech?
A leech lets go when its victim dies.

What do you call a lawyer with an IQ of 50?
Your Honour.

What do you call skydiving lawyers?
Skeet.

What's the difference between a good lawyer and a great lawyer?
A good lawyer knows the law, a great lawyer knows the judge.

Did you hear about the new microwave lawyer? You spend five minutes in his office and get billed for five hours.

What's the definition of a lawyer?
The larval stage of a politician.

Why are lawyers like rhinoceroses?
They're thick-skinned, short-sighted and always ready to charge.

How can you tell if a lawyer is well hung?
You can't get a finger between the rope and his neck.

99 per cent of lawyers give the rest a bad name.

A man received a bill from his lawyer. It said: "For crossing the road to speak to you and discovering it was not you: $40."

Why do you never see lawyers on the beach?
Cats keep covering them in sand.

It was so cold last winter, I saw a lawyer with his hands in his own pockets.

What's the difference between a female lawyer and a pit bull?
Jewellery.

If you were stranded on a desert island with Hitler, Mussolini and a lawyer, and you had a gun with only two bullets, what would you do?
Shoot the lawyer twice.

Hell hath no fury like the lawyer of a woman scorned.

How do you keep a lawyer from drowning?
Take your foot off his head.

What do you call a hitchhiking lawyer?
Stranded.

A lawyer is someone who writes a 90-page document and calls it a brief.

Life lesson: if your lawyer has a ponytail, you're going to prison.

What did the lawyer do after his wife said: "I love you"?
He cross-examined her.

How does a lawyer sleep?
First he lies on one side, then he lies on the other.

Lawyer to convicted killer: "There's good news and bad news. The bad news is you're getting the electric chair. The good news is I got the voltage lowered."

What do you call a lawyer who doesn't chase ambulances?
Retired.

Why did the lawyer cross the road?
To get to the car accident on the other side.

Two young lawyers race their cars over a cliff to see who hits the bottom first. Who wins?
Society.

How do you save a drowning lawyer?
Throw him an anchor.

Did you hear about the new sushi bar that caters exclusively for lawyers? It's called Sosumi.

What's the difference between a lawyer and a catfish?
One's a scum-sucking bottom dweller, the other's a fish.

When lawyers die, why are they buried in holes 20 feet deep?
Because deep down they're all nice guys.

Why do lawyers have bad eyesight?
They spend so much time going through the small print.

Why didn't the lawyer have any clothes to wear to work?
Because he'd lost his suit.

Lawyer's creed: a man is innocent until proven broke.

How do you get a lawyer out of a tree?
Cut the rope.

A terrorist group hijacked a planeload of lawyers. They said they'd release one an hour unless their demands were met.

What do you call 10 lawyers buried up to their necks in sand?
Football practice.

What did the lawyer name his daughter?
Sue.

Why won't sharks attack lawyers?
Professional courtesy.

Why did New Jersey get all the toxic waste and California all the lawyers?
New Jersey got to pick first.

What do you get when you cross a Mafia godfather with a lawyer?
An offer you can't understand.

LAZINESS

My wife said to me: "I'm fed up with you being so lazy. Pack your bags and leave!" I said: "You pack them."

Hard work never killed anybody, but why take the risk?

Doctor: "There's nothing wrong with you. You're just lazy."
Man: "Now give me the medical term so I can tell my wife."

I'm not lazy, I'm a relaxaholic.

Hard work pays off in the future. Laziness pays off now.

Did you hear about the man who was so lazy, he married a pregnant woman?

I went to the supermarket with my wife, and she called me lazy. I almost fell out of the trolley!

Job interviewer: "How would you describe yourself in five words?"
Applicant: "Lazy."

I'm so lazy I have a snooze button on my smoke alarm. *Tim Vine*

My brother's so lazy he has moss growing on his north side.

If you're too lazy to start anything, you may get a reputation for patience.

It might look like I'm doing nothing, but at the cellular level I'm actually quite busy.

I'm a recovering workaholic.

Progress is made by lazy people looking for an easier way to do things.

I started with a lazy eye, and it just spread from there.

It takes more muscles to frown than to smile, which explains why fat people are always so jolly.

The only problem with doing nothing is you never know when you've finished.

I'm struggling to finish writing my book, *The A to R of Laziness*.

Definition of laziness: trying to pee harder to remove the poop stain on the toilet bowl.

Some people are like blisters. They don't show up until the work is done.

There's no excuse for laziness but I'm working on it.

LETTERS

What did the letter O say to the letter Q?
"Dude, your dick is hanging out."

The letter N is annoying because it always wants to be the centre of attention.

Part of the alphabet has been destroyed in a terrorist attack. It's not yet known which letter had anything to do with the atrocity, but early reports suggest G had.

If ever I saw an amputee being hanged, I'd just yell out letters. **Demetri Martin**

Why is the letter G scary?
Because it turns a host into a ghost.

Why are there are only 24 letters in the alphabet?
Because ET went home.

LIFE

The trouble with life is there's no background music.

Never take life too seriously: nobody gets out alive.

Monday is a terrible way to spend one-seventh of your life.

Good news is just life's way of keeping you off balance.

I believe you should live each day as if it was your last, which is why I don't have any clean laundry, because who wants to wash clothes on the last day of their life? *Jack Handey*

After a year in therapy, my psychiatrist said to me: "Maybe life isn't for everyone."

Life is like being a pubic hair on the side of a toilet bowl. Eventually you will get pissed off.

I used to have a handle on life, but it broke.

It's reached the point where you can no longer enjoy the simple things in life – like taking a long slow swig of cold beer – without some idiot behind you sounding his horn.

The best way to find your niche in life is to live in a crevice.

Sometimes it seems I just spend half my life breathing in.

I've learnt that the people you care most about in life are taken from you too soon while the less important ones just never go away.

First Buddhist: "How's life?"
Second Buddhist: "I've had better."

The world will end the day after the warranty expires.

How do you know that you're leading a sad life?
When a nymphomaniac tells you: "Let's just be friends."

Get even: live long enough to be a problem to your children.

I chose the path less travelled, but only because I was lost.

Life is like a roll of toilet paper: long and useful, but it always ends at the wrong moment.

Snow White didn't achieve much in her life, but she did manage to turn one of the dwarves purple. So at least she dyed Happy.

Sometimes I wish life had subtitles.

I remember when I used to eat lettuce, tomato and cucumber non-stop. I guess those were my salad days.

What if the hokey cokey really is what it's all about? **Bob Monkhouse**

Life is a test, and I didn't take very good notes.

All the desirable things in life are either illegal, expensive, fattening or married to someone else.

Every time I find the meaning of life, they change it.

Just when you think you've won the rat race, along come faster rats.

I tried to get a life once, but they were out of stock.

Life is like a box of chocolates: if you're fat, it doesn't last long.

Life is like a box of chocolates – empty due to my wife.

You can't have everything. Where would you put it?

There are no winners in life, only survivors.

I just had a GPS installed in my life. It keeps urging me to go back four years and turn left at the entrance to the church.

Life is like taking a shower. One wrong turn and you're in hot water.

I try to take one day at a time, but sometimes several days attack me at once.

How do we know life is a bitch?
Because if it was a slut, it would be easy.

Life would be easier if you could mark people as spam.

On the keyboard of life, always keep one finger on the escape key.

I've turned my life around. I used to be depressed and miserable; now I'm miserable and depressed.

Life may not be worth living but what else are you going to do with it?

I was on a roll today till I realized it was my lunch and now it's ruined.

At first we thought the world was flat. Next we decided it was round. Now we know it's crooked.

Thanks to ID theft, I was living the life of Riley.

Living on Earth may be expensive, but it does include an annual free trip around the sun.

Life's like a bird. It's pretty cute until it craps on your head.

I recently took up meditation. It beats sitting around doing nothing.

Everything in life comes with a string attached . . . even when you are born.

Life is like a bowl of cherries and I'm in the pits.

As you journey through life, take a moment every now and then to think of others – you never know, they could be plotting something.

Life is nothing like the brochure.

There are three stage of sex in a man's life: tri-weekly, try weekly and try weakly.

The most precious thing we have is life, yet it has absolutely no trade-in value.

You know it's going to be a bad day when the bird singing outside your window is a vulture.

You know it's going to be a bad day when you go to put on the clothes you wore home from the party and there aren't any.

You know it's going to be a bad day when the plumber floats by on your kitchen table.

You know it's going to be a bad day when your twin sister forgets your birthday.

You know it's going to be a bad day when the pest exterminator crawls under your house and never comes out.

You know it's going to be a bad day when your accountant's letter of resignation is postmarked Panama.

You know it's going to be a bad day when you find Yellow Pages open at "hitmen".

You know it's going to be a bad day when you call the Samaritans and they put you on hold.

You know it's going to be a bad day when a black cat crosses your path and drops dead.

You know it's going to be a bad day when your horn sticks on the freeway behind 20 Hell's Angels.

You know it's going to be a bad day when you see your stockbroker hitchhiking out of town.

You know it's going to be a bad day when you find a TV news team waiting at your office.

You know it's going to be a bad day when your suggestion box starts ticking.

You know it's going to be a bad day when your cat chokes on your goldfish.

You know it's going to be a bad day when the fortune teller charges you half-price.

You know it's going to be a bad day when your blind date turns out to be your ex-wife.

Life: it's just an f in lie.

Yesterday evening I had to change a light bulb. After that I crossed the road and walked into a bar. That was when I realized my life is a joke.

Most people are searching for something: the meaning of life, true love or their place in the world. Me? I'm just trying to find Wally.

LIGHT BULB JOKES

How many psychiatrists does it take to change a light bulb?
Only one, but the bulb really has to want to change.

How many Irishmen does it take to change a light bulb?
Two. One to hold the bulb and another to drink whiskey until the room spins.

How many lawyers does it take to change a light bulb?
How many can you afford?

How many pessimists does it take to change a light bulb?
None. The old one is probably screwed in too tight.

How many Country and Western singers does it take to change a light bulb?
Two. One to change it, and one to sing about how heartbroken he is at the loss of the old one.

How many archaeologists does it take to change a light bulb?
Three. One to change it, and two to argue about the age of the old one.

How many Catholics does it take to change a light bulb?
Two. One to do the screwing, one to hear the confession.

How many movie directors does it take to change a light bulb?
One, but he wants to do it 17 times.

How many firemen does it take to change a light bulb?
Four. Three to cut a hole in the roof and one to change the light bulb.

How many baritones does it take to change a light bulb?
None. They can't get up that high.

How many civil servants does it take to change a light bulb?
53. One to change the light bulb, 52 to do the paperwork.

How many mystery writers does it take to change a light bulb?
Two. One to screw it almost all the way in, and then one to give it a surprising twist at the end.

How many economists does it take to change a light bulb?
None. If the light bulb really needed changing, market forces would already have caused it to happen.

How many Jewish mothers does it take to change a light bulb?
None. "Don't worry about me, I'll sit here all alone in the dark."

How many vegans does it take to change a light bulb?
Two. One to change it, and one to check for animal ingredients.

How many climate-change zealots does it take to change a light bulb?
Three. One to change it, one to say how much warmer he thinks it might be than the previous bulb, and one to write a factual paper on the findings.

How many Mafia hitmen does it take to change a light bulb?
Three. One to screw it in, one to keep lookout, and one to shoot any witnesses.

How many circus performers does it take to change a light bulb?
Four. One to change it, and three to sing, "Ta da!"

How many British MPs does it take to change a light bulb?
Four. One to change the bulb, and three others to claim for it on expenses.

How many advertising executives does it take to change a light bulb?
None . . . because, "Look! It's getting brighter! It's definitely getting brighter!"

How many photographers does it take to change a light bulb?
"Just one more. Just one more."

How many American footballers does it take to change a light bulb?
Two. One to screw it in, the other to recover the fumble.

How many doctors does it to take to change a light bulb?
It depends on whether the bulb has health insurance.

How many visitors to an art gallery does it take to change a light bulb?
Two. One to change it and one to say, "My four-year-old could have done that!"

How many Jehovah's Witnesses does it take to change a light bulb?
Three. One to change the bulb and turn it on, the other two to knock on your door and ask if you've seen the light.

How many paranoids does it take to change a light bulb?
"Who wants to know?"

How many accountants does it take to change a light bulb?
"What sort of answer did you have in mind?"

How many fishermen does it take to change a light bulb?
One, but you should have seen the bulb. It was this B-I-G!

How many Russians does it take to change a light bulb?
That's a military secret.

How many auto mechanics does it take to change a light bulb?
Two. One to screw in all the bulbs he has until he finds one that fits, and the other to tell you he thinks he'll have to replace the whole socket.

How many Californians does it take to change a light bulb?
Nine. One to turn the bulb, and eight to share the experience.

How many California therapists does it take to change a light bulb?
Just one, but it takes 36 visits.

How many cops does it take to screw in a light bulb?
None. It turns itself in.

How many feminists does it take to change a light bulb?
Feminists don't screw at all. That's what sperm banks are for.

How many Amish does it take to change a light bulb?
"What's a light bulb?"

How many philosophers does it take to change a light bulb?
"Define 'light bulb'."

How many boring people does it take to change a light bulb?
One.

How many sound engineers does it take to change a light bulb?
"One, two. One, two. One, two."

How many folk guitarists does it take to change a light bulb?
Three. One to change it, and two to complain that it's gone electric.

How many actors does it take to change a light bulb?
Five. One to climb the ladder and four to say. "It should have been me."

How many surrealists does it take to change a light bulb?
Fish.

How many social workers does it take to change a light bulb?
None. But it takes six to write a paper titled "Coping with Darkness".

How many Chinese people does it take to change a light bulb?
Thousands, because Confucius say: "Many hands make light work."

How many divorced men does it take to change a light bulb?
Who knows? They never get to keep the house!

How many divorced women does it take to change a light bulb?
Four. One to change the bulb, three to form a support group.

How many health and safety officers does it take to change a light bulb?
Four. Two to hold the ladder, one to change the bulb, and one to observe that correct procedure is being followed.

How many supermodels does it take to change a light bulb?
"What do you want me to do, ruin my nails?"

How many televangelists does it take to change a light bulb?
One, but for the message of light to continue to shine, send in your donations today.

How does a spoilt rich girl change a light bulb?
She says: "Daddy, I want a new apartment."

One.
How many psychics does it take to change a light bulb?

LOVE

I fell in love with my girlfriend at second sight. The first time I met her, I didn't know her father was a millionaire.

I gave blood today. I know it's not the usual sort of thing you give your wife on Valentine's Day, but it came from the heart.

What's the definition of endless love?
Two blind men playing tennis.

My mate is in love with two school bags. He's bisatchel. *Tim Vine*

If love is blind, why is lingerie so popular?

Love is blind – but marriage is an eye-opener.

Two nihilists fell in love. They had nothing in common.

Learning to love yourself is important. Just don't let your partner catch you doing it.

In my case, love may not have been blind but it was certainly in need of an eye test.

You know what breaks my heart? High cholesterol.

I'm in trouble with my girlfriend after she asked where I was taking her on Valentine's Day. It seems that "over the coffee table" was not what she wanted to hear.

Money can't buy love, but it can rent a very close imitation.

I told my wife: "I love you, plain and simple." She raged: "How dare you call me plain and simple?"

It is better to have loved a short man than never to have loved a tall.

Love isn't constant: it comes in spurts.

I've learned that you cannot make someone love you. All you can do is stalk them and hope they panic and give in.

How can you tell if two octopuses are in love?
They walk arm in arm in arm in arm . . .

MAGIC

I tried my hand at being a magician, but when someone revealed all my tricks, I became disillusioned.

How do you get a magician to do 100 card tricks?
Ask him to show you one.

The closest I'll ever get to being a magician is convincing my dog that I really threw the ball.

Did you hear about the magician who was driving down the road?
He turned into a driveway.

A man asked a magician how he did a particular trick. The magician replied: "I could tell you, but then I'd have to kill you." "OK," said the man. "Just tell my wife."

How are digital cameras like magicians?
They don't do exposure.

I'm not very good at magic. I can only do half a trick. I'm a member of the Magic Semi-Circle. *Tim Vine*

David Copperfield's greatest trick was getting Charles Dickens to write a book about him before he was born.

MANNERS

Trying to be a gentleman, I stood aside and held the door open for my girlfriend, but all she said was: "Do you mind leaving me alone while I'm having a shit?!"

The only substitute for good manners is fast reflexes.

Etiquette is knowing which finger to put in your mouth when you whistle for the waiter.

Man to dinner party guest: "How dare you break wind before my wife?"
Guest: "Sorry, I didn't realize it was her turn."

MARRIAGE

What's the difference between being a lion tamer and being married?
A lion tamer only gets his head bitten off once.

Getting married is like buying a washing machine – you'll never need to do it by hand again.

Marriage is the only war where you sleep with the enemy.

What did the wife do when she saw her husband staggering around the backyard?
Reloaded.

My wife came home from work yesterday and asked me to console her. So I hit her over the head with my X-box.

Did you hear about the couple who got married in a bookshop? It was a novel experience.

Marriage is like a bank account. You put it in, you take it out, you lose interest.

My wife and I were inseparable – sometimes it took four people to pull us apart.

Playboy has introduced a new magazine for married men. Every month the centrefold is the same woman.

Husbands are proof that women have a sense of humour.

Why didn't the man speak to his wife for 18 months?
He didn't want to interrupt her.

An X-ray specialist married one of his patients. Everybody wondered what he saw in her.

How can you tell when your wife is dead?
The sex is the same, but the dishes pile up.

My wife and I have been married 22 years – 46 with the windchill factor.

What happened to the married couple who bought a water bed?
They started to drift apart.

A married man should forget his mistakes – there's no use two people remembering the same thing.

Mike: "I'm a man of few words."
Marty: "I'm married, too."

I've just been given two weeks to live – my wife's gone away for a fortnight.

My parents have been together forever. They've passed their silver and gold anniversaries. The next one is rust. *Rita Rudner*

Love is one long sweet dream and marriage is the alarm clock.

A spouse is someone who will stand by you through all the problems you wouldn't have had if you'd stayed single.

Why is an engagement ring like a tourniquet to a bachelor?
It stops his circulation.

Marriage is like taking a bath. After you've been in it for a while, it isn't so hot.

She's been married so many times, they don't give her a new licence any more – they just punch the old one.

What's the difference between a new wife and a new dog?
After six months the dog is still pleased to see you.

What's the difference between a new husband and a new dog?
A new dog only takes a month to train.

I told my wife that a husband is like a fine wine: he gets better with age. The next day she locked me in the cellar.

Husband: "I'm going to make you the happiest woman in the world."
Wife: "Well, I'll miss you."

Why do most men die before their wives?
They want to.

What's the secret of a happy marriage?
Clear history, delete files.

I still remember the very words I said to my girlfriend on the day we became engaged: "I thought you were on the bloody pill!"

Jackie: "My husband's really kind and caring."
Jill: "Yes, mine's ugly, too."

Husband: "Honey, why do you always answer me back with a question whenever I ask you anything?"
Wife: "Is that what I do?"

I've been happily married for nine years – and nine out of twenty-five isn't bad.

Before marriage, a man yearns for the woman he loves. After marriage, the "y" becomes silent.

My wife and I have an open marriage – I just haven't told her yet.

I took my wife to a wife-swapping party. I had to throw in some cash.
Henny Youngman

Courtship is like looking at the pictures in a seed catalogue; marriage is what comes up in your garden.

What's the difference between a bachelor and a married man?
A bachelor comes home, sees what's in the refrigerator, and goes to bed; a married man comes home, sees what's in the bed, and goes to the refrigerator.

My wife keeps complaining I never listen to her . . . or something like that.

Did you hear about the husband who had been trying to drown his sorrows for years, but she was too good a swimmer?

Mike: "My wife's one in a million."
Marty: "Really? I thought she was won in a raffle."

They say marriage is an institution, but who wants to live in an institution?

What is a husband?
An attachment you screw on the bed to get shelves put up.

Wife: "Why do you keep reading our marriage licence?"
Husband: "I'm looking for a loophole."

Marriage is a thing which puts a ring on a woman's finger and two under the man's eyes.

I got married to Miss Right. I just didn't know her first name was "Always".

Husband: "If you learned how to cook and iron, we could do without the maid."
Wife: "And if you learned how to make love, we could do without the gardener."

Getting married for sex is like flying business class just to recharge your phone.

Sometimes my secretary reminds me of my wife. I was running my hand up her skirt the other lunch break when she said: "Remember, you have a wife."

Husbands are like fires: they go out if left unattended.

Mike: "My wife's an angel."
Marty: "You're lucky – mine's still alive."

I always get breakfast in bed from my wife . . . provided I sleep in the kitchen.

Marriage is not a lottery. You get a chance in a lottery.

When you're dating, you picture the two of you being together for ever; when you're married, you wonder who will die first.

When they're dating, a man holds his wife's hand in public; when they're married, he flicks her ear in public.

I lost my virginity when I was 17, but I found it again when I got married.

A smart husband is one who thinks twice before saying nothing.

Before we got married I caught her in my arms. Now I catch her in my pockets.

My wife says we don't spend enough time together, so I moved the X-box into the kitchen.

What's the only way to have your husband remember your anniversary? **Get married on his birthday.**

We're equal partners in our marriage. I'm the silent one.

I said to my wife: "Do you think the excitement and romance has gone out of our marriage?" She said: "I'll discuss it with you during the next commercial break."

Adam and Eve had the perfect marriage. He didn't have to hear about all the men she could have married, and she didn't have to hear how great his mother's cooking was.

Every man likes to think he's marrying a nymphomaniac. But after three months the nympho leaves and you're just left with the maniac.

Marriage is the process of finding out what kind of man your wife would have preferred.

Did you hear about the wife who took her husband to the cleaners? Their shower had broken.

My wife said: "When I'm gone, you won't find another woman like me." I said: "What makes you think I'd want another woman like you?"

Why do men twist their wedding rings? **They're trying to work out the combination.**

Wife: "Why do you keep reading our marriage licence?" **Husband: "I'm looking for the expiry date."**

Marriage is a ceremony that turns a dreamboat into a barge.

My wife and I were married in a toilet. It was a marriage of convenience.

For an anniversary present I bought my wife a custard pie. She threw it straight back in my face.

Mike: "To lose a wife can be hard."
Marty: "In my case, it's been impossible!"

My wife is always ordering me around. In fact, I don't think I've bought her one drink since we've been together.

A husband is someone who takes out the trash and gives the impression he just cleaned the whole house.

Men claim to be in charge but in reality a husband controls his wife in much the same way that a barometer controls the weather.

What's the difference between a girlfriend and a wife?
About 45 pounds.

Marriage is like the witness protection programme: you get new clothes, you live in the suburbs, and you're not allowed to see your friends any more. *Jeremy Hardy*

When a man steals your wife, there is no better revenge than to let him keep her.

The formula for a happy marriage is the same as for living in California: when you find a fault, don't dwell on it.

My wife is an earth sign, I'm a water sign. Together we make mud.

Marriage is the only sport in which the trapped animal has to buy the licence.

She didn't want to marry him for his money, but it was the only way she could get it.

Jackie: "Aren't you wearing your wedding ring on the wrong finger?"
Jill: "Yes, I am. I married the wrong man."

In marriage, it only takes a few seconds to go from a warm welcome to a heated argument.

A man may be a fool and not know it – but not if he is married.

In the first year of marriage, the man speaks and the woman listens. In the second year, the woman speaks and the man listens. In the third year, they both speak and the neighbours listen.

Husband: "I hear you've been telling everyone that I'm an idiot."
Wife: "Sorry, I didn't know it was a secret."

My first wife was temperamental: 50 per cent temper and 50 per cent mental.

Marriage is a relationship where one person is always right and the other is the husband.

Wife to husband: "No woman would look twice at you – unless she couldn't believe her eyes the first time!"

A married couple can only achieve domestic harmony if the husband is playing second fiddle.

My wife and I always compromise. I admit I'm wrong, and she agrees with me.

Jackie: "What was your first husband's name?"
Jill: "Brad. But I called him Bradawl because he was a little boring tool."

When a man opens the door of his car for his wife, you can be sure of one thing: either the car is new or the wife.

I know a man who's so henpecked he's still taking orders from his first wife.

My wife is one in a million – yes, she's that insignificant.

A retired husband is often a wife's full-time job.

There are two steps to a successful marriage: first, let your wife think she is having her own way, and second, let her have her own way.

Marriage isn't a sprint, it's a marathon. I've run a marathon, and I was glad when it was over.

Did you hear about the dwarf who married a six-foot woman?
His mates put him up to it.

Son: "How much does it cost to get married, Dad?"
Father: "I don't know, son – I'm still paying for it."

There's only one thing I don't like about my new Thai bride – she keeps leaving the toilet seat up.

Mike: "I'm getting married next month."
Marty: "Against whom?"

After I held the door open for a pretty blonde, my wife complained: "You never hold the door open for me." I said: "That's not true. What about the time you threatened to leave?"

Wife: "Will you love me when I'm old and ugly?"
Husband: "Darling, of course I do."

The first part of our marriage was very happy. Then, on the way back from the ceremony . . . *Henny Youngman*

Did you hear about the couple who hated doing puzzles? Fifty years together, and never a crossword.

Boy: "Can I have your daughter's hand?"
Girl's father: "Why not? You've had the rest of her."

Wife: "Let's go out and have some fun tonight."
Husband: "Great, but if you get home before I do, leave the hall light on."

My wife does bird impressions. She watches me like a hawk.

Why did the polygamist cross the aisle?
To get to the other bride.

Jackie: "I can't think why you got married in the first place."
Jill: "It was that old story about opposites attract. He wasn't pregnant and I was."

An Arab offered me 40 camels for my wife. I said: "Sorry, I don't smoke."

Did you hear about the wife who had her husband eating out of the palm of her hand? It saved on the washing-up.

My wife said she wanted more freedom. "No problem," I said, "I'll extend the kitchen."

Mike: "How's your headache?"
Marty: "Out shopping."

When does a man finds it easy to understand a wife?
When it isn't his wife.

My wife talks so much, I get hoarse just listening to her.

The Invisible Man married an invisible woman. The kids were nothing to look at. **Tommy Cooper**

My wife dresses to kill, and cooks the same way.

Wife: "I never know what to do with my hands when I'm talking."
Husband: "Try covering your mouth."

A bachelor is a rolling stone who gathers no boss.

My marriage was just a conversation that got out of hand.

Mike: "What's the first thing that your wife does when she gets up in the morning?"
Marty: "She sharpens her tongue."

We're a fastidious couple. I'm fast and she's hideous.

Why a man should ever want to marry is a mystery. Why a man should want to marry two women is a bigamistery.

My wife complained today that I treat her like a child. I didn't how to react, so I gave her a gold star and a smiley face for sticking up for herself.

A small boy asks his father: "Dad, how did you get married to Mom?" The father turns to his wife and says: "See, even our son can't believe it!"

When a man holds a woman's hand before marriage, it's love; after marriage, it's self-defence.

I know a couple that get on like a house on fire. They both feel trapped, and are slowly suffocating to death. **Jimmy Carr**

Wife: "One more word from you, and I'm going back to my mother."
Husband: "Taxi!"

My wife and I went to see a marriage counsellor. She sat us down and said: "If you're both happy, we'll start." I said: "If we were both happy, we wouldn't be here."

A bachelor is a man who has taken many a girl out but has never been taken in.

I can remember when I got married, I can remember where I got married, I just can't remember why.

Mike: "I hate how my wife keeps talking about her ex-husband."
Marty: "That's nothing. Mine keeps talking about her *next* husband."

Missing: wife and dog. Reward for dog.

I read recently that love is entirely a question of chemistry, which must be why my wife treats me like toxic waste.

If you want your wife to listen, talk to another woman.

My wife always complains that I never notice her. So remembering something for a change, I called her at work today to wish her Happy Birthday. It turns out she died two years ago.

My wife and I were happy for 25 years – then we met.

Jackie: "How come you've kept the same husband for eight years?"
Jill: "His complexion matches my furniture."

To some, marriage is just a word; to others, it's a sentence.

Two years ago, I married a lovely young virgin, and if that doesn't change soon, I'm going to divorce her.

When I got married I disappointed a lot of women. Now I can concentrate on disappointing just the one.

Marriages are made in Heaven. Then again, so are thunder and lightning.

Marriages are made in Heaven, but mine is so fragile I think it was made in Taiwan.

Bachelors treat all women as sequels.

Mike to Marty: "There's nothing I wouldn't do for my wife, and there's nothing she wouldn't do for me. And that's how we go through life – doing nothing for each other."

My wife says I'm a model husband – a small replica of the real thing.

He's a model husband, but not a working model.

After 10 years of marriage, you watch the TV after sex; after 20 years of marriage, you watch the TV during sex; and after 30 years of marriage, you watch the TV instead of sex.

My wife is so tired at the end of the day she can hardly keep her mouth open.

A bigamist is a man who can have his Kate and Edith too.

After marriage, a husband and wife are like the two sides of a coin: they can't face each other but still they stay together.

Wife: "You'll be sorry. I'm going to leave you!"
Husband: "Make up your mind. Which is it going to be?"

Marriage is like a game of noughts and crosses: when the wife is cross, the husband gets nought.

A husband can have several small mouths to feed and one big one to listen to.

I'm so henpecked, I have to wash and iron my own apron.

Your marriage is in trouble if your wife says, "You're only interested in one thing", and you can't remember what it is. *Milton Berle*

Wife: "Look at how devoted that couple are. See how he kisses her whenever they meet. Why don't you do that?"
Husband: "I'd love to, but I hardly know her."

Mike: "Is your wife outspoken?"
Marty: "Not by anyone I know of."

A happily married man is one who understands every word his wife didn't say.

A man arrives home to find his wife wearing a sexy negligee. "Tie me up," she purrs, "and you can do anything you want." So he ties her up and goes off to play golf.

A bachelor is a guy with just a single thought – staying that way.

You can tell a husband is losing interest in his wife when his favourite sexual position is next door.

Why is it healthy for women to be married?
Because banging your head up against a brick wall burns off 150 calories an hour.

Marriage is like a mousetrap. Those on the outside are trying to get in. Those on the inside are trying to get out.

My wife's always telling me that I don't look at things from her point of view. So I went and looked out of the kitchen window but it didn't help.

A husband is someone who can guess what his wife is going to say before she repeats it.

I joined Bachelors Anonymous. Whenever I feel tempted to marry, they send over a fierce woman in wrinkled tights to nag me for an hour.

A man is the head of the family and the wife is the neck. The neck turns the head exactly the way it wants . . .

Our marriage guidance counsellor said we needed to talk about the elephant in the room. I turned to my wife and said: "See, even she thinks you're fat!"

Boy: "Is it true, Dad, that in some parts of Africa a man doesn't know his wife until he marries her?"
Father: "That happens in every country, son."

The only pressing engagement a married woman has is the ironing.

Jackie to Jill: "My neighbour is always running down her husband, but look at me: my husband is stupid, lazy, selfish and unreliable yet you never hear me say a bad word about him."

How do you know if your husband is dead?
The sex is the same, but you get the remote.

Reporter: "Sir, you've been happily married for 45 years. What's your secret?"
Husband: "You'll have to speak up. I'm as deaf as a post, and have been for 45 years."

My wife and I got married for better or worse. She couldn't do better; I couldn't do worse.

A wife is someone who may suffer in silence but usually has a lot to say about it later.

What's the difference between a mother and a wife?
One brings you into the world crying; the other ensures you continue to do so.

Husband: "Oh, doctor. My wife's dislocated her jaw. Can you come out to see her in, say, four or five weeks' time?"

A good wife always forgives her husband when she's wrong.

My wife wanted a new fridge, and because I like sex I said: "Yeah."
John Bishop

Why do married men hang strobe lights from their bedroom ceilings?
To create the illusion that their wives are moving during sex.

If it weren't for marriage, women would have to spend most of their adult lives arguing with complete strangers.

A husband lays down the law to his wife, then accepts all her amendments.

Wife: "How shall we celebrate our twentieth wedding anniversary?"
Husband: "How about with a two-minute silence?"

I found out today that my marriage isn't legal because her dad didn't have a licence for that shotgun.

MARTIAL ARTS

I'm kicking myself that I didn't take up karate earlier.

Did you hear about the karate expert who joined the army? The first time he saluted, he killed himself.

What do you call a pig that does karate?
A pork chop.

I have a black belt in karate. It's not that I'm any good, I just never wash it.

I have a black eye in karate.

Karate makes sense. If you practise breaking boards in half, you'll be able to protect yourself the next time a board attacks you.

After half a dozen karate lessons, I can now break a four-inch board with my plaster cast.

MASTURBATION

Why couldn't the scarecrow masturbate?
He was just clutching at straws.

My wife caught me masturbating while studying a magic eye picture. I said: "It's not what it looks like!"

What do you call a 90-year-old man who can still masturbate?
Miracle Whip.

If a woman is uncomfortable watching you masturbate, do you think: a) you need more time together, b) she's a prude, c) she should have sat somewhere else on the bus?

Mothers have Mother's Day and fathers have Father's Day, so what do single men have?
Palm Sunday.

What do you call someone who cries while he masturbates?
A tearjerker.

I'm really great at sex. Now all I need is a partner.

Did you know that if a man masturbates four times a week, it reduces the risk of him getting prostate cancer? I've tallied up my weekly counts and I'm immortal. *Sean Lock*

I just got home from the World Blindfold Masturbation Championships. No idea where I came.

Masturbation: the leading cause of tissue damage.

What's the most sensitive part of a man's body during masturbation?
His ears, listening for footsteps.

What's the ultimate rejection?
When you're masturbating, and your hand falls asleep.

The toughest thing when your girlfriend catches you masturbating is explaining to her that technically it's all her fault.

MATH

Did you hear about the man who is determined to count backwards all the way from a million? He says he'll stop at nothing.

Why did I divide sin by tan? Just cos.

Did you hear about the mathematician who turned off his heating so he could be cold and calculating?

What is half of infinity?
nity.

Alcohol and calculus don't mix: Don't Drink and Derive.

Why are dwarfs good at math?
Because it's the little things that count.

There are 10 types of people: those who understand binary, and those who don't.

I used to be good at math – until they decided to add the alphabet to it.

Confused about an invoice, a boss asked his secretary: "If I were to give you $20,000 minus 14 per cent, how much would you take off?" "Everything but my earrings," she replied.

I failed my math exam so many times, I lost count.

If God had intended us to use the metric system, Jesus would have had only 10 disciples.

What do mathematics teachers call retirement?
The aftermath.

I'm terrible at math. The equation 2n + 2n is 4n to me.

Why did the algebra book kill himself?
Because nobody understood him.

Why did one math textbook say to the other?
"I don't know about you, but I've got a lot of problems."

What's the scariest thing in geometry?
A vicious circle.

Boy: "Dad, will you help me find the common denominator?"
Father: "Don't tell me they haven't found it yet! I remember looking for it when I was a boy."

Did you hear about the math teacher who ordered too much graph paper? He didn't know where to draw the line.

What did the number 0 say to the number 8?
"Nice belt."

Numbers have never been my thirte.

Father: "If I had six coconuts and I gave you two, how many would I have left?"
Son: "I don't know. At school we do all our arithmetic in apples and oranges."

Teacher: "If I had seven oranges in one hand and eight oranges in the other hand, what would I have?"
Little Johnny: "Big hands."

Teacher: "Who knows what comes after 8, 9, 10?"
Little Johnny: "Jack, Queen, King."

Teacher: "If you had five dollars in your left pocket and three dollars in your right pocket, what would you have?"
Little Johnny: "Someone else's pants."

Teacher: "How many degrees in a circle?"
Little Johnny: "Fahrenheit or Celsius?"

Teacher: "If you got 10 dollars from 10 people, what would you have?"
Little Johnny: "A new bike."

Teacher: "If I laid three eggs here and three eggs over there, how many would I have?"
Little Johnny: "I'm not sure. Let's see you do it first."

Teacher: "If I had eight flies on my desk and I swatted one, how many would be left?"
Little Johnny: "The dead one."

Teacher: "If I have four bottles in one hand and three bottles in the other hand, what do I have?"
Little Johnny: "A drink problem, Miss?"

Teacher: "Did your parents help you with your math homework questions?"
Little Johnny: "No. I got them wrong all by myself."

Teacher: "If you had five apples on your desk, and the boy next to you took two, what would you have?"
Little Johnny: "A fight."

Teacher: "Why are you doing your math multiplication on the floor?"
Little Johnny: "Because you told us to do it without using tables."

Teacher: "What comes after six?"
Little Johnny: "The milkman."

Four-thirds of all Americans don't understand fractions.

MEMORY

I had amnesia once – maybe twice.

I woke up this morning and forgot which side the sun rises from. Then it dawned on me.

Everyone has a photographic memory – some just don't have film.

I took my old nan back to the first house she ever lived in – in Alzheimer Street. It should have been a trip down Memory Lane . . .

My short-term memory's not as good as it used to be. Also my short-term memory's not as good as it used to be.

My uncle came out of the closet yesterday. He's not gay, but he's got Alzheimer's, and he thought it was the car.

Doctor: "I have very bad news. You have cancer and Alzheimer's."
Patient: "Well, at least I don't have cancer."

My wife has the worst memory – she never forgets anything.

Seen it all, done it all, can't remember most of it.

Mike: "I've lost my memory."
Marty: "When did it happen?"
Mike: "When did what happen?"

What's the best thing about Alzheimer's?
You meet new people every day.

I've got the memory of an elephant. I distinctly remember going to the zoo once and seeing an elephant.

My memory has got so bad it has caused me to lose my job. I'm still employed; I just can't remember where.

My grandfather suffers from Mallzheimer's disease. He goes to the mall and forgets where he parked the car.

Did you hear about the man who discovered a cure for amnesia but kept forgetting what it was?

First old man: "Can you remember the name of the first woman you ever kissed?"
Second old man: "I can't even remember the name of the last one!"

What do you get from a forgetful cow?
Milk of Amnesia.

I went to see the doctor because I couldn't remember anything. I thought it was amnesia, but it turns out I just have a really boring life.

A man collecting in a shopping mall asked a woman for a donation to an Alzheimer's charity. "But I gave to you just now," she said. "Don't you remember?"

My poor nan has had Alzheimer's for years – but I guess I should be grateful for the $10 I get for my birthday every week.

My friends have been teasing me about my Alzheimer's. But the joke's on them – I don't have a toaster.

MEN

What's the difference between a man and childbirth?
One is a constant pain and almost unbearable, the other is simply having a baby.

Jackie to Jill: "I like my men the way I like my coffee – ground up and in the freezer."

How do men sort their laundry?
"Filthy" and "Filthy but Wearable".

Why do men find it difficult to make eye contact?
Breasts don't have eyes.

Build a man a fire and he's warm for a night. Set a man on fire and he's warm for the rest of his life.

How do you scare a man?
Sneak up behind him and throw rice.

What do you call a handcuffed man?
Trustworthy.

A man who refused to fight used to be called a coward. Now he's called a bachelor.

How do we know God made Adam before Eve?
Because you always make a rough draft before the final copy.

If women didn't ask so many questions, men wouldn't have to lie to them.

A woman without a man is like a neck without a pain.

Men do cry, but only when assembling furniture. *Rita Rudner*

What's the difference between going to a singles bar and going to a circus?
At a circus the clowns don't talk.

Why are real men happy to do the housework?
Because their wives tell them to be.

Men have two emotions: hungry and horny. If you see him without an erection, make him a sandwich.

A man should never tell a woman that he's unworthy of her love. She knows.

Men's brains are like the prison system: not enough cells per man.

Why do men prefer electric lawnmowers?
So they can find their way back to the house.

Why are men like photocopiers?
Apart from reproduction, they're not much good for anything else.

Jackie: "Why do you say that man at the bar is getting on your nerves? He's not even looking at you."
Jill: "That's what's getting on my nerves."

How does a man show that he's planning for the future?
He buys two cases of beer instead of one.

A guy knows when he's in love when he loses interest in his car for a couple of days. *Tim Allen*

I'm happy to live in a free country where a man can do as his wife pleases.

What's the difference between a g-spot and a golf ball?
Men will spend 20 minutes looking for a golf ball.

Why are men like placemats?
Because they only show up when there's food on the table.

Why do men chase women they have no intention of marrying?
For the same reason dogs chase cars they have no intention of driving.

What's a man's idea of foreplay?
Brushing his teeth.

Men's troubles can be attributed to three things – women, money, and both.

To women, why are men like bank accounts?
Without a lot of money, they don't generate much interest.

He took his misfortune like a man – he blamed it on his wife.

How can you tell if a man is a male chauvinist?
He thinks "harass" is two words.

Why do men like women in leather?
Because they smell like new cars.

It takes only four men to wallpaper a house, but you have to slice them thinly.

Men are like mini-skirts. If you're not careful, they'll creep up your legs.

What do all men in singles bars have in common?
They're married.

How is Colonel Sanders a typical man?
All he's concerned with is legs, breasts and thighs.

The best way to get a man to do something is to suggest he's too old for it.

If a man tells a woman she's beautiful, she'll overlook most of his other lies.

Trying to pin a man down can be like trying to nail blancmange.

Why are men like mascara?
Because they run at the first sign of emotion.

Why is a launderette a bad place to pick up a woman?
Because a woman who can't even afford a washing machine will never be able to support you.

Why did God put men on Earth?
Because a vibrator can't mow the lawn.

Men are like high heels – they're easy to walk on once you get used to it.

Apparently 60 per cent of women believe in ghosts. That's because they've seen how quickly guys can disappear after sex. *Jay Leno*

There comes a time in every man's life when he must stand up and tell his mother he's an adult. This usually happens at around 45.

Mike: "I'm a self-made man."
Marty: "At least you're not trying to blame anyone else."

Scientists have discovered something that can do the work of five men – a woman.

For the man who was everything: a calendar to remind him when his payments are due.

Man cannot live by bread alone – unless he's locked in a cage and that's all you feed him.

Why do men buy their partners flowers?
To accompany a weak alibi.

Men are proof of reincarnation – you can't get that dumb in just one lifetime.

What do you give the man who has everything?
Antibiotics.

What did the Virgin Mary say when she saw the Three Wise Men?
"Typical! You wait ages then three come at once!"

Actually there were Four Wise Men on the road to Bethlehem, but one said he knew a short cut.

For a woman, sleeping with a man is like a soap opera. Just when it's getting interesting, he's finished till next time.

Show me a man with his head held high, and I'll show you a man having trouble with his bifocals.

What do most men consider a gourmet restaurant?
Any place without a drive-up window.

When is the only time you can change a man?
When he's in nappies.

How many men does it take to change a toilet roll?
Nobody knows; it's never happened.

God promised women that ideal husbands could be found in all four corners of the world. Then he made the Earth round.

A man's ultimate fantasy is to have two women at once – one cooking, one cleaning.

Men are like chocolates – they never last long enough and they always leave stains when they get hot.

Most men would rather scrub the kitchen floor during a big football match than discuss anything emotional.

Men think monogamy is something you make dining tables out of.
Kathy Lette

Why can men read maps better than women?
Because only a man can understand the concept of an inch equalling a hundred miles.

Every man should have a wife – preferably his own.

What's a man's idea of a romantic night out?
A candlelit football stadium.

How can you tell the difference between men's real gifts and their guilt gifts?
Their guilt gifts are more expensive.

What's a man's idea of a golden opportunity?
A blonde.

How can you tell if a man is sexually excited?
He's breathing.

Why are men like cement?
After getting laid, they take a long time to get hard.

Only a man would buy an $800 car and put a $6,000 music system in it.

Apparently a fifth of British men have no idea how to turn on the washing machine. I find chocolates or flowers usually do the trick.

If you want a committed man, look in a mental hospital.

Why were men given larger brains than dogs?
So they won't hump women's legs at cocktail parties.

Why are men like parking spots?
The good ones are always taken and the ones that are left are handicapped.

What's the fastest way to a man's heart?
Through his chest with a sharp knife.

If it's not Valentine's Day and you see a man in a flower shop, you can probably start up a conversation by asking: "What did you do?"

What's a man's idea of foreplay?
Half an hour of begging.

A modern man will stand for anything – except a woman on the bus.

What's the difference between a man and a condom?
Condoms have changed: they're no longer thick and insensitive.

Why are women called "birds"?
Because they tend to pick up worms.

Why is it so difficult for women to find men who are sensitive, caring and good-looking?
Because those men already have boyfriends.

A woman's work that is never done is the stuff she asked her husband to do.

A lot of men *can* multi-task. They can talk and annoy you at the same time.

Women are always saying that men can't multi-task. Yet when we pee while having a shower, they complain!

Why are men like lava lamps?
They're fun to look at, but they're not all that bright.

What should you give a man who has everything?
A woman to show him how to work it.

By the time most men learn how to behave, they are too old to do anything else.

Why do only 10 per cent of men go to Heaven?
Because if they all went, it would be Hell.

What's the difference between a man and a broken clock?
Even a broken clock is right twice a day.

Why do men like to marry virgins?
To avoid criticism.

What do you call a man with 99 per cent of his brain missing?
Castrated.

What do you call a man who expects to have sex on the second date?
Slow.

What's the difference between a man and Bigfoot?
One is covered in matted hair and smells awful; the other has big feet.

Why are men like public toilets?
All the good ones are engaged, and the rest are full of crap.

Men are like a pack of cards. You need a heart to love them, a diamond to marry them, a club to batter them and a spade to bury them.

Some men are discovered; others are found out.

Why are men like linoleum?
If you lay them right the first time, you can walk all over them for the next 50 years.

What has eight arms and an IQ of 60?
Four men watching a football game.

Why are men like guns?
Keep one around long enough, and eventually you're going to want to shoot it.

Why are men like chocolate bars?
They're sweet, smooth and head straight for your hips.

What do you call an intelligent, handsome, caring, sensitive man?
A rumour.

What do men and pantyhose have in common?
They either cling, run or don't fit right in the crotch.

What's the one thing that keeps most men out of college?
High school.

Why are men like coolers?
Load them with beer and you can take them anywhere.

Man: "I don't know why you wear a bra – you've got nothing to put in it."
Woman: "Well, you wear underpants, don't you?"

What do you say to a man with two black eyes?
Nothing, he's already been told twice.

Why is psychoanalysis quicker for men than for women?
Because when it's time to go back to childhood, he's already there.

Why do men prefer blondes?
Men always like intellectual company.

How is a man like a snowstorm?
Because you don't know when it's coming, how many inches you'll get or how long it will stay.

What does it mean when a man is in your bed, gasping for breath and calling your name?
You didn't hold the pillow down long enough.

Why do men name their penises?
Because they don't like the idea of a stranger making 90 per cent of their decisions.

I've never seen a woman make a fool out of a man without a lot of co-operation.

What's a man's idea of a seven-course meal?
A hot dog and a six-pack.

When two men fight over a woman, it's the fight they want, not the woman.

What do anniversaries and toilets have in common?
Men always miss them.

Why are men like popcorn?
Because they satisfy you, but only for a little while.

When is the only time a man thinks about a candlelit dinner?
When there's been a power failure.

Jackie: "I got a set of golf clubs for my husband."
Jill: "Great trade!"

Jesus was a typical man. They always say they'll come back, but you never see them again.

Why is food better than men?
Because you don't have to wait an hour for seconds.

Why are men like lawnmowers?
They're hard to get started, they emit noxious odours, and half the time they don't work.

Why don't men eat between meals?
There is no "between" meals.

By the time a man is old enough to read a woman like a book, he's too old to start a library.

Why do women live longer than men?
Someone has to stick around and clean up the mess after them.

What are the three biggest tragedies in a man's life?
Life sucks, job sucks, wife doesn't.

MEXICANS

A Mexican family were driving along the highway when they saw a sign saying, "30 Only". So they stopped and 12 of them got out.

Why were there only 5,000 Mexican soldiers at the Battle of the Alamo?
They only had two vans.

Why did the Mexican shoot his wife?
Tequila.

What do you call a Mexican who's had his car stolen?
Carlos.

What do you call a Mexican with a vasectomy?
A dry Martinez.

Why is there so little Mexican literature?
Because spray paint wasn't invented until 1949.

What do Mexicans do when they are cold?
They use chicken fajitas.

How do you stop a Mexican tank?
Shoot the guy pushing it.

MIDDLE AGE

The good thing about being middle-aged is that the glass is still half-full. The bad thing is that pretty soon your teeth will be floating in it.

Have you heard about the new bra for middle-aged women? It's called the "sheep dog" because it rounds them up and points them in the right direction.

You know you've reached middle age when the only thing you care to exercise is caution.

Thirty is a nice age for a woman – especially if she happens to be 40.

I covered myself from head to toe in mirrors this morning. I think I'm at that age where you do a lot of reflecting.

Middle-aged women no longer have upper arms: they have wing-spans. Instead of being women in sleeveless shirts, they're flying squirrels in drag.

They say that 40 is the new 30, but try telling that to a speed camera.

My mother's going through the change, and she's been getting quite depressed. It's been tough for me, too, having to call her Dad.

A woman is looking at herself naked in the mirror. She says to her husband: "Darling, I'm old and fat. Cheer me up. Pay me a compliment." He says: "Your eyesight's still good."

I'm not getting older. I just collect wrinkles.

Forty has been a difficult age for her to get past – in fact, it's taken her at least seven years.

My wife never lies about her age. She just tells people she's the same age as me, and then lies about my age.

A wife of 40 should be like money. You should be able to change her for two of 20.

In middle age, the growth of hair on a woman's legs slows down, which gives her plenty of time to care for her newly acquired moustache.

Jackie: "I don't look 37, do I?"
"No, darling," says Jill, "but I bet you did when you were."

I'm young at heart, but slightly older in other places.

Youth is when you're allowed to stay up on New Year's Eve; middle age is when you're forced to.

My wife dropped a cup the other day and wailed: "What's wrong with me?!" I named six things before I realized it was a rhetorical question.

She finally admitted her age, but she forgot to say how many years ago she reached it.

I find I don't like to do things now that I did 20 years ago – like look in the mirror.

Every time I go to a college reunion I find my old classmates are so fat and bald they hardly recognize me.

She holds her age well – she's been 29 for years.

Middle age is when you're willing to get up and give your seat to a lady, but can't.

Middle age is when you choose your cereal for the fibre, not the toy.

Middle age is when women stop worrying about being pregnant, and men start worrying they look like they are.

Middle age is when you start turning out the lights for economic rather than romantic reasons.

Middle age is when broadness of the mind and narrowness of the waist change places.

Middle age is when you start discussing rain gutters.

Middle age is when you leave nightclubs before the end to "beat the rush".

Middle age is when you can remember your children's names, but not always the right ones.

Middle age is when, before going out anywhere, you ask what the parking is like.

Middle age is when, instead of throwing out an old pair of trainers, you keep them for use in the garden.

Middle age is when your high school yearbook is home to three different species of mould.

Middle age is when you step on the scales and the balance is no longer in your favour.

Middle age is when you buy your first T-shirt without anything written on it.

Middle age is when you'd pay good money to be strip-searched.

Middle age is when you buy your jeans for comfort rather than style.

Middle age is when you recognize the classic rock songs that have been turned into elevator muzak.

Middle age is when you have nightmares about forgetting to move the trash cans to the street for the garbage collector.

Middle age is when you find yourself saying: "Is it cold here or is it just me?"

Jackie: "Remember 1970s fashions? Did you have hot pants?"
Jill: "I still do, but that's the menopause for you."

What's the difference between a clown and a man having a mid-life crisis?
The clown knows he's wearing ridiculous clothes.

MIND

I used to have an open mind but my brains kept falling out.

Don't confuse an open mind with one that's vacant.

His open mind should be closed for repairs.

The best way to change someone's mind is with a machete.

Of all the things I've lost, I miss my mind the most.

I haven't lost my mind: it's backed up on disk somewhere.

He has a one-track mind, and the traffic on it is very light.

Husband: "I have half a mind to leave you."
Wife: "And half a mind is all you have."

My mind works like lightning. One brilliant flash and it's gone.

When I'm not in my right mind, my left mind gets pretty crowded.

He went to a mind reader last week and was only charged half-price.

I've changed my mind three times today. It seems to work better now.

Wife: "There's something preying on my mind."
Husband: "Don't worry, it will soon die of starvation."

I thought about cloning a new, more efficient brain, but then I realized I was getting a head of myself.

People with narrow minds usually have broad tongues.

I'm practising ygolohcysp: reverse psychology

He's so narrow-minded he only has one eyebrow.

Did you hear about the office worker who let his mind wander? It hasn't come back yet.

The best way to change a woman's mind is to agree with her.

They say you only use 10 per cent of your brain. What about the other 30 per cent?

Wife: "I'm going to give you a piece of my mind!"
Husband: "Are you sure you can afford it?"

When a thought crosses his mind, it's a long and lonely journey.

The mind is like a parachute; it works much better when open.

If your mind goes blank, don't forget to turn off the sound.

MODERN TERMS

Abracadabbler: an amateur magician.
Accordionated: being able to drive and fold a road map simultaneously.
Affluenza: a bloated, sluggish and unfulfilled feeling that results from trying to keep up with the Joneses.
Algaebra: what the Little Mermaid wears over her chest.
Antiboyotics: when administered to teenage girls, they improve school grades and reduce money spent on make-up.
Apocalypstic: the tiny smudge you came home with on your collar that makes your wife act like it's the end of the world.
Assmosis: the process by which some people absorb success by sucking up to the boss.
Authoritis: writer's cramp.
Badaptation: a lousy movie version of a good book.
Beelzebug: Satan in the form of a mosquito that gets into your bedroom at three in the morning and cannot be cast out.
Blamestorming: workers sitting around in a group to discuss who was at fault.
Bozone layer: the substance surrounding stupid people and which stops bright ideas from penetrating.
Caterpallor: the colour you turn after finding half a worm in the fruit you're eating.

Decaflon: the gruelling event of getting through the day consuming only things which are good for you.

Deifenestration: to throw all talk of God out of the window.

Elbonics: the unspoken language where two people jostle for one armrest in a theatre.

Epiphunny: the moment of sudden revelation when one gets the joke.

Floordrobe: a floor littered with discarded clothes, a practice much favoured by teenagers.

Foreploy: any misrepresentation about yourself for the purpose of obtaining sex.

Frisbeetarianism: the belief that after death the soul flies up onto the roof and gets stuck there.

Giraffiti: vandalism spray-painted very, very high.

Glibido: all talk and no action.

Greyhound: a very short skirt, only an inch from the hare.

Hipatitis: terminal coolness.

Hippochondriacs: people who worry a lot about their weight.

Ignoranus: a person who's both stupid and an asshole.

Incorrigibelle: a beautiful woman who never learns from her mistakes.

Inoculatte: to take coffee intravenously.

iTwat: someone who has both an iPhone and an iPad.

Karmageddon: it's like the Earth explodes and it's like a serious bummer, man.

Manufracture: to make items which break after little use.

Mouse potato: the Internet generation's equivalent of a couch potato.

Nagivator: a bossy person who sits in the passenger seat and gives directions to the driver.

Namesis: someone who shares your name, but is much wealthier and more successful than you.

Osteopornosis: a degenerate disease.

Polarvoid: the state of having no baby pictures, a condition that usually befalls the second-born child.

Pseudonymphomania: the compulsive desire to have sex under an assumed name.

Reintarnation: coming back to life as a hillbilly.

Sarchasm: the gulf between sarcastic wit and the person who doesn't get it.

Seagull manager: a manager who flies in, makes a lot of noise, craps on everything, and then leaves.

Sheeple: people who have to go out and buy the latest gadget just because they think everyone else is.

Spamnesia: failure to reply to friends' emails because your computer thinks they're junk.

Testiculating: waving your arms around and talking bollocks.

Tumfoolery: when a middle-aged man sucks in his stomach while being introduced to an attractive woman.

Wuzband: a former husband.

MOMMY, MOMMY

"Mommy, Mommy, why is Daddy running away?"
"Shut up, and help me reload."

"Mommy, Mommy, are you sure this is how you learn to swim?"
"Shut up, and get back in the sack."

"Mommy, Mommy, why is Daddy so pale?"
"Shut up, and keep digging."

"Mommy, Mommy, why am I running around in circles?"
"Shut up, or I'll nail your other foot to the floor."

"Mommy, Mommy, can I lick the bowl?"
"Shut up, and flush."

"Mommy, Mommy, Daddy's on fire!"
"Quick, fetch the sausages."

"Mommy. Mommy, why is Daddy zig-zagging down the garden?"
"Shut up, I'm trying to take aim."

"Mommy, Mommy, Emily's been run over by a steamroller!"
"Quick, fetch the maple syrup.

"Mommy, Mommy, Daddy just fell off the roof!"
"I know, dear. I saw him pass the window."

"Mommy, Mommy, can I play in the sandbox?"
"Not till I find a better place to bury Daddy."

"Mommy, Mommy, Daddy's been run over in the street."
"Don't make me laugh, you know my lips are chapped."

"Mommy, Mommy, Daddy's thrown up."
"Shut up, and get a fork before your sister gets all the big chunks."

"Mommy, Mommy, Daddy went through the meat grinder."
"Shut up, and eat your burger."

"Mommy, Mommy, I don't like shark fishing."
"Shut up, and stop squirming."

"Mommy, Mommy, I don't want to see Niagara Falls."
"Shut up, and get back in the barrel."

"Mommy, Mommy, my head hurts."
"Shut up, and hold the dartboard."

"Mommy, Mommy, the kids at school say I'm a freak."
"Shut up, and comb your face."

"Mommy, Mommy, why can't we get a waste disposal unit?"
"Shut up, and keep chewing."

"Mommy, Mommy, what's a nymphomaniac?"
"Shut up, and help me get Grandma off the doorknob."

"Mommy, Mommy, what's a transvestite?"
"Shut up, and unhook Daddy's bra."

"Mommy, Mommy, how far is it to Europe?"
"Shut up, and keep swimming."

"Mommy, Mommy, Grandpa's going out."
"Well, throw some more gasoline on him then."

"Mommy, Mommy, what happened to all your scabs?"
"Shut up, and eat your cornflakes."

"Mommy, Mommy, I don't like tomato soup."
"Shut up, we only have it once a month."

"Mommy, Mommy, why do the other kids say I have a big nose?"
"You don't, but lift your head up or you'll scrape the floor."

"Mommy, Mommy, there's something in Daddy's eye."
"Shut up, and eat around it."

"Mommy, Mommy, when will we have this nice yellow pudding again?"
"Shut up, you know that Grandma's leg is no longer infected.

"Mommy, Mommy, why are we pushing the car off the cliff?"
"Shhh, you'll wake Daddy."

"Mommy, Mommy, can I play with Grandma?"
"Not today; we already dug her up three times this week."

MONEY

I won a tidy sum on the lottery and gave my homeless brother a brand-new home – it was the box from my new 65-inch TV.

A fool and his money can throw one hell of a party.

I recently came into some money. It was a waste of a fiver – I thought it was a tissue.

Money can't buy everything – that's what credit cards are for.

Who was the greatest financier that ever lived?
Noah, because he was able to float a company when the whole world was in liquidation.

What's the best way to keep your bills down?
Use a paperweight.

I won $2 million on the lottery, so I decided to donate a quarter to charity. Now I have $1,999,999.75.

What's better than winning the lottery?
Winning it the day after your divorce comes through.

Nothing dispels enthusiasm like a small admission fee.

Egypt is having problems with factions trying to hive off the country's assets since the 2011 uprising. So beware of any pyramid schemes.

What's the quickest way to double your money?
Fold it in half.

Wife: "Be honest with me, darling. Do you only love me because my father left me a fortune?"
Husband: "Don't be silly. I'd love you no matter who left you a fortune."

Did you hear about the husband whose credit card was stolen? He didn't report it because the thief was spending less than his wife did.

I'm saving my money. One day it might be worth something.

There is a way of transferring money that is even faster than electronic banking. It's called marriage.

I won the lottery last night. I haven't told my wife yet because I can't use my phone on the plane.

Did you hear about the man who was so mean, when he found a pack of corn plasters he bought a pair of tight shoes?

A budget is an orderly method of going into debt.

A wife opens the mail and tells her husband brightly: "The bank says this is our final notice. Isn't it nice that they're not going to bother us any more?"

Money isn't everything. There's also MasterCard and Visa.

Wife: "Now that we've won the lottery, what should we do about the begging letters?"
Husband: "Keep sending them."

The cost of a faulty jetpack is going through the roof.

When I give to charity, I like to give direct to the homeless. That way I know exactly where my money is going – straight to the liquor store.

A lot of money is tainted: taint yours and taint mine.

Whoever invented the copyright symbol should have a fortune by now.

If money doesn't grow on trees, why do banks have branches?

Earn cash in your spare time: blackmail friends.

Why did the man put his money in the freezer?
He wanted cold, hard cash.

Foreign aid is the transfer of money from poor people in rich countries to rich people in poor countries.

My girlfriend just saved me a lot of money – she married someone else.

The back of a man's anorak was jumping up and down, and people were giving him money. I said: "Do you make a living from that?" He said: "Yes, it's my livelihood."

Boy: "I'd go through anything for you."
Girl: "Let's start with your bank account."

If a sewage worker wins the lottery, does he become part of the effluent society?

Credit cards help you live within your income and beyond your means.

Anyone with money to burn will always find himself surrounded by people with matches.

I decided to join a Reincarnation Club, but they said membership was $750. Then I thought: What the hell? You only live once . . .

Husband: "What have you been doing with all the grocery money I gave you?"
Wife: "Turn sideways and look in the mirror."

All I ask for is the opportunity to prove that money can't buy happiness.

Money can't buy happiness, but it can rent it for a couple of hours.

My friend has had to tighten her belt, but that's anorexia for you.

It's not hard to meet expenses – they're everywhere.

What is a long-term investment?
A short-term investment that failed.

Materialism is buying things we don't need with money we don't have to impress people that don't matter.

I'm saving up for a rainy day. So far I've got an umbrella, a waterproof cape and a pair of gumboots.

What's the best thing you can say about misers?
They make good ancestors.

Whenever I go near a bank, I get withdrawal symptoms.

If money could talk, it would say goodbye.

MONKEYS

What do you call a monkey with a stick of dynamite up its butt?
A baboom.

Why did the monkey fall out of the tree?
Because he was dead.

Why did the second monkey fall out of the tree?
Because he was tied to the first monkey.

Why did the third monkey fall out of the tree?
Peer pressure.

Why did the squirrel fall out of the tree?
He was doing an impression of a monkey.

I saw a monkey in the jungle with a tin opener. I said: "You don't need a tin opener for a banana." "I know," he said. "This is for the custard."

What did the baboon say when his sister had a baby?
"Well, I'll be a monkey's uncle!"

The smaller the monkey, the more it looks like it would kill you at the first opportunity.

Two monkeys are getting into a bath. One goes: "Ooh ooh ah ah ah ah ah." The other says: "We'll put some cold in then."

MOTORCYCLES

Harley-Davidsons don't leak oil: they mark their territory.

What do you call a laughing motorcycle?
A Yamahaha.

Why do Hell's Angels wear leather?
Because chiffon wrinkles too easily.

I got into a fight with a burly biker who said he was going to mop the floor with my face. I said: "You'll be sorry – because you won't be able to get in the corners very well."

What's the difference between a Harley and a Hoover?
The position of the dirtbag.

What did the biker say when his baby murmured: "Mother"?
"Hey, the baby just said half a word!"

You're a biker when your idea of jewellery is chains and barbed wire.

You're a biker when you can tell what kind of bugs they are by the taste.

You're a biker when you're only sunburnt on the back of your hands and neck.

You're a biker when you wake up next to your partner, and your first thought is if your bike will start.

You're a biker when you don't think it's a good party until someone rides his bike into the living room and does doughnuts.

You're a biker when your best suit is all leather.

You're a biker when your other suit is a rain suit.

You're a biker when you have motorcycle parts in the dishwasher.

You're a biker when your best friends are named after animals.

You're a biker when you carry a picture of your bike in your wallet.

MOVIES

Our local cinema owner died last night. His funeral is on Wednesday at 2.10, 4.30 and 7.50.

Did you hear about the guy who watched *The Lord of the Rings* over and over again? It was just force of Hobbit.

There's a new movie out called *Harry Wizard*. He's a potter.

A woman goes into a video store and says: "Can I take *The Elephant Man* out?" The clerk says: "Are you sure he's your type?"

Did you ever see the French movie *And*? I think it was released in this country as *ET*. **Milton Jones**

Why does ET have such big eyes?
Because he saw the phone bill.

What's ET short for?
Because he's got little legs.

The problem with sex in the movies is the popcorn usually spills.

How did Darth Vader know what Luke Skywalker was getting for Christmas?
He felt his presents.

I went to see *X-Men: First Class* at the cinema. However, when I got there I was a little short of cash so I had to settle for *X-Men: Economy*.

Did you hear about the leper who went into a video shop and said: "Have you got *My Left Foot*?"

Are orphans allowed to watch PG movies?

Did you hear about the new pirate movie? It's rated ARRR!

What did the director of *The Mummy* say after filming was finished?
"That's a wrap."

There's a new DVD about driveway foundations. It's hardcore.

Did you hear about the man who watched a love scene at a drive-in movie theatre for a whole hour before he realized he was facing the wrong way?

I saw that movie about a gang who take time off from looting ships around Jamaica to improve their posture – *Pilates of the Caribbean*.

Where can you borrow a DVD of *Jaws*?
From a loan shark.

A man goes into a video store and says: "Have you got that movie featuring Long John Silver?" "Sorry," says the sales clerk, "we don't sell pirate videos."

Arnold Schwarzenegger has been offered a new role in a sequel to *The Terminator*. In this one, he travels back in time and kills the person who suggested he run for Governor. **Conan O'Brien**

The pig that played Babe was just a ham actor.

Rick Astley asked if he could borrow my collection of Disney Pixar films. "Sure," I said, "you can have *Toy Story, A Bug's Life* and *Finding Nemo*, but I'm never gonna give you *Up*."

I made a video starring my six-foot-tall girlfriend who has severe hearing difficulties. It was my first movie in high deaf.

What's the right age to tell a movie that it's adapted?

I was watching *Mary Poppins* and thought: Surely those chimney sweeps could make more money as professional dancers?

"Now pay attention, 007. This looks like an ordinary suitcase, but if you push this button, a handle comes out and you can wheel it."

I've just watched the uncut version of *Scarface*. It's just called *Face*.

As a child I watched *Mary Poppins* so many times I suffered from a condition with my sight: umdiddleiddleiddleum-diddleeye. **Milton Jones**

I wanted to read an Internet plotline of that new film about high-performance sports cars. But then I realized there were spoilers.

Apparently if you go to the movies alone, you're considered a loner and a bit weird. So I took my cat with me.

I call my girlfriend "babe" because she looks just like the movie star.

Have you heard about the sequel to *The Exorcist*? In the new version a woman hires the Devil to get a priest out of her son.

I watched a movie last night with my girlfriend. I was on the edge of my seat. It's about time she lost some weight.

Then I watched a movie about a baby hen. It was a real chick flick.

An adult movie is a film viewed by people over 30 with a cast of 25-year-olds doing what 18-year-olds do, with a plot for a 6-year-old.

When I'm feeling ill, I love to curl up in front of an old black and white movie, mainly because I'm off colour.

A Hollywood producer is an executive who wears a worried look on his assistant's face.

After watching a few zombie films I've decided that in the event of a zombie apocalypse, I'm going to be a cameraman because they never seem to attack them.

I hate the way Hollywood always changes everything. For instance, *Twister* the movie is nothing like the board game. **Tony Cowards**

Did you know Disney are remaking *Jungle Book* as *Jungle Kindle*?

Feeling a bit lonely and frustrated, I went online and ordered a DVD titled *Bald and Barely Legal*. When it arrived, I found it was a documentary about old tyres.

Why was the Margaret Thatcher movie *The Iron Lady* given an 18 certificate?
Because it's unsuitable for miners.

The Iron Lady really is a lousy sequel to *Iron Man*.

Did you hear about the guy who thought *20,000 Leagues Under the Sea* was about baseball?

I've seen better films on day-old soup!

The badness of a movie is directly proportional to the number of helicopters in it.

Did you hear about the man who regularly dreamt he had sex with famous movie stars? He had erotic dreams about Cameron Diaz once a week but he had Keira Knightley.

I was thrown out of the movie theatre for bringing in my own food. I was devastated – it's been ages since I've had a good barbecue.

What Disney movie is about a stupid boyfriend?
Dumb Beau.

What Disney film features a lot of swearing and cursing?
101 Damnations.

My grandmother was called Pearl and her husband was called Dean, but we always thought of them as Granny and Grand Papa-pa-pa-pa-pa-pa-pa-pa-pa-pah . . . **Milton Jones**

My goat ate my DVD of *One Flew Over the Cuckoo's Nest*, which is surprising because he hated the book.

I just watched a new movie about fishing. There was a great cast in it.

Who's Afraid of Virginia Woolf?
Virginia Sheep.

How do you know if you're watching a gay Western?
All the good guys are hung.

Last week, I tried that whole walking-away-in-slow-motion thing that movie heroes do when something is exploding. I really wish I hadn't.

When Tom Cruise got his first Oscar nomination, I bet he felt five foot tall.

Why do Mexican movie directors shout "enchilada" at the end of filming?
Because it's a wrap.

The Scarecrow didn't have the brains, Tin Man didn't have the heart, and the Lion didn't have the courage. So Dorothy remained a virgin.

Some horses break into the movies, but usually they're saddled with bit parts.

I've just spent 30 minutes in the HMV store deciding which movie to download when I get home.

I know *Charlie and the Chocolate Factory* backwards. Such a sad ending. ***Chris Addison***

How come in movies anyone getting out of a taxi always manages to pull the exact fare out of their pocket without even looking?

How come in movies you can always find a parking spot outside or opposite the building you're visiting?

How come in movies detectives never have wrong hunches?

How come in movies cops who are about to retire invariably die on their last day?

How come in movies the TV news story that affects you personally always appears as soon as you switch on?

How come in movies getaway cars never start first time, but police cars do?

How come in movies all bombs are fitted with electronic timing devices that have large digital displays so you know exactly when they're going to explode?

How come in movies these same bombs are always defused in the last three seconds, never earlier?

How come in movies any fight at a wedding reception results in the destruction of the cake?

How come in movies all beds have special L-shaped sheets that reach to armpit level on a woman but only up to the waist of the man lying beside her?

How come in movies when someone steals a car, the driver's seat is always in the correct position?

How come in movies the Eiffel Tower is visible from any room in Paris?

How come in movies if you decide to start dancing in the street, anyone you bump into will know all the steps?

Did you hear about the movie called *Constipation*? It hasn't come out yet.

Madonna's last movie was so bad that even when it was shown on a plane people got up and walked out.

Mission: Impossible III? How can it be impossible if he's already done it twice?

Movie synopsis: *Mission: Impossible IV*. Tom Cruise tries to see what's on top of the fridge.

She was the kind of girl you take to the movie when you want to see the picture.

Have you heard of that new film about a tractor? I just saw the trailer.

What musical is about a train conductor?
My Fare, Lady.

I went to a video store and said: "Can I take out *Batman Forever*?" They said: "No, you'll have to bring it back tomorrow." **Tim Vine**

Have you seen that new movie *Cardboard*? It's very popular at the Box Office.

The new Justin Bieber move is amazing in 3-D. It's like you could actually reach out and punch him.

And there's a 3-D movie of *Glee*. Apparently the 3-D is so good, it feels like the characters are literally pulling you out of the closet.

I saw a movie about some guy who experienced amazing revelations while eating his cereal. It was called *Breakfast Epiphanies*.

I saw a movie about a beaver the other day. It was the best dam movie I've ever seen.

MUSIC

Did you hear about the band called 999 Megabytes? They haven't done a gig yet.

I used to be in a band called Missing Cat. You probably saw our posters. **Stewart Francis**

I used to be in a band called The Hinges – we supported The Doors.

I used to be in a band called Origami, but we folded.

I used to be in a band called T-Mobile, but we kept breaking up.

I used to be in a band called White Line. We were described as middle of the road.

My mates and I are in a band called Duvet – we do covers.

Before that we started a band called The Sewers. You probably never heard of us – we were underground.

I'm in a band called Stuck In The Departure Lounge. Check us out.

I was in a band called The Prevention – we were told we were better than The Cure.

I was in a band called Dusk – we were on before The Darkness.

I was in a band called Rome. We were sacked.

There's a new band called The Blank Cheques. They're currently unsigned.

A bunch of my friends burp medleys of rock songs. They call themselves The Gastric Band.

There's a new Elbow tribute band called Arse. They're so good you can't tell them apart.

Is it true that Ashley Cole cheated on Cheryl because she mimed her orgasms?

What is Prince's favourite vegetable?
Little Red Courgette.

Mike: "Who sang 'Ain't No Sunshine'?"
Marty: " 'Oh, I know, I know, I know, I know, I know, I know, I know, I know, I know . . .' "

The Beatles have a new album out, but it's only drum and bass.

Rap is to music what Etch-a-Sketch is to art.

It's taken over 30 years, but today a cold-case team finally arrested and charged Video for the murder of the Radio Star.

A former French international footballer was charged today with battering Sophie Ellis-Bextor to death at his Paris apartment. Police say it was a case of murder on Zidane's floor.

A man sees a woman fishing while listening to her iPod. He mouths: "Caught any, love?" Confused, the woman removes her headphones and replies: "You're close. It's Nirvana!"

How did Bob Marley like his doughnuts?
Wi' jammin'.

And how do the Wailers like their doughnuts?
They like jammin', too.

If female genitalia could speak, it would sound exactly like Enya. *Dylan Moran*

What happens if you play blues music backwards?
Your wife returns to you, your dog comes back to life, and you get out of prison.

What's the difference between a moose and a blues band?
The moose has the horns up front and the asshole behind.

Why did the jazz musician like the wooden board?
Because it had a nice groove in it.

Did you know that it took Stevie Wonder eight years to write "Superstition"? He dropped his pencil on the first day.

To vote for Ringo, press the Richard Starkey now.

How scary must it be for a scuba diver to see Adele rolling in the deep?

Where does Baghdad's Chief of Police keep his CDs?
In a rack.

Jackson Five – now with no artificial colours.

I set up a Buddy Holly tribute website. It had a few hits but then it crashed.

What's the name of Pakistan's number one Elvis impersonator?
Ahmal Shukup.

If Elvis were alive now, he'd be scratching at the inside of his coffin.

I phoned up to buy tickets for an Elvis tribute act. The voice said: "Press 1 for the money, 2 for the show . . ."

I went into a record store and asked where the CDs for Aerosmith and Run-D.M.C. were. The guy said: "Walk this way."

Warning: if you receive an email offering two free tickets to see James Blunt, don't open it, because it contains two free tickets to see James Blunt.

What's the difference between a Rihanna video and a porn video?
The music is better in a porn video.

What's the difference between Bono and God?
God doesn't walk around Dublin thinking he's Bono.

Glastonbury was very wet and muddy. There was trench foot, dysentery, peaches . . . all the Geldof daughters. **_Sean Lock_**

My wife said my obsession with Oasis has gone too far. I said: "Maybeee . . ."

Why did Noel Gallagher cross the road?
Because the Beatles did.

What did the waiter say when Liam Gallagher ordered soup?
"You gotta roll with it."

What's blue and sings alone?
Dan Aykroyd.

What is "karaoke" Japanese for?
"Tone deaf".

Which female rock singer has fallen on hard times?
Cyndi Pauper.

What has 300 legs and a dozen teeth?
The front row at a Willie Nelson concert.

What was Meat Loaf's favourite musical instrument at school?
The dinner bell.

I've written a song about a tortilla. Well, it's more of a rap.

Amy Winehouse, Jim Morrison, Kurt Cobain, Janis Joplin, Brian Jones and Jimi Hendrix all died aged 27. Justin Bieber turns 27 in 2021. Just be patient!

Have you heard about the new tribute band OCDC? They play all their hits, but in alphabetical order.

The song was very catchy – but so was the Bubonic Plague.

I tried to write a drinking song once, but I couldn't get past the first bar.

LEGO drum kits: if you can't beat them, join them.

I saw one of the Righteous Brothers in the street last week – the one who's still alive.

Wife: "Why do you always go out on the balcony when I start singing?"
Husband: "I don't want the neighbours to think I'm beating you."

Mike: "If you were stuck on a desert island and could have three records, what would they be?"
Marty: "The long-distance swimming one would be good."

At any time, the temptation to sing "The Lion Sleeps Tonight" is never more than a whim away.

I heard a man singing "Do . . . Re . . . Mi" the other day. I thought: He'll go Far. *Tim Vine*

Piracy is killing the music industry. Well, you try playing the guitar with a hook.

What's the name of India's newest karaoke star?
Gerupta Singh.

Mark Knopfler used to pay me to look after his hens while he was away on tour. I just gave them a handful of corn every day. It was money for nothing and I got some chicks for free.

What do you call a French singer with laryngitis?
Charles Aznavoice.

I'm fed up with my mates promising to come to a Whitesnake gig with me and then never showing up. Here I go again on my own.

After Conrad Murray was found guilty of the involuntary manslaughter of Michael Jackson, I bet the Boogie was mighty relieved.

I'm leaving my girlfriend because of her obsession with The Temptations. Or is it just my imagination?

What happened when Mick Jagger went to the doctor with a cut lip?
The doctor gave him a puncture repair kit.

If Mama Cass had shared her ham sandwich with Karen Carpenter, they'd both be alive today.

Which Europe song is about the demise of LP records?
"The Vinyl Countdown."

My girlfriend's father is so posh he calls Roger Daltrey's old band The Whom.

People said I'd never get over my Phil Collins obsession. Take a look at me now.

I went to a karaoke bar last night and discovered they didn't play any 70s disco music. At first I was afraid . . . I was petrified. *Stewart Francis*

What did the folk singer say when he won the $20 million lottery?
"I'll just keep working till it's gone."

What happens when a jazz musician's clothes are all worn out?
It's ragtime.

When my wife sings, people clap their hands . . . over their ears.

At the end of his daughter's short piano recital, her proud father asked a musician friend: "What do you think of her execution?" The friend replied: "I'm in favour of it."

Choir: a group of people whose enthusiastic singing allows the rest of the congregation to lip-sync.

I conducted an orchestra the other day. It's more fun than you can shake a stick at.

What's the difference between chimpanzees and orchestra conductors? **Chimps can communicate with humans.**

Why is a conductor like a condom? **It's safer with one, but more fun without.**

What's the difference between a conductor and a sack of fertilizer? **The sack.**

Why did the composer spend all his time in bed? **He wrote sheet music.**

Did you hear about the eighteenth-century Austrian composer who wore a turban? Haydn Sikh.

What is the Cuban National Anthem? **"Row, Row, Row Your Boat".**

Who's 25 Cent? **50 Cent's half-brother.**

I went to London's Royal Albert Hall once, but it was full of pushchairs. It was Last Night of the Prams. *Tim Vine*

I went to see an orchestra play in Bermuda. It was great until the guy playing the triangle suddenly disappeared.

What was Beethoven's favourite fruit? **Ba-na-na-NA!**

Beethoven was so deaf he thought he was a painter.

Our local IBS society put on a version of *The Sound of Music*. The most popular song was "How Do You Solve a Problem Like My Rear?"

What do you call a horse that plays the violin in a musical? **Fiddler on the hoof.**

Did you hear about the band that got a call to do a gig at a fire station? When they got there, they found it was a hoax.

Rap is like scissors. It always loses to rock.

I'm in a heavy metal band. I play lead.

If Jimmy cracks corn and no one cares, why is there a song about him?

Back in the sixties and seventies, Mick Jagger was always undergoing paternity tests. But it was like getting blood out of a Stone.

Meat Loaf: a man who can light up a room just by moving away from the window.

What does James Last say when he walks into an elevator?
"This place rocks!"

I bought Bonnie Tyler's old car last year on eBay. It's terrible. Every now and then it falls apart.

I was listening to the radio the other day and I thought: Why do all these old bands keep copying *Glee* songs?

My friend and I wear toupees in our George Michael and Andrew Ridgeley tribute band. We're called Wig Wham. ***Tony Cowards***

What does Björk do when she's feeling horny?
She watches pjorn.

I spent all day searching for a U2 track, but I still haven't found what I'm looking for.

The Eagles eventually left Hotel California when they realized the door said "PULL" rather than "PUSH". They never mention this in the song.

How do you make Lady Gaga cry?
Poker face.

What did the Christmas gift paper salesman shout outside the black music awards?
"50 Cents a rapper."

When I heard REM had split up, I fainted in the curry house. That's me in the korma . . .

A music lover is a man who, when told that Pamela Anderson sings in the bath, puts his ear to the keyhole.

Whoever said a cat scratching its claws down a blackboard was the worst sound ever had obviously never attended a karaoke night.

We now have rappers who used to be gangsters telling us not to download music because it's stealing.

I do backing vocals. It's me who says, "This vehicle is reversing."

Which band's first manager was a one-legged gingerbread man?
Limp Bizkit.

Did you hear about the man who could hear a Bee Gees song coming from his vegetable rack? It turned out to be chives talking.

Lady Gaga's lyrics are so obscure. Perhaps she has hidden a gender.

The Eurovision Song Contest is the Paralympics of music.

I don't like country music, but I don't like to denigrate those who do. And for those who like country music, denigrate means "put down".
Bob Newhart

What do you call a woman with two fannies?
N-Dubz.

I've just read a Velvet Underground biography. It's not brilliant, but it's a good loo read.

Why did they let the turkey join the rock band?
Because he had his own drumsticks.

LeAnn Rimes. No, it doesn't.

I just booked a Chinese Journey tribute act to sing at my dad's funeral. All together now: "Don't stop bereaving . . ."

When my girlfriend said she was leaving me because of my obsession with the Monkees, I thought she was joking. And then I saw her face . . .

U2's first album is being re-mastered without any guitars on it. It rather takes The Edge off it.

When The Edge was at school, he was a border.

Boy: "Can I go to a 50 Cent concert?"
Father: "Sure. Here's a dollar. Take your sister."

What sings, gnaws trees and drives girls wild?
Justin Beaver.

I got ripped off by ticket touts. I thought I'd bought tickets to see The Cure, but it turned out they were for Placebo instead.

Jedward: the reason why double-barrelled shotguns were invented.

MUSICAL INSTRUMENTS

What do you call someone who hangs around with musicians?
A drummer.

What do you call a drummer who doesn't have a girlfriend?
Homeless.

What's the difference between a drummer and a pigeon?
A pigeon is capable of leaving a deposit on a new Ferrari.

What's the difference between a drummer and a pizza?
A pizza can feed a family of four.

What do you give a drummer with a scratch card?
A coin to scratch it with.

How is a drum solo like a sneeze?
You can tell it's coming, but you can't do a thing about it.

How do you know if there's a drummer at your door?
The knocking always speeds up.

What's the difference between a drummer and Dr Scholl's footpads?
Dr Scholl's bucks up the feet.

What's the best way to confuse a drummer?
Put a sheet of music in front of him.

Mike: "How late does the band play?"
Marty: "About half a beat behind the drummer."

What do you say to a drummer with a pretty girl on his arm?
"Nice tattoo."

My doctor advised me to give up playing the drums. He lives in the flat below.

What's the definition of a successful drummer?
One whose girlfriend has got two jobs.

What's the difference between a drummer and a drum machine?
With a drum machine you only have to punch the information in once.

Why is a drum machine better than a drummer?
Because it can keep good time and won't sleep with your girlfriend.

What has three legs and a dick on top of it?
A drum stool.

Did you hear about the drummer who finished high school?
Me neither.

What's the last thing a drummer says in a band?
"Hey, guys, why don't we try one of my songs?"

You know you're a drummer if you spend an hour tuning your snare, even though no one can hear the difference.

You know you're a drummer if you play the drum part on a song and ask whether anyone recognizes it.

You know you're a drummer if you've ever dropped a stick while playing and not noticed.

You know you're a drummer if your style of dancing involves slapping your thighs and pounding your feet.

You know you're a drummer if your drum kit cost more than your car.

You know you're a drummer if you've ever tried playing another instrument with drumsticks.

You know you're a drummer if you've ever taken over 30 seconds to realize that the rest of the band has stopped playing.

Mike: "Why did you put your drums up for sale?"
Marty: "I saw my neighbour arriving home with a gun."

How can you tell if a bagpipe is out of tune?
Someone is blowing into it.

Why do bagpipers walk when they play?
They're trying to get away from the noise.

What's the definition of a gentleman?
Someone who knows how to play the bagpipes, but doesn't.

How is playing the bagpipes like throwing a javelin blindfolded?
You don't have to be very good to get people's attention.

What's the difference between a set of bagpipes and a Harley-Davidson?
You can tune a Harley.

I thought learning to play the bagpipes was hard until I realized I was strangling an ostrich.

Why are accordionists' fingers like lightning?
They rarely strike the same spot twice.

What's the definition of an optimist?
An accordion player with a pager.

What's an accordion good for?
Learning how to fold a map.

What do you call an accordionist's girlfriend?
His latest squeeze.

What's a bassoon good for?
Kindling an accordion fire.

The accordion was invented by a man who couldn't decide how big the one that got away was.

What do you call an oboeist who is deaf?
Principal.

An oboe is an ill woodwind that nobody blows good.

What's the best way to tune a banjo?
With wirecutters.

What's the difference between a trumpeter and a hooker?
A hooker has a better sense of rhythm.

Why can't gorillas play the trumpet?
Gorillas are too sensitive.

Why was the modest member of the brass section fired?
Because he refused to blow his own trumpet.

How can you spot a trumpeter's kids at a playground?
They're the ones who don't know how to swing.

How can you spot a trombonist's kids at a playground?
They're the ones who don't know how to use the slide.

What kind of calendar does a trombonist use for his gigs?
Year-at-a-glance.

What's the difference between a dead trombonist lying in the road and a dead squirrel lying in the road?
The squirrel might have been on his way to a gig.

What's the least-used sentence in the English language?
"Is that the trombonist's Ferrari?"

How do you improve the aerodynamics of a trombonist's car?
Take the Domino's Pizza sign off the roof.

What do you get when you cross a French horn player with an ant?
An ant that can't march.

Why did God give French horn players one more brain cell than horses?
So they wouldn't shit during a parade.

How does a woman know when she's dating a French horn player?
When he kisses her, he has his hand up her backside.

Why is the French horn a divine instrument?
Because a man blows into it, but God knows what comes out of it!

What's the difference between a saxophone solo and a round of machine-gun fire?
The round of machine-gun fire only repeats itself 100 times a minute.

Why did the chicken cross the road?
To get away from the cello recital.

What's the difference between a cello and a chainsaw?
The grip.

What's the difference between a cellist and a dog?
A dog knows when to stop scratching.

How do you get two cellists to play in perfect unison?
Shoot one of them.

How can you tell if a cello is out of tune?
The bow is moving.

What's the latest crime wave in New York?
Drive-by cello recitals.

Why do cellists stand for long periods outside people's houses?
They can't find the key and they don't know when to come in.

What do a cello and a lawsuit have in common?
Everyone is happy when the case is closed.

Why do cellists leave their cases on the dashboard of their car?
So they can park in handicapped zones.

Why shouldn't cellists take up mountain climbing?
Because if they got lost, no one would search for them.

Why shouldn't you drive off a cliff in a Mini with three cellos in it?
You could fit in at least one more.

What's the difference between a vacuum cleaner and a viola?
A vacuum cleaner has to be plugged in before it sucks.

What's the difference between a viola and fingernails scraping on a blackboard?
Vibrato.

What's another name for viola auditions?
Scratch lottery.

Why should you never try to drive a roof nail with a viola?
You might bend the nail.

What's the range of a viola?
Thirty yards if you've got a good arm.

Viola players spend half the time tuning their instruments and the other half playing out of tune.

What's the definition of perfect pitch?
Throwing a viola into a dumpster without hitting the rim.

Why did people use to tremble with fear when a man came into a bank carrying a viola case?
They thought he was carrying a viola and might be about to use it.

Why do so many viola players date drummers?
It makes them feel superior.

How do you keep your violin from getting stolen?
Put it in a viola case.

What's the difference between a viola and a coffin?
The coffin has the dead person on the inside.

What's the difference between viola players and terrorists?
Terrorists have sympathizers.

What's the difference between a cello and a viola?
A cello burns longer.

What's the difference between a violin and a viola?
None. The violin just looks smaller because the violinist's head is bigger.

If a drummer and a viola player caught a cab, which one would be the musician?
The cab driver.

What's the best thing to play on a double bass?
Solitaire.

How do you make a double bass sound in tune?
Chop it up and turn it into a xylophone.

Why are harps like elderly parents?
Both are unforgiving, and hard to get in and out of cars.

Did you hear about the guitarist who was so bad, she couldn't even pluck her eyebrows.

Guitarist: "The drummer broke one of the strings in my guitar, and he won't tell me which one."

What do you get when you drop a piano down a mine shaft?
A flat miner.

Why was the piano invented?
So the musician would have a place to put his beer.

Mike: "The keys on your piano are yellow. It must be really old."
Marty: "No, the elephant was a heavy smoker."

Why is crossing the street like playing the piano?
C sharp or B flat.

Mother: "Where's your brother?"
Boy: "He's in the house playing a piano duet. I finished first."

If you drop an accordion, a set of bagpipes and a viola off the top of a 20-storey building, which one hits the ground first?
Who cares?

A man walks into a music store and says: "I'd like to buy that accordion over there for my band." The cashier says: "You must be a drummer. That's the radiator."

Show me a man who claims to be a medieval stringed instrument, and I'll show you a lyre.

I traded in my wife's piano for a clarinet. You can't sing while playing the clarinet.

A kettle drum and a pair of cymbals fell down a 200-foot cliff. B-boom! Tcchh!

NAMES

What do you call a woman with one leg?
Eileen

What do you call a woman who sets fire to her gas bill?
Bernadette

What do you call a woman draped across the centre of a tennis court?
Annette

What do you call a woman standing a long, long way in the distance?
Dot

What do you call a woman with a sunbed on her head?
Tanya

What do you call a woman with a police car on her head?
Nina

What do you call a woman trapped in a Chinese food processor?
Brenda

What do you call a woman who is tied up to a jetty?
Maud

What do you call a woman with a hairy top lip?
Tash

What do you call a guy at your front door with no arms and no legs?
Matt

What do you call a guy in a pile of leaves with no arms and no legs?
Russell

What do you call a guy waterskiing with no arms and no legs?
Skip

What do you call a guy stuffed in a mailbox with no arms and no legs?
Bill

What do you call a guy in a pot of boiling water with no arms and no legs?
Stu

What do you call a man with no arms and no legs who is hanging on your wall?
Art

What do you call his arms and legs?
Pieces of Art

What do you call a guy in a meat grinder with no arms and no legs?
Chuck

What do you call a guy who is a good swimmer but has no arms and no legs?
Bob

What do you call a guy whose legs are cut off at the knees?
Neil

What do you call a man with no shins?
Tony

What do you call a man with three eyes?
Seymour

What do you call a man with a pole through his leg?
Rodney

What do you call a man with a car on his head?
Jack

What do you call a man with a crane on his head?
Derek

What do you call a man with a spade on his head?
Doug

What do you call a man without a spade on his head?
Douglas

What do you call a man with a seagull on his head?
Cliff

What do you call two men hanging on either side of a window?
Curt and Rod

What do you call a guy who's feeling ill?
Paulie

What do you call a man with 60 rabbits up his butt?
Warren

What do you call a man with a three-inch penis?
Justin

What do you call a man with a lump of wood on his head?
Edward

What do you call a man with two lumps of wood on his head?
Edward Wood

What do you call a man with three lumps of wood on his head?
Edward Woodward

What do you call a man with four lumps of wood on his head?
I don't know, but Edward Woodward would.

NATIVE AMERICAN INDIANS

Why were the Indians the first people in America?
They had reservations.

What happened when the Native American Indian decided to return to his first wife?
It was back to squaw one.

I bought my wife a genuine Native American Indian washing machine – a rock.

Did you hear about the Native American Indian who drank 10 gallons of Darjeeling? He was found dead in his tea-pee.

What happened to Tonto when the Lone Ranger's horse trod on his hand?
He had his palm crossed with Silver.

Tourist: "Why is your wife called Five Horses?"
Indian chief: "Nag, nag, nag, nag, nag."

Why did the chief's car stop?
Injun trouble.

My grandfather was an old Indian fighter. My grandmother was an old Indian.

Squaw: "Those Cherokee smoke signals, what do they mean?"
Chief: "It is either a declaration of war, or their barbecue is out of control."

What did the Indian say when the white man tied his penis in a knot?
"How come?"

What's the American Indian word for "lousy hunter"?
Vegetarian.

A soldier cradled the dying General Custer in his arms at the Little Big Horn. Custer gasped: "I'll never understand Indians. A few minutes ago they were singing and dancing . . ."

I have a friend who is half-Indian: Ian.

NAVY

Why did the navy change from using bar soap to powder soap?
Because it takes longer to pick up.

How do you separate the men from the boys in the navy?
With a crowbar.

Why did the admiral decide not to buy a new hat?
He was afraid of cap sizing.

Did you hear about the man who joined the navy to see the world and spent five years in a submarine?

A guy in our unit could balance a ball on the end of his nose. I said: "Let me guess: you were in the Seals?"

Obesity is now such a problem in the navy that they've created a new rank: Really Big Rear Admiral.

Recruiting officer: "How would you feel about working on a submarine?"
Sailor: "Would I have to sleep with the windows closed?"

Did you hear about the hopeless naval captain? He grounds the warship he walks on.

NEIGHBOURS

My next-door neighbour started banging on my door last night, screaming about underwear going missing from her washing line. I tell you, I nearly shat her pants.

Last night the sex was so good, even the neighbours had a cigarette afterwards.

I come from a really tough neighbourhood. I once bought a waterbed and found a guy at the bottom of it. *Rodney Dangerfield*

Love thy neighbour, but make sure her husband is away first.

The nice thing about living in a small town is that when I don't know what I'm doing, someone else does.

My neighour is a nuisance. He keeps borrowing back everything I take from him.

Did you hear about the man who threw snow on his neighbour's driveway and yelled: "Now do you get my drift?"

I love my next-door neighbour's house. It's right up my street.

A pretty blonde moved in across the street, so I went over and returned a cup of sugar. She said: "You didn't borrow this." I said: "I will."

Neighbours are the only people who listen to both sides of an argument.

What's the best way to meet your neighbours?
Play loud music at two o'clock in the morning.

My neighbour is in *Guinness World Records* for having 43 concussions. He lives very close – just a stone's throw away. *Stewart Francis*

My neighbour had a penis extension. Now his house looks really silly.

NEW YORK

What should you do if you see a New Yorker jogging?
Trip him up and give the lady's purse back to her.

Often the first thing that strikes a visitor to New York is a taxi.

Remember, in New York it's bad manners to lie down inside someone else's chalk body outline.

When visiting New York, avoid paperwork for your next-of-kin by keeping your dental records on you.

What's the difference between Batman and a New Yorker?
Batman can go out without Robin.

What do New Yorkers put in their stockings at Christmas?
Their heads.

Did you hear about the New Yorker who went 65 days without food? He gave his order to the wrong waiter.

Why did the New Yorker sleep under his car?
He wanted to get up oily.

What do you call a New Yorker who never farts in public?
A private tutor.

The New York City Marathon is the only marathon in the world where the starter's gun gets return fire. ***David Letterman***

A tourist in New York stops a passer-by and says: "Excuse me, could you possibly tell me how to get to the Empire State Building, or should I go fuck myself again?"

You're a New Yorker if your door has more than three locks.

You're a New Yorker if you think being able to swear at people in their own language makes you multilingual.

You're a New Yorker if you envy cabbies for their driving skill.

You're a New Yorker if you get arthritis in your middle finger from over-use.

You're a New Yorker if you go to a hockey game for the fighting.

You're a New Yorker if you consider eye contact an overt act of aggression.

You're a New Yorker if the most frequently used part of your car is your horn.

Why did the New Yorker cross the road?
"What's it to you?!"

NEW ZEALAND

A New Zealand farmer is carrying a sheep under each arm. His mate asks: "You sheerin'?" "No way," says the farmer, "these two are all mine."

Why does New Zealand have some of the fastest racehorses in the world?
Because the horses have seen what the Kiwis do with their sheep.

Surely after all these years they can just call it Zealand now.

NEWSPAPERS AND MAGAZINES

Did you read about the ice cream store proprietor who was murdered? The local newspaper got two scoops: strawberry and vanilla.

I just read in the paper about a guy who goes around stealing coffee from the poor. I don't know how he sleeps at night.

Did you hear about the raisin who cheated on his wife? It was in the newspaper, in the currant affairs section.

I read a story: "Hundreds and Thousands to Join Strike Action". Chocolate flakes, crushed nuts and rainbow drops have yet to decide.

I read in the paper that a man was lucky to be alive after being hit by a train. I reckon I'm luckier: I've never been hit by a train.

The paper says: "Borrowers are still struggling to get on the first rung of the housing ladder." Surely that's because they're so tiny.

I used to be a freelance journalist but I wasn't very good. Lance is still in prison.

Did you hear about the group of journalists who formed a clothing-optional track club? Their motto was "All the Nudes That's Fit to Sprint".

I saw an article about peripheral vision . . . out of the corner of my eye.

A newspaper editor was captured by cannibals and eaten by their leader. He therefore became editor-in-chief.

I called the newspaper to place an ad, but I couldn't tell the lady about it because it was classified.

Did you hear about the magazine that hired a chiropractor to do a spinal column?

A man read a newspaper ad: "Dial Sexy, local rate calls." So he phoned, and a woman answered: "Good afternoon, Dyslexia help line."

NUDITY

A large hole was found in a fence surrounding a nudist colony. Police are looking into it.

Who is the most popular man at a nudist colony?
The one who can carry two cups of coffee and 12 ring doughnuts.

Who is the most popular woman at a nudist colony?
The one who can eat the last two doughnuts.

How do you find a blind man in a nudist colony?
It's not hard.

Never play strip poker with a nudist – they have nothing to lose.

Where does a nudist put his keys after he locks his car?

As I sit here naked in Robert Pattinson's hotel room, it occurs to me that I might have mixed up my bucket list with my wife's.

Streakers beware: your end is in sight.

A nudist camp is a place where the peeling is mutual.

The local naturists' club has introduced Dress Down Friday. Now on Fridays none of the women trim their bikini lines.

What was the name of the Spanish male nudist?
Señor Willy.

Did you hear about the man who was such a committed nudist that he wouldn't even put dressing on his salad?

Why did the nudist couple break up?
They had been seeing too much of each other.

I just received a text inviting me to the local nudist club. I thought: Why not? I haven't got anything on.

Nudists are like people who do amateur dramatics: those who are most enthusiastic are those who should do it least. *Jeremy Hardy*

My wife says she really hates it when our next-door neighbour sunbathes topless in the garden. Personally, I'm sitting on the fence.

Do nudists suffer from clothestrophobia?

What's the worst thing about being made police chief in a nudist colony?
Pinning on the badge.

Did you hear about the flasher who was thinking of retiring? He decided to stick it out for one more year.

If God had meant us to be naked, we would have been born that way.

What sign did they put up at the nudist camp?
"Sorry. Clothed For Winter".

What did the elephant say to the naked man?
"It's cute, but can it pick up peanuts?"

The police are still hunting for a man who terrorizes nudist camps with a bacon slicer. Inspector Wilkins had a tip off this morning, but hopes to be back on duty tomorrow.

I scared my postman today by coming to the door naked. I'm not sure what scared him more: me being nude or the fact I knew where he lived.

NUNS

What's the definition of innocence?
A nun working in a condom factory thinking she's making sleeping bags for mice.

What's the definition of suspicious?
A nun doing press-ups in a cucumber field.

What's the difference between a nun and a woman taking a shower?
The nun has hope in her soul.

What do you call a nun with a washing machine on her head?
Sistermatic.

What do you call a nun who's had a sex-change operation?
A transister.

A boy was on his first day at Catholic school. The nun asked him: "Do you know where little boys and girls go when they do bad things?" The boy said: "Probably behind the bike sheds."

How do you get rid of a nun's hiccups?
Tell her she's pregnant.

Are you allowed to kiss a nun?
Yes, but don't get into the habit.

What do you get when you cross an apple and a nun?
A computer that won't go down.

A nun goes into a shop and asks for 82 bananas. The shopkeeper says he could give her a discount if she ordered a box of 100. "OK," says the nun, "I suppose we could eat the other 18."

What do you call a sleepwalking nun?
A roamin' Catholic.

What do you call a nun in a wheelchair?
Virgin Mobile.

Nun: "There's a case of syphilis in the convent."
Mother Superior: "Good, I was getting tired of the Chardonnay."

How do you get a nun pregnant?
Dress her up as an altar boy.

Why do nuns have flat hair?
Force of habit.

OLD AGE

What does a 75-year-old woman have between her breasts that a 25-year-old woman doesn't?
Her navel.

Even at 83, my uncle is a three-times-a-night man. He really shouldn't drink so much tea before going to bed.

I don't know how I got over the hill without making it to the top.

When you get old, every doctor says the same thing. It's either something you have to live with or something you have to live without.

Nostalgia is heroin for old people. – *Dara O'Briain*

Why do nursing homes give Viagra to their male patients?
To stop them rolling out of bed.

I'm young at heart, but considerably older in other places.

Two old men were having an argument. One said: "I'm so angry, I'm taking you off my pallbearer list!"

Doctor: "The best thing for you to do at your age is give up sex and alcohol."
Old man: "I don't deserve the best. What's the next best?"

Did you hear about the old man who lost his glasses, and couldn't look for them until he'd found them?

Why shouldn't women over 60 have babies?
Because they'll put the baby down and forget where they've left it.

She's so decrepit that if she were a building, she'd be condemned.

An elderly female streaker runs past a bus stop. One old man says: "What was she wearing?" "I don't know," says another, "but whatever it is, it needs ironing."

When you get old, safe sex means not falling out of bed.

Do you realize that in about 40 years we'll have thousands of old ladies running around with tattoos?

An old man was sitting on his porch when a driver stopped to ask for directions. "How do you get into town?" he called out. The old man replied: "Usually my son takes me."

The best contraceptive for old people is nudity.

Having sex at 77 is still wonderful. It just gets more difficult to see who you are having it with.

Why are old people always doing puzzle books? Surely by the time you're in your seventies there's enough stuff that puzzles you without forking out a fiver. *Frankie Boyle*

When you get old, your wild oats turn into prunes and All Bran.

What happened when the old woman streaked through the flower show?
She won the prize for Best Dried Arrangement.

Her age is a millinery secret. She keeps it under her hat.

My granddad's 75 but he can still cut the mustard. He just needs help opening the jar.

Doctor: "You have acute angina."
Old lady: "Oh, doctor, you say the sweetest things."

My father said: "Everything's finally starting to click for me – my knees, my elbow, my neck."

Old man: "I think I'm getting senile. I keep forgetting to zip up."
Doctor: "That's not senility. Senility is when you forget to zip down."

My aunt is 86, but she doesn't need glasses. She drinks straight out of the bottle.

Did you hear about the sad case of the deaf old man who went to Bangkok to buy a La-Z-Boy?

It's easier to get older than it is to get wiser.

I did a gig at an old people's home. Tough crowd. They wouldn't respond to my knock-knock jokes until I showed ID. *Frank Skinner*

Old woman in church: "I've just done a silent fart. What do you think I should do?"
Husband: "Put a new battery in your hearing aid."

When I was a kid I could toast marshmallows over my birthday candles. Now I could roast a turkey.

My old uncle says arthritis is the cruellest disease: it makes all your joints stiff except the one you want.

Old man: "I feel just like a newborn baby – no hair, no teeth, and I think I just wet my pants."

My aunt's teeth are like stars – they come out at night.

Two old ladies are sitting in church. One whispers: "I think my butt is falling asleep." The other says: "I know. I've heard it snore three times already."

Doctor: "I need a urine, stool and semen sample from you."
Old man: "OK, doc, I'll just leave you my underpants."

The older a man gets, the farther he had to walk to school as a boy.

A flasher exposed himself to three old ladies. The first old lady had a stroke, the second old lady had a stroke, but the third old lady had arthritis and couldn't reach that far.

Two old ladies are discussing their dead husbands. One says: "Did you have mutual orgasms?" "No," says the other, "I think we were with the Prudential."

At age 71, my uncle said he was bisexual. He was saying 'bye to sex.

My grandfather keeps a record of everything he eats. It's called a tie.

I'm at the age where I want two women in bed. Then if I fall asleep, they'll have someone to talk to.

Why don't old ladies have Brazilians?
Don't know. It's a bit of a grey area.

Old age is when you have too much room in your house, but not enough room in your medicine cabinet.

Old age is when you stoop to pick something up and try to think of other things you can do while you're down there.

Old age is when almost everything hurts, and what doesn't hurt doesn't work.

Old age is when your favourite piece of software is a pillow.

Old age is when it takes you a couple of tries to get over a speed bump.

Old age is when it takes longer to rest than it did to get tired.

Old age is when your doctor no longer gives you an X-ray, he just holds you up to the light.

Old age is when you wake up with that "morning-after" feeling, and you didn't do anything the night before.

Old age is when by the time the last birthday cake candle is lit, the first candle has burnt out.

Old age is when you are cautioned to slow down by your doctor instead of the police.

Old age is when your friends compliment you on your new alligator shoes and you're not wearing any.

Old age is when you finally get your head together, but the rest of your body starts falling apart.

For old people, "happy hour" is a nap.

Visitor: "Have you lived here all your life?"
Old man: "I don't know. I haven't died yet."

I'm getting old. When I squeeze into a tight parking space, I'm sexually satisfied for the day. *Rodney Dangerfield*

Doctor: "Have you ever been bedridden?"
Old lady: "Yes, many times – and I've been taken over a kitchen worktop too."

You know you're old when your idea of "getting a little action" means not needing to take a laxative.

You know you're old when all of your favourite movies are re-released in colour.

You know you're old when conversations with people your own age often turn into "duelling ailments".

You know you're old when the little grey-haired old lady you help across the street is your wife.

You know you're old when you start picking your teeth out of the popcorn.

You know you're old when you sit in your rocking chair and can't get it going.

You know you're old when "getting lucky" means finding your car in the parking lot.

You know you're old when every time you suck in your gut, your ankles swell.

You know you're old when your reclining chair has more gadgets than your car.

You know you're old when you can't tell the difference between a heart attack and an orgasm.

Old people use a lot more four-letter words, like "what?" and "when?"

What's six feet long and smells of urine?
A line dance at a nursing home.

You don't know real embarrassment until your hip sets off a metal detector.

What does it mean when an old man always calls his wife "honey"?
That he forgot her real name years ago.

Regular naps prevent old age, especially if you take them while driving.

Did you hear about the old man whose forehead was so wrinkled he could screw his hat on?

Reporter: "What's the best thing about being 106?"
Old woman: "No peer pressure."

It's good being 75 because in a hostage situation you are likely to be released first.

It's good being 75 because people no longer view you as a hypochondriac.

It's good being 75 because things you buy now won't wear out.

It's good being 75 because there is nothing left to learn the hard way.

It's good being 75 because you can enjoy hearing about other people's operations.

It's good being 75 because you can eat dinner at 4 p.m.

It's good being 75 because your eyesight won't get much worse.

It's good being 75 because no one expects you to run anywhere.

It's good being 75 because your secrets are safe with your friends, since they can't remember them either.

Why did the old man take Viagra?
So that his dick would stick out far enough to stop him peeing on his slippers.

Did you hear about the old lady who entered a contest for most prominent veins? She didn't win, but she came varicose.

First old lady: "Did you come on the bus?"
Second old lady: "Yes, but I made it look like an asthma attack."

OPERA

What's the difference between a soprano and a Rottweiller?
Lipstick.

What's the difference between a soprano and a Porsche?
Most musicians have never been in a Porsche.

Did you hear about the soprano who sang in church last week? Afterwards 200 people changed their religion.

Why did the soprano break into song?
Because she couldn't find the key.

Did you hear about the soprano who performed to an audience of dwarfs? She got a standing ovation, but didn't know it.

What do you see if you look up a soprano's skirt?
A tenor.

I went to the opera once, but I didn't enjoy it. I couldn't even tell who won.

What's the definition of an opera?
Where a man gets stabbed and starts singing instead of bleeding.

I go to the opera whether I need the sleep or not.

Why was the soprano like a reluctant sailor?
She never hit the high C's.

What's the difference between an opera conductor and a baby?
A baby sucks its fingers.

Why do sopranos keep touring from city to city?
It keeps assassins guessing.

OPINIONS

A smart wife will always ask her husband's opinion – after she has made up her mind.

If I want your opinion, I'll ask you to fill out the necessary forms.

Wife to husband: "When I want your opinion, I'll give it to you!"

When I want your opinion, I'll remove the duct tape.

My opinions are my wife's, and she says I'm lucky to have them.

OPTOMETRISTS

What did the Asian optometrist call his shop?
Asif Eyecare.

Optometrist: "Have your eyes ever been checked?"
Patient: "Never. They've always been blue."

Optometrist: "You need glasses."
Patient: "But I'm wearing glasses."
Optometrist: "Then I need glasses."

What do optometrists listen to?
iTunes.

A Polish man goes to the optometrist who shows him the eye chart with the letters P V O W K S C Z Y. The optometrist says: "Can you read it?"
The Pole says: "Read it!? I know him!"

How do we know optometrists live long?
Because they dilate.

Mike: "Guess who I bumped into today at the optometrists."
Marty: "Everyone?"

My eyesight is so bad I have to wear contact lenses just to find my glasses.

Have you heard about the new Viagra eye drops? Your vision will be wrecked, but at least you'll look hard.

What did the lens say to the policeman?
"I've been framed, officer."

I thought I saw an eye doctor on an Alaskan island, but it turned out to be an optical Aleutian.

Optometrist: "Read the bottom line."
Patient: "Copyright 2007. Made in China."

I hate wearing glasses, but I need them to drive. So I got a prescription windshield.

Why should you never listen to an optometrist's jokes?
They get cornea and cornea.

Sign at an optometrist's: "If you don't see what you're looking for, you've come to the right place."

Patient: "How do you know I need new glasses before you've even examined my eyes?"
Optometrist: "I could tell as soon as you first walked in through the window."

Wouldn't it be ironic if everyone went blind in the year 2020?

PARENTS

I read somewhere that 26 is too old to still live with your parents. It was on a note, in my room.

My parents stayed together for 40 years, but that was out of spite.

My father ran the marathon but my mother competed in the 100 metres. It's tough growing up with mixed-race parents.

I'm sure wherever my dad is, he's looking down on me. He's not dead, just very condescending. *Jack Whitehall*

I said to my parents: "Mum, Dad, I've decided to live on my own from now on." "That's OK," they said. "Your luggage is outside," I added.

My dad didn't like me much. He only took me fishing once. I remember swimming back to shore and thinking . . .

My father used to ground me – and then run electricity through me.

I've just tracked down my biological father, who walked out on my mother when I was 10, and given him what he deserves – 34 years of Father's Day presents.

Alcohol was my father's answer to everything. He didn't drink; he was just lousy at quizzes.

My dad accidentally gave me soapflakes instead of cornflakes for breakfast. I wasn't just mad, I was foaming at the mouth!

My dad only hit me once. It was with a Land Rover.

My dad wore the trousers in our family – at least, after the court order.

My father brought me up single-handedly. It's not easy being the son of a pirate.

My parents came up for the weekend. I keep them in the cellar. **Milton Jones**

My parents are in the iron-and-steel business. My mother irons and my father steals.

Son: "Where are the Himalayas, Dad?"
Father: "If you put things away, you'd know where to find them."

My father has looked down on me ever since he became a stilt walker.

Boy: "You messed up my childhood!"
Father: "How could I? I wasn't even there!"

I was proud that my dad made a name for himself, although the police called it identity fraud.

A scoutmaster was surprised to see a young boy arrive for summer camp with an umbrella. "Why the umbrella?" he asked. The boy said: "Didn't you ever have a mother?"

My mother was a travel agent for guilt trips.

My mother hated me. Once she took me to an orphanage and told me to mingle. **Joan Rivers**

Son: "Can I go outside and watch the solar eclipse?"
Mother: "OK, but don't stand too close."

She took after her mother who took after her father who took after the nanny.

I came home and found my mother slumped in her chair with needles in her arms. She often falls asleep while she's knitting.

My mother was a cultivated woman. She was born in a greenhouse.

We have a beautiful little girl we named after my mom. In fact, Passive Aggressive Psycho turns five tomorrow. *Stewart Francis*

My mother always believed that labelling children was wrong, which caused chaos in the maternity ward.

When I left home, my mother said: "Don't forget to write." I thought, That's unlikely. After all, it's a fairly basic skill.

PARTIES

Did you hear about the boy and girl who went to a fancy-dress party as a barcode? They were clearly an item.

I went to a seafood disco party last week and pulled a mussel.

What did Samuel Morse say when he was invited to a party?
"I'll be there on the dot. Can't stop now, must dash."

I went to a postman's birthday party last week. We played "pass the 'sorry you weren't in' note".

How do you know when you're at a bulimic stag party?
The cake jumps out of the girl.

Why don't skeletons like parties?
They have no body to dance with.

My wife's not happy. I took her to a party at the weekend, but I didn't tell her it was a swingers party. And she hates Glenn Miller!

A man gave his girlfriend a piggy back to a fancy dress party. "What have you come as?" asked the host. The man replied: "I'm a turtle and this is Michelle."

I didn't want to go to the 1980s music-themed party, but my friend was adamant.

I approve of America's two-party system – one on Friday night and one on Saturday night.

Going to a party with your wife is like going fishing with a game warden.

On my way to a Harry Potter fancy-dress party, I saw some broomsticks in a shop. "How much are they?" I asked. The shopkeeper said: "They're a Quidditch."

I saw an eighties party advertised, so I went as Boy George, only to find that everyone else there was over 80.

Did you hear about the man who went to a fancy-dress party wearing an early-nineteenth-century French military uniform and carrying a fake grenade? He was Napoleon Blownapart.

I went to a fancy-dress party as an oven, but when I got there my friend was also dressed as an oven. He said: "I thought you were coming as a parrot." "No, I said I'm going as a cooker, too."

Last week, I went to a really awkward party in an igloo. I tried to break the ice, but that only made things worse.

Why did the guy bring toilet paper to the party?
He was a party pooper.

At this year's office party my aim is to get so drunk that people will finally stop talking about how drunk I got last year.

21 per cent of people cheat at their office Christmas party. I'm ashamed to admit I also cheated at mine: I sat down before the music stopped.
Jimmy Carr

A man who wore only a pair of Y-fronts to a fancy-dress party explained that he was a premature ejaculation. "What do you mean?" asked the hostess. He said: "I've come in my pants."

I met this girl at a party. She said people called her Vivaldi. I asked: "Is that because you're a brilliant violinist?" She said: "No, it's because my name's Viv and I work on the checkout at Aldi."

Do arsonists have housewarming parties?

At every party there are two kinds of people: those who want to go home and those who don't. The trouble is, they're usually married to each other.

How can you tell when a girl has been to a boring party?
She comes home with the same amount of lipstick she went out with.

Did you hear about the old woman with varicose veins who went to a fancy-dress party as a road map?

Who did the mortician invite to his party?
Anyone he could dig up.

I hate being the only drunk person at a party. It totally ruined my son's fifth birthday.

You know it's been a good office party when your P45 arrives at your house before you do.

Neighbour: "Did you hear me pounding on the wall last night?"
Party host: "Don't worry about it. We were making a fair bit of noise ourselves."

How can a man tell if he's had a good time at a party?
By the look on his wife's face.

Did you hear about the guy who went to a fancy-dress party as nitrogen?
He was in his element.

I went to a bulimia party. The place was heaving.

PENS AND PENCILS

If number 2 pencils are the most popular, why are they still number 2?

What did the pencil sharpener say to the pencil?
Stop going around in circles and get to the point.

I bought a $7 pen because I always lose pens and I got sick of not caring. **Mitch Hedberg**

The inventor of cats' eyes got the idea when his car headlights reflected in the eyes of an oncoming cat. If the cat had been walking away, he would have invented the pencil sharpener.

I was going to design a pencil with erasers at both ends, but then I thought: 'What would be the point?'

Highlighter pens are the future. Mark my words.

I've decided to marry a pencil. I can't wait to introduce my parents to my bride, 2B.

PERSONALITY

Some people say I'm superficial, but that's just on the surface.

Somebody called me pretentious the other day. I nearly choked on my latte.

Pretentious? *Moi*?

I've gone to find myself. If I should return before I get back, keep me here.

Why be difficult when, with a bit of effort, you can be impossible?

I tried to embrace my feminine side, but it put a restraining order on me.

I'm the kind of guy who doesn't take orders from anyone, which is probably why I lost my job as a waiter.

I used to be indecisive, but now I'm not so sure.

He's not the worst person in the world, but until a worse one comes along, he'll do.

I must be useful, because last night a girl called me a tool.

Charm is that indefinable something possessed by women with stunning figures.

I hate having to explain myself. Don't ask me why.

I'm an apathetic sociopath – I'd kill you if I cared.

My friends say I'm too easy to please. I was delighted when they told me.

I'm not weird. I'm a limited edition.

I wear my heart on my sleeve . . . ever since the botched transplant.

They broke the mould when they made him, but some of it grew back.

My wife says I'm too impulsive, but what the hell does she know? She only met me yesterday.

I'll tell you who's famous for his foibles: Aesop.

You may have a heart of gold, but so does a hard-boiled egg.

I'm humble, and proud of it.

She's such a social climber, she wore crampons to a cocktail party.

I often get into trouble because I misplace things – like the last time I was in a bar I got a black eye because I misplaced my hand on a girl's knee.

They told me I was gullible, and I believed them.

Becoming aware of my character defects leads me to the next step – blaming my parents.

You have a striking personality. How long has it been on strike?

I am in touch with reality, but it's a bad connection.

He's a balanced kind of guy – a chip on each shoulder.

Mike: "The trouble with you is you're your own worst enemy."
Marty: "Not while my wife's alive I'm not."

As I said before, I never repeat myself.

He's neither right-handed nor left-handed, just under-handed.

I do have initiative; I just need to be told when to use it.

I'm not anti-social. I'm just not user-friendly.

You know what really floats my boat? Water.

My mate from the pub said I was posh. Naturally I ordered the butler to show him the door.

I've told you a million times, I never exaggerate.

I'm not a competitive person. I'll be the first to admit it. **Stewart Francis**

I laugh in the face of danger, except if I'm involved.

I've been told that I'm a great listener . . . by many large-breasted women.

I don't have an attitude: I have a personality you can't handle.

Did you hear about the man who took everything with a pinch of salt? Now he has hypertension.

I don't follow tradition – and neither did my father nor his father before him.

I tried to get in touch with my inner child, but he's not allowed to talk to strangers.

A positive attitude may not solve all your problems, but it will annoy enough people to make it worth the effort.

I'm a kleptomaniac, but I'm taking something for it.

I've been doing a lot of soul searching lately. James Brown's name seems to come up a lot.

Integrity is everything. I'll sell you mine for fifty bucks.

PESSIMISM

I was born to be a pessimist. My blood type is B Negative.

Remember, when one door closes, another slams in your face.

I went to the annual meeting of the Society of Pessimists. It was very disappointing. The room was half-empty.

I've always been unlucky. I had a rocking horse once and it died.
Tommy Cooper

I wouldn't say I'm unlucky, but opportunity only knocked on my door to complain about the noise.

I'm so unlucky. Recently I bought a non-stick pan, and I can't get the label off.

A lot of guys have lucky pants. I have unlucky pants.

Every morning is the dawn of a new error.

Welcome to Shit Creek. Sorry, we're out of paddles.

Last week I forgot how to ride a bicycle.

With my luck, when my ship comes in, I'll probably be at the airport.

When you're finally holding all the cards, why does everyone decide to play chess?

I'm such a pessimist, my problem is not that the glass is half-empty, it's that somebody stole the glass.

Have you heard about the pessimists' Advent calendar? When one door opens, another one closes.

I want to join the Pessimists' Club, but they probably won't accept me.

Into every life some rain must fall – usually when your car roof is down.

If I had a pound for every time someone called me a pessimist, I still probably wouldn't be able to afford anything worthwhile.

Always borrow money from pessimists – they don't expect it back.

I got home and there was a note on my door. It said: "Knocked. You weren't in. – Opportunity."

PETS

I just made my hamster a strong coffee – I don't want him falling asleep at the wheel.

Did you hear about the gardener who mashed his daughter's pet hamster because he had heard that you could get tulips from hamster jam?

What's the difference between a hamster and a cow?
Hamsters rarely survive the branding.

What has four legs and flies?
A dead hamster.

How do you make a hamster drink?
Put it in a blender.

A man walks into a pet shop and asks to buy a wasp. The shopkeeper says: "We don't sell wasps." The man says: "But there's one in the window."

Where did Quasimodo keep his pet rabbit?
In a hutch, back of Notre Dame.

I went into a pet shop to buy a goldfish. The sales clerk said: "Do you want an aquarium?" I said: "I don't care what star sign it is."

What pet can you wear on your face to keep cool?
A chinchilla.

For sale: Dead canary. Not going cheap.

Sign in a pet shop window: Free legless parrot. No perches necessary.

My budgie broke his leg so I made him a little splint out of two matchsticks. His face lit up when he tried to walk . . . mainly because I'd forgotten to remove the sandpaper from the bottom of his cage.

What always succeeds?
A budgie with no teeth.

I went back to my local pet shop and said: "I want my money back for this budgie sunbed." The guy said: "That's a toasted-sandwich maker."

Did you hear about the girl who kissed her canary and caught chirpes? Her doctor told her it was untweetable.

My daughter won first prize in an unusual-pet contest. She entered a tin of sardines.

What do you call a parrot wearing a raincoat?
Polyunsaturated.

Two parrots sitting on a perch. One says to the other: "Can you smell fish?"

When your parrot sees you reading a newspaper, does he wonder why you're sitting there staring at carpeting?

What should you do if your parakeet has a temperature of 112 degrees? **Baste him.**

I rang the vet to complain about his excessive fees. He just put the phone down . . . as quickly and humanely as possible.

PICK-UP LINES

"Is this seat empty?"
"Yes, and this one will be, too, if you sit down."

"What do you think of my dancing?"
"Are you trying to get fit or are you having one?"

"Can I have the last dance?"
"You've just had it."

"How about a drink?"
"I like your approach. Now let's see your departure."

"Your place or mine?"
"Both. You're going to yours, and I'm going to mine."

"So what's your sign?"
"No Entry."

"Whisper those three little words that would make my night."
"Go to hell!"

"I wish they'd turn the lights down."
"So do I. I can still see you."

"Do you mind if I smoke?"
"I don't care if you burn."

"I'm a photographer; I've been looking for a face like yours."
"I design gargoyles; I've been looking for a face like yours."

"I know how to please a woman."
"Well, please leave me alone."

"How about a date?"
"Sorry, I don't date outside my species."

"What do I have to give you to be able to kiss you?"
"Chloroform."

"Haven't I seen you some place before?"
"Yes, that's why I don't go there any more."

"How did you get to be so beautiful?"
"I must have been given your share."

"Will you go out with me on Saturday?"
"Sorry, I'm having a headache this weekend."

"I'd go to the end of the world for you."
"Yes, but would you stay there?"

"Come out with me. Lower your standards a little."
"I did, and the answer's still no."

"Didn't we go on a date once? Or was it twice?"
"It must have been once; I never make the same mistake twice."

"Let's go someplace else."
"I'm busy right now. Can I ignore you some other time?"

"Am I the first man you've ever slept with?"
"Of course. Why do all you men ask such silly questions?"

"Nice legs. When do they open?"
"Nice mouth. When does it shut?"

"If I could see you naked, I'd die happy."
"If I could see you naked, I'd die laughing."

"You're one in a million."
"And that just about sums up your chances."

"So how do you like your eggs in the morning?"
"Unfertilized."

"I'd really like to get into your pants."
"No, thanks, there's already one asshole in there."

"I've got some condoms, so I think we should sleep together tonight."
"What's the hurry? Are they near their expiry date?"

"I could really light your fire."
"Not with that little match you couldn't."

"Don't go thinking about me while I'm gone."
"I wasn't thinking about you while you were here."

"What would you say if I asked you to marry me?"
"Nothing. I can't talk and laugh at the same time."

"I promise I'll write."
"Are you allowed to use sharp objects where you stay?"

"When can I see you again?"
"How about never?"

Bad pick-up line: "You remind me of my dead ex-girlfriend."

Bad pick-up line: "Can I buy you a drink or do you just want the money?"

Bad pick-up line: "If you were a booger, I'd pick you first."

PINOCCHIO

When did Pinocchio first realize he was made of wood?
The day his hand caught fire.

Where is Pinocchio's website?
On the splinternet.

What did Raggedy Ann say to Pinocchio as she was sitting on his face?
"Tell the truth! Tell a lie! Tell the truth! Tell a lie!"

PLASTIC SURGERY

When it comes to plastic surgery, a lot of people turn their noses up.
Tim Vine

I was sacked from my job as a plastic surgeon for using helium instead of silicone. It all went tits up.

She's had so many facelifts, she pees through her ears.

My girlfriend had a face lift, a tummy lift, and a buttock lift. Now she's nearly two feet off the ground.

I couldn't afford plastic surgery, so I just paid a few dollars for the doctor to touch up my X-rays.

I gave my wife plastic surgery – I cut up her credit cards.

Why do plastic surgeons always look tired?
Because they've been grafting all day.

Before plastic surgery she used to look her age; now she doesn't even look her species.

I need cheering up. I lent my friend $8,000 for plastic surgery. Now I don't know what he looks like. *Emo Philips*

Does anyone have any tips on how to reverse plastic surgery? I'm all ears.

People in Los Angeles don't get older, they just get tighter.

Never go to a plastic surgeon whose favourite artist is Picasso.

Patient: "Will it hurt?"
Plastic surgeon: "Only when you get my bill."

A plastic surgeon's office is the only place where you can pick your nose in public.

Doctor: "You'll be another man after these cosmetic procedures."
Patient: "Great, doc, and don't forget to send your bill to the other man."

What is liposuction?
Letting the fat out of the bag.

What did the woman say to the doctor after undergoing plastic surgery?
"So long, and thanks for the mammaries."

Most people who have plastic surgery are disappointed with the results, although they always look pleasantly surprised. *Jimmy Carr*

Did you hear about the careless plastic surgeon? He stood in front of a fire and melted.

When two plastic surgeons opened for business in the same street there were a few raised eyebrows.

Did you hear about the woman who had her face lifted so often that every time she crossed her legs her mouth snapped shut?

PMS

There's no need for women to behave the way they do on their period. It's an ovary action.

If men had periods, they'd boast about the size of their tampons.

Have you heard about the new Greek tampon called Abzorba the Leak?

What's the difference between PMS and BSE?
One attacks the poor cow's brain and sends it mental; the other is an agricultural problem.

What do you get when you cross PMS with GPS?
A crazy bitch who will find you!

Why should you never trust a woman?
How can you trust something that bleeds for a week and doesn't die?

How can you tell which bottle contains the PMS medicine?
It's the one with the teeth marks.

OK, so maybe "Who lit the fuse on your tampon?" wasn't the most sensitive thing to say.

Have you heard about the new line of Tampax with bells and tinsel? It's for the Christmas period.

What's the best thing about fingering a gypsy when she's on her period?
You get your palm red for free.

POEMS

Roses are red, violets are blue; sugar is sweet, but revenge is, too.

Roses are red, violets are blue; if I had your face, I'd be in a zoo.

My darling, my lover, my beautiful wife; marrying you screwed up my life.

Love may be beautiful, love may be bliss; but I only slept with you because I was pissed.

I thought that I could love no other; until, that is, I met your brother.

At beautiful places I only see you; because your fat butt is blocking the view.

They say true lovers need time apart; today could be a good day to start.

My feelings for you no words can tell; except for maybe "Go to Hell!"

I felt the earth move beneath my feet; perhaps you should have less to eat.

Calvin Klein, Dior, Chanel; and still you can't disguise the smell.

There's nothing I wouldn't do for you; that I haven't done for your teammates, too.

I see your face when I am dreaming; that's why I always wake up screaming.

Kind, intelligent, loving and hot; that describes everything you're not.

I want to feel your sweet embrace; but keep that paper bag on your face.

My love for you is everlasting; is your sister still single – I'm only asking?

What inspired this amorous rhyme? Two parts vodka, one part lime.

Hickory dickory dock, three mice ran up the clock. The clock struck one, but the other two escaped with minor injuries.

Roses are red, violets are red, the weather forecast is red. My TV needs fixing.

POLICE

I got pulled over by the police last night. They asked me where I was between 6 and 11. I told them I was in junior school.

I've just moved into a new flat directly over a police station. It would appear that I am above the law.

A traffic cop barked: "Pull over!" I said: "No, it's a cardigan, but thanks for noticing."

A fellow walked up to me and said: "You see a cop around here?" I said: "No." He said: "Stick 'em up!" *Henny Youngman*

Police chief: "Why are you putting handcuffs on that building?"
Rookie cop: "I'm making a house arrest."

Did you hear about the man who went around beating people up for no reason? He was charged with impersonating a police officer.

Police have arrested a man for selling pills that promise eternal life. Records show that it was the fourth time he has been arrested. The previous arrests were in 1765, 1849 and 1937.

Female cop: "Sir, you have the right to remain silent. Anything you say will be held against you."
Suspect: "Breasts."

Did you hear about the guy who was picked up for stealing human hearts from a morgue? It was a cardiac arrest.

Cop: "Are you going to come quietly or do I have to use earplugs?"

Police informant: "I think I know who threw that Scrabble set into the road?"
Cop: "OK. What's the word on the street?"

Man: "Why do you want me to accompany you to the station, officer?"
Policeman: "Because I'm scared of the dark."

If you're being chased by a police dog, try not to go through a tunnel, then on to a little seesaw, then jump through a hoop of fire. They're trained for that. *Milton Jones*

Police were called to the World Gurning Championships at the weekend after things started to turn ugly.

Why did the policeman stay in bed all day?
He was an undercover officer.

Mike: "It says in the paper that the police are looking for a bank robber with one eye."
Marty: "Why don't they use two?"

How can you spot a police glow worm?
It has a flashing light.

The Keystone Kops were frequently criticized for excessive use of farce.

Did you hear about the rookie cop who handed out 44 parking tickets before he realized he was at a drive-in movie?

My "take no prisoners" attitude is starting to irritate my superiors at the police station.

A cop pulled me over today and said: "Papers." So I said: "Scissors. I win!"

How do police handcuff a one-armed man?

I travelled home last night by pogo stick, but got stopped by the police for jumping a red light. *Tony Cowards*

Thieves broke into a police station and stole all the toilets. Police say they have nothing to go on.

Why did the policeman get ratty?
Because Moley forgot to lock the front door.

Did you hear about the Los Angeles cop who found a stolen car on Sunset Boulevard? He pushed it on to Vine Street because he couldn't spell "Boulevard".

I got cautioned by the police for taking a dip in my local swimming pool. Apparently you're not allowed hummus in the water.

On what charge did the cop book a driver who had swerved to avoid tin tacks that had fallen from a truck?
Tacks evasion.

Did you hear about the police informant named Maurice? He was known as Mo the grass.

How many police officers does it take to break an egg?
None, "it fell down the stairs."

What was the address of the new police station?
Letsby Avenue.

A policeman stopped me the other night. He said: "Would you blow into this bag, sir?" I said: "What for?" He said: "My chips are too hot." *Tommy Cooper*

Did you hear about the detective who thought he'd found the mass grave of 1,000 snowmen? It turned out to be a carrot field.

Officers in Chicago say they want to interview a man wearing high heels and lacy knickers, but the chief says they must wear their normal uniforms.

My horoscope said: "You're going places and can't be stopped." Unfortunately the officer who gave me a ticket obviously hadn't read it.

A Las Vegas MC was arrested by police. Brandishing the cuffs, the cop snarled: "Put your hands together." The MC said instinctively: "For Mr Neil Diamond."

Police officer: "Do you think I should put on the cuffs?"
Criminal: "No, you look good in short sleeves."

I listen to the police band on my radio. Once I dialled 911 and dedicated a crime to my girlfriend.

Did you hear about the mime artist who was arrested? Officers told him he had the right to remain silent.

I always used to think my granddad was a police frogman, but it turns out he was just a French policeman. *Milton Jones*

Police officer: "I'm arresting you for trespassing."
Man: "On what grounds?"

No matter how much you may fancy him, it's never advisable to go up to a police marksman and say: "Will you take me out?"

How do you join the police?
Handcuff them together.

POLISH PEOPLE

How can you tell a Polish firing squad?
It stands in a circle.

How can you tell which is the groom at a Polish wedding?
He's the one with the clean bowling shirt.

Did you hear about the Polish helicopter crash?
The pilot got cold, so he turned off the fan.

Why did the Polish guy fall out of the window?
He was ironing the curtain.

Did you hear about the Polish guy who got an old-style camera for his birthday?
He just got back his first roll of film, 24 shots of his right eye.

I went to Poland once. It was the worst of the Teletubby-themed amusement parks.

Did you hear about the Polish guy who thought his wife was trying to kill him? On her dressing table he had found a bottle of Polish Remover.

Why do so many Polish names end in "ski"?
Because they can't spell "toboggan".

A Polish man had his vasectomy done at Sears. Now when he makes love, the garage door goes up.

Did you hear about the Pole whose wife gave birth to twins? He demanded to know who the other man was.

What's delaying the Polish space programme?
The development of a working match.

How did the Polish guy burn his face at Hallowe'en?
He went bobbing for French fries.

What does the bride of a Polish man get that's long and hard on her wedding night?
His surname.

Why did the Polish truck driver go on vacation to England?
So he could get the other arm suntanned.

Did you hear about the Polish guy who locked his keys in the car? It took an hour to get his wife out.

How do you spot the Polish guy at the car wash?
He's the one on the bike.

Poland just bought 10,000 septic tanks. As soon as they learn how to drive them, they're going to invade Russia.

Doctor: "Have you had a check up recently?"
Polish woman: "No, just a couple of Hungarians and an Estonian."

Did you hear about the Polish attempt on Mount Everest? They ran out of scaffolding.

What sign is at the bottom of Polish swimming pools?
No Smoking.

POLITICAL CORRECTNESS

Suggs is marching against racism and homophobia – it's just Madness gone politically correct.

Being politically correct means always having to say you're sorry.

When a man talks dirty to a woman, it's sexual harassment. When a woman talks dirty to a man, it's $3.95 a minute.

I don't buy fat-free milk, because I don't want to encourage cows with negative body image issues.

I am not stupid; I suffer from minimal cranial development.

I am not lazy; I am energetically declined.

I am not clumsy; I am uniquely coordinated.

I am not a psychopath; I am socially misaligned.

I do not hog the blankets; I am thermally unappreciative.

I do not eat like a pig; I suffer from reverse bulimia.

I do not have a beer belly; I have developed a liquid grain storage facility.

I am not going bald; I am in follicle regression.

I do not have body odour; I have non-discretionary fragrance.

I am not weird; I am behaviourally different.

I am not old; I am chronologically gifted.

I am not late; I have a rescheduled arrival time.

I am not ignorant; I am factually unencumbered.

I am not overweight; I am gravity-enhanced.

I am not a bad dancer; I am overly Caucasian.

I am not short; I am anatomically compact.

I am not a lousy cook; I am microwave-compatible.

I am not unemployed; I am involuntarily leisured.

I am not drunk; I am chemically inconvenienced.

I am not ugly; I am aesthetically challenged.

I am not a male chauvinist pig; I have swine empathy.

The Internet has become too politically correct. What's all this nonsense about disabled cookies? In my day they were broken biscuits.

POLITICS

How can you tell when a politician is lying?
His lips are moving.

What do you get when you ask a politician to tell "the truth, the whole truth and nothing but the truth"?
Three different answers.

The Prime Minster held a meeting with the cabinet today. He also spoke to the bookcase and argued with a chest of drawers. *Ronnie Barker*

Why don't politicians like golf?
Because it's too much like their work: trapped in one bad lie after another.

There are two sorts of politicians: those who can talk nonsense on any subject under the sun, and those who don't need a subject.

Car salesman: "The car is fitted with an airbag." Woman: "I don't need one – I'm married to a politician."

Politicians should serve two terms: one in office, one in prison.

Did you hear about the politician who had the ear of the Prime Minister? No? That's why the Prime Minister didn't hear about it either.

Why are politicians like gay men?
Neither will give you a straight answer.

Honesty in politics is much like oxygen. The higher up you go, the scarcer it becomes.

Politicians are like ships – noisiest when lost in a fog.

Barack Obama is a combination of Martin Luther King and Spock. *Robin Williams*

In a democracy, a man can choose his own form of government – blonde, brunette or redhead.

The more you see of today's politicians, the more you think Guy Fawkes was simply ahead of his time.

Politicians are people who divide their time between running for office and running for cover.

What do politicians and porn actors have in common?
Both are experts at switching positions in front of a camera.

When politicians get the flu, you never know which way they'll vote. Sometimes the eyes have it, and sometimes the nose.

Why do socialists drink herbal tea?
Because proper tea is theft.

When the best actors are chosen by other actors, it's called the Oscars. When the best actors are chosen by the people, it's called an election.

What happens when you give Viagra to a politician?
He gets taller.

Little girl: "Do all fairy tales begin with, 'Once upon a time . . .'?"
Father: "No, some begin with, 'If I am elected . . .' "

A politician has to be able to see both sides of an issue so he can get around it.

In democracy, it's your vote that counts; in feudalism, it's your count that votes.

Conservative Party spin doctor's motto: I'm gonna sell you a Tory.

Describing Tony Blair as a Middle East peace envoy is like asking a mosquito to find a cure for malaria. **Rory Bremner**

A politician is a man who stands for what he thinks the voters will fall for.

If the opposite of pro is con, does that make Congress the opposite of progress?

How long does a US congressman serve?
Until he gets caught.

Why did Al Gore get a nipple ring?
Because he heard that George W. Bush got a Dick Cheney.

How can you spot Al Gore in a bunch of Secret Service agents?
He's the stiff one.

George W. Bush went into Burger King and asked for two whoppers. The guy serving said: "You're an intellectual giant and were the best President we ever had."

How did Gordon Brown meet his wife?
He was out in a bar one night, sneezed, and she caught his eye.

There's a lot in the media about the brothers Ed and David Miliband, but you never hear much about their other siblings Steve and Glenn.

Why did David Cameron go to a candlelit restaurant with George Osborne?
Before tackling the economy, he said he needed a mandate.

Gaddafi. What an idiot! A dictator, and he only made himself colonel. A guy who put chicken in a bucket made it to colonel! **Rich Hall**

How do we know Colonel Gaddafi was a teddy boy?
He was found in drainpipes.

Why is it that political leaders don't seem to know the answers until they write their memoirs?

THE POPE

What happened to the Pope when he went to Mount Olive?
Popeye nearly killed him.

In a new book, the Pope exonerates the Jews for the death of Jesus. Well, not a moment too soon. He really nipped that one in the bud. *Jay Leno*

What's the difference between the Pope and your boss?
The Pope only expects you to kiss his ring.

I think the Pope could have made more of an effort on his latest tour. He wore the same clothes every day.

How does the Pope buy things online?
Via his PaPal account.

On Christmas Eve, why didn't the Pope feel the need to give an address?
Because everyone knows he lives in the Vatican.

What's black and white and tells the Pope to get lost?
A nun who's just won the lottery.

I read that the Pope loves cats. It said he's a Cataholic. *Milton Jones*

POVERTY

Being poor has its advantages. For example, your keys are never in your other trousers.

Just about the time when you think you can make ends meet, somebody moves the ends.

My wife and I used to work on a submarine, but it was tough keeping our heads above water.

I'd like to help the homeless but they're never home.

Beggar: "Lady, I haven't eaten a thing in four days."
Woman: "I wish I had your willpower."

What do you call a hobo with short legs?
A low-down bum.

No matter how much you give a homeless person for tea, you never get that tea. *Jimmy Carr*

When I was growing up, we were so poor we couldn't even afford to pay attention.

When I was a kid, we were so poor we couldn't afford summer holidays. My mother told me to watch the television if I was bored. Sometimes I was even allowed to switch it on.

We were so poor my parents couldn't afford to buy me a yo-yo for Christmas. All I got was a yo.

Beggar: "Any change?" Man: "No, still the same house and job, but thanks for asking."

The homeless problem would be solved if the *Big Issue* had naked women in it.

We were so poor, when I was ill I could only afford to have one measle at a time.

My parents could never afford to buy me shoes, so they painted my feet black and laced up my toes.

We're so poor that I had to get my wife to sell one of her kidneys to pay for Christmas. If things get any worse, I might have to cancel Sky Sports.

I'm having an out-of-money experience.

Maybe a good way of solving the world's problems is to get the hungry to eat the homeless.

As a kid I was made to walk the plank. We couldn't afford a dog. *Gary Delaney*

Beggar: "Do you have any loose change?"
Man: "No, it's good and secure, thanks."

I smashed open my piggy bank today . . . and found I had just enough money to buy a new piggy bank.

Wife: "How much money do we have in the bank?"
Husband: "I don't know. I haven't shaken it lately."

I wish the buck stopped here. I could use a few.

Beggar: "I haven't tasted food all week."
Man: "Don't worry, it still tastes the same."

I started out with nothing and I still have most of it left.

You know you're broke when American Express calls and says: "Leave home without it!"

You know you're broke when you clean your house in the hope that you'll find loose change.

You know you're broke when you give blood every day – just for the free cup of tea.

You know you're broke when you wash toilet paper.

You know you're broke when you're on a telemarketer blacklist of people not to call.

You know you're broke when you go to KFC to lick other people's fingers.

You know you're broke when at communion you go back for seconds.

Caravans are a fun way of telling your kids that you're poor. *Jimmy Carr*

PREGNANCY

What's the difference between a heavily pregnant woman and a supermodel?
Nothing, if the husband knows what's good for him.

Why did the pregnant woman eat rubber?
She wanted to have a bouncing baby.

A girl showed her boyfriend a pregnancy test she had taken. The result was positive. "Should we keep it?" he asked. "No point," she said. "You can only use them once."

Why do the wives of cab drivers rarely get pregnant?
Because cab drivers have a habit of pulling out unexpectedly.

Why did the woman in labour start shouting: "Shouldn't! Wouldn't! Couldn't!"?
She was having contractions.

I come from a small town whose population count never changes. Whenever a woman gets pregnant, a man leaves town.

Obstetrician: "Will the father be present during the birth?"
Pregnant woman: "No, he and my husband don't get along."

What's the difference between a pregnant woman and a light bulb?
You can unscrew a light bulb.

How did Burger King get Dairy Queen pregnant?
He forgot to wrap his whopper.

My best friend's girlfriend is six months pregnant. She asked me if I wanted to feel the baby. On reflection, I think she meant on the outside.
Jimmy Carr

Did you hear about the "morning after" pill for men? It changes your blood group.

Woman: "I'm two months pregnant. When will my baby move?"
Doctor: "With any luck, right after he finishes school."

A woman's most common craving during pregnancy is for the father to be pregnant.

A girl broom told a boy broom she was pregnant. "How can you be pregnant?" said the boy broom. "We haven't even swept together."

Why is a pregnant girlfriend like burnt toast?
In both cases the guy thinks: If only I'd taken it out sooner.

My girlfriend told me she was pregnant, but she didn't want anyone else to know. I said: "OK. Mum's the word."

The only time a woman wants to be a year older is when she is expecting a baby.

What do you do when your daughter is pregnant and claims she hasn't slept with anyone?
Start a religion.

Man: "I don't understand how my wife is pregnant – we haven't had sex for over a year."
Doctor: "It's what we call a grudge pregnancy – somebody's obviously had it in for you."

My girlfriend had a phantom pregnancy. Now we have a little baby ghost. *Jimmy Carr*

Wife: "I worry that now I'm pregnant and fat you won't fancy me any more, and you'll run off with someone young and slim. What's your biggest fear?"
Husband: "Snakes."

What two things in the air can make a woman pregnant?
Her legs.

PRISON

What happened when the short fortune-teller escaped from prison?
There was a small medium at large.

What do prisoners use to call each other?
Cell phones.

A man escapes from prison and cautiously makes his way home. "Where the hell have you been?" rages his wife. "You escaped six hours ago!"

Why are prison walls never built to scale?

Why was the sword swallower sent to prison?
He coughed and killed two people.

Under a new scheme, prisoners are repairing broken letters on shop signs. The government hopes it will deliver reformed characters.

My buddy is serving 20 years for something he didn't do. He didn't wipe his fingerprints off the gun.

A cop was escorting a prisoner to jail when his hat blew off. "Shall I run and get it for you?" asked the prisoner. "You must think I'm stupid," said the cop. "You stand here and I'll get it."

Prisoners complain behind bars; husbands complain in them.

Did you hear about the man who found prison to be character-building because it gave him the courage of his convictions?

I recently got a job in a prison brothel. It has its pros and cons.

Prison warden: "Break it up, you two! What's the fight about?"
Prisoner: "He called me a dirty number."

Solitary confinement: it's not for everyone.

An offender was fined $100 and told that if he was caught again, he would be thrown in jail. Fine today, cooler tomorrow.

A man facing the electric chair is asked by the prison chaplain if there is anything he can do for him in his dying moments. "Yes," says the prisoner, "you can hold my hand."

Why did the escaped convict saw the legs off his bed?
He wanted to lie low.

Did you hear about the warden who gave the prisoners acne cream in the hope that it would stop them breaking out?

PROCRASTINATION

My mother said: "You won't amount to anything because you procrastinate." I said: "Just you wait."

A procrastinator's work is never done.

Procrastination is the art of keeping up with yesterday.

Never put off till tomorrow what you can do today. It may be made illegal by then.

Never put off till tomorrow what you can forget about entirely.

I always wanted to be a procrastinator, but I never got around to it.

Today's greatest labour-saving device is tomorrow.

There is no time like the present for postponing what you ought to be doing.

Son: "What does 'procrastination' mean, Dad?"
Father: "I'll tell you later."

Procrastinators unite! . . . Tomorrow.

PSYCHIATRISTS

A woman walks into a psychiatrist's office leading a kangaroo. She says: "Doctor, I'm worried about my husband. He thinks he's a kangaroo."

What happens when a psychiatrist spends the night with a hooker?
In the morning each of them says: "That'll be $400 please."

Patient: "I keep acting like a yo-yo."
Psychiatrist: "Sit down . . . sit down . . . sit down . . ."

A psychiatrist is someone who finds you cracked and leaves you broke.

Psychiatrist: "So how long have you believed in reincarnation?"
Patient: "Ever since I was a puppy."

Why did Frankenstein's monster visit the psychiatrist?
He thought he had a screw loose.

I told my psychiatrist that nobody understands me. Now I have to pay him extra for an interpreter.

Did you hear about the man who thought he had turned into a can of deodorant? But he wasn't Sure.

My psychiatrist told me I was crazy, and I said I wanted a second opinion. So he said I was ugly, too.

Did you hear about the psychiatrist who used shock treatment? He gave you his bill in advance.

Two psychiatrists pass in the hall. The first says: "Hello." The second thinks: I wonder what he meant by that.

My psychiatrist helped me a lot. Before, I would never answer the phone because I was scared of it. Now I answer it whether it rings or not.

After 18 months of baring my soul in therapy sessions, something my psychiatrist said brought tears to my eyes. It was: *"No hablo Inglés."*

A man told a psychiatrist: "Doctor, I keep thinking I'm *Time* magazine." The psychiatrist said: "I can see you have a lot of issues."

For my birthday, my psychiatrist kindly sent me a basket of fruit. It was shrink-wrapped.

Did you hear about the mechanic who went to the psychiatrist? He lay down under the couch.

A man walks into a psychiatrist's with a fried egg on his head. The psychiatrist asks: "Why have you got a fried egg on your head?" The man says: "If it was boiled, it would roll off."

According to Freud, what comes between fear and sex?
Fünf.

Is a street on which several psychiatrists live called a mental block?

Psychiatrist: "Madam, why are you wearing a dress made of sponges?"
Patient: "I'm self-absorbed."

Therapy is expensive; popping bubble-wrap is cheap. You choose.

Patient: "I have this urge to paint myself gold. Why?"
Psychiatrist: "It sounds to me as if you have a gilt complex."

What did the psychiatrist tell the genie?
"Your emotions are all bottled up."

My psychiatrist can cure alcoholism. He charges so much, you can't afford a drink.

Did you hear about the guy who was diagnosed as psychoceramic? He was a crackpot.

Why didn't Cleopatra think she needed psychiatric help? Because she was the Queen of Denial.

I don't think I'm mentally ill. I just do what my Rice Krispies tell me.

How do crazy people go through the forest?
They take the psycho path.

It seems my psychiatrist didn't mean it when she told me to bare all.

My gay friend's visit to the psychiatrist was a waste of time. He spent the first 20 minutes rearranging the couch.

Why go to a psychiatrist when you can stay at home and talk to the ceiling for free?

My psychiatrist is great. He lumped all my nagging little worries into one big complex.

A man calls the psychiatrist at a mental hospital and asks who's in room 12. "Nobody," says the psychiatrist. "Good," says the man. "I must have escaped."

Occasionally I question my sanity; sometimes, worryingly, it replies.

What's the difference between the psychiatrists and the patients at a mental hospital?
The patients eventually get better and go home.

Patient: "Why did you charge me a group rate?"
Psychiatrist: "You've got multiple personalities."

How do you spot a psychiatrist in a nudist camp?
He's the one listening instead of looking.

Psychiatrist to patient: "I think your problem is low self-esteem. It's very common among total losers."

Why is Saudi Arabia free of mental illness?
There are nomad people there.

A man walks into a psychiatrist's wearing only shorts made from clingfilm. The psychiatrist says: "Well, I can clearly see you're nuts."

Psychiatrist: "So how long have you been under the illusion that you are a world-famous psychoanalyst?"
Patient: "It started when I was Jung . . ."

The voices in my head may not be real, but they have some good ideas.

The voices in my head are telling me to stop being delusional and to remember that I have earphones on.

Psychiatrist to nurse: "Just say we're very busy. Don't keep saying, 'It's a madhouse.'"

What did one behaviourist say to another after sex?
"That was wonderful for you. How was it for me?"

A man walks into a psychiatrist's office with a pancake on his head, fried eggs on each shoulder, and strips of bacon over his ears. He says: "Doc, I'm worried about my brother."

PSYCHICS

A psychic showed me the girl I was going to marry. It was love at second sight.

A man visited a psychic who told him that a lot of money would be coming his way. That afternoon he was hit by a Securicor truck.

Why was the psychics' convention cancelled?
Unforeseen circumstances.

If I had a crystal ball . . . I'd sit down really carefully.

A psychic tells a woman: "Your husband will soon meet a terrible, violent death." "One question," says the woman. "Will I be acquitted?"

Why do psychics always ask you for your name?

I almost had a psychic girlfriend but she left before we met. *Steven Wright*

Do people with psychic powers get nostalgic about next week?

Is there an expiry date on fortune cookie predictions?

It's tough to make predictions, especially about the future.

I'm a terrible psychic – I don't know about you.

REDHEADS

What's the difference between a ginger guy and a brick?
A brick will get laid.

What is every ginger's wish?
To go prematurely grey.

Why are the Harry Potter films unrealistic?
They show a ginger kid with two friends.

What do you call a good-looking guy with a redhead?
A hostage.

Why do ginger people get sunburnt easily?
It's nature's way of telling us they should be locked indoors.

Baldness: a second chance for gingers.

How do you get a redhead to argue with you?
Say something.

How do you know when you've satisfied a redhead?
She unties you.

What's the difference between a terrorist and a redhead?
You can negotiate with a terrorist.

What's safer, a redhead or a piranha?
A piranha: they only attack in groups.

What do redheads miss most about a great party?
The invitation.

What's the most frustrated animal in the world?
A ginger rabbit.

What do you get if you cross Raggedy Ann with the Pilsbury Dough Boy?
An angry redhead with a yeast infection.

Why did God invent colour blindness?
So that someone would fancy ginger kids.

When do ginger kids start smoking?
When sunlight touches them.

I bought one of those anti-bullying wristbands when they first came out. I say "bought", I actually stole it off a short, fat ginger kid. ***Jack Whitehall***

Apparently there are no naturally bald people – just ginger-haired ones with initiative.

What's the difference between a redhead and a bag of garbage?
Garbage gets taken out once a week.

How do you get a redhead's mood to change?
Wait ten seconds.

How do you know when a redhead has been using a computer?
There's a hammer embedded in the monitor.

How does every redhead joke begin?
By looking over your shoulder.

REDNECKS

What does a redneck say by way of foreplay?
"Hey, sis, get in the back of the truck!"

Who is the poorest person in Arkansas?
The Tooth Fairy.

What's considered bisexual in Alabama?
Someone who likes sheep and goats.

How do you know when you're at a redneck wedding?
Everyone is sitting on the same side of the church.

Did you hear the governor's mansion in Alabama burned down? It nearly destroyed the whole trailer park.

What's the definition of a redneck virgin?
A girl who can run faster than her brother.

Why do they throw out a sack of manure at redneck weddings?
To keep the flies off the bride.

Why is it so difficult to solve a redneck murder?
All the DNA is the same.

In India, a red dot on the forehead means you're married. In Alabama, it's a black eye.

A redneck driver is pulled over by a traffic cop. The cop says: "Got any ID?" The redneck says: " 'Bout what?"

Why did the redneck think the Three Wise Men were firemen?
Because he heard someone say, "They came from afar."

Have you seen the redneck version of *Star Wars*? It ends with the line, "Luke, I am your father . . . and your uncle."

Did you hear about the redneck Jedi? His father's name was Garth Vader.

What's the difference between a good ol' boy and a redneck?
The good ol' boy raises livestock, the redneck gets emotionally involved.

Cut and bruised and their clothes ripped to shreds, two rednecks stagger out of a zoo. One says to the other: "That lion dancing sure ain't as restful as they make out."

What are the toughest six years of a redneck's life?
Third grade.

What's the most popular chat-up line in Arkansas?
"Mmm, nice tooth!"

What do people do with broken-down cars in West Virginia?
Build a house next to them.

What's the last thing you usually hear before a redneck dies?
"Hey, y'all, watch this!"

Did you hear about the redneck who took his pregnant wife to the grocery store because they had free delivery?

A redneck girl watches her brother saddle up a horse. "Why have you put that saddle on backward?" she asks. He says: "How do you know which way I'm going?"

Did you hear about the redneck who took a roll of toilet paper to a crap game?

Did you hear about the redneck who studied five days for a urine test?

Did you hear about the redneck who put iodine on his paycheque because he got a cut in pay?

How many rednecks does it take to eat a possum?
Two. One to eat, and one to watch for cars.

Why has the minimum drinking age in Arkansas been raised to 32?
To keep alcohol out of high schools.

What do tornadoes and redneck divorces have in common?
Someone's gonna lose a trailer home.

How can you tell if a redneck is married?
There are tobacco spit stains on both sides of his pickup truck.

What's the difference between a northern fairy tale and a southern fairy tale?
A northern fairy tale begins "Once upon a time"; a southern fairy tale begins "Y'all ain't gonna believe this shit . . ."

You might be a redneck if you go to a family reunion to find a date.

You might be a redneck if you leave the local dump with more than you took there.

You might be a redneck if you listen to the police scanner to find out how your relatives are doing.

You might be a redneck if you think fast food is running over a possum at 75 m.p.h.

You might be a redneck if your living-room sofa came from a Ford.

You might be a redneck if you've ever told your wife to move over in bed so there's more room for your dog.

You might be a redneck if your dad walks with you to school because you're both in the same grade.

You might be a redneck if you've ever waited in line to have your picture taken with a freak of nature.

You might be a redneck if your wife's dress shoes have steel toes.

You might be a redneck if bikers back down from your mom.

You might be a redneck if you have more than three cousins named Rufus.

You might be a redneck if you have a disassembled motorcycle engine anywhere in your house.

You might be a redneck if any of your children are named after your hunting dog.

You might be a redneck if your Christmas stocking is filled with ammo.

You might be a redneck if your family tree doesn't fork.

You might be a redneck if your sister is the third generation of women in your family to conceive a baby as a result of an alien abduction.

You might be a redneck if the value of your truck depends on how much gas is in it.

You might be a redneck if you think a woman who is "out of your league" bowls on a different night.

You might be a redneck if you've been married three times and still have the same in-laws.

You might be a redneck if you own a special baseball cap for formal occasions.

You might be a redneck if the centrepiece on your dining-room table is an original signed work by a famous taxidermist.

You might be a redneck if the rear tyres on your car are at least twice as wide as the front ones.

You might be a redneck if your mother keeps a spit cup on the ironing board.

You might be a redneck if you've ever been too drunk to fish.

You might be a redneck if your house doesn't have curtains but your truck does.

You might be a redneck if you've ever parked a Camero in a tree.

You might be a redneck if you throw a beer can out of the truck window and your wife shoots it.

You might be a redneck if your mom's lost at least one tooth opening a beer bottle.

You might be a redneck if you and your dog use the same tree.

You might be a redneck if you think watching professional wrestling is foreplay.

You might be a redneck if your front porch collapses and four dogs get killed.

You might be a redneck if you have a wind chime in your yard made out of empty beer cans.

You might be a redneck if you go Christmas shopping for your mom, your sister and your girlfriend – and you only need to buy one gift.

You might be a redneck if your grandfather died and left everything to his widow, but she can't touch it till she's 14.

You might be a redneck if you have five cars that are immobile and a house that isn't.

You might be a redneck if your penknife has ever been referred to as "Exhibit A".

You might be a redneck if you've ever had to scratch your sister's name out of a message that begins, "For a good time, call . . ."

You might be a redneck if your wife has a beer belly, and you find it attractive.

You might be a redneck if you mow the grass in your front yard and find a vehicle.

You might be a redneck if you think loading the dishwasher means getting your wife drunk.

You might be a redneck if your toilet paper has page numbers on it.

You might be a redneck if your house has been surrounded by the FBI at least twice this year.

You might be a redneck if the billboard that reads "SAY NO TO CRACK" reminds you to pull up your jeans.

You might be a redneck if birds are attracted to your beard.

You might be a redneck if your wife's job requires her to wear an orange vest.

You might be a redneck if you've ever painted a car with house paint.

You might be a redneck if the directions to your house include the words "Turn off the paved road".

You might be a redneck if you've ever given rat traps as gifts.

You might be a redneck if your wife's hairdo has ever been ruined by a ceiling fan.

You might be a redneck if you use weedkiller in your living room.

You might be a redneck if you think the stock market has a fence around it.

You might be a redneck if one of your kids was born on a pool table.

You might be a redneck if you think "He needed killin" is a valid defence for murder.

You might be a redneck if you've ever used a toilet brush as a backscratcher.

You might be a redneck if your wife owns a homemade fur coat.

You might be a redneck if your masseuse uses hog lard.

You might be a redneck if you had to remove a toothpick for your wedding pictures.

Did you hear about the divorced redneck who wondered if his ex-wife was still his sister?

RELATIONSHIPS

My ex-wife was deaf. She left me for a deaf friend of hers. To be honest, I should have seen the signs. *Tim Vine*

I'm one bad relationship away from having 30 cats.

My girlfriend ended our relationship after I had one of those penis extensions. She said she couldn't take it any longer.

My mate and his other half separated last week. That'll teach him to fall asleep on railway tracks.

When I broke up with my girlfriend, she started crying and said I was a self-centred bastard. You should have seen the look on my face.

I'm single by choice, though not my choice.

When I'm not in a relationship I shave one leg so it feels like I'm sleeping with a woman.

My girlfriend has left me. She said I was too passive, and didn't stand up for myself enough. I can't argue with that.

Not all men want a relationship just for sex. Some want their washing done too.

I just read a letter from my girlfriend saying she is breaking up with me because I can't throw anything away. It's dated 5 May 1989.

Jackie: "I'm shocked you've broken up with Alex. I thought it was love at first sight."
Jill: "It was, but the second and third sights changed my mind."

My wife kicked me out, so I've been living in a telephone box. I just wanted somewhere to call home.

Some couples' idea of commitment is jointly buying a box set of *The Wire*.

My girlfriend asked me: "Do you want to get married?" "Sure," I said. "When I meet the right girl."

What's a man's idea of honesty in a relationship?
Telling you his real name.

My girlfriend says that I'm afraid of commitment . . . well, she's not my girlfriend, more a wife. *Stewart Francis*

My girlfriend likes to role-play. For the past three years, she's been playing my ex-girlfriend.

My girlfriend said she wanted me to put the magic back into our relationship. But I don't think sawing her in half was quite what she had in mind.

I told the ambulancemen the wrong blood type for my ex, so now she knows what rejection feels like.

My girlfriend said: "I need some space." I replied: "That's because you're so fat." Surprisingly that didn't win her round.

In our relationship, I bring home the bacon and my girlfriend carries the rest of the shopping.

My girlfriend and I like to dress as Adrian Balboa and Apollo Creed. We're going through a Rocky patch.

My workmate Lorne dumped his girlfriend, after which she was left looking forlorn.

My friend's wife left him last week. She said she was going out for some milk and never came back. I asked him how was coping. He said: "Not bad. I've been using some of that powdered stuff."

My girlfriend and I broke up yesterday. I just don't know what went wrong between Tubby and me.

My girlfriend left me the other day because apparently I'm too cold and formal. So I sent her a letter of complaint.

Me and my girl are in a long-distance relationship. That's restraining orders for you!

My girlfriend's leaving me because I don't take anything seriously lol.

Did you hear about the broken-hearted tractor salesman? He got a John Deere letter.

My girlfriend and I have decided to take our relationship to the next level. We're moving into the flat upstairs.

My girlfriend left me because of my obsession with health and safety. I said: "Mind the door doesn't hit you on your way out."

A girl told her boyfriend: "You have to make sacrifices in a relationship." So he went out and slaughtered a goat.

My girlfriend told me to put the magic back into our relationship. So I disappeared.

I liked my new girlfriend but after looking through her drawer and finding a nurse's uniform, a French maid outfit and a policewoman's uniform, I decided to dump her because it's obvious she can't hold down a job.

Did you hear about the girl who went out with a monorail enthusiast but left him because he had a one-track mind?

How do men define a 50/50 relationship?
You cook, we eat.

My girlfriend threatened to leave me today because apparently I'm a smart arse. She said: "We're at a crossroads in our relationship: one way is love and trust, the other is divorce." I said: "I think you'll find that's called a T-junction." *Jimmy Carr*

What did the plumber say when he broke up with his girlfriend Florence?
"It's all over, Flo."

My wife and I are incompatible. I lost my income, she lost her patability.

Mike: "I think I'm going to leave my wife. She hasn't spoken to me in three months."
Marty: "Don't be too hasty. A good woman like that is hard to find."

My girlfriend left me after finding me in bed with my best friend. I tried to explain to her that it was only because his kennel was being repaired.

A wise man once said to my brother: "If you love her, let her go . . . and come out with your hands up."

Long-distance relationships are like fat people – they rarely work out.

When my wife left me, I couldn't sleep. She took the bed.

My girlfriend says I'm too immature for her. I say that's absolute nonsense, and my teddy agrees with me.

Even my inflatable doll has dumped me. She said I kept letting her down.

"Dear Alex, I'm so sorry I broke things off with you, and realize now I was wrong. Please take me back. Jill. P.S. Congratulations on your big lottery win."

RELIGION

I was christened by a vicar in a gorilla suit. It was a blessing in disguise.

Jesus said to John: "Come forth, I'll give you eternal life." But John came fifth, and won a toaster.

My next-door neighbour worships exhaust pipes – he's a Catholic converter.

How do you get holy water?
Boil the hell out of it.

What happened to the church janitor who was also the organist?
He had to watch his keys and pews.

People who want to share their religious views with you almost never want you to share yours with them.

If we are all God's children, what's so special about Jesus? *Jimmy Carr*

Sunday school teacher: "Why did Joseph and Mary take Jesus with them to Jerusalem?"
Small girl: "Because they couldn't get a babysitter."

Christianity: one woman's lie about having an affair that got seriously out of hand.

Our new young minister said such a large ceremony would be a baptism of fire. I said: "I think you might find the flames will scare the baby."

Who tracks down lost vicars?
The Bureau of Missing Parsons.

The bishop came to our church today, but I don't think he was a real bishop. He never moved once diagonally.

Did you hear about the "Dial a Prayer" service for agnostics? You call the number and no one answers.

When our church relocated, it had an organ transplant.

Sunday school teacher: "In your Bible drawing, who is the man in an airplane wearing goggles?"
Child: "Oh, that's Pontius the pilot."

A true test of faith is when the collection plate comes around and you only have a $20 bill.

I'm puzzled when they say Jesus was a carpenter, because I've got all of their records and I don't remember him singing on any of them.

My friend decided some years ago that he would have to sleep with a woman before agreeing to marry her. He looks upon it as one of the perks of being a vicar.

Did you hear about the guy who told religious jokes and was put on the Sects Offenders List?

I love Jesus. He's born, I get presents. He dies, I get chocolate.

Mormons and Jews are combining to form a new super-religion. Their headquarters will be in Salt Beef City.

Woman in restaurant: "Is that seat saved?"
Churchgoer: "No, but we're praying for it."

If they make it illegal to wear the veil at work, beekeepers are going to be furious. *Milton Jones*

What do you call a Far Eastern monk who sells reincarnations?
A used karma dealer.

A pastor asks the Sunday school class what "Amen" means. Little Johnny puts up his hand and says: "Tha-tha-tha-that's all, folks!"

Jesus walked into a hotel, handed the receptionist a box of nails and said: "Can you put me up for the night?"

The minister at our church is really self-obsessed. It's all hymn, hymn, hymn.

A Muslim found the face of Allah in a tub of margarine. His neighbour from Nepal saw it and said: "I can't believe it's not Buddha."

Why do Muslim women wear veils?
So they can blow their noses without getting their hands dirty.

My church accepts any denomination, but they prefer tens and twenties.

The vicar was like a totally different person in church. I guess it was his altar ego.

After buying a hot dog at a stall at a religious convention, a Buddhist asks: "Where's my change?" The seller replies: "Ah, change must come from within."

So what if Jesus turned water into wine? I once turned a whole student loan into vodka. *Sean Lock*

Going to church does not make you a Christian any more than standing in a garage makes you a car.

How do we know Adam was a Baptist?
Only a Baptist could stand next to a naked woman and be tempted by a piece of fruit.

An old lady walks into a Catholic church just as the priest is coming down the aisle swinging an incense pot. She says: "Father, I love your dress, but do you know your handbag's on fire?"

Why don't Baptists make love standing up?
Because it could lead to dancing.

I'm guessing the whole "touch wood" thing didn't really work for Jesus.

Priest: "When are you going to have a ham sandwich, Rabbi?"
Rabbi: "At your wedding, Father."

My wife converted me to religion. Until I married her, I didn't believe in Hell.

Abbot: "Why is that obese monk meditating in the kitchen?"
Housekeeper: "Well, you did say we should get a deep, fat friar."

Religion is insurance in this world against fire in the next.

I've nothing against Mormons, but I wouldn't want my sisters to marry one.

Catholic: "I hate England. It's cold and wet and full of Protestants."
Protestant: "Why don't you go to Hell? It's hot and dry and full of Catholics."

What do priests and Christmas trees have in common?
The balls are just for decoration.

Jesus opened the fridge. One of the disciples asked: "Is it wine yet?" "No," said Jesus, reading the bottle. "It says it's 'still water'."

What kind of fun does a priest have?
Nun.

"Lord, give me the strength to change the things I can, the grace to accept the things I cannot, and a great big bag of money."

How do you know when you're living in a rough neighbourhood?
The local church has a bouncer.

There's a remote tribe that has started worshipping the number zero. These days, nothing is sacred.

"Turn at the entrance to temptation and go forth to meet the Lord!" That's the last time I buy a cheap GPS from a preacher.

What religion is a woman who has had a sex-change operation? **Hethen.**

I've found Jesus. He was behind the sofa the whole time!

It's difficult isn't it when you're in a mosque and everyone's praying . . . and you really enjoy leapfrog? *Milton Jones*

A vicar was leaving his parish after 25 years. "We're sorry to see you go, Vicar," said one old lady. "Before you came, we didn't know what sin was."

What did Jesus say as he was being nailed to the cross? **"Don't touch my Easter eggs, I'll be back in a day or two."**

Religion: giving people hope in a world torn apart by religion.

RESTAURANTS

I work as a waiter. The pay isn't great, but it puts food on the table.

Did you hear about the new restaurant called Karma? There's no menu. You just get what you deserve.

There's another new restaurant called Karma 2. It serves just desserts.

How did the man tackle his new job at a burger restaurant? **With relish.**

I just had lunch at an excellent Christian restaurant called The Lord Giveth. They also do takeaways. *Tim Vine*

The soup was so thick that when I stirred it, the room went around.

Sitting in a restaurant, I was suddenly hit on the back of the head by a prawn cocktail. I turned round, and this big guy shouted: "That's just for starters!"

Mike: "Will you join me in a bowl of soup?" **Marty: "I don't think there's room for both of us."**

Did you hear about the superior chef who had an attitude problem? He had a French fry on his shoulder.

Last night the steak I ordered mooed at me. I thought, That's rare.

I'm not saying it was a bad restaurant, but they've only just introduced same-day service.

A word of advice: never do a runner from a Kenyan restaurant.

Did you know that every new McDonald's creates twenty jobs? Ten dentists and ten heart surgeons.

The downside of fame? I can't walk out of a nice restaurant without immediately getting harassed and hounded by a waiter holding the bill.
Conan O'Brien

I was in a restaurant and I heard a voice say: "Can I take your order, sir?" I looked down and saw this man with no shoulders, no torso, no arms and no legs. I said: "You must be the head waiter."

My uncle is such a noisy eater that when he started on his soup in the restaurant, four couples got up to dance.

Last week a customer in my restaurant complained that his food was over-seasoned. I took his comments with several pinches of salt.

Waiter: "How did you find the steak, sir?"
Customer: "With a magnifying glass."

I don't think the Thanksgiving turkey had been plucked properly. We were all spitting feathers.

A Cambodian, a Malaysian, a Chinese, a Korean, a Laotian, a Vietnamese, a Mongolian and a Burmese walk into a smart restaurant. The manager says snootily: "Sorry, you can't come in here without a Thai."

The other night I ate at a real family restaurant. Every table had an argument going.

Have you heard about the exclusive Parisian restaurant that makes omelettes using only one egg? Apparently in France one egg is *un oeuf*.

I was sitting in the restaurant when my girlfriend called to say: "Sorry, I can't make dinner tonight." I said: "Don't worry, that's the chef's job."

Two old ladies are in a restaurant. One says: "The food in here is simply terrible." The other one adds: "And such small portions!"

I start my job at a restaurant tomorrow. I can't wait.

I went to a restaurant the other day called Taste of the Raj. The waiter hit me with a stick and got me to build a complicated railway system. *Harry Hill*

What's a dumbwaiter?
One who asks if the kids want dessert.

Chef to waiter: "Push the soup of the day. It's a week old."

What's the definition of a fancy restaurant?
One that serves cold soup on purpose.

A clean tie attracts the soup of the day.

I like going into McDonald's and ordering an Egg McMuffin and a McChicken, just to see which one comes first.

Waiter: "Sorry, sir, there's a 45-minute wait for a table."
Customer: "I'm 92 years old; I may not have 45 minutes left!"

Did you hear about the new Elvis Presley-themed steak restaurants? They're for people who love meat tender.

I was eating in an open-air café when it started raining. It took me an hour and a half to finish my soup.

Did you hear about the fight at the seafood restaurant? Four fish got battered.

I went to a drive-through McDonald's, but it was more expensive than I thought, particularly by the time I'd hired the car.

Last week I went to a French–Cuban fusion restaurant: Chez Guevara.

Having a smoking section in a restaurant is like having a peeing section in a swimming pool.

I used to have a favourite restaurant, but nobody goes there any more. It's too crowded.

There was no place to eat last night, so I went to a kebab shop and had a doner . . . which my body rejected. *Emo Philips*

Chef: "Didn't I tell you to notice when the soup boiled over?!"
Waiter: "I did. It was 4.15."

Customer: "Waiter, how do you prepare the chicken?"
Waiter: "We don't. We just tell it straight that it's going to die."

Why shouldn't you order pelican pizza?
The bill will be enormous.

A man walked into a fast-food restaurant and said: "I'll have an alligator sandwich, and make it snappy!"

"Waiter! There's a fly in my soup."
"Don't worry, sir, the spider in the bread roll will get it."

"Waiter! There's a fly in my soup."
"No, sir, that's the essential vitamin bee."

"Waiter! What's this fly doing in my soup?"
"Looks like the backstroke, sir."

"Waiter! What's the meaning of this fly in my soup?"
"I don't know, sir. I'm a waiter, not a fortune-teller."

"Waiter! There's a dead beetle in my soup."
"Yes, sir, they can't swim as well as flies."

"Waiter! There's a wasp in my soup."
"Yes, sir, it's the fly's day off."

"Water! What's this in my soup?"
"No idea, sir. All insects look the same to me."

"Waiter! Your thumb's in my soup."
"Don't worry, sir. The soup's not hot."

"Waiter! There's a button in my soup."
"Thank you, sir. I wondered what had happened to it."

"Waiter! I can't find any chicken in this chicken soup."
"Well, sir, would you expect to find angels in angel cake?"

"Waiter! Is there soup on the menu?"
"No, sir, I wiped it all off."

"Waiter! There's a fly in my soup."
"Actually that's the chef. The last customer was a witch doctor."

"Waiter! There's a fly in my soup."
"Yes, sir. It's the rotting meat that attracts them."

"Waiter! There's a dead fly in my wine."
"Well, sir, you did ask for something with a little body to it."

"Waiter! Why is your thumb on my steak?"
"I don't want it to fall on the floor again."

"Waiter! This coffee tastes like mud."
"Yes, sir, it's fresh ground."

"Waiter! Coffee without cream, please."
"Sorry, sir, we're out of cream. Would you like it without milk?"

"Waiter! If this is coffee, please bring me some tea. But if this is tea, please bring me some coffee."

"Waiter! Is this milk fresh?"
"Fresh? Three hours ago it was grass!"

"Waiter! Do they ever change the tablecloths in this restaurant?"
"I don't know, sir. I've only worked here for a year."

"Waiter! This water is cloudy."
"No, sir, the water is fine. It's the glass that's dirty."

"Waiter! The water here tastes strange."
"It shouldn't do, sir. The manager himself passed it only yesterday."

"Waiter! What do I have to do to get a glass of water in this place?"
"Set yourself on fire, sir."

"Waiter! This food isn't fit for a pig."
"Sorry, sir, I'll bring you some that is."

"Waiter! What time is it, please?"
"Sorry, sir, this isn't my table."

"Waiter! I demand to speak to the manager!"
"Sorry, sir, he's out for lunch."

"Waiter! I've tasted fresher fish than this!"
"Not in here you haven't, sir."

What's worse than a fly in your soup?
A fly in my soup.

Last night I ordered an entire meal in French, and even the waiter was surprised. It was a Chinese restaurant. *Tommy Cooper*

RETIREMENT

Old quarterbacks never die, they just pass away.

Old cashiers never die, they just check out.

Old wrestlers never die, they just lose their grip.

Old college deans never die, they just lose their faculties.

Old gardeners never die, they just go to pot.

Old insurance agents never die, it's against their policy.

Old archers never die, they just bow and quiver.

Old cartographers never die, they just lose their way.

Old sailors never die, they just get a little dingy.

Old electricians never die, they just lose contact.

Old dieticians never die, they just waist away.

Old mathematicians never die, they just go off on a tangent.

Old sculptors never die, they just lose their marbles.

Old investors never die, they just roll over.

Old police officers never die, they just cop out.

Old dry cleaners never die, they just get depressed.

Old chess players never die, they just go to pieces.

Old bowls players never die, they simply jack it in.

Old auditors never die, they just lose their figures.

Old washerwomen never die, they just peg out.

Old environmentalists never die, they are just recycled.

Old judges never die, they just cease to try.

Old professors never die, they just lose their class.

Old foresters never die, they just pine away.

Old poker players never die, they just shuffle off.

Old chauffeurs never die, they just lose their drive.

Old lawyers never die, they just lose their appeal.

Old engineers never die, they just lose their bearings.

Old pilots never die, they just go to a higher plane.

Old cartoonists never die, they just go into suspended animation.

Old steelmakers never die, they just lose their temper.

Old garage mechanics never die, they just retire.

Old farmers never die, they just go to seed.

Old students never die, they just get degraded.

Old milkmaids never die, they just lose their whey.

Old US postal carriers never die, they just lose their zip.

Old beekeepers never die, they just buzz off.

Old watchmakers never die, they just run out of time.

Old florists never die, they just make alternative arrangements.

Old limbo dancers never die, they just go under.

Old accountants never die, they just lose their balance.

Old daredevils never die, they just get discouraged.

Old yachtsmen never die, they just keel over.

Old cowboys never die, they just get deranged.

Old tanners never die, they just go into hiding.

Old chemists never die, they just don't react any more.

Old number theorists never die, they just get past their prime.

Old fishermen never die, they just smell that way.

Old bosses never die, much as you want them to.

Old vampires never die, they just . . . don't.

The worst thing about retirement is having to drink coffee on your own time.

When the human cannonball retired, they couldn't find a replacement of the right calibre.

The best time to think about your retirement is before your boss does.

What was Bob the Builder called after he retired?
Bob.

RIDDLES

What's brown and sticky?
A stick.

What do a coffin and a condom have in common?
Both are filled with stiffs, but one's coming and the other's going.

How do you make a cigarette lighter?
Take out the tobacco.

What's the difference between medium and rare?
Six inches is medium, eight inches is rare.

What's the definition of perfect balance?
A pregnant hunchback.

What has 18 legs and catches flies?
A baseball team.

What did the girl oyster say to the boy oyster?
"You never open up to me."

What happened when the waltzers broke down at the theme park?
They had to hire a spin doctor.

Why was the washing machine laughing?
Because it was taking the piss out of the knickers.

Why did the traffic light turn red?
Because it had to change in the middle of the street.

What's long and thin, covered in skin, red in parts, and goes in tarts?
Rhubarb.

Where do you weigh whales?
At a whale weigh station.

What makes the Leaning Tower of Pisa lean?
It doesn't eat much.

What's pink and hard?
A pig with a flick knife.

What do you get if you cross a bullet and a sycamore in winter?
A cartridge in a bare tree.

What do you get if you cross an elephant and a rhino?
El-if-i-no.

What is soft and yellow and goes round and round?
A long-playing omelette.

How do you make a Maltese Cross?
Set fire to his jumper.

What has hindsight?
A stag during the rutting season.

Why did the ink spots cry?
Because their father was in the pen doing a long sentence.

What's the biggest drawback in the jungle?
An elephant's foreskin.

What's orange and sounds like a parrot?
A carrot.

When is a tractor not a tractor?
When it turns into a field.

What's the difference between a bad marksman and a constipated owl?
The bad marksman shoots but can't hit.

Why did the crab walk forwards?
Because he was drunk.

What is small, red and whispers?
A hoarse radish.

Why did the willow weep?
He was unpoplar.

Why is the sky so high?
So that birds don't bump their heads.

How do you make a Venetian blind?
Poke his eye out.

Where do you weigh pies?
Somewhere over the rainbow . . . weigh a pie.

What do you see when the Pilsbury Dough Boy bends over?
Doughnuts.

What's the quietest place in the world?
The complaints department at the parachute packing plant.

Why did Snoopy want to quit the comic strip?
He was tired of working for Peanuts.

What do Tupperware and a walrus have in common?
They both like a tight seal.

If you don't feel very well, what do you probably have?
A pair of boxing gloves on.

What's yellow and smells of bananas?
Monkey sick.

What goes clip?
A one-legged horse.

What has 100 balls and fucks rabbits?
A shotgun.

Why do mermaids wear seashells?
Because they're too big for B-shells and too small for D-shells.

What's the difference between an ornithologist and a stutterer?
One's a bird watcher, the other's a word botcher.

What do you get when you cross an anteater with a vibrator?
An armadildo.

Who robs banks and squirts ink?
Billy the Squid.

Why was the blind man's leg wet?
Because his dog was blind too.

What is a thespian pony?
A little horse play.

How do you make a Swiss Roll?
Push him down a mountain.

What's hard and straight going in, and soft and sticky coming out?
Chewing gum.

What's the difference between a photocopier and the flu?
One makes facsimiles and the other makes sick families.

Where does bad light end up?
Prism.

What causes a riot?
Three dyslexics.

What's another name for a water otter?
A kettle.

What goes in dry, comes out wet and satisfies two people?
A tea bag.

What's the difference between a good vacuum cleaner and a Swiss admiral?
A good vacuum cleaner sucks and never fails.

If Ireland fell into the sea, which county wouldn't sink?
Cork.

What has two legs and bleeds?
Half a dog.

What did the big cracker say to the little cracker?
My pop is bigger than yours.

What goes, "Click . . . is that it? Click . . . is that it? Click . . . is that it?"
A blind man with a Rubik's cube.

What's the difference between a businessman and a dog?
A businessman wears a suit, a dog just pants.

What do you call the useless bit of fatty tissue at the end of a penis?
A man.

What do you do with a wombat?
Play wom.

What's pink, wrinkly and hangs out your pants?
Your mother.

How do whales listen to music?
On an iPod.

What's got 400 legs and no pubic hair?
The front row at a Justin Bieber concert.

What did the big chimney say to the little chimney?
"You're too young to be smoking."

What's red and sits in the corner?
A naughty fire engine.

What can you serve that you can't eat?
A tennis ball.

If a quiz is quizzical, what's a test?

Why was everyone so poor in Biblical times?
Because there was only one Job.

What's the difference between a clever spoonerism and a fart?
One's a shaft of wit . . .

What does an envelope say when you lick it?
Nothing. It just shuts up.

What is a Yankee?
The same as a quickie, but a guy can do it alone.

What's green, has two legs and a trunk?
A seasick tourist.

What did Cinderella say while she was waiting for her photos?
"Some day my prints will come."

How do you turn a fox into an elephant?
Marry it.

What can a goose do, a duck can't and a lawyer should?
Stick his bill up his ass.

What did the water say as it passed through the filter?
"I hope I made myself clear."

If Eve wore a fig leaf, what did Adam wear?
A hole in it.

What did the plate say to the bowl?
"Dinner's on me."

What's the difference between a pickpocket and a peeping tom?
A pickpocket snatches watches . . .

What's yellow and hides in Afghanistan?
The Talibanana.

What's the difference between a pheromone and a hormone?
You can't hear a pheromone.

How do you make a fruit cordial?
Tell him you like his shirt.

What's worse than a bull in a china shop?
A hedgehog in a condom factory.

What has a bottom at the top?
A pair of legs.

Why don't mountains get cold in the winter?
They wear snow caps.

Why does Tigger have no friends?
Because he plays with Pooh.

Why don't scarecrows have any fun?
Because they're stuffed shirts.

Why do ghouls and demons go around together?
Because demons are a ghoul's best friend.

What's the definition of bipolar?
A sexually curious bear.

Why don't people like dilemmas?
Because they have horns.

What washes up on small beaches?
Microwaves.

What's got a trunk, four legs and lots of keys?
A piano up a tree.

What does Colombia produce that no other country produces?
Colombians.

What do you call someone who can't tell the difference between a spoon and a ladle?
Fat.

What's brown and hides in the attic?
The diarrhoea of Anne Frank.

What's a volcano?
A mountain with hiccups.

Why did the crab get arrested?
Because he was always pinching things.

What's the difference between an orchestra manager and a crooked accountant?
One books the fiddles . . .

How do you make antifreeze?
Steal her blanket.

When do you go at red and stop at green?
When you're eating a watermelon.

What's the only thing you can look down on and approve of at the same time?
Cleavage.

What do you call a person who keeps on talking when people are no longer interested?
A teacher.

What did the egg say to the boiling water?
"It's going to take a while for me to get hard. I just got laid by a chick."

What's a bigamist?
An Italian fog.

What does Speedy Gonzales have beneath his carpet?
Underlay, underlay.

What part of Popeye never rusts?
The part he puts in Olive Oyl.

Why are mountains so funny?
Because they're hill areas.

What's brown and sounds like a bell?
Dung.

Why are embroiderers bad-tempered?
They're always getting the needle.

What's blue and square?
An orange in disguise.

What's the moral of the story about Jonah and the whale?
You can't keep a good man down.

Which country was once run by napkins?
The Serviette Union.

What did the candle say to the flame?
You get on my wick.

What's long, hard and full of semen?
A submarine.

What has orange hair, big feet, baggy pants, and comes out of a test tube?
Bozo the clone.

How is a bicycle like a duck?
Both have handlebars, except the duck.

What's grey and comes in pints?
An elephant.

What is the height of patience?
A woman lying down with her legs apart under a banana tree.

What is the height of frustration?
A boxer trying to scratch his balls.

What do you get if you cross Colonel Sanders and Diana Ross?
Chicken Supreme.

What has one horn and gives milk?
A milk truck.

What did Sherlock Holmes say to his assistant when he saw the yellow door?
"It's a lemon entry, my dear Watson."

What's red and white and sits in trees?
A sanitary owl.

What did one candle say to the other?
"Going out tonight?"

What's a hospice?
About three gallons.

How do snowmen get around?
They ride an icicle.

What did the envelope say to the stamp?
"Stick with me and we'll go places."

What's the difference between light and hard?
You can sleep with a light on.

What do you have if you have one large green ball in your left hand and one large green ball in your right hand?
The undivided attention of the Incredible Hulk.

What do you call a boomerang that doesn't work?
A stick.

ROYALTY

If Queen Elizabeth II is ever asked for ID, does she just take a £10 note from her purse?

What does the Queen do when she passes gas?
She issues a royal pardon.

When a royal pardon turns out unexpectedly, what follows?
A royal flush.

A man came out of Buckingham Palace covered in white paint. "What happened to you?" asked a policeman. The man said: "I've just been decorated by the Queen."

Did you hear about the Prince Charles commemorative teapot? It never reigns, but it pours.

I was assistant to Princess Diana for a while, but I realized that no matter how hard I worked they were never going to make me Princess Diana.

Why didn't the gay prince want a bookmark for his birthday?
He preferred to bend the pages over.

RUSSIANS

What's the difference between a Russian funeral and a Russian wedding?
One less drunk.

Did you hear about the Russian abortion clinic? There's a 12-month waiting list.

What's the difference between America and Russia?
In America, you find a party; in Russia, the party finds you.

There are only two kinds of Russian soup: one made from beet and cabbage, the other from cabbage and beet.

What was the name of the Russian who invented a cure for the common cold?
Benylin Forchestikov.

In the west, you watch television; in Russia, the television watches you.

Is it safe to eat apples from Chernobyl?
Yes, but you have to bury the core at least 10 feet deep.

Inside every Russian lady . . . there's another Russian lady.

Did you hear about the new chain of Russian coffee shops? It's called Tsarbucks.

Why do Russians go around in threes?
So that there is one who can read, one who can write and one who can keep an eye on the two intellectuals.

Did you hear about the new Russian condom? It's called Red Riding Hood.

SALESPEOPLE

Salesman: "You still haven't paid for the new windows we installed nine months ago."
Man: "Well, you said after a year the windows would pay for themselves."

Did you hear about the man who was such a great salesman he could sell underarm deodorant to the Venus de Milo?

The telemarketer asked me if I ever read magazines. I said I did, periodically.

A woman buys a wall mirror. The store salesman says: "Do you want a screw for that?" "No, thanks," says the woman, "but I'll let you kiss me for two tins of paint."

Telemarketer: "I'm conducting a survey. What do you know about dwarfs?"
Man: "Very little."

Salesman: "Would you like to buy a pocket calculator?"
Man: "No, thanks. I already know how many pockets I have."

Three times last week, a guy knocked on my door trying to get me to buy a jet washer. I hate high-pressure salesmen.

I went to a garage sale, but when I got there the people didn't want to sell their garage after all.

How do salespeople traditionally greet each other?
"Hi, I'm better than you."

I got arrested for selling flags in the street: trading standards.

Two women knocked at my door and started preaching to me about the virtues of brown bread. I think they were Hovis Witnesses.

Did you hear about the salesman who talked to himself? He kept selling himself things he didn't want.

I had a leaflet through my door saying "Jumble Sale". So far I've got "seal" and "ales".

Customer: "You said this sweater was pure wool, but the label says 100 per cent cotton."
Salesman: "Oh, that's just to keep the moths away."

A man who knocked on our door had a blue face, frost on his top lip and icicles hanging from his beard. Afterwards I said to my wife: "Don't worry, it was only a cold caller."

Have you ever wondered how silly a balloon seller in the High Street feels when he's down to his last balloon?

I have to say the last used-car salesman I dealt with was a bit on the aggressive side. But after I bought the car he did release my wife and kids.

SAYINGS

Letting the cat out of the bag is a whole lot easier than putting it back in.

Whoever coined the phrase "quiet as a mouse" has never stepped on one.

If it really was the thought that counted, many more women would be pregnant.

Imitation is not the sincerest form of flattery. Stalking is.

He who hesitates is not only lost, but also miles from the next exit.

When isn't it a good time to ask someone to cut you some slack?
When you're bungee jumping.

An apple a day keeps the doctor away. So does not having health insurance.

An apple a day keeps the doctor away, but an onion a day keeps everyone away.

Sure, you can't take it with you – but you can hide it where no other bastard can find it.

Familiarity breeds children.

The lion shall lie down with the lamb, but the lamb probably won't get much sleep.

But what if bygones want to be something else?

If you're not part of the solution, you must be a consultant.

If you can keep your head while others around you are losing theirs, you probably haven't grasped the seriousness of the situation.

If you can keep your head while others around you are losing theirs, you may want to land your helicopter somewhere else.

Where there's smoke, there's dinner.

No matter how much you push the envelope, it will still be stationery.

If your grandmother sucked eggs, you'd teach her some table manners.

Birds of a feather flock together and crap on your car.

Why do people say: "Your guess is as good as mine"? No, it's not. My guesses are the best.

Never let the grass grow under your feet – it tickles.

My father always used to say: "When one door closes, another one opens." Whereas my mother used to say: "George, isn't it about time you got that bloody car fixed? It's embarrassing."

Whoever said anything is possible obviously never tried slamming a revolving door.

Two can live as cheaply as one – for half as long.

If it ain't broke, fix it until it is.

How is it that when we skate on thin ice, we can get in hot water?

People in glasshouses should get dressed in the basement.

If a tree falls in the woods and nobody hears it, then my illegal logging operation is a success.

If there's one thing today has taught me it's that you don't learn something new every day.

Laugh and the world laughs with you, snore and you sleep alone.

Selling sea shells by the sea shore: easier done than said.

How did a fool and his money get together in the first place?

Remember, you've got to break some eggs to make a real mess on your neighbour's car.

You're only young once, but you can be immature forever.

They say you don't miss things until they're gone. But I don't miss having chronic diarrhoea.

Keep your nose to the grindstone and your shoulder to the wheel. It's cheaper than plastic surgery.

It's a small world, but I wouldn't like to paint it. **Steven Wright**

The early bird gets the worm, but the second mouse gets the cheese.

The early bird who catches the worm usually works for someone who comes in late and owns the worm farm.

The things that come to those who wait may be the things left by those who got there first.

People change. My friend is now a bedside lamp.

Out of the mouths of babes often comes cereal.

"One man's rubbish is another man's treasure" may be a perceptive phrase, but it's a cruel way to tell a child he's adopted.

A bird in the hand makes blowing your nose difficult.

A bird in the hand is safer than one overhead.

When the shit hits the fan, your toilet is probably in the wrong place.

Rainy days and automatic weapons always get me down.

Those that forget the pasta are doomed to reheat it.

If all is not lost, where is it?

The meek shall inherit the Earth, but not until the rest of us are done with it.

The meek shall inherit the Earth, but not its mineral rights.

Where there's a will, there are dozens of relatives.

A picture is worth a thousand words, but it takes longer to load.

Talk is cheap because supply exceeds demand.

Talk is cheap until you hire a lawyer.

Doesn't expecting the unexpected make the unexpected become the expected?

Two wrongs don't make a right, but two Wrights did make an airplane.

The pen may be mightier than the sword, but it is slightly less effective in armed combat.

Change is inevitable, except from a vending machine.

The darkest hour is just before the dawn, unless you're using an energy-saving light bulb.

The bigger they are, the harder they hit.

Time waits for no man, but it always stands still for a woman of 39.

Don't judge a book by its movie.

It's a small world, until you chase your hat down the street.

Every dog has its day; only a dog with a broken tail has a weak-end.

A problem shared is a buck passed.

A woman's word is never done.

"Better out than in," my uncle always used to say. He was the worst heart surgeon ever.

Money is the root of all wealth.

Prick Up Your Ears: the 2012 Male Contortionist of the Year Awards.

Can a short person "talk down" to a taller person?

What happens when someone beats you to the punch?
You have to drink beer instead.

Lead me not into temptation. I can find the way myself.

If an apple a day keeps the doctor away, why don't Daleks hide in orchards?

Variety is the spice of life, but monotony buys the groceries.

One good turn gets most of the blankets.

SCHOOL

I started a lot of fights at school because I had Attention Deficit Disorder. Of course, that meant I never finished them . . .

It wasn't school I hated, just the principal of it.

Mother: "Hurry up, you'll be late for school."
Son: "What's the rush? They're open till 3.30."

Did you hear about the cross-eyed teacher who couldn't control his pupils?

I was so popular in school everybody hated me.

Father: "Let me see your report card."
Son: "You can't. My friend's borrowed it. He wants to scare his parents."

Why was the boy's rubber band pistol confiscated during algebra class?
Because it was a weapon of math disruption.

On my first day at school my parents dropped me off at the wrong nursery. There I was . . . surrounded by trees and shrubs.

I used to resent being sent to boarding school as a kid, but now I can get on a plane better than anybody else.

Mother: "So how did your first day at school go? What did you learn?"
Son: "How to talk without moving my lips."

"But I don't want to go to school today, Mommy."
"You have to. You're 48, and you're the school principal."

When the teacher said I was average, she was just being mean.

Our local primary school has had to build a "naughty ramp" as the "naughty step" didn't comply with accessibility regulations.

When I was at school, I was perpetually punched in the head by other kids. So my dad sent me off to learn boxing . . . where I was perpetually punched in the head by other kids. *Lee Evans*

IKEA has sponsored our local school. Now assembly takes ages.

At school I was teacher's pet. She couldn't afford a dog.

Mother: "What did you learn in school today?"
Son: "Not enough. I have to go back tomorrow."

Mother: "Why aren't you doing well at history?"
Son: "The teacher keeps asking about things that happened before I was born."

Mother: "Let me see your school report."
Son: "OK, but don't show it to Dad. He's been helping me!"

Mother: "How were the exam questions?"
Son: "They were easy. But I had trouble with the answers."

Father: "Why is your January report card so bad?"
Son: "You know what it's like. Things are always marked down after Christmas."

Boy: "I can't go to school today. I don't feel well."
Mother: "Where don't you feel well?"
Boy: "In school."

At school the teacher said I was in a class of my own. It was only later I found out the official term was "quarantine".

Aunt: "Are you in the top half of your class?"
Boy: "No, I'm one of the students who make the top half possible."

At the end of her first week at school, a little girl said to her mother: "I'm wasting my time there. I can't read, I can't write, and they won't let me talk."

My school was so posh that gym was called james.

Teacher to parent: "There's one good thing I can say about your son – with grades like these, he couldn't have been cheating."

Mother: "Why have you stopped studying?"
Boy: "Because it's dangerous. I read about someone who was shot dead because he knew too much."

My exam results were all underwater – below C level.

Who's to blame for the rise of drugs in schools?
Supply teachers.

Teacher to pupil: "I'm glad your writing has improved because now I can see how bad your spelling is."

Boy to mother: "My teacher doesn't know anything. All she does is ask questions."

I went to the school of hard knocks. You had to – the doors were really thick.

Did you hear about the boy who skipped school to go bungee jumping? He was suspended.

Teacher: "Simon, can you say your name backwards?"
"No Mis."

A boy tells his mother: "My teacher thinks I'm going to be famous. She says all I have to do is mess up one more time and I'm history!"

You know there's a problem with the education system when you realize that out of three Rs only one begins with an R. *Dennis Miller*

My parents only sent me to boarding school so they wouldn't have to help with my homework.

In high school I was in the French club. All we would do was occasionally surrender to the German club.

The teachers always hated me, even when I was the principal.

What did the gangster's son tell his father after failing his school exam?
"They questioned me for two hours, Dad, but I never told them anything."

Whiteboards are remarkable.

Boy to friend: "Sorry, I can't come out to play this evening. I promised my dad that I would stay in and help him with my homework."

The main purpose of education is to keep them off the streets – the teachers, that is.

Why did the teacher always put the lights on?
Because the class was so dim.

Teacher: "Johnny, you know you can't sleep in my class."
Little Johnny: "I know, Miss. But maybe if you were a little quieter, I could."

Teacher: "In 1940, what were the Poles doing in Russia?"
Little Johnny: "Holding up the telegraph lines."

Teacher: "Your essay on 'My Dog' is exactly the same as your brother's."
Little Johnny: "Of course it is, Miss. It's the same dog."

Teacher: "Did your father help you with your homework last night?"
Little Johnny: "No, Miss. He did all of it."

Teacher: "How can one person make so many silly mistakes in one day?"
Little Johnny: "I get up early, Miss."

Teacher: "When you're dead, what do you want to be remembered for?"
Little Johnny: "Ever."

Teacher: "Didn't you hear me call you?"
Little Johnny: "Yes, but you said I mustn't answer you back."

Teacher: "Why are you standing on your head?"
Little Johnny: "I'm just turning things over in my mind."

Teacher: "Why is the Mississippi such an unusual river?"
Little Johnny: "Because it has four eyes but can't see."

Teacher: "Why does a surgeon wear a mask when he's performing an operation?"
Little Johnny: "So that if he messes up, the patient won't know who did it."

Teacher: "You clearly haven't studied your geography. What's your excuse?"
Little Johnny: "Well, my dad says the world is changing every day, so I decided to wait until it settles down."

Teacher: "That's quite a cough you have there, Johnny. What are you taking for it?"
Little Johnny: "I don't know, Miss. How much are you offering?"

Teacher: "Come on, any five-year-old should be able to solve this problem."
Little Johnny: "No wonder I can't do it. I'm nearly ten."

Teacher: "I hope I didn't see you looking at Timmy's test paper."
Little Johnny: "I hope you didn't see me, too!"

Teacher: "This note from your father looks like your handwriting."
Little Johnny: "That's because he borrowed my pen."

Teacher: "Are you getting any parental guidance, Johnny? Tell me, what's your father like?"
Little Johnny: "Beer and women, Miss."

Teacher: "Where is your homework?"
Little Johnny: "I didn't do it, Miss, because I didn't want to add to your already heavy workload."

Teacher: "Where is your homework?"
Little Johnny: "Our central heating broke down, so we had to burn my homework to stop us from freezing."

Teacher: "Why haven't you given me your homework?"
Little Johnny: "I made it into a paper airplane and someone hijacked it."

Teacher: "Where is your homework?"
Little Johnny: "I lost it fighting a boy who said you weren't the best teacher in school."

Teacher: "For the last six months you've brought me a bag of raisins every week. Why have you stopped"?
Little Johnny: "My rabbit's dead, Miss."

Teacher: "Johnny, please don't whistle while you're studying."
Little Johnny: "I wasn't studying – just whistling."

Teacher: "Would you two boys at the back of the room stop passing notes?"
Little Johnny: "We're not passing notes. We're playing cards."

Teacher: "Name three collective nouns."
Little Johnny: "Waste basket, vacuum cleaner and garbage truck."

Teacher: "Do you say your prayers before eating?"
Little Johnny: "I don't have to. My mom is a good cook."

Teacher: "When is the best time to pick pears?"
Little Johnny: "When the farmer's not around."

Teacher: "George Washington not only chopped down his father's cherry tree, but also admitted it. So why didn't his father punish him?"
Little Johnny: "Because George still had the axe in his hand."

Teacher: "Why was George Washington buried at Mount Vernon?"
Little Johnny: "Because he was dead."

Teacher: "Does anyone know which month has 28 days?"
Little Johnny: "All of them."

Teacher: "What was the name of Noah's wife?"
Little Johnny: "Joan of Ark."

Teacher: "Why are you picking your nose in class?"
Little Johnny: "Because my parents won't let me do it at home."

Teacher: "I told you to stand at the end of the line."
Little Johnny: "I tried, but somebody was already there."

Teacher: "Why have you got cotton wool in your ears? Do you have an infection?"
Little Johnny: "You keep saying things go in one ear and out the other, so I'm trying to keep them all in."

Teacher: "You missed school yesterday, didn't you?"
Little Johnny: "Yes, but not very much."

Little Johnny: "I don't think I deserve zero for my homework."
Teacher: "Me neither, but it was the lowest mark I could give."

Teacher: "So Johnny can't come to school today? That's too bad! Who is speaking?"
Voice on phone: "This is my father."

What did the inflatable teacher say to the inflatable boy who took a pin into the inflatable school?
"You've let me down, you've let the school down, but most of all you've let yourself down."

The secret of teaching is to appear to have known all your life something you only learnt that morning.

At school I was teacher's pet. She kept me in a cage at the back of the class.

You know you're a teacher if you believe the staff room should be equipped with a Valium salt lick.

You know you're a teacher if you believe chocolate is a food group.

You know you're a teacher if you think people should be required to obtain a government permit before being allowed to reproduce.

You know you're a teacher if you get a secret thrill out of laminating something.

You know you're a teacher if you know 100 good excuses for being late.

You know you're a teacher if you can tell when it's a full moon without ever looking outside.

You know you're a teacher if you believe "shallow gene pool" should have its own box in the report card.

Dr Watson: "Holmes, what's another name for a primary school?"
Sherlock Holmes: "Elementary, my dear Watson."

SCIENCE

Why did the scientist fit a door knocker?
He wanted to win a no-bell prize.

Why do protons have mass?
I didn't even know they were Catholic.

Two hydrogen atoms are talking. One says: "I think I've lost an electron." The other asks: "Are you sure?" The first replies: "Yes, I'm positive."

The guy who split the atom is probably thrilled that we use "sliced bread" as our measure of greatness.

Last week a hypnotist convinced me that I was a soft, malleable metal with an atomic number of 82. I'm easily lead.

Scientists have just found the gene for shyness. They would have found it earlier, but it was hiding behind two other genes.

Does the name Pavlov ring a bell?

It's true that the Earth rotates, but scientists are always putting their own spin on it.

What do you call a robot that always takes the longest route round?
R2 detour.

Why are robots never afraid?
Because they have nerves of steel.

A scientist conducting a large experiment with liquid chemicals was trying to solve a problem when he fell in and became part of the solution.

What is the study of soda carbonation?
Fizzics.

Animal testing is a terrible idea. They get nervous and give the wrong answers.

Einstein's girlfriend told him: "I need two things from you, time and space." A puzzled Einstein looked at her and asked: "What's the second thing?"

I heard that in relativity theory, time and space are the same thing. Apparently Einstein discovered this when he kept showing up five miles late for meetings.

Do you want to hear a joke about sodium?
Na.

Dopeler effect: the tendency of stupid ideas to seem smarter when they come at you rapidly.

The only perfect science is hindsight.

Clones are people two.

After many attempts a scientist successfully cloned his own genes. He was so thrilled, he was beside himself.

A nuclear physicist is someone who has many ions in the fire.

It was recently discovered that research causes cancer in rats.

Biology is the only science where multiplication and division mean the same.

Friction can be a drag.

What is the most important thing to learn in chemistry?
Never lick the spoon.

What kind of aftershave do genetic scientists wear?
Eau de clone.

How can you tell a male chromosome from a female chromosome?
Pull down its genes.

In pursuit of scientific answers, animals have been tortured for the past 100 years. They're still not talking. I'm starting to think they don't know anything. *Jimmy Carr*

I'll tell you what gets me down – gravity.

What is a physicist's definition of sex?
A couple oscillating in a field.

Why are quantum physicists so poor at sex?
Because when they find the position, they can't find the momentum, and when they have the momentum, they can't find the position.

Atomic ache: what you get when you eat uranium.

The new theory on inertia doesn't seem to be gaining much momentum.

I love the three types of radiation. I like alpha and gamma, but I prefer the other type. I think it's beta.

What's a quark?
The sound a posh duck makes.

I've discovered a new compound that needs to be added to the periodic table. It's made up of B, O and O. It's the element of surprise.

Scientists believe that most people lean forward slightly when they nod their head. I'm inclined to agree.

THE SCOTS

How do you take a census in Scotland?
Throw a 10 pence coin in the street.

What's the difference between a Scotsman and a canoe?
A canoe tips occasionally.

It's incredible to think that every single Scotsman started out as a Scotch egg. *Milton Jones*

Why do Scottish families have double glazing?
So their children can't hear the ice cream van.

What's the difference between a Scotsman and a coconut?
You can get a drink out of a coconut.

Angus goes round to Jock's house and finds him carefully stripping the wallpaper from the walls. "You're decorating, I see," says Angus. "No," says Jock, "I'm moving house."

Did you hear about the Scotsman who gave up playing golf after 22 years? He lost his ball.

How do you disperse a crowd of angry Scots?
Pass round a collection box.

What do you call a Scotsman who always stops at the finest hotels?
A taxi driver.

Why was the Scotsman glum despite winning £5 million on the lottery?
It pained him to think of the pound he'd wasted on a second ticket.

How was the Scottish nuisance phone caller caught?
He kept reversing the charges.

A Scotsman arrived home to find a plumber's van outside his house. "Please God," he said. "Let it be her lover!"

Scottish newspaper ad: Lost – £5 note. Sentimental value.

Sign outside a Scottish cinema: "Free admission for old-age pensioners, if accompanied by both parents."

Did you hear about the Scotsman who complained to a magazine that if it didn't stop printing Scottish jokes he wouldn't borrow it to read any more?

What was the name of the Scottish cloakroom attendant?
Angus McCoatup.

I'm half-Scottish, half-Indian, which means, unlike most Scots, I don't get sunburn watching fireworks. ***Danny Bhoy***

Being from Scotland I love the summer. It's my favourite day of the year.

Outside a Glasgow police station was a poster: "Man Wanted For Murder". Over 100 Scotsmen applied for the job.

Did you hear about the Scottish football captain who lent the referee a coin for the toss? He demanded the ref's whistle as security.

Scots are very practical. If you say, "My father just died", most people will say: "Oh, that's a shame." A Scotsman will say: "What size were his feet?"

Did you hear about the Scotsman who was poisoned? He refused to die until he had got his money back on the empty bottle.

How can you spot a Scottish trawler?
It's the one not being followed by seagulls.

Did you hear about the Scotsman who promised his sister a food mixer as a wedding present? He bought her a wooden spoon.

And what about the Scotsman who told his children that the tooth fairy had been kidnapped by dental extremists?

I asked a Scotsman: "Did you have spots as a teenager?" He said: "Ach, nee."

How did the Scotsman save money on a personal address book?
He took a telephone directory and simply crossed out the names and addresses of the people he didn't know.

Why are many Scottish churches circular?
So nobody can hide in the corners during the collection.

One in three Scottish girls is obese. As are the other two. *Jimmy Carr*

Why was the Scotsman worried about getting a taxi to take him and his new girlfriend home?
Because she was so beautiful he could barely keep his eyes on the meter.

SECRETS

Of course I can keep secrets. It's the people I tell them to who can't keep them.

Some people have skeletons in their closet. I have a whole graveyard.

Never tell a secret to a pig. It may squeal.

There are two kinds of secrets: one is not worth keeping and the other is too good to keep.

My girlfriend is good at keeping secrets. We were engaged for three months before I knew it.

I never repeat gossip, so listen carefully the first time.

It turns out my girlfriend Big Amy had a secret husband. If only there'd been some clue . . .

SEX

Sex is the only activity where you start at the top and work your way to the bottom while getting a raise.

It seems they've finally found a cure for erectile dysfunction – that was a long time coming.

How do you make your girlfriend cry while you are having sex?
Phone her up and tell her about it.

Why is sex like a game of bridge?
If you have a good hand, you don't need a partner.

What did the banana say to the vibrator?
"What are you shaking for? She's going to *eat* me."

How do you make your wife scream after an orgasm?
Wipe your dick on the curtains.

What do you get if you mix Viagra and Prozac?
A guy who is ready to go but doesn't really care where.

What are the three words men hate to hear most during sex?
"Are you done?"

What are the three words women hate to hear most during sex?
"Honey, I'm home."

I read that men who make love twice a week live 12 years longer than men who are celibate. I said to my wife: "You're trying to kill me, aren't you?"

What's the square root of 69?
Ate something.

I bought my wife a sex manual but half the pages were missing. We went straight from foreplay to post-natal depression. ***Bob Monkhouse***

For a man, what's the best thing about a blow job?
Ten minutes of silence.

I went out with a girl who punched me in the face every time she had an orgasm. I didn't mind too much until I found out she was faking them.

Sex is nobody's business but the three people involved.

Mike: "Did you know that every condom has a serial number?"
Marty: "No, I've never had to unroll one that far."

All those in favour of Viagra, please rise.

Husband: "Why can't I tell when you have an orgasm?"
Wife: "Because you're never there when it happens."

Why don't women blink during foreplay?
There isn't time.

Masochist: "Hurt me!"
Sadist: "No."

After having sex with a girl, there's nothing worse than looking down to see a split, leaking condom hanging off the end of your dick, particularly when you weren't wearing one to start with.

Women just don't like me. When I called one of those phone sex lines, the woman said she had a headache.

Why does it take a million sperm to fertilize one egg?
They won't stop to ask for directions.

Celibacy leaves a lot to be desired.

I went to bed with two Thai girls last night. It was just like winning the lottery – we had six matching balls.

Sex is like a cassette. Insert, Play, Fast Forward, Pause, Eject.

My wife told me she wanted to have sex in the back seat of the car. She wanted me to drive. **Rodney Dangerfield**

Husband: "Fancy a quickie?"
Wife: "As opposed to what?"

I used to live for sex; now I'd die for some.

After a particularly disastrous sex session, I said to my wife: "Someday we'll look back on this, laugh nervously and change the subject."

Sex alone is not enough to build a relationship, but with two people . . .

I bought some of those super-sensitive condoms the other day. They're great. They hang around afterwards and talk to the woman.

I once had sex for an hour and five minutes. I'll always remember it because it was the night the clocks went forward.

During sex most married men fantasize that their wives aren't fantasizing.

Mike: "My wife and I have what we call Olympic sex."
Marty: "Sounds great!"
Mike: "Not really. It only happens once every four years."

A girl told me she wouldn't sleep with me if I was the last person on Earth. If I was the last person on Earth, she wouldn't have a say in the matter.

I remember the first time I had sex with my wife was across a table. It was amazing, although some of the guests thought it rather spoiled the reception.

What do you call a man who's just had sex?
Anything you like: he's asleep.

I went to a premature ejaculation class this morning, but they told me it was tomorrow.

What's the difference between erotic and kinky?
Erotic is using a feather; kinky is using the whole chicken.

I was making love to this girl and she started crying. I said: "Are you going to hate yourself in the morning?" She said: "No, I hate myself now!"

What do you call kinky sex with chocolate?
S&M&M.

Mike: "I never had sex with my wife before we were married. How about you?"
Marty: "I'm not sure. What was her maiden name?"

What food kills a woman's sex drive?
Wedding cake.

My wife said I only ever want sex with her when I'm drunk. That's not true. I usually want a kebab as well.

Wife: "Why do you never call out my name when we're making love?"
Husband: "I don't want to wake you."

I haven't had sex for about 1 year, 3 months, 18 days and 47 minutes. It doesn't bother me though.

Viagra is now available in powder form to put in your tea. It doesn't enhance your sexual performance, but it does stop your biscuit going soft.

What do condoms and cameras have in common?
Both capture the moment.

At my age I like threesomes – in case one of us dies. *Rodney Dangerfield*

What did the penis say to the condom?
"Cover me, I'm going in!"

As I lay in bed, I felt a hand reach into my boxer shorts and start to play with my balls. It was nice, but I wasn't in the mood. "Not tonight," I said. "I'm tired." "It doesn't work like that in here," said my cellmate.

I had sex with my girlfriend over a table and got her pregnant. Then she had me over a barrel.

My wife surprised me last night by saying she wanted to go on top. But that's the wonderful unpredictability of bunk beds.

Why do men like having sex with the lights on?
It makes it easier to put a name to the face.

Incest: I can relate to that.

Jackie: "Which do you prefer – sex or cake?"
Jill: "What kind of cake?"

My sex is life is like my Ferrari 599 GTO. I don't have a Ferrari 599 GTO.

Being single is like a vacuum. It sucks when you are turned on.

I've bought some of that 007 Viagra. It makes you roger more.

What's the best way to stop a guy smoking after sex?
Fill his water bed with gasoline.

Man: "Doctor, I suffer from premature ejaculation. Can you help?"
Doctor: "No, but I can introduce you to a woman with Attention Deficit Disorder."

My wife said she wanted to make me happy in the bedroom. So now the bedroom has a 42-inch TV, a fridge full of beer, and she sleeps in the lounge.

My wife's a sex object. Every time I ask for sex, she objects. **Les Dawson**

I accidentally called a phone sex line for married people. It was just a long uncomfortable silence till the woman's voice said: "Hurry up, I need to check the casserole."

What's the speed limit of sex?
68, because at 69 you have to turn around.

Husband: "Shall we try swapping positions tonight?"
Wife: "That's a good idea. You stand by the ironing board while I sit on the sofa and fart."

I asked my wife if she wanted a cigarette after sex. She said: "No, one drag is enough."

I think my girlfriend must have had sixty-one boyfriends before me because she calls me her sixty-second lover.

For a man, what is the downside of a threesome?
He'll probably disappoint two women instead of one.

The big difference between sex for money and sex for free is that sex for money usually costs a lot less.

My sex life is unbelievable. Whenever I tell people I have a sex life, they don't believe me.

Husband: "That was great sex! I never knew you had it in you!"
Wife: "That's funny. Neither did I. But I guess size isn't everything."

What are the two things that a woman should never do in bed?
Point and laugh.

I went to bed with a blind girl last night, and she said I had the biggest dick she'd ever laid her hands on. I said: "You're pulling my leg."

Oral sex makes one's day, but anal sex makes one's hole weak.

When they have sex, what do most men like their wives to do?
The shopping.

My wife said I was like an animal in bed last night . . . whatever a sloth is.

Before we make love my husband takes a painkiller. *Joan Rivers*

Man: "Am I the first man you ever made love to?"
Woman: "You might be. I must say your face does look familiar."

What should you do if your girlfriend starts smoking in bed?
Use a lubricant.

What did Adam say to Eve?
"Stand back! I don't know how big this thing gets."

Man: "Since I first saw you, I've wanted to make love to you really badly."
Woman: "Well, you've succeeded."

I bought one of those inflatable dolls last week. To be honest, it was a bit of a let-down.

With my first wife, it was just sex, sex, sex. Three times in 20 years.

Did you hear about the guy who was into bestiality? His sex life has gone to the dogs.

I have a tremendous sex drive. My girlfriend lives 50 miles away.

Man: "Do you approve of sex before marriage?"
Vicar: "Not if it delays the service."

It's horrible when you're having sex and you have to stop halfway through, like when the doorbell goes or the saucepan boils over . . . or you run out of money. *Frank Skinner*

There's a new addition to the *Kama Sutra*. It's called the plumber position: you stay in all day and nobody comes.

Viagra is like Disneyland – a one-hour wait for a two-minute ride.

What matters is not the length of the wand but the magic in the stick.

The trouble with safe sex is it's a tight squeeze and you have to remember the combination.

They say rhino horn is an aphrodisiac, which you'd probably need if your girlfriend looked like a rhino.

Husband: "I can't remember the last time we made love."
Wife: "I can, and that's why we're not doing it again!"

I went to London last weekend and had sex with a model . . . which led to me being thrown out of Madame Tussaud's.

My wife thinks having sex doggie-style means making me sit up and beg for it.

I tried some of that aphrodisiac rhino horn, and now I can't stop charging at Land Rovers.

Why is a man more intelligent when he's having sex?
Because he's plugged into a woman.

Mike: "The woman I slept with last night is really big – everywhere – but she's very sensitive about it."
Marty: "Did you put your foot in it?"
Mike: "No, but I probably could have."

I always call out my wife's name during sex . . . just to make sure she's not around.

I have a lot of issues with sex . . . mostly *Playboy, Penthouse* and *Hustler*.

My girlfriend and I often role-play in the bedroom. She pretends she's Catwoman, and I pretend that I love her. *Frankie Boyle*

What's the definition of making love?
Something a woman does while a guy is shagging her.

Did you hear about the woman who lost her virginity, but still had the box it came in?

If a man doesn't climax, it's his fault; if a woman doesn't climax, it's his fault.

What does a woman's asshole do when she is having an orgasm?
He's usually at home with the kids.

Silence doesn't necessarily mean your sexual performance was so good it left her speechless.

My wife's so ungrateful. The other day I gave her a massive orgasm, and she just spat it out.

Woman to man: "Does time fly when you're having sex – or was it really just 45 seconds?"

Did you hear about the man who wanted people to pretend to spank him? He was a pseudo-masochist.

Why did Miss Piggy have trouble speaking?
She had a frog in her throat.

An empty aluminium cigar tube filled with angry wasps makes an inexpensive vibrator.

My wife only ever has sex with me for a purpose. Last night it was to time an egg.

Sex when you're married is like going to a 7-Eleven shop. There's not as much variety, but at three o'clock in the morning it's always there.

My girlfriend said I was lousy in the bedroom department, but she doesn't realize how difficult it was to keep an erection with the store manager shouting at me.

My wife and I take turns at oral sex. First she talks about it, then I talk about it.

Impotence is nature's way of saying "no hard feelings".

Last night in bed, my wife said we should try some role reversal. So I said I had a headache.

Sex is like air – it's not important unless you aren't getting any.

A medical report states that the human male is physically capable of enjoying sex up to and even beyond the age of 80. Not as a participant of course . . . *Denis Norden*

Mike: "After 20 years of marriage, sex is down to three times a year."
Marty: "Same here. In fact, if my wife didn't sleep with her mouth open, I'd get none at all."

I tried phone sex once, but the holes in the dialler were too small.

My friend's really unlucky. She hasn't had sex with a man for years in case of disease, but last year she caught *E. coli* from a cucumber.

My wife says our sex life has become boring and that I'm easily distracted. Oh, well, better get back to it, I suppose.

SHE'S LIKE . . .

She's like train tracks – she's been laid across the country.

She's like a hardware store – 10 cents a screw.

She's like a doorknob – everyone gets a turn.

She's like a Hoover – she sucks, blows, and finally gets laid in the closet.

She's like a race car driver – she burns a lot of rubbers.

She's like a Workmate – accepts tools of all sizes.

She's like a birthday cake – everybody gets a piece.

She's like an escalator – guys go up and down on her all day.

She's like a streetlamp – you can find her turned on at night on any street corner.

She's like a gas station – you have to pay before you pump.

SHE WAS ONLY . . .

She was only a plumber's daughter, but she sure gave my heart a wrench.

She was only a pilot's daughter, but she kept her cockpit clean.

She was only an architect's daughter, but she knew all the angles.

She was only a whisky maker's daughter, but I loved her still.

She was only a road worker's daughter, but she knew how to get her asphalt.

She was only an electrician's daughter, but she had all the right connections.

She was only a draughtsman's daughter, but she knew where to draw the line.

She was only a constable's daughter, but she wouldn't let the Chief Inspector.

She was only a meteorologist's daughter, but she had a warm front.

She was only an actuary's daughter, but she knew her surrender value.

She was only a minister's daughter, but I wouldn't put anything pastor.

She was only a baseball pitcher's daughter, but you should have seen her curves.

She was only a blacksmith's daughter, but she knew how to forge ahead.

She was only a fisherman's daughter, but when she saw my rod she reeled.

She was only a surgeon's daughter, but she knew how to operate.

She was only a stableman's daughter, but all the horse manure.

She was only a photographer's daughter, but she was really developed.

She was only a barman's daughter, but she knew how to pull them.

She was only a greengrocer's daughter, but her melons were the juiciest in town.

She was only a barrister's daughter, but she kept a tight hold on her briefs.

She was only a carpenter's daughter, but she always had tools in her box.

She was only an undertaker's daughter, but anyone cadaver.

She was only a violinist's daughter, but when she took off her G-string all the boys fiddled.

SHIPS

Passenger to ship's officer: "Which one of these is the non-smoking lifeboat?"

Why didn't the sailors play cards?
Because the captain was sitting on the deck.

It's rarely a good sign when you see the captain running towards you wearing a life-jacket.

Did you hear about the shipwreck survivor who clung to a huge bar of soap and was eventually washed ashore?

Consider this: the Ark was built by amateurs, the *Titanic* was built by professionals.

On the one hand, Captain Hook was pretty awesome.

How do you make a pirate angry?
Take the P out of him.

Wife: "When you proposed to me, you said you had an ocean yacht."
Husband: "Just shut up and row!"

Why did the pirate refuse to say, "Aye, aye, captain"?
Because he only had one eye.

Counting the number of metal bolts along the side of a ship is not just fascinating, it's riveting.

If I were a pirate with only one eye, there's no way I'd risk losing the other by having a parrot with a sharp beak on my shoulder. *Karl Pilkington*

Where on a ship can you find a pirate's bathroom?
The poop deck.

What did the pirate order when he went to a fish restaurant?
Pieces of skate.

What happened to the survivors of a collision between a red ship and a blue ship?
They were marooned.

A new book speculates that the designer of the *Titanic* had a lisp. That's unthinkable.

What do you get when you cross the Atlantic with the *Titanic*?
Just over halfway.

Did you hear about the man who opened a yacht showroom? Sails went through the roof.

My grandfather was on a ship which sank on 5 November. He let off all the flares, but the people on the other ships just went "Ooooooh!"

The pirate captain was standing in his treasure pile. He didn't have much – his booty was only shin-deep.

Which pirate drools continuously?
Long John Saliva.

Ancient ships were much more fuel-efficient. They got thousands of miles to the galleon.

Wife: "I put all your clothes in that little closet with the glass window."
Husband: "You mean the porthole . . .?"

When I was a deep-sea diver, I never found any sunken ships. They said I was reckless. – *Tim Vine*

Why did the tugboat drown itself?
It heard that its mother was a tramp and its father was a ferry.

Why could Long John Silver never find an aspirin?
Because his parrots ate 'em all.

How much does it cost a pirate to get his ears pierced?
A buck an ear.

Why did the passengers rush to see the musicians on the *Titanic*?
Because someone shouted "A band on ship."

SHOES

Did you hear about the man who put on a pair of clean socks every day? By the end of the week he couldn't get his shoes on.

A man says to a hobo: "How come you're only wearing one shoe? Did you lose one?" "No," says the hobo. "I found one."

Why did the man clean shoes for a living?
Because he took a real shine to it.

I met a Dutch girl with inflatable shoes last week. I phoned her up to arrange a date, but unfortunately she'd popped her clogs.

Why was the baby shoe unhappy?
His father was a loafer, and his mother was a sneaker.

The best way to forget all your troubles is to wear tight shoes.

What do you call a shoe made from a banana?
A slipper.

How did the idiot come to wear his shoes on the wrong feet?
He put them on while his legs were crossed.

Why did the woman wear pumps?
She had water on the knees.

"I stand corrected," said the man in the orthopaedic shoes.

Wife: "No wonder you're in pain! You've got your shoes on the wrong feet!"
Husband: "But they're the only feet I have."

I only own one running shoe. It's my personal trainer.

Why was the Italian stiletto unhappy?
She went on a date with a Cuban heel.

Why did my wife cross the road?
To go back to the first shoe shop we went in three hours ago!

SHOPPING

Did you hear about the guy who bought a sponge door? Don't knock it.

I bought a hip-hop back scratcher from Jay-Z. Now I've got 99 problems but the itch ain't one.

My wife and I always hold hands. If I let go, she goes shopping.

I went to the supermarket to buy some alphabet soup, but they said it was out of print.

Once you've seen one shopping centre, you've seen a mall.

I used to work in a health shop, and people would come in and say, "Evening Primrose Oil?" I'd say, "Please call me Kevin."

If you feel the world is moving too fast, take comfort from the queue for the supermarket checkout.

I wish I hadn't bought that corrugated iron. If anything it's made my clothes *more* creased.

My wife said she was going window shopping. She came home with a bay and two stained-glass.

I was in the supermarket the other day, and I met a lady in the aisle where they keep the generic brands. Her name was Woman.

I complained to the supermarket manager: "This vinegar has got lumps in it." He said: "Those are pickled onions."

Two tigers are walking down the aisle of a supermarket. One says to the other: "Quiet in here today, isn't it?"

When faced with a dozen different brands of light bulb, how do you decide which to buy?
By process of illumination.

Why was one of the clerks worried when the store's sticker gun went out of control?
She found there was a price on her head.

How can you spot people who can't count to 10?
They're the ones in front of you in the supermarket express lane.

I asked the supermarket manager: "Why are all those pears sitting around a table?" "Oh," he said, "they're Conference pears."

Buy one, get one free: does it have to be in that order?

My girlfriend came home from a shopping trip with five big white toy bears. I'm afraid she may have buy polar disorder.

A supermarket is a place where you can spend 20 minutes searching for instant coffee.

My mother is the kind of woman you don't want to be in line behind at the supermarket. She has coupons for coupons. *Chris Rock*

My wife will buy anything marked down. Last week she bought an escalator.

A jellyfish walked into a hardware shop and bought ten drills.

I bought a new water softener. Now my water is so soft, when it drips it doesn't make a sound.

Two men are looking in a shop window. One points to a shirt and says: "That's the one I'd get." At which point a Cyclops appears and beats him up.

Last week I bought a fridge magnet. They really work. So far I've got 11 fridges.

I bought some Häagen-Dazs ice cream, and as the cashier rang it up, I asked: "How do you pronounce that?" She said slowly: "Four dollars and 59 cents."

All my wife does is shop. Once she was sick for a week and three stores went under.

I went to the paper shop this morning, but it had blown away.

I bought some batteries but they were not included. So I had to buy them again.

The sign at the supermarket checkout said: "Eight items or less." So I changed my name to Les.

A fun thing to do in the checkout line is to take one thing from the cart in front of you and see if they notice. I did it last week, but the woman didn't see the joke. Perhaps I shouldn't have taken her baby.

The staff at my local supermarket are so bad that when I used the self-service checkout, I was named employee of the month.

I walked up to the cheese counter . . . which interrupted him and so he had to start again.

I bought a *Lord of the Rings*-themed kitchen. My wife loves the hob bit.

My wife and I went into a bed store, and saw a bed we really liked. But we couldn't decide whether or not to buy it. In the end we decided to sleep on it.

On the 13th second of the 13th minute of the 13th hour of the 13th day of the 13th month, I realized the cut-price calendar I'd bought was crap.

I bought a new mouse mat today. Hopefully that will stop them leaving footprints all over my kitchen floor.

People who "put something by" each week are simply not shopping hard enough.

I just spent $300 on a pair of binoculars. I think they saw me coming.

Woman: "I asked for six apples, but you've only given me five."
Greengrocer: "I know, but one was rotten, so I saved you the trouble of throwing it away."

I bought myself a steam cleaner because my steam is absolutely filthy.

Customer: "Can I try on that dress in the window?"
Store assistant: "No, madam, you'll have to use the fitting room like everyone else."

I've just bought a new aftershave that smells like breadcrumbs. The birds love it.

A man walks into a hardware shop and says: "One mousetrap, please, and can you hurry? I have to catch a bus." "Sorry," says the sales assistant, "but our traps aren't that big."

I bought a coin press last week, but there are no instructions. I can't make head or tail of it.

My wife wanted to buy a $1,500 garden slide, but it had an 80-degree incline. I thought, That's a bit steep.

I haven't seen my wife for three days. I don't know whether she's left me or gone shopping.

I bought a soldering iron last week. It made a right mess of my clothes.

I own a shop selling "Closed" signs. We haven't had a single customer.

A man goes into a bookshop and asks the woman at the desk: "Do you keep stationery here?" "No," she says, "sometimes I wriggle about a bit."

Last week I bought a brand-new boomerang. But I just don't seem able to throw the old one away.

SHOW BUSINESS

A friend told me last week that he'd been a mime artist for the past 10 years. I said: "You kept that quiet!"

I need a new assistant for my knife-throwing act. I also need a large rug and a spade.

What's the best way to kill a variety act?
Go for the juggler.

I used to work with a guy who started his show by taking the tops off bottles of beer with his butt. Not much of an act, but a hell of an opener.

SIGNS

I saw a sign that said "These doors are alarmed". Well, I didn't frighten them.

I saw a billboard poster that said "Learn to read". I thought, Who is it aimed at?

I think there was a sign writers' strike in town today, but it was hard to tell. Their placards were blank.

Why do the signs that say "Slow Children" have a picture of a running child?

I saw a sign that said: "Have you seen this man?" So I phoned up and said: "No." *Kevin Bridges*

Sign outside a brothel: "It's a business doing pleasure with you".

Notice in a farmer's field: "The farmer allows walkers to cross the field for free, but the bull charges".

Sign on a lawn at a drug rehab centre: "Keep off the grass".

Sign on a Scottish golf course: "Please refrain from picking up lost balls until they have finished rolling".

Sign outside a police station: "If you drink and drive, we'll provide the chasers".

Sign in a bank: "We can loan you enough money to get completely out of debt".

Sign on a plumber's van: "Don't sleep with a drip. Call your plumber".

Sign outside a car exhaust repair shop: "No appointment necessary. We hear you coming".

Sign on Spike Milligan's office door: "Do not disturb. I'm disturbed enough already".

Sign in a bar: "Those drinking to forget please pay in advance".

Sign in a music store: "Out to lunch. Bach at 2.0. Offenbach at 2.30".

Sign on the van of Mr Singh the builder: "You've had the cowboys, now try the Indians".

Sign on a divorce lawyer's wall: "Satisfaction guaranteed or your honey back".

Sign in a company reception area: "We shoot every third salesman, and the second one just left".

Sign in a clothing store: "Come inside and have a fit".

Sign in a veterinarian's waiting room: "Back in five minutes. Sit! Stay!"

Sign on a diaper service truck: "Rock a dry baby".

Sign in an airplane: "After use, please return stewardess to upright position".

Sign in an elevator: "Eighth-floor button out of order. Please push three and five instead".

Sign on an electrician's truck: "Let me check your shorts".

Sign on a broken perfume bottle: "Out of odour".

Sign at the tyre store: "We skid you not!"

Sign in a DIY store: "Husbands choosing colours must have note from wives".

Sign in a pet store: "Buy one dog, get one flea".

Sign on a plumber's truck: "A flush beats a full house".

A man was asked to design a warning sign for deer to stop them crossing busy roads. He came up with "The Buck Stops Here".

I saw a sign outside my house saying: "We are digging this road". I thought to myself: Thanks, I really like it, too.

I saw a billboard that read "Future events". I thought, That's a sign of things to come. *Tim Vine*

I saw a sign that made me piss myself yesterday. It said "Toilets Closed".

SKUNKS

Did you hear about the blind skunk? He fell in love with a fart.

What do you call two skunks having a 69?
Odor Eaters.

What's black, white and red all over?
A skunk with nappy rash.

What do you get if you cross a skunk with a hot-air balloon?
Something that stinks to high heaven.

What did the judge say when he saw the skunk in the witness box?
"Odour in court!"

What's the difference between a skunk and a squirrel?
The skunk uses cheaper deodorant.

Did you hear about the skunk that fell in a lake and stank to the bottom?

What do you get if you cross an owl with a skunk?
Something that smells but doesn't give a hoot.

Why did the skunk buy three boxes of tissues?
Because he had a stinking cold.

Did you hear about the skunk that went to church? He had his own pew.

SKYDIVING

Why don't blind people go skydiving?
It scares the hell out of their dogs.

How does a blind skydiver know when he's approaching the ground?
His dog's lead goes slack.

You don't need a parachute to skydive. You only need a parachute to skydive twice.

Why did the skydiver quit his job?
He fell out with his boss.

Why do female skydivers wear jockstraps?
So they don't whistle on the way down.

What's the hardest part about skydiving?
The ground.

Novice skydiver: "If my main parachute doesn't open and my reserve parachute doesn't open, how long till I hit the ground?"
Instructor: "The rest of your life."

SLEEP

I like to sleep with the bedside lamp on, even though my wife thinks it's weird. I don't see why. I think it makes a great hat.

I woke up the other morning and found that everything in my room had been replaced by an exact replica. ***Steven Wright***

Why did the insomniac marry the man with a nervous tic?
So she could get forty winks.

I won't rest until I find a cure for insomnia.

Sleeping comes naturally to me. I could do it with my eyes closed.

I haven't slept for six days, because that would be too long.

A man tells the doctor he is having trouble sleeping. The doctor advises: "Sit on the edge of the bed – you'll soon drop off."

I slept through the alarm this morning. Luckily it was only a small fire.

If you want your wife to pay undivided attention to every word you say, talk in your sleep.

My wife just found out I replaced our bed with a trampoline. She hit the roof.

I usually sleep with my laptop next to me in bed, but it got angry when it discovered I'd got the Internet on my phone and so I ended up sleeping on the couch.

Man: "Doctor, I suffer from insomnia."
Doctor: "Don't lose any sleep over it."

I woke up this morning with a dead leg. No idea who it belongs to. *Tony Cowards*

Rule of bed: the one who snores will fall asleep first.

Jackie: "Do you ever wake up grumpy?"
Jill: "Sometimes, but other times I let him sleep."

I sleep better naked. I just wish the flight attendant had been more understanding.

I had trouble sleeping last night. I tried counting black sheep but I couldn't see them in the dark.

If children refuse to sleep during nap time, are they guilty of resisting a rest?

Insomnia is a contagious disease often transmitted from babies to parents.

Did you hear about the guy who bought an electric blanket because he wanted his wife to be hot in bed?

Warm baths do not cure insomnia. Two bottles of wine cure insomnia.

I missed my nap today. I slept right through it. *Henny Youngman*

What's a good cure for sleepwalking?
Sprinkle tin tacks on your bedroom floor.

I bought a bottle of sleeping tablets. The label said: "WARNING: may cause drowsiness".

Last night I lay in bed looking up at the stars in the sky, and I thought: Where the hell is the ceiling?

The early worm gets eaten by the bird, so sleep late.

I got out the wrong side of bed this morning, and I've been grumpy ever since. That's because my bed is next to the window and I live on the third floor.

Insomnia is what you think you've got when you lie awake all night for an hour.

Why do we feel safe under blankets? It's not like a murderer will come in thinking, I'm gonna kill . . . oh, damn, he's under a blanket!

I stayed awake all night trying to remember whether I have amnesia or insomnia.

Why do husbands often talk in their sleep?
It's the only chance they get.

Insomnia is the triumph of mind over mattress.

This morning I woke up to the unmistakable smell of pigs in a blanket. But that's the price you pay for letting the relatives stay over.

Doctor: "How much sleep do you usually need?"
Man: "About 15 minutes more."

I grew up in a house with three brothers, so we all had to share beds. I didn't know what it was like to sleep in a bed alone until I got married.

A noise woke me up this morning. It was the crack of dawn.

When I woke up this morning, my girlfriend asked if I'd slept well. I said: "No, I made a few mistakes." *Steven Wright*

A man tells the doctor: "I snore so loudly, I keep myself awake." The doctor suggests: "Have you tried sleeping in another room?"

A lot of couples sleep in separate beds when they get older, but it's rarely a good sign when she suggests it on your wedding night.

First we slept in separate rooms, then it became separate houses and separate towns.

I'm not saying my wife and I no longer sleep in the same bed, but if I want to stroke her back I have to catch two buses and a tram.

My wife thinks we should sleep in separate beds. Good idea. I've chosen the blonde's at number 32.

Why do women rub their eyes when they get up in the morning?
Because they don't have balls to scratch.

SLUGS AND SNAILS

People take the life of a snail with a pinch of salt.

What's the definition of a slug?
A homeless snail.

Two slugs are slithering along the path when they get stuck behind two snails. "Oh, no!" groan the slugs. "Caravans!"

Why did the snail go to assertiveness classes?
To bring him out of his shell.

I thought pulling the shell off my racing snail would help it move faster, but instead it became sluggish.

I don't like eating snails. I prefer fast food.

SNAKES

Two pythons had an argument. Afterwards, the male python coiled his body and planted a kiss on the female's mouth. The female python said: "You can't get round me just like that you know."

What do you call a snake who works for the British government?
A civil serpent.

Why did some snakes disobey Noah when he said: "Go forth and multiply"?
They couldn't, because they were adders.

I met an Indian who worked with cobras. He was a charming man.

My friend was bitten by a rattlesnake, and I tried to save him by telling him an amusing story. If I'd known the difference between antidote and anecdote, I guess he'd be alive today.

Why can't you trust snakes?
They speak with forked tongues.

Why did the boa constrictors get married?
They had a crush on each other.

What did St Patrick say to the snakes when he was driving them out of Ireland?
"Are ye all right in the back there, lads?"

SOCCER

Why is a blind man like a bad football team?
Both struggle to hold on to a lead.

What do you say to a Spanish soccer player with no legs?
"Grassiass."

Two flies are playing football in a saucer. One says to the other: "We need to improve our game – next week we're in the cup."

What do you call a Scotsman at the World Cup finals?
Ref.

Husband to wife: "I know I said I loved you more than football, darling, but that was during the close season."

A bad football team is like an old bra – no cups and little support.

Did you hear about the thieves who broke into the football club and stole the most valuable item in the trophy room? Police are looking for someone carrying a rolled-up carpet.

Did you hear about the thieves who stole all of the club's silverware acquired over the previous 40 years – knives, forks, spoons, everything?

Footballer Michael Owen has released a new fragrance. It's called My Cologne.

Why doesn't Pakistan have an international football team?
Because every time they get a corner, they open a shop.

I'm the kind of person who likes to think outside of the box, which has rather hindered my career as a goalkeeper.

The World Cup in South Africa was amazing. The last time I saw African kids that excited, Madonna was at their school with a net. *Russell Howard*

I went to a football match where both sets of supporters were chanting: "You're not singing any more." It was a charity match for the deaf.

Did you hear about the player who hit the bar . . . after every game?

Tony Blair gave the half-time team talk at a game, but nobody believed him when he warned that the opponents could mount a serious attack in the next 45 minutes.

After dating the team's goalie for a while, my sister decided he was definitely a keeper.

Why did women's football take so long to catch on?
Because it took ages to persuade 11 women to wear the same outfit in public.

They say football is a game of two halves. Not for me. I can get through six pints while watching it on TV at the pub.

Why don't teenage boys make good goalkeepers?
They find it hard to keep a clean sheet.

What did the US soccer coach do after winning the World Cup?
He turned off his Play Station.

What did the footballer say when he accidentally hiccupped during a game?
"Sorry, it was a freak hic."

How did the soccer pitch end up as a triangle?
Someone took a corner.

What do Scottish football teams and a three-pin plug have in common?
They're both useless in Europe.

My team's unbeaten in 20 games this season which were all 4–1 and one 4–4. I love playing for the Musketeers.

Why did the soccer coach flood the pitch?
He wanted to bring on the sub.

The trouble with the Homeless Football World Cup is that all the players fight over who's going to be on the bench. *Tony Cowards*

Why did they call the goalkeeper Dracula?
Because he was afraid of crosses.

Why did they call the goalkeeper Cinderella?
Because he was late for the ball.

Did you hear about the accident-prone goalkeeper who put his head in his hands and dropped it?

Did you hear about the clueless manager who bought a microwave so he could get his substitutes warmed up quicker?

When a woman says, "We need to talk", why is it never about football?

My wife says she's leaving me because I think more about football than I think of her. I'm really going to miss her – we've been together for nearly nine seasons now.

SOCIAL WORKERS

What's the difference between a Rottweiler and a social worker?
It's easier to get your kids back from a Rottweiler.

Two social workers see a man lying on the pavement covered in blood. As they walk past, one says to the other: "Whoever did that really needs help."

SPACE

What do you call an overweight alien?
Extra cholesterol.

What did the alien say to the gas pump?
"Don't you know it's rude to stick your finger in your ear while I'm talking to you?"

Why was the thirsty alien hanging around the computer keyboard?
He was looking for the space bar.

Did you hear about the mysterious chip pan in the sky? It was described as an unidentified frying object.

I found an alien pleasuring himself in my freezer. He said: "I come in peas."

Why is an astronaut like an American footballer?
Both like to make safe touch-downs.

Did you hear about the astronaut who broke the law of gravity? He got a suspended sentence.

The star asked the sun: "Why is the moon always up so late?"
The sun said: "It's just a phase."

How do you know when the moon is broke?
It's down to its last quarter.

If space is a vacuum, who changes the bags?

I'm being abducted by aliens at 4.47 p.m. tomorrow. They want me because I can see into the future.

Did you hear about the astronaut who took a book to read in space? He couldn't put it down.

Two American astronomers are visiting a French observatory. One asks: "Comet Halley view?"

What did the alien say when he entered the library?
"Take me to your reader."

SPEECH

Don't talk to me about freedom of speech!

Freedom of speech is wonderful – right up there with the freedom not to listen.

In a nation of free speech, why are there telephone bills?

An after-dinner speaker is someone who rises to the occasion and then stands too long.

I recently gave a talk to a group of backpackers. They were on the edge of their seats. **Stewart Francis**

Ancient orators tended to Babylon.

I went to see one of those motivational speakers last week. Well, I nearly did.

"Malities. Malities. Malities. Malities. Well, that's the formalities out of the way . . ."

SPIDERS

Why do black widow spiders kill their males after mating?
To stop the snoring before it starts.

I just killed a huge spider crawling along the floor with my shoe. I don't care how big a spider is, nobody steals my shoe!

My son wanted a pet spider, so I went to the local pet store but they were $90. Blow that! I thought. I can get one cheaper off the web.

SPORTS

I went bobsleighing last night. I killed 18 people called Bob.

As the Polish bobsleigh team set off on their first run, the brake man suddenly fell to the floor, clutching his leg. "Go on without me," he cried. "I'll only slow you down."

I'm a curling addict. I need a hit, and I want to get stoned.

Luge is sliding along an ice chute at 90 m.p.h. on what is essentially a tea tray.

I'm not very interested in tobogganing, but I would do it if pushed. **Gary Delaney**

Skiing can be very time-consuming. I spent one day skiing and six in hospital.

If you're going to try cross-country skiing, start with a small country.

Skiers are always jumping to contusions.

A skier is someone why pays an arm and a leg for the privilege of breaking them.

I got a useful pamphlet with my new skis. It tells you how to convert them into a pair of splints.

A small girl watching a water-skier says to her father: "That man is so silly. He'll never catch that boat!"

What's the hardest part of rollerblading?
Telling your parents you're gay.

Did you hear about the two silkworms who had a race? It ended in a tie.

A kitchen knife and a spoon had a race. Who won?
Neither. It ended in a drawer.

Why was the electrician disqualified from the running race?
Because he made a short circuit.

How do you start a jelly race?
"Get set . . ."

How do you start a teddy bear race?
"Ready, teddy, go!"

How do you start a firefly race?
"Ready, steady, glow!"

Did you hear who won the Bangkok marathon? I heard it was a Thai.

What's the toughest part of the Chinese Marathon?
That moment when you hit the wall.

I was watching a marathon where one runner was dressed as a chicken and another as an egg. I thought, This could be interesting.

I'm going to compete in a marathon dressed as Michael Jackson. I'm not sure which race yet.

I was asked to run the London Marathon for charity, but I had to decline as I've no experience of organizing something that big.

Marathon runners with bad footwear suffer the agony of defeat.

Did you hear about the two fat guys who ran the New York Marathon? One ran in short bursts, the other in burst shorts.

I once ran for my school – but only because the bus was late.

I couldn't really sprint at school. I preferred to take my time and build up my endurance levels, which benefited me in the long run.

Why did the runner protest after tripping over a large wicker basket full of food on the final bend?
He felt he'd been hampered.

Rugby is a game played by gentlemen with odd-shaped balls.

I was fired from the tug-of-war team for not pulling my weight.

Why did the Indy car driver make eight pitstops during the race?
He kept asking for directions.

To neigh or not to neigh. That is equestrian.

TV announcer: "Who will take the second shot in this snooker game? Find out after the break."

I don't think I'm as popular as I thought – I've been put in goal for my local darts team.

I played darts with my brother last week, but it was really hard getting him to stick in the board.

My wife didn't understand darts, so I had to explain some of the finer points.

Did you hear about the dumb guy who turned up for the Olympics with a roll of barbed wire under his arm, and came third in the fencing?

The Olympic flag now has only four rings – green, blue, red and black. The Greeks had to pawn the gold one.

I wanted to go to the Paralympics, but I couldn't get a parking space anywhere near the stadium.

Where are the Olympics for people with minor afflictions? Dressage for haemorrhoid sufferers? The 4x100 relay for multiple personality disorders? *Hal Cruttenden*

My girlfriend can't wrestle, but you should see her box!

I love rowing. It's oarsome.

Show me a crazy rower who has fallen out of a one-man boating race, and I'll show you a man who is out of his scull.

The indecisive rower could not choose either oar.

Volleyball is just a competitive version of don't let the balloon touch the floor.

There are drug tests everywhere in sport. Even the old men who play bowls have been giving urine samples, although they didn't mean to.

If you have a referee in boxing, a referee in soccer and a referee in rugby, what do you have in bowls?
Prunes and custard.

My brother used to be a sports repairman. He fixed football matches, horse races, boxing fights . . .

My granddad races pigeons. I don't know why – he never beats them.

STATISTICS

A recent survey showed six out of seven dwarfs aren't Happy.

I just got back from a statistical probability conference. It was average.

Statistics show that 55 per cent of workers would have sex with a co-worker at a Christmas party. The other 45 per cent were women.

Three out of four Canadians make up 75 per cent of the population.

Statistically two out of three isn't bad. Unless you come home from the park with two out of three kids. Then it's bad.

Statistics are like mini-skirts. They give you ideas but hide the most important thing.

Figures show that every two minutes in England a woman gives birth. This woman must be stopped.

63 per cent of men have had sex in the shower; the other 37 per cent have never been in prison.

Smoking is the leading cause of statistics.

Statistics show that at the age of 80, there are five women to every man. What a lousy time for a man to get those odds!

If four out of five people suffer from diarrhoea, does that mean that one person enjoys it?

Statistics show that 90 per cent of men don't know how to use a condom. These people are called dads.

STOCKBROKING

Why did God create stock market analysts?
To make weather forecasters look competent.

Never trust a stockbroker who's married to a travel agent.

The only way to make a killing on the stock markets is to shoot your broker.

I put my money in boxing gloves, but I took a big hit.

"I'm thinking of leaving my husband," said the broker's wife. "Our sex life is lousy. All he ever does is stand at the end of the bed and tell me how good things are going to be."

The market may be bad, but I slept like a baby last night. I woke up every hour and cried.

Why is the man responsible for investing your money called a broker?

There was an unexpected rally in the markets today. A stockbroker who jumped out of a window on the twelfth floor saw a computer screen on the fifth floor and did a U-turn.

The stock market today was up and down like a whore's drawers.

Three of my stocks went off the financial page and into the help-wanted section. **Bob Hope**

Why is the fall in the stock market not all bad?
It won't be so hard to keep up with the Dow Joneses.

When it comes to the stock market, I'm neither a bull nor a bear: more an ass.

A market analyst is an expert who will know tomorrow why the things he predicted yesterday didn't happen today.

Today's stock market report: helium was up, feathers were down and paper was stationary.

Knives were up sharply, but pencils lost a few points.

Fluorescent tubing was dimmed in light trading.

Escalators continued their slow decline and mining equipment hit rock bottom.

Balloon prices were inflated, diapers were unchanged and the market for raisins dried up.

I received a Christmas card from my stockbroker today. It wished me, but in no way guaranteed me, a Happy Christmas.

STRESS

What's the difference between stress, tension and panic?
Stress is when your wife is pregnant, tension is when your girlfriend is pregnant, and panic is when both are pregnant.

I read an article which said that typical symptoms of stress are: eating too much, impulse buying and driving too fast. That sounds like my idea of a perfect day.

Don't take your worry to bed with you – make her sleep in a separate room.

I don't suffer from stress. I'm a carrier.

Stress is when you wake up screaming and realize you haven't fallen asleep yet.

I'm becoming increasingly worried and concerned that there isn't enough anxiety in my life.

I'm so stressed I might go potholing. I tend to cave under pressure.

Who are the most nervous musicians?
Guitarists. They're always fretting.

Worrying works. 90 per cent of things I worry about never happen.

Your family could be stressed if the school principal has your number on speed dial.

Your family could be stressed if you are trying to get your four-year-old to switch to decaffeinated.

Your family could be stressed if the cat is on Valium.

Your family could be stressed if no one has time to wait for microwave dinners.

Your family could be stressed if conversations often begin with, "Put the gun down, and then we can talk."

You're too stressed if you find the sun too loud.

You're too stressed if antacid tablets become your sole source of nutrition.

You're too stressed if you can travel without moving.

You're too stressed if you and reality file for divorce.

You're too stressed if you believe that if you think hard enough, you can fly.

You're too stressed if trees begin to chase you.

STUDENTS

How does a high school boy propose marriage?
"You're having a what?!"

A student who changes the course of history is probably taking an exam.

I took a geography course that was so hard, I couldn't find the classroom.

The library at the University of Iowa burnt down last week. The students were very upset – some of the books hadn't been coloured in yet.

Neighbour: "What are you going to be when you graduate?"
Student: "Penniless."

I've just received my degree in Calcium Anthropology – the study of milkmen.

At university my girlfriend took English and I took medicine. But I'm better now.

I studied to be a bone specialist – the tutor said I had a head for it.

Did you hear about the realistic Politics exam? Students got extra marks for *not* answering the question.

I took a college course in speed waiting. Now I can wait an hour in just 10 minutes.

Mike: "What's your son taking at university?"
Marty: "Every penny I've got."

Did you hear about the young man who studied semaphore? His interest is flagging.

College exams are nature's laxatives.

I've been revising for a practical exam on pest control. I was up all night swatting.

Did you hear about the student who cheated in his Ethics exam?

What's the difference between a soccer pitch and a media studies degree?
A soccer pitch has goals.

What's the difference between a camel and a medical student?
A camel can go five days without drinking.

Did you hear about the medical student who removed the appendix from one of his textbooks?

Studying is healthy, so best leave it to the sick.

Why is a degree like a condom?
It's rolled up when you get it, it represents a lot of effort, and it's worthless the next day.

I've just taken my hive-building exams. I'm hoping to get a B in at least one of them.

If students wrote the Bible, the Last Supper would have been eaten the next morning – cold.

If students wrote the Bible, the Ten Commandments would actually be only five; double spaced and written in large font.

If students wrote the Bible, Paul's letter to the Romans would become Paul's email to abuse@romans.gov.

If students wrote the Bible, instead of God creating the world in six days and resting on the seventh, he would have put it off until the night before it was due and then pulled an all-nighter.

You're a college student if 6 a.m. is when you go to sleep, not when you wake up.

You're a college student if you schedule your classes around sleep habits and TV soaps.

You're a college student if you wash dishes in the bathroom sink.

You're a college student if you wear the same underpants for a week and think nothing of it.

You're a college student if your idea of a square meal is Pop-Tarts.

You're a college student if you've travelled with bags of dirty clothes.

You're a college student if you throw out bowls and plates because you don't feel like washing them.

You're a college student if your trash is overflowing and your bank account isn't.

You're a college student if you live in a house with three couches, none of which match.

You're a college student if you stay up late to finish homework, then sleep through the class in which it was due.

You're a college student if the food in your fridge may or may not be older than your little brother.

You're a college student if finding random people in your house is perfectly normal.

You're a college student if you have more beer than food in your fridge.

You're a college student if weekends start on Thursday.

You're a college student if you know the pizza delivery boy by name.

You're a college student if you don't think three miles is too far to walk to a party.

STUPIDITY

A chip on the shoulder is an indication of wood higher up.

Did you hear about the clueless pirate who wore a patch over both eyes?

When you're arguing with an idiot, try to make sure he isn't doing the same thing.

If he were any more stupid, he'd have to be watered twice a week.

Did you hear about the man who realized he could exactly replicate the sound of banging two coconut shells together simply by riding a horse along a cobbled street?

He has two brains. One is lost; the other is out looking for it.

Even if he had two guesses, he couldn't tell which way an elevator was going.

If shit was wit, he'd be constipated.

The only thing he took up in school was space.

Why do people ask, "What the hell were you thinking?" Obviously I was thinking I was going to get away with it and not have to explain it.

Did you hear about the man who thought a *pas de deux* was a father of twins?

It is OK to be ignorant in some areas, but some people abuse the privilege.

Did you hear about the man who put ice in his condom to keep the swelling down?

What's the difference between genius and stupidity?
Genius has its limits.

He has a small piece of brain lodged in his skull.

Approaching a low bridge, a trucker yells: "Oh, no! The bridge is 9 feet high, and this truck is 10 feet." "Just carry on," says his co-driver. "There are no cops around."

A word to the wise is not necessary. It's the stupid who need all the advice.

He is a waste of two billion years of evolution.

My son complains of headaches. I tell him all the time: "When you get out of bed, it's feet first."

Did you hear about the man who thought the International Date Line was a matchmaking service?

He's not a complete idiot. Some parts are missing.

You look at him and think: The wheel is turning, but the hamster is dead.

Guillotining him would only make an aesthetic difference.

Did you hear about the guy who took an IQ test, but the results were negative?

The less he knows on any subject, the more stubbornly he knows it.

Why did the idiot steal a police car?
He saw 911 written on the back and thought it was a Porsche.

He got into the gene pool while the lifeguard wasn't looking.

He's so dumb he can't count his balls and get the same answer twice.

Did you hear about the idiot who thought sugar diabetes was a boxer?

The only reason some people get lost in thought is because it's unfamiliar territory.

I filled my tank up with petrol this morning. Now all my goldfish are dead.

What's the difference between ignorance and apathy?
I don't know and I don't care.

Did you hear about the man who thought Plato was a brand of dishwasher?

He's a gross ignoramus – 144 times worse than a regular ignoramus.

Why did the idiot want to go to Jeopardy?
He had heard there were thousands of jobs there.

He's at his wits' end – but it was only a short journey.

I refuse to have a battle of wits with an unarmed person..

Did you hear about the man who painted his sundial with luminous paint so he could tell the time at night?

If ignorance were a disability, he'd get a full pension.

Most people don't act stupid. It's the real thing.

His train of thought is still boarding at the station.

Did you hear about the man who bought a sleeping bag? He spent two hours trying to wake it up.

A contestant in a spelling bee was asked to spell Mississippi. "Which," he said, "the river or the state?"

SUCCESS

There are two rules for success. First, don't tell everything you know.

Success is relative. The more success, the more relatives.

If at first you do succeed, try not to look astonished.

If at first you don't succeed, skydiving probably isn't for you.

If at first you don't succeed, destroy all evidence that you tried.

If at first you don't succeed, redefine success.

If at first you don't succeed, look in the bin for the instructions.

If at first you don't succeed, try management.

If at first you don't succeed, call it version 1.0.

No man is really successful until his mother-in-law acknowledges it.

Bragging: the patter of tiny feats.

If everything's going your way, you're driving in the wrong lane.

The road to success is marked with many tempting parking spaces.

There is no secret of success. Did you ever know a successful man who didn't tell you all about it?

The dictionary is the only place where success comes before work.

It's lonely at the top, but you eat better.

Anybody can win, unless there happens to be a second entry.

Whenever I find the key to success, someone changes the lock.

Success always occurs in private, and failure in full view.

Eagles may soar, but weasels don't get sucked into jet air intakes.

The road to success is always under construction.

If at first you don't succeed, you'll get a lot of free advice from people who didn't succeed either.

My claim to fame is that I used to be the world's youngest person.

SUICIDE

Did you hear about the man who tried to kill himself with an overdose of aspirin? After taking two, he started to feel a lot better.

Bungee jumping is for suicidal people who are indecisive.

Bungee jumping is suicide with strings attached.

Why did the kleptomaniac who lost both hands commit suicide?
He just couldn't take any more.

If someone with multiple personality disorder threatens to kill himself, is it considered a hostage situation?

Did you hear about the suicidal twin who killed her sister by mistake?

I was so depressed, I was going to jump out of a twelfth-floor window, so they sent a priest up to talk to me. He said: "On your marks . . ."

Commit suicide: 100,000 lemmings can't be wrong.

When I was a teenager, my dad's suicide attempt hit me hard. He landed on me when he jumped out the window.

Suicide notes: they're a dying art form.

I have a paper cut from writing my suicide note. It's a start. . . **Steven Wright**

I called the suicide hotline and was put through to a call centre in Pakistan. When I told them I was suicidal, they got very excited and asked if I could drive a truck.

Patient: "Doctor, I have suicidal tendencies. What should I do?"
Psychiatrist: "Pay me in advance."

Did you hear about the man who deliberately overdosed on nitrous oxide? He was killing himself with laughter.

Suicide is the sincerest form of self-criticism.

A man committed suicide by overdosing on decongestant tablets. All they found was a pile of dust.

Old man to chauffeur: "Jenkins, I'm 90 and have had enough of life. Kindly drive over the next cliff."

I've agreed to help my wife in an assisted suicide. I'm paying for her driving lessons.

I phoned the Samaritans to say that I was about to throw myself under a train. They told me to stay on the line.

SUPERHEROES

Iron Man is a superhero; Iron Woman is a command.

How does Batman's mother call him to dinner? "Dinner, dinner, dinner, dinner, Batman."

What did Batman say to Robin before they got in the Batmobile?
"Get in the Batmobile, Robin."

What do you call Batman and Robin after they've been run over by a steamroller?
Flatman and Ribbon.

If you were born in Gotham City and your first name is "The", there's a good chance you'll grow up to be a villain.

Did you hear that Wonder Woman's boyfriend was treated for heroine addiction?

Why is Superman's shirt so tight?
Because he's wearing a size S.

Why is Super-Man stupid?
Because he wears his underwear over his pants.

Where's Spider-Man's home page?
On the worldwide web.

I call my granddad Spider-Man. He hasn't got any special powers, he just finds it difficult getting out of the bath.

Why does Superman stop bullets with his chest, but he ducks if you throw a revolver at him?

I can stop a speeding bullet – only once, though.

I bet if Aquaman and Jesus had a fight, Jesus would walk all over him.

SURGERY

Surgeon to patient: "The bad news is I've had to amputate both your legs. The good news is the guy in the next bed wants to buy your slippers."

Patient: "Doctor, I can't feel my legs!"
Surgeon: "Don't worry, that's because I've had to amputate your arms."

Never entrust your life to a surgeon with more than three Band Aids on his fingers.

You know the operation hasn't gone well when you find your pacemaker has only a 30-day guarantee.

Wife: "I just can't afford that operation right now."
Husband: "Oh, well, you'll just have to talk about the old one for another year."

A vasectomy means never having to say you're sorry.

Nearing the end of an operation, the patient suddenly wakes up and demands the right to close his incision. Reluctantly the surgeon hands him the needle and says: "Suture self."

As soon as the surgeon felt the patient's wallet, he knew there was nothing more he could do.

When the transplant surgeon said he was a man after my own heart, I didn't realize he meant it literally.

What's the worst thing about getting a lung transplant? The first couple of times you cough, it's not your phlegm.

A man needed a blood transfusion, but the hospital ran out of blood, so they substituted borscht. Now his heart never skips a beet.

A monologue is a conversation between a woman who has just had an operation and one who hasn't.

"There's only a one in 100 risk of anything going seriously wrong," the surgeon told the patient. "Besides, I've done 99 of these operations before and they've all been fine."

The colder the X-ray table, the more of your body is required on it.

Two surgeons argued bitterly over who should operate on a patient's femur. It became a real bone of contention.

Doctor to patient: "There's nothing wrong with you that an expensive operation can't prolong."

Did you hear about the jolly surgeon who had his patients in stitches?

To improve my sense of smell, I had surgery that implanted a dog's olfactory glands. Now I have to drive with my head out of the window.

My brother was rushed to hospital, and they operated on him just in time. Two days later, and he would have got better without it.

What is a surgeon's favourite type of music?
Hip op.

Did you hear about the man who had an operation for haemorrhoids?
All his troubles are behind him now.

When did the man have a change of heart?
After he was wheeled into the operating room.

Jackie: "Did you recover from your operation?"
Jill: "Not yet. The doctor says I still have two more payments."

Have you ever taken something apart, had a look inside, then put everything back, only to find you have a few bits left over? Well, that's kind of why my brother's no longer a surgeon.

SWIMMING

If one synchronized swimmer drowns, do the rest have to drown too?

If swimming is good for your figure, why are whales so fat?

Why did the swimmer do the backstroke?
He'd just had lunch and didn't want to swim on a full stomach.

I always wanted to go swimming with dolphins. But when it came to it they both died in the car on the way to the baths. *Milton Jones*

With anything new it's always a good idea to start at the bottom, except when you're learning to swim.

A man knocked on the door and said he was collecting for a swimming pool. So I gave him a glass of water to start him off.

I can swim 100 yards in 5 seconds – going over a waterfall.

I entered a swimming contest last week. I won the 100-metre butterfly. What on earth am I going to do with an insect that big?

TAXES

IRS: we've got what it takes to take what you've got.

If God had meant us to pay taxes, he'd have made us smart enough to fill in the return form.

A harp is a piano after taxes.

How is a tax loophole like a good parking spot?
As soon as you see one, it's gone.

After a man pays his income tax, he knows how a cow feels after she's been milked.

When making out your tax return, it's better to give than to deceive.

Why does a slight tax increase cost you $200 and a substantial tax cuts saves you 30 cents?

A fine is a tax for doing wrong; a tax is a fine for doing well.

A fool and his money are soon parted. The rest of us wait until filing our income tax returns.

Do not steal: the taxman hates competition.

Making out your own income tax return is like a do-it-yourself mugging.

Notice how when you put "the" and "IRS" together, it spells "theirs".

If my business gets much worse, I won't need to lie on my next tax return.

What's the difference between a taxidermist and a tax collector?
The taxidermist only takes the skin.

I tried paying my income tax with a smile, but they wanted a cheque.

Did you hear about the fire at the tax office? Fire crews managed to put it out before any serious good was done.

TAXICABS

I used to be a cabbie but I drove away all my customers.

I said to the taxi driver: "King Arthur's Close." He said: "Don't worry, we'll lose him at the next set of lights." *Tommy Cooper*

Mike: "How come you paint one side of your cab red and the other side blue?"
Marty: "Whenever I get into an accident, the witnesses contradict each other."

The town's taxi drivers wanted to remain open over the Christmas period but after initially being divided over the issue, the council closed ranks.

Man: "Can you take me to Chelsea?"
Taxi driver: "Sure. What part?"
Man: "All of me!"

I was in a taxi last night, and I asked the driver what he liked about the job. He said he has freedom, he's his own boss, and no one tells him what to do. I said: "Turn left here."

TENNIS

I see Serena Williams has been seeded – it must have been a brave man who did that.

Why is tennis the noisiest sport?
Because you can't play it without raising a racket.

Watching Wimbledon tennis under the roof is like watching porn at lunchtime. It gets the job done, but we all know it's wrong.

Dad: "Stop watching porn! I can hear it in my room!"
Son: "I'm not watching porn. That's Maria Sharapova playing tennis!"

Female tennis players must be able to control their grunting. Can't they just try and pretend that their parents are in the next room? *Jeremy Hardy*

How do we know they played tennis in Ancient Egypt?
Because the Bible tells how Joseph served in Pharaoh's court.

Mixed doubles tennis is often played by athletic couples who want to burn a few calories while arguing.

The only tennis player better than Roger Federer is Roger Federest.

Why should you never date a tennis player?
Because love means nothing to them.

My tennis club has 200 members. Only 30 actually play tennis, the rest of us are waiting for a court.

What time does Andy Murray go to bed?
Tennish.

Andy Murray goes into a library and asks for a couple of books about great tennis serves. "No," says the librarian, "you'll never return them."

TERRORISTS

What sort of holiday does a terrorist go on?
A suspicious package holiday.

Two terrorists are driving with a bomb in the front seat of their car. "Slow down," says one. "You might set off the bomb." "Don't worry," says the other, "there's a spare bomb in the back."

Suicide bombers: what makes them tick?

Three Afghan police officers were injured when their vehicle crashed into a tree. The Taliban said they planted it.

Terrorism is a curse. What happened to the days when you could look at an unattended bag on a train or a bus and think, I'll have that?

What was Osama Bin Laden's favourite make of trainers?
Jihadidas.

What was Bin Laden's favourite dessert?
Terrormisu.

I used to go out with a girl who was a terrorist, but I got tired of the constant sniping.

Suicide bombing: now there's a bright idea. I want to see how the instructor does it. "Right lads, I'm only going to show you this once. . ."
Billy Connolly

Did you hear about the terrorist who went into a military equipment shop and tried to buy a grenade on his debit card? It all went wrong when the cashier asked him for his pin.

What happened to the blonde terrorist who tried to blow up a bus?
She burned her lips on the exhaust pipe.

Two female terrorists are walking along a city street. One says to the other: "Be honest: does my bomb look big in this?"

Looking back, I wasn't a very good suicide bomber.

TEXAS

If God had meant Texans to ski, he would have made bullshit white.

Did you hear about the Texan who spent his summers in a little place he'd bought up north? Canada.

Why doesn't Texas slide off into the Gulf?
Because Oklahoma sucks.

Did you hear about the Texan who moved to Oklahoma and raised the IQ level of both states?

A Texan goes to the dentist. "Your teeth are fine," says the dentist. "No work needed." "Drill anyway," says the Texan. "I feel lucky."

Why are rectal thermometers banned in Texas?
Fear of brain damage.

Texas is a place where they barbecue everything but ice cream.

Canadian: "I've heard that Texan clocks go as well as Swiss ones."
Texan: "Yup. In fact, some go even faster."

Canadian: "I guess every American state has its share of dwarfs."
Texan: "Sure, but our dwarfs are bigger."

Texans are living proof that Indians screwed buffaloes.

Did you hear about the Texan who was as crude as his oil?

And did you hear about the Texan who took elocution lessons so that his oil would be refined?

First Texan: "Weren't you in Paris on vacation last month?"
Second Texan: "I don't know. My wife bought the tickets."

One of the first things schoolchildren in Texas learn is how to compose a simple sentence without the word "shit" in it.

What does a wealthy Texan buy his sick wife?
A get well car.

Texas is the only place in the world where you have to be on the lookout for phony $1,000 bills.

TIME

Wear a watch and you'll always know what time it is. Wear two watches and you'll never be sure.

I live in California and my watch is three hours fast. I can't fix it, so I'm moving to New York.

How long a minute is depends on which side of the bathroom door you're on.

My new stopwatch is brilliant. It can go from 0–60 in a minute.

What is always behind the times?
The back of the clock.

Calendars: their days are numbered.

Time is what keeps everything from happening at once.

I walked into my Sarcastics Anonymous meeting five minutes late. "Oh," they said, "nice of you to join us!"

Where do you go to get your broken watch repaired?
A second-hand shop.

Did you hear about the man who was going to look for his missing watch but could never find the time?

I won a year's supply of calendars – in other words, one.

If time heals all wounds, how come the belly button always stays the same?

Why did the boy throw the clock out the window?
He wanted to see time fly.

An alarm clock is a device for waking childless households.

We are all time travellers, moving at the speed of exactly 60 minutes per hour.

If you want more time, wear more watches.

A woman's "I'll be ready in five minutes" is exactly the same as a man's "I'll be home in five minutes".

Why did the clock phone the ruler?
Because desperate times call for desperate measures.

Time may be a great healer, but it's a lousy beautician.

I went to buy a clock. The man in the shop said: "Analogue?" I said: "No, just a clock."

Time is the best teacher, but it kills all its students.

Every time history repeats itself, the price goes up.

Did you hear about the man who was worried because his sundial was slow?

In these uncertain times, I should get myself a watch that works.

What time is it when the clock strikes 13?
Time to get a new clock.

What did the Leaning Tower of Pisa say to Big Ben?
"If you've got the time, I've got the inclination."

Why did the man stamp on his watch?
Because he had time to kill.

Wife: "Our wall clock almost killed Mother. It fell only seconds after she got up from the couch."
Husband: "That damn clock always was slow."

I bought a waterproof, shockproof, anti-magnetic, unbreakable watch. I lost it.

TOILET STUFF

Did you hear about the constipated composer? He couldn't finish his last movement.

Ban toilet cleaner: germs have feelings too.

If diarrhoea runs down only one leg, is it monorrhea?

Air freshener – because there's no louder way of telling the whole house you've just had a shit.

What do you call a Turkish guy with a weak bladder?
Mustafa Pee.

I phoned the Incontinence Hotline, but they asked me to hold.

I phoned the Incontinence Hotline, and the operator said: "Where are you ringing from?" I said: "The waist down."

Why can't you hear a pterodactyl using the toilet?
Because it has a silent P.

Diarrhoea is hereditary – it runs in your jeans.

If you have diarrhoea, never trust a fart.

Did you hear about the man who ate a globe? He put the world in motion.

I bought a toilet brush, but I don't really like it. I think I'll go back to using paper.

A mute incontinent: goes without saying.

I was delivering leaflets on flatulence awareness. Unfortunately I let one rip.

What's the difference between a West End theatre and a public toilet?
The theatre is for arts and farces.

Did you hear about the giant with diarrhoea? No? It's all over town.

If you're an American when you enter the bathroom, and you're American when you leave the bathroom, what are you while you're in the bathroom?
European.

I used to clean out public toilets, and after three years I was promoted. They gave me a brush.

Can a dwarf be caught short?

Did you hear about the man who fell into a sewer and drowned? He couldn't swim but he went through the motions.

Disabled toilets: ironically the only toilets big enough to run around in.
Jimmy Carr

Constipation: same shit, different day.

Why do men whistle while they're sitting on the toilet?
It helps them remember which end to wipe.

Did you hear about the guy who often used the wrong toilet in pubs? He had a reputation as a bit of a ladies' man.

Why did the baker have brown hands?
Because he kneaded a poo.

What goes in and out and stinks of pee?
Your granny doing the hokey cokey.

Constipation is the thief of time, but diarrhoea waits for no man.

I'm one of those people who like to read while they're having a shit. Which is probably why I'm banned from Waterstones.

TOM SWIFTIES

"I need a pencil sharpener," said Tom bluntly.

"I'm the chief washer-up," said Tom judiciously.

"Rowing a boat hurts my hands," said Tom callously.

"I've only enough carpet for the hall and landing," said Tom with a blank stare.

"That little devil didn't tell the truth," Tom implied.

"Pass me the shellfish," said Tom crabbily.

"I'd love to learn a new card game," said Tom wistfully.

"I'm going to be intestate," said Tom unwillingly.

"I couldn't believe there were 469 sheep in the flock," Tom recounted.

"I only have diamonds, clubs and spades," said Tom heartlessly.

"Who would want to steal modern art?" asked Tom abstractedly.

"What a magnificent bra!" said Tom upliftingly.

"My girlfriend Ruth has fallen off the back of my motorbike," yelled Tom, riding on Ruthlessly.

"This must be an aerobics class," Tom worked out.

"I've mixed up my gloves," said Tom intermittently.

"I've been reading Voltaire," said Tom candidly.

"The doctor removed my left ventricle and atrium," said Tom half-heartedly.

"What a charming doorway!" said Tom entranced.

"I've run out of wool," said Tom, knitting his brow.

"This wind is really strong," blustered Tom.

"I know who turned off the lights," Tom hinted darkly.

"You have the right to remain silent," said Tom arrestingly.

"I guess I'll have to write my name again," said Tom resignedly.

"I don't work here on a regular basis," said Tom casually.

"So it's a duel you want?" Tom shot back.

"Who wants Parmesan?" asked Tom gratingly.

"In a former life, I was a great opera singer," said Tom, feeling callous.

"I have no recollection of the last 24 hours," said Tom lackadaisically.

"Let's go to McDonald's," said Tom archly.

"A spirit transported me from one side of the room to the other," said Tom, visibly moved.

"I'm sure we can fool them into thinking this is pollen," said Tom beguilingly.

"I'll order the Chinese soup," said Tom wantonly.

"Why is this phone flex tangled?" asked Tom coyly.

"I've gone back to my wife," was Tom's rejoinder.

"That just doesn't add up," said Tom nonplussed.

"A million thanks, Monsieur," said Tom mercifully.

"You're a real zero!" said Tom naughtily.

"The situation is grave," said Tom cryptically.

"My stereo's half fixed," said Tom monotonously.

"I'm burning aromatic substances," said Tom incensed.

"Hurry to the back of the ship," said Tom sternly.

"Some you lose," said Tom winsomely.

"Very well, you can borrow it again," Tom relented.

"Give me some pre-packed cheese slices," said Tom craftily.

"The seesaw is upside down," said Tom saucily.

"I'm losing my hair!" Tom bawled.

"I've removed all the feathers from this chicken," said Tom pluckily.

"I want this statue to look like the *Venus de Milo*," said Tom disarmingly.

"I'm about to hit the golf ball," Tom forewarned.

"There's someone at the front door," Tom chimed in.

"Another working week begins," said Tom mundanely.

"I want a motorized bicycle," Tom moped.

"Nice mirror," Tom reflected.

"Would you like some soda?" asked Tom caustically.

"It's a piece of laboratory equipment," Tom retorted.

"The average frequency of my voice is 160Hz," said Tom in measured tones.

"Careful with that saw!" said Tom offhandedly.

"I work at a bank," said Tom tellingly.

"I love redheads," said Tom gingerly.

"I unclogged the drain with a vacuum cleaner," said Tom succinctly.

"I mustn't let the fire go out," Tom bellowed.

"I have a BA in social work," said Tom with a degree of concern.

"Cocaine?! I've never touched the stuff!" Tom snorted.

"Your fly is undone," was Tom's zippy reply.

"I flatly deny this!" said Tom, under pressure.

"Why can't you use your own toothbrush?" Tom bristled.

"I've just struck oil," Tom gushed.

"I've injured my leg," said Tom lamely.

"I'll do your conveyancing, but I'll be slow and overcharge you," said Tom solicitously.

"This trout is excellent," said Tom superficially.

"I hope you like my bid for this contact," said Tom tenderly.

"I knew the gun wasn't loaded," said Tom blankly.

"What's an angle over 90 degrees?" asked Tom obtusely.

"I have writer's block," said Tom contritely.

"I bought fifty burgers, but now I've only ten left," said Tom with fortitude.

"I had no luck at the races," Tom endorsed.

"So only one person arrived at the party before I did?" Tom second-guessed.

TRAINS

Did you hear about the man who had always wanted to be run over by a steam train? Eventually it happened – he was chuffed to bits.

What happened when a young man was caught having sex with a girl in a train carriage?
He was arrested for having a first-class ride with a second-class ticket.

I sat on the train this morning opposite a stunning Thai girl. I kept thinking to myself: Please don't get an erection, please don't get an erection. But she did.

Did you hear about the man who tried to cheat the train company by buying a return ticket and not going back?

Station porter: "Miss the train, sir?"
Passenger: "No, I didn't like the look of it, so I chased it out of the station!"

Britain's trains are great – we have the best replacement bus service in the world.

I got on the train this morning, and a man was sitting in my seat. I said: "Go on, then. You drive the thing!"

Did you hear about the man who only rode the New York subway to have his clothes pressed?

I was sitting opposite an Indian lady on the train. She shut her eyes and stopped breathing. I thought she was dead until I saw the red dot on her head and realized she was just on standby.

How can you tell when a train has gone?
It leaves its tracks behind.

A woman rings the lost property office of the train company and asks if they've found a missing vulture. "OK, madam," says the clerk, "what colour is it?"

Ah, return tickets: they take me back.

The best time to miss a train is at a level crossing.

Did you hear about the man who thought he couldn't travel on the London Underground because a sign said: "Dogs must be carried on the escalator", and he didn't have a dog?

TRANSVESTITES

Did you hear about the fat, alcoholic transvestite? All he wanted to do was eat, drink and be Mary.

What's the biggest crime committed by transvestites?
Male fraud.

Did you hear about the transvestite who was disappointed when he went drag racing?

A male transvestite escaped from police custody last week. Officers fear he may now be a broad.

TRUTH

Confession is good for your soul, but bad for your career.

Never tell a lie unless it is absolutely convenient.

The best way to lie is to tell the truth – carefully edited truth.

Never trust a man who says he's the boss at home. He probably lies about other things too.

The trouble with half-truths is you never know which half you've got.

Honesty is the best policy, but insanity is a better defence.

I'd like to be the last man on Earth. Then I'd know if all those women were telling the truth.

TURTLES

Is a turtle without a shell homeless or just naked?

Why is turtle wax so expensive?
Because turtles only have tiny ears.

Why did the turtle cross the road?
To get to the Shell station.

A truck load of tortoises crashed into a train load of terrapins. What a turtle disaster!

Mike: "Can you do an impression of a tortoise?"
Marty: "I'm going to stick my neck out and say yes."

What did the turtle tell police after he was mugged by a gang of snails?
"It all happened so fast."

TV

Sky News: it's still blue with white clouds.

The History Channel + 1: where history repeats itself.

National Geographic + 1: where lightning does strike twice.

I think the Discovery Channel should be on a different channel each day.

Did you hear about the woman who phoned the Shopping Channel and told the operator she was just browsing?

Americans love the Home Shopping Network because it's commercial-free.

Did you hear about the Jewish game show – *The Price Is Too Much*?

Did you hear about the new TV contest Cher is hosting to find her doppelgänger? It's called *Cher and Cher Alike*.

Waking the Dead – just one letter away from being the most controversial show on TV.

There's a new US cop show where all the forensic scientists are avatars. It's called *CGI Miami*.

Did you hear about the new Channel 4 show in which farmers go to each other's harvests and secretly rate them? It's called *Combine With Me*.

Did you hear about the man who was so old, he could remember when *X Factor* was Roman sunscreen?

I just saw a daytime TV show where they found Joe Strummer's skeleton in the loft of a house. It was called *Clash in the Attic*.

I saw that show about a group of married women who have absolutely nothing in common. I think it was called *Disparate Housewives*.

Recently we bought the box set of *Doctor Who* and watched it back to back. Unfortunately I wasn't the one facing the screen. **Milton Jones**

How do Daleks keep their skin soft?
EXFOLIATE!

I watched a shocking documentary while sitting with both feet behind my head. It made for uncomfortable viewing.

Sex on TV can't hurt you – unless you fall off.

Last night, I watched a compelling documentary about sniffing adhesives. I was glued to the screen.

"Dad, tell us again how when you were a boy you had to walk all the way across the room to change channels."

I'm getting tired of cable TV. Day after day it's the same 121 channels.

The six o'clock news is where they begin with "good evening", and then proceed to tell you why it isn't.

I don't mind *America's Got Talent*. My only problem with it is that it's on TV.

My wife said: "You'll never guess who I saw in town!" "OK then," I said. "I'll carry on watching the football."

There's a new TV show about origami. It's paper view.

A man sits down to watch a DVD, and a message says: "This movie has been altered to fit your television screen." He turns to his wife and asks: "How do they know what size screen we have?"

I just watched a documentary on shovels – ground-breaking stuff.

There's nothing but porn on TV these days. It makes me so angry I sit on the end of my bed and shake my fist at it. **Stewart Francis**

The best thing about Alzheimer's is that you never have to watch repeats on TV.

Why didn't Lady Penelope ever sleep with any of the *Thunderbirds* pilots?
She knew it would lead to a complicated, tangled mess.

What do you call a Teletubby that's been burgled?
A Tubby.

Roy Rogers: "More hay, Trigger?"
Trigger: "No, thanks, Roy. I'm stuffed."

There's a new TV show about two detectives who solve crimes over the phone: *Star Key and Hash*.

Why do we press harder on the buttons when the battery in the remote control is dead?

Breaking news: ne ws.

8.28 p.m. My wife is leaving me because of my obsession with *Big Brother*.

Tonight I'm going to try something different. I'm going to sit on the TV and watch the sofa.

The human race is faced with a cruel choice: work or daytime TV.

A new study reveals that guests on daytime talk shows are mainly female. Of course, most of them weren't born that way.

Daytime TV is very educational. It teaches you not to sit around wasting your life . . . watching daytime TV.

Are daytime phone-in competitions too easy? a) Yes. b) Barack Obama. c) The Great Wall of China.

I watch so many episodes of *CSI* that when I turn off the set now I wipe my fingerprints off the remote.

I can't help thinking that *CSI* is just the adult version of *Scooby Doo*.

Men don't care what's on TV; they only care what else is on TV.

Save money on a bigger TV simply by moving your couch closer to the existing one.

Hitler may have been an evil dictator, but he has single-handedly saved the History Channel.

If it weren't for Thomas Edison, we'd all be watching TV by candlelight.

What county in Ireland hates *South Park*?
Kilkenny.

Why won't Homer Simpson eat toast?
Because he can't bear the thought of having to spread marge.

I used to watch golf on TV, but the doctor said I needed more exercise. So now I watch tennis on TV.

Did you watch that TV documentary about obesity in the navy? It got the biggest ratings.

Anne Robinson is sad to be leaving *The Weakest Link*, but her surgeon's going to put a brave face on her. *Jack Whitehall*

I was at a fight last night when an episode of *Jerry Springer* broke out.

Why did Captain Kirk go into the ladies' toilet?
To boldly go where no man has been before.

What did Mr Spock find in the *Enterprise* toilet?
The captain's log.

How many ears does Mr Spock have?
Three. A right ear, a left ear, and a final front ear.

Reality is for people who can't handle *Star Trek*.

Why won't Dubai let *The Flintstones* be shown when Abu Dhabi do?

UGLINESS

I'm not saying my girlfriend was unattractive, but in bed I used to mentally dress her.

If good looks are a curse, my brother is blessed.

He looks like a talent scout for a cemetery.

After a heavy night's drinking, I woke up next to a really ugly woman. That's when I knew I'd made it home safely.

Somebody once gave him a dirty look – and he's kept it ever since.

If she was cast as Lady Godiva, the horse would steal the show.

I offered to be a face donor, but they turned me down.

He was such an ugly baby, his incubator had tinted windows.

My girlfriend says I'm not conventionally handsome. Isn't that like telling a penguin it's not a conventional flyer?

When she walks into a room, the mice jump on chairs.

My wife opened her birthday present and as she held it in her hands she said: "This is nice, but why a mirror?" I said: "In case you forget why I'm leaving you."

He looks like his face was designed in a wind tunnel.

I've seen better-looking faces on a pirate flag.

Pharmacist: "In order to buy arsenic you need a legal prescription. I'm sorry, a picture of your husband isn't enough."

If ugliness was a crime he'd be serving three life sentences.

Man: "Doc, I'm so ugly. What can I do about it?"
Doctor: "Hire yourself out for Hallowe'en parties?"

Ugly women are like prime numbers. Nothing will go into them except themselves.

They broke the mould *before* they made him.

My girlfriend's so ugly, when she worked in a pet store people kept asking how big she would get.

Husband to wife: "You look a million dollars – all wrinkled and green."

He was born ugly and built to last.

Did you hear about the girl who was so ugly, she had to hand out whistles to construction workers?

Most people need a licence to be that ugly.

I said my girlfriend was like the sun. She was flattered until I told her it was only because nobody can bear to look directly at her.

To look at his face, you'd think his hobby was stepping on rakes.

You look at his face and think, Was anybody else hurt in the accident?

Some people's looks turn heads; his turn stomachs.

The last time I saw anything resembling his face, it was being wiped.

My wife is as pretty as a flower – a cauliflower.

He looks like something the dog just buried in the backyard and is trying to forget where.

Instead of donating my body to science, people say I should donate my face to science fiction.

How do you know if you're really ugly?
Dogs hump your legs with their eyes closed.

They say a pretty face is a passport; hers expired years ago.

I've been registered as blind. I can see perfectly, but my wife came with me to the appointment and the doctor just put two and two together.

If she's still ugly, have another beer.

UNITED STATES

Chasing the American Dream does not count as exercise.

How is the US government tackling childhood obesity?
By building stronger seesaws.

Apparently 72 per cent of American women are now overweight. Shocking figures!

Speaking as a Londoner, I don't fancy going to America because they drive on the right side of the road. I tried it the other day and it's bloody dangerous!

Why wasn't Christ born in Chicago?
They couldn't find three wise men and a virgin.

War is God's way of teaching Americans geography.

Arriving in Boston, a hungry tourist asks a cabbie: "Where can I get scrod around here?" The cabbie says: "I must have heard that request a thousand times, but that's the first time anyone's used the pluperfect subjunctive!"

Did you hear about the chicken who knew the first leg of his journey would take him to Buffalo? From there he decided to wing it.

Only in America do banks leave both doors open but chain the pens to the counters.

People say as a criticism: "Only 30 per cent of Americans have a passport." I say the rest of the world should be glad the other 70 per cent don't know there's anywhere outside America. ***Reginald D. Hunter***

I've never seen the Catskill Mountains, but I did see mine catch a bird once.

The average American would drive his car to the bathroom if the doors were wide enough.

I come from a stupid family. During the Civil War my great-great-great-grandfather fought for the west.

The town of Fairbanks, Alaska, has passed a law outlawing all dogs. In future it will be known as Dogless Fairbanks.

Monday was Martin Luther King Day in America. Or as it's known in the South, Monday.

What do you call an intelligent person in Minnesota?
A tourist.

What do Americans call a TV set that operates for five years without need of repair?
An import.

I went to Las Vegas to forget. Then I went to San Francisco to forget Las Vegas.

I just got back from an all-expenses trip to Las Vegas, and that's what it was – all expenses.

I come from Montana, which is very flat. Wonderfully flat. You can watch your dog run away for three days. ***Rich Hall***

"Ladies and gentlemen, this is your captain speaking. We are about to land at Salt Lake City airport. Passengers are reminded to set their watches back 25 years . . ."

I had to move from Cincinnati. I couldn't spell it.

Which state is round at each end and high in the middle?
Ohio.

Fifteen years ago, Americans had Johnny Cash, Steve Jobs and Bob Hope – now they have no cash, no jobs, and no hope.

What is the most common educational level in New Mexico?
Kindergarten dropout.

Why do Vermont police cars have stripes on the sides?
So the cops can find the handles.

Did you hear about the Vermont guy who thought the Canadian border paid rent?

Did you hear about the incident at the Vermont State Library?
Somebody stole the book.

A man walks into a Vermont store and asks for some invisible ink. "Certainly," said the storekeeper. "What colour?"

You're American if going out for a walk means getting the mail.

You're American if speaking a second language means you're an immigrant.

You're American if you drive around looking for the closest parking space – at the gym.

You're American if your idea of a four-course meal includes two courses of burgers.

You're American if you consider yourself to be well-travelled even though you've never left your own country.

You're American if you can't pronounce the name of the country you're invading.

VACATION

I've just been on a once-in-a-lifetime holiday. I'll tell you what, never again! *Tim Vine*

I went on safari once to Kenya and was shocked to see two male lions mating with each other in full view. I thought: Have they no pride?

A husband and wife are on safari in Africa. "Look," he says, "lion tracks! You see where they go and I'll find out where they came from."

I once drove across America in six days – four days of driving and two to refold the maps.

I went on holiday and got through six Jeffrey Archer novels. I must remember to take more toilet paper next time.

When my wife packs for vacation, the only thing she leaves behind is a note to the milkman.

The only book that really tells you where you can go on vacation is your cheque book.

I met my wife when I was working at a travel agent's. She was looking for a vacation and I was the last resort.

What's a man's idea of an extended vacation?
Two weeks stretched out on a sun bed.

Frightened tourist: "Are there any bats in this cave?"
Guide: "Yes, but don't worry. The snakes eat most of them."

Last year, I went on a ballooning holiday. I put on four stone. *Milton Jones*

When in Colombia, say no to anyone wanting you to deliver a suitcase of powdered sugar to their grandmother in Miami.

If you look like your passport photo, you're almost certainly not well enough to travel.

Jackie: "When you went to London, did you see them changing the guards?"
Jill: "Why, were the old ones dirty?"

My wife wanted to see the world, so I bought her an atlas.

I spent two weeks in Kenya on a Land Rover safari. It was a complete waste of time. I didn't see any Land Rovers.

It's possible to spend your entire vacation on a winding mountain road behind a large motor home.

Guide at Runnymede: "The Magna Carta was signed in 1215."
US tourist: "Damn! Missed it by 10 minutes!"

An American tourist is admiring Windsor Castle: "It's an awesome building," he says, "but I'm surprised they built it directly under the flight path to Heathrow."

A friend said: "You want to go to Brighton, it's good for rheumatism." So I did and I got it. *Tommy Cooper*

A half-man, half-bull took a trip around Europe, but only went to three places. It was a minor tour.

I just got back from vacation, and I'm glad to say my credit cards are all in remission.

A woman went to the capital of France on a wine-tasting vacation, but drank too much, fell from her hotel window and ended up in a body cast. She vowed never again to get plastered in Paris.

Last week, I went on a trip to a postcard factory. It was OK. Nothing to write home about.

Isn't Disney World just a people trap run by a mouse?

My dream vacation is to rest in the shade of a gorgeous blonde.

Can't help feeling my ostrich friend isn't making the most of our trip to the beach. *Milton Jones*

An American tourist in England asks a police officer: "Can you tell me the way to Bath?" The officer says: "Well, first you turn on the taps . . ."

If you don't want to go away on vacation, you can achieve the same effect by staying at home and tipping every second person you see.

Safari tourist: "Is it true that a crocodile won't attack if you're carrying a torch?"
Tour guide: "It depends on how fast you carry the torch."

Thomson Cruises specialize in shorter trips. They advertise them as Tom Cruises.

Did you hear about the man who crossed the Atlantic twice without taking a shower? He was a dirty double-crosser.

I found a shell on the beach. Luckily it didn't explode.

London tour guide: "Ladies and Gents . . . that concludes our tour of the toilets."

Think twice before boarding a cruise ship where the passengers are supplied with oars.

Mike: "Did you enjoy your vacation? Feel any change?"
Marty: "Not a penny."

My holiday luggage got lost at the airport. Luckily the sniffer dog found it.

Wife: "Oh, no! I've just remembered I left the electric iron on at home."
Husband: "Don't worry, I remembered I left the taps running."

A cruise is when you go for days and days – and see nothing but food.

On vacation, a girl can either go to the mountains and see the scenery or go to the beach and *be* the scenery.

If you spread out all the sand in North Africa, it would cover the Sahara Desert.

I was arguing with my wife about holidays the other day. I want to go to Greece; she wants to come with me.

When I go away, the thing I enjoy most is trying to squeeze my body into a small suitcase. In fact, I can hardly contain myself. ***Tim Vine***

I like to go on vacation late in the season to avoid the rush of people taking their holidays early in the season to avoid the rush.

A dream vacation would be one where all your family gets along.

I went to the Canary Islands this year, but I didn't see one canary. Next year I'm going to the Virgin Islands . . .

"My wife's gone to the West Indies." "Jamaica?" "No, she went of her own accord."

"My wife's gone to Indonesia." "Jakarta?" "No, she went by plane."

"My wife's gone to South America." "Chile?" "No, it's very hot there at the moment."

"My wife's flown to stay near Lake Michigan." "Chicago?" "No, she was a passenger."

"My wife's gone on holiday to India." "Mumbai?" "No, her dad paid for it."

"My wife was robbed in Western Australia." "Perth?" "No, but they took her pathport and driving lithenth."

"My wife went to a casino in the Himalayas." "Tibet?" "Of course. Why else would she go?"

"My wife's gone to a music concert in South Korea." "Seoul?" "No, R & B."

"My wife's band went on tour in south-east Asia." "Singapore?" "Yes, and the bassist's rubbish, too."

VAMPIRES

Why do vampires drink blood?
Because coffee keeps them awake all day.

How can you tell if a vampire is lazy?
He uses leeches.

Why did the vampire give up acting?
He couldn't find a part he could get his teeth into.

Why did the vampire read the *New York Times*?
He heard it had good circulation.

Why does Dracula have no friends?
Because he's a pain in the neck.

I went out thieving with a couple of vampires the other day. They put me up on their shoulders so I could reach stuff. I got arrested and charged with shoplifting on two counts. *Tim Vine*

A vampire's motto: blood is thicker than water, and tastier too.

What happened at the vampires' reunion?
All the blood relations went.

Police officer: "What are you doing on this road, Dracula?"
Dracula: "Looking for the main artery, officer."

If vampires have no reflection, how come they have such neat hair?

Did you hear about the elderly vampire? He was a bit long in the tooth.

Why did the vampire give his girlfriend a blood test?
To see if she was his type.

What happened when the vampire went to the blood bank?
He asked to make a withdrawal.

Why wouldn't the vampire eat his soup?
It clotted.

On reflection, vampires aren't that scary.

VEGETABLES

I bought some rocket salad yesterday, but it went off before I could eat it.

The best way to serve cabbage is to someone else.

A carrot was involved in a terrible car crash. The neurosurgeon told his family: "I'm afraid he's going to be a vegetable for the rest of his life."

I didn't work my way to the top of the food chain to eat vegetables.

Many celebrities are into lettuce. Elton John, he's a rocket man.

I don't know if you've ever fallen asleep whilst eating a plate of cauliflower, and then woken up and thought you were in the clouds.
Milton Jones

What's the difference between boogers and broccoli?
Kids won't eat broccoli.

What do you get when an epileptic falls into a lettuce patch?
Seizure salad.

Did you hear about the guy who put a bag of petits pois in a blender because he wanted to visualize whirled peas?

What's the kindest vegetable?
A sweet potato.

Why did the King Edward potato tell the princess potato not to marry John Motson?
"Because he's just a commentator."

Two snowmen were standing in a field. One looked at the other and said: "Can you smell carrots?"

A man walks into a greengrocer's and asks for five pounds of potatoes. The greengrocer says: "We only sell kilos." "OK," says the man, "I'll have five pounds of kilos."

VEGETARIANS

I'm not a vegetarian because I love animals, but because I hate plants.

Red meat is bad for you. Furry green meat is even worse.

Why does vegan cheese taste bad?
It hasn't been tested on mice.

Can vegetarians eat animal crackers?

If vegetarians eat vegetables, should we be wary of humanitarians?

Some vegetarians look so much like the food they eat they could almost be classed as cannibals.

I decided that becoming a vegetarian was a missed steak.

What do you call a vegetarian with diarrhoea?
A salad shooter.

I follow a strict vegan diet. I eat only vegans.

I have no beef with vegetarians.

How do you attract a vegetarian?
Make a noise like a wounded vegetable.

Note to vegetarians: my food shits on your food.

WAR

My granddad lost his vocal cords in the war. He doesn't like to talk about it.

What do you call someone who fought in the war and survived mustard gas and pepper spray?
A seasoned veteran.

My grandfather was bayoneted in the war. He was pronounced dead on a rifle.

Why did so many black GIs get killed in Vietnam?
Because every time the sergeant shouted "Get down!" they stood up and started dancing.

Countries are making nuclear weapons like there's no tomorrow. *Emo Philips*

During World War Two my granddad was posted to Japan. You should have seen the size of the envelope!

Cluster bombing from B52s is extremely accurate – they always hit the ground.

All the time my granddad was in the army his wife sent him nagging letters. He couldn't even enjoy the war in peace.

A nuclear war can ruin your entire day.

In a nuclear war all men will be cremated equal.

My granddad used to say that during World War Two the only bomb you had to worry about was the one with your name on it . . . which used to scare the hell out of our neighbours, Mr and Mrs Doodlebug.

My grandfather is a Cold War veteran. He can't afford to put the heating on.

WEATHER

A man never truly realizes how cold his hands are until he has to pee.

I'm having trouble keeping my hands warm with fingerless gloves. Any tips?

Snow is the only time four inches can keep a woman in bed all day.

Since the snow came, all my wife has done is look through the window. If it gets any worse, I'll have to let her in.

Today has been 80 degrees in the shade. I was clever. I stayed in the sun. *Tommy Cooper*

Have you heard about the witch who became a weather forecaster? She predicted sunny spells.

I love it when it snows: my garden looks like everyone else's.

What's the difference between council gritters and the yeti?
There have been sightings of the yeti.

It was so cold this morning I had to scrape ice off the car windshield with my store discount card. But I only got 10 per cent off.

I had a terrible week away. It only rained twice, but once was for three days and the other time was for four.

If there were no golf balls, how would we measure hail?

One cave man says to the other: "I don't care what you say, we never had such strange weather before they started using bows and arrows."

What is worse than raining cats and dogs?
Hailing taxis.

My dad says Manchester's weather is like Iraqi Muslims – either Sunni or Shi'ite. *Jason Manford*

Mike: "How did you find the weather while you were away?"
Marty: "I just went outside and there it was."

People say: "Isn't snow pretty?" But I lost my sister because of the snow. She's an albino.

It was so cold out, it was like a Motown day: Three Degrees, Four Tops.

It's raining cats and dogs. Well, as long as it doesn't reindeer.

Fog is a natural weather phenomenon that usually occurs around an airport while surrounding areas are clear.

A government official informs a man that due to state boundary changes his farm will now be in New Hampshire. "Thank heaven!" he says. "I don't think I could stand another of those Maine winters!"

I call my umbrella Adam because one of its ribs is missing.

I can tell if it's raining by my corns. If they get wet, it's raining.

The weather forecasters said there would be three inches of snow last night, but when I woke up this morning there was miles of it!

The British summer: eight weeks of warm rain.

Did you hear about the man who was hit on the head by a giant hailstone? He was knocked out cold.

RIP dense water vapour. You'll always be mist.

Droughts are because God didn't pay his water bill.

All of us could learn a lesson from the weather: it pays no attention to criticism.

We have an automatic air-conditioner. Whenever the weather gets hot, it automatically breaks down.

My brother came in from the garden holding a flaming ball of hydrogen. I said: "My, you've caught the sun!" **Mark Little**

Why are hurricanes always given friendly names like Irene or Katia? Surely Hurricane Bastard would be more appropriate.

Florida in July is when hot water comes out of both taps.

Florida in July is when trees are whistling for dogs.

Florida in July is when the cows are giving evaporated milk.

Florida in July is when you learn that a car seat buckle makes an effective branding iron.

Florida in July is when potatoes cook underground.

Florida in July is when you learn that you can steer your car with just two fingers.

Florida in July is when you learn that asphalt has a liquid state.

It doesn't rain in Florida. The sun just drips perspiration.

Sometimes it's so hot in Florida that even the statues have armpit stains.

Husband: "Did you hear the thunder and lightning last night?"
Wife: "You should have woken me. You know I can never sleep through a storm."

WEDDINGS

I made my girlfriend's dreams come true by marrying her in a castle, although you wouldn't have thought it from the look on her face as we were bouncing around.

Two aerials met on a roof, fell in love and got married. The ceremony wasn't great, but the reception was brilliant. *Tommy Cooper*

The batteries on my camcorder died halfway through my best friend's wedding speech. I'm never going to hear the end of it.

In church on her wedding day, what three words are foremost in a bride's mind?
"Aisle, altar, hymn."

June is the traditional month for weddings. The other 11 months are for divorce.

I'll never forget our wedding. I've tried, but my wife won't let me.

What's the difference between a nudist wedding and an ordinary wedding?
At a nudist wedding you don't have to ask who the best man is.

Women cry at weddings, men afterwards.

The length of a marriage is inversely proportional to the amount spent on the wedding.

What do you call it when people start throwing rice at each other at an Indian wedding?
A pilau fight.

She has walked up the aisle so often they're trying to make her pay for the carpet.

Why do mothers always cry at weddings?
Because girls tend to marry men like their fathers.

Always get married early in the morning. That way if it doesn't work out, you haven't wasted the whole day.

I should have known it was a mistake to get married. Even after I said "I do", the vicar looked at my bride and then asked me: "Is that your final answer?"

A limbo dancer married a locksmith. The wedding was low key.

Why did the husband like to watch his wedding video backwards?
So he could see himself walking out of the church a free man.

Forward planning means saving a piece of wedding cake for your divorce lawyer.

My bride looked absolutely beautiful standing at the altar with a tear running down her cheek. Apparently.

Soon after Sam and Ella got married, they suffered food poisoning.

Man: "Are you a friend of the groom?"
Woman: "Certainly not. I'm the bride's mother."

My sister had a fairytale wedding: Grimm.

I gave my sister away at her wedding. I stood up and shouted: "She used to be a man!"

Did you hear about the nuclear physicists' wedding? The bride was absolutely radiant.

After paying for the wedding, about all a father has left to give away is the bride.

I remember my friend's wedding day. The bride looked stunning, the groom looked stunned.

A Hollywood wedding is one where they take each other for better or worse – but not for long.

A best man's speech should be like a mini-skirt: short enough to be interesting, but long enough to cover the bare essentials.

Shotgun wedding: a case of wife or death.

I was invited to the wedding of T-Mobile and Orange. The reception afterwards was poor. There was only one bar.

It was an emotional wedding. Even the cake was in tiers.

Why does the bride smile when she walks up the aisle?
She knows she's given her last blow job.

Did you hear about the two skiers who got married? After the wedding it was downhill all the way.

I always seem to cry at weddings, especially the one I went to last week where the vicar said to me: "I'm afraid your bride hasn't turned up."

WEIGHT

I have put on a lot of weight. I used to be 7lb 4oz.

I'm not saying she was fat, but after sex I rolled over three times and I was still on her.

Wife: "George, do these jeans make my ass look like the side of the house?"
Husband: "No, our house isn't blue."

My wife's so fat, when she fell down the stairs I thought *EastEnders* was finishing.

They say no man is an island, but he comes close.

Even his double chin has a double chin.

I went to Weightwatchers last night and threw Maltesers all over the floor. I then watched the best game of Hungry Hippos I've ever seen!

My wife more than kept her girlish figure. In fact, she doubled it.

He has flabby thighs, but fortunately his stomach covers them.

Can fat people go skinny dipping?

I'm sure I've put on weight. I haven't actually weighed myself; it's just a gut feeling.

You know you're fat when you drop something and think to yourself: Do I really need it?

Obesity is not to be taken lightly.

What's the best way to burn calories?
Set fire to a fat man.

She said she was going to play the field, but she looked better suited to grazing in one.

This morning our seriously overweight neighbour suddenly burst in the kitchen. It made a hell of a mess.

They say that not "cleaning your plate" is the best way to lose weight. I haven't done the dishes in months but I've still put on 20 pounds.

What do fat people like most about the Internet?
The cookies.

When you have a fat friend there are no seesaws, only catapults.
Demetri Martin

I've worked out that I only need to date two more fat girls before I can honestly say I've been out with tons of women.

What's the best way to pick up a fat chick?
With a crane.

After I had queued patiently at the bank, the teller finally served me. She said: "Sorry about your wait." I said: "You're not exactly skinny yourself!"

Walking through town, I saw a group of fat Goths. They were morbidly obese.

I threw away my weight-loss DVD after three weeks because I noticed that the people on it weren't losing weight either.

A diet is a selection of foods for people who are thick and tired of it.

Did you hear about the man who went to the paint store because he wanted to lose weight? He heard you could get thinner there.

Weird scientific fact: the heavier the woman, the easier she is to pick up.

My wife has put on a lot of weight. But she's had a lot on her plate.

What do we want? A cure for obesity! When do we want it? After dinner!

I joined a Weightwatchers class last week. We meet in the basement, although we were on the first floor when we started.

I thought black was meant to be slimming, but it always makes my wife look like the opening to a tunnel.

They say that travel broadens one. He must have been around the world.

She was the flabbiest stripper I've ever seen. When she ran off the stage she started her own applause. **Les Dawson**

I broke up with a girl once because she lied about her weight. I say that, she died in a bungee-jumping accident.

Why is a fat woman like a moped?
They're both fun to ride until your friends see you with one.

She'd make a good burglar because her ass would wipe out her footprints.

Jackie: "Is your husband a Weightwatcher?"
Jill: "Yes, he watches every girl under 120 pounds."

Obese kids have simply got very slow metabolisms and very fast chip-eating hands.

A successful diet is the triumph of mind over platter.

My wife went on a crash diet. She wrecked three cars, a small van and a motorbike.

Doctors say seven million people are overweight. Of course, these are only round figures.

A fat boy comes home from school and tells his mother proudly: "I got the highest score in PE today . . . By the way, what is BMI?"

My wife is the double of Kate Moss. Kate Moss is 8 stone and my wife is 16 stone.

I'm not fat: I'm just hard to kidnap.

Mike: "I see what you mean about your belly. Have you tried to diet?"
Marty: "Yes, but whatever colour I use, it still looks fat."

My wife got upset because I said I thought her butt looked a little big in the picture I was looking at . . . on Google Earth.

Why is it that every time you lose weight, it finds you again?

I'm not saying my wife is fat, but if I had to pick five of the fattest people I could think of, she'd be three of them.

How do you get a fat girl into bed?
Piece of cake. *Sean Lock*

The only thing bigger than an obese man's stomach is his appetite.

My wife complained: "Everything I eat goes straight to my butt." I said: "Yes, that's generally how the digestive system works."

It's not the minutes spent at the table that makes one fat, it's the seconds.

Have you heard about the new dating site for obese people? It's called Fat Chance.

My weight is perfect for my height, which varies.

She wanted to lose a lot of ugly fat, but her husband wouldn't agree to a divorce.

My wife is on a new diet: coconuts and bananas. She hasn't lost weight, but you should see her climb a tree! *Henny Youngman*

"Thank you for calling the weight loss helpline. If you'd like to lose half a pound right now, press 1 18,000 times."

My wife asked me: "Do my ankles look fat?" I said: "What ankles?"

Dieting is the one time when a man is happy to see his spare tyre go flat.

It's hard to be as fit as a fiddle when you're shaped like a cello.

My wife said: "At work, my opinion carries a lot of weight." I said: "So do your legs."

I broke up with my girlfriend last night. She said: "Is it really over?" I told her: "It couldn't be more over if you started singing."

A large lady walks into a store and says: "I'd like to see a bikini that will fit me." The sales assistant says: "So would I!"

My wife's got a million-dollar figure. Unfortunately it's all in loose change.

Why did the fat boy crawl over the front of his girlfriend's car?
She told him there was a chip on the windshield.

THE WELSH

What's the most common lie a Welshman tells?
"I was only trying to help that sheep over the fence."

What do you call a Welshman with lots of girlfriends?
A shepherd.

How does a Welshman find a sheep in tall grass?
Very satisfying.

Why do Welshmen wear button-fly jeans?
Because sheep can hear a zipper at 100 yards.

I asked my Welsh mate how many sexual partners he'd had. He started counting, but then fell asleep.

What's the definition of safe sex in Wales?
Branding the sheep which kick.

Did you hear they've just discovered a new use for sheep in Wales?
Wool.

Did you hear about the new online dating site for Welshmen?
EweTube.

What do you call a Welshman with a sheep under each arm?
A pimp.

Have you heard about the Welsh Muslim festival? It's called Ramalamb.

What do you call four sheep tied to a post in Wales?
A leisure centre.

Did you hear about the Welshman who thought he'd caught a nasty STD? It turns out he was just allergic to wool.

Although Sir Anthony Hopkins is Welsh, why has he never been accused of having sex with sheep?
It's all down to the silence of the lambs.

Did you hear about the Welshman who bought his girlfriend a pen for her birthday, but she kept getting out?

Where else but Wales can you get sex, a nice warm jumper and a casserole – all from the same date?

Did you hear about the Welsh vicar who lives over a shop? They call him Evans Above.

A friend said to me: "I can never do the Welsh accent properly. Every time I try it, it sounds like Pakistani." I said: "You'll just have to try harder, Tariq."

WOMEN

A good woman is like a good bar – liquor in the front and poker in the rear.

If women ruled the world, there would be no war – just a bunch of jealous countries not talking to each other.

Give a woman an inch, and she thinks she's a ruler.

Did you hear about the woman who had spent years searching for a tampon that fitted her properly? Eventually she just threw in the towel.

Why are hurricanes named after women?
They're wet and wild when they come, and they take your house when they leave.

If you don't think women are explosive, try dropping one.

Why is a car like a hysterectomy?
A woman can't reverse either of them.

What do you show a woman who has been driving accident-free for five years?
Second gear.

My wife's going to be a mummy any time now. Only the head left to wrap.

What's the difference between a woman and a cell phone?
You can put a cell phone on silent.

When a man says "fine", he means everything is fine. When a woman says "fine", she means "I'm really hacked off and you have to find out why."

If your wife keeps coming out of the kitchen to nag you, what have you done wrong?
Made her chain too long.

What are the seven dwarfs of menopause?
Itchy, Bitchy, Sweaty, Sleepy, Bloated, Forgetful and Psycho.

A woman can hold a grudge until it dies of old age . . . and then she will have it stuffed and mounted.

How do women get minks?
The same way minks get minks.

What's a woman's idea of a tragedy?
Marrying a man for love and then discovering he has no money.

A woman enjoys a man of strong will – as long as it's made out to her.

If you want to know how old a woman is, just ask her sister-in-law.

Why hasn't a woman gone to the moon?
Because it doesn't need cleaning yet.

Women make better bosses. No study or survey. My wife just told me.
Denis Leary

How can you spot a macho woman?
She rolls her own tampons.

How is a woman like a condom?
Both spend more time in your wallet than on your dick.

Women like quiet men: they think they're listening.

What's six inches long, two inches wide and drives women wild?
Money.

What do you call a woman with a screwdriver in one hand, a knife in the other, a pair of scissors between the toes on her left foot, and a corkscrew between the toes on her right foot?
A Swiss army wife.

A siren is what a woman looks like before marriage and sounds like after.

Why is a woman different from a computer?
A woman won't accept a three-and-a-half-inch floppy.

Women are like police: they can have all the evidence in the world but they still want a confession.

Why does a woman close her eyes during sex?
Because no woman wants to see a man enjoying himself.

The only time a woman is interested in a man's company is when he owns it.

Women are like computers. They take too long to warm up and a better model always comes along once you've already got one.

Why did God invent shopping carts?
To teach women how to walk on their hind legs.

The years that a woman subtracts from her age are not lost. They are added to the ages of other women.

If women are so great at multi-tasking, why can't they have a headache and sex at the same time?

It's easy to handle women if you know how. The trouble is, nobody knows how.

Did you hear about the woman who changed her name from Annie Key because people kept hitting her?

How do you fix a woman's watch?
You don't. There's a clock on the stove.

Why are women like stones?
You skip the flat ones and don't bother picking up the heavy ones.

Why do women have two sets of lips?
One to argue, one to apologize.

What do you call a woman who works as hard as a man?
Lazy.

What is a man's definition of the perfect woman?
A nymphomaniac whose father owns a pub.

What's the worst thing a woman can get on her thirtieth wedding anniversary?
Morning sickness.

What's the difference between a woman and a battery?
A battery has a positive side.

Why do brides always wear white?
Because all kitchen appliances are that colour.

Why are there so few women superheroes?
Because by the time they'd got changed, the entire world would have been wiped out.

Militant feminists: I take my hat off to them. They don't like that. *Milton Jones*

Women are like roads: the more curves they have, the more dangerous they are.

What's the difference between a nice girl and a good girl?
A nice girl goes out on a date, goes home and goes to bed; a good girl goes out on a date, goes to bed, and then goes home.

What is six inches long and makes a man groan as soon as a woman touches it?
A gear stick.

Why don't women need driving licences?
Because there are no roads from the kitchen to the bedroom.

What do women and dog turds have in common?
The older they get, the easier they are to pick up.

If your dog is barking at the back door and your wife is yelling at the front door, who do you let in first?
The dog. At least he'll stop after you let him in.

Men wake up as good-looking as when they went to bed. Women somehow deteriorate during the night.

I thought women were supposed to love a man in uniform. Well, I've been out clubbing in my McDonald's uniform for the last three nights and I've had no success at all.

What does a woman make best for dinner?
Reservations.

Women are like blue jeans. They look good for a while, but eventually they fade and have to be replaced.

How do you blind a woman?
Put a windshield in front of her.

Women like jewellery. They're like raccoons: show them some shiny stuff and they'll follow you home. *Alonzo Bodden*

Why do men fart more than women?
Because women won't shut up long enough to build up pressure.

Why are there so few sex phone lines for women?
Because if a woman wants someone to talk dirty to her, she only has to go to work.

Why did God make Man first?
He didn't want a woman looking over his shoulder.

What's the definition of a tree?
Something that stands still for 70 years, then suddenly jumps out in front of a woman driver.

Mike to Marty: "I like my women the way I like my coffee – cold and bitter."

The difference between Man and Woman?
Man stands up to get knocked down; Woman lies down to get knocked up.

After years of trying to figure out women, I'm giving up and moving on to a much simpler subject: quantum physics.

Running after women never hurt anybody; it's the catching that does the damage.

What's long and hard and makes women groan?
An ironing board.

Why are women like police cars?
Both make a lot of noise to let you know you did something wrong.

Did you hear about the women's self-help group for compulsive talkers? It's called On and On Anon.

Even if you can't read a woman like a book, it's nice to thumb the pages.

A woman can humiliate any man simply by saying: "Hold my purse."

There are two kinds of women: the kind you dream about and the kind you marry.

I don't think feminists realize that by keeping their name after marriage they are jeopardizing their future children's banking security. *Gary Delaney*

How can you tell if your girlfriend's frigid?
When you open her legs, the lights go on.

Why are women like convertibles?
Both are more fun with their tops down.

A woman is someone who can stand for 20 minutes at a door talking because she hasn't got time to come in.

Why do women have smaller feet than men?
So they can stand closer to the kitchen sink.

Why did God create Eve?
To iron Adam's leaf.

After years of research, scientists have finally found what makes women happy: nothing.

I'm all for women's movement. I hate it when they just lie there.

Women should be more like golf caddies – either holding your balls or getting the tee ready.

A woman is the only hunter who uses herself for bait.

What do you call a woman covered in tattoos?
The scenic route.

What would have happened if Three Wise Women had gone to Bethlehem?

They would have asked for directions, cleaned the stable and brought practical gifts, like a nice casserole.

What is a woman's favourite position?
CEO.

What's the difference between a woman running down the road and a sewing machine?
A sewing machine only has one bobbin.

Women are like olive oil. They claim to be virgin . . .

What do you do if your boiler explodes?
Buy her flowers.

A gold digger is a woman who pulls the wool over a man's eyes and then fleeces him.

What's the difference between a woman and a volcano?
A volcano never fakes an eruption.

What's the only thing that can cheat a woman out of having the last word?
An echo.

Women are like jazz music: 3/4 jazz time and 1/4 rag time.

They say a woman's work is never done. Maybe that's why they get paid less. *Sean Lock*

What paralyses women from the waist down?
Marriage.

Why was a woman in the Bible turned into a pillar of salt?
Because she was dissatisfied with her Lot.

What's the difference between a bitch and a whore?
A whore sleeps with everyone at the party, and the bitch sleeps with everyone at the party but you.

If there was a parallel universe, would women still not be able to park in it?

Feminism: because not all women can be beautiful.

Intuition is the ability women have to read between the lines on a blank page.

What's the difference between a Sumo wrestler and a feminist?
A Sumo wrestler shaves his legs.

Why did the woman cross the road?
More to the point, what was she doing out of the kitchen?

Women are so good at multi-tasking that my friend's wife once used the toaster while having a bath. Well, that's what he told the coroner.

One day, long, long ago, there lived a woman who did not nag or complain. But it was a long time ago, and it was just that one day.

WORDS

In the beginning was the word. And the word was "aardvark".

I was going to join a debating team, but someone talked me out of it.

What is a Freudian slip?
When you say one thing but mean your mother.

Lite: the new way to spell "Light", now with 20 per cent fewer letters.

Palindromes date all the way back to Eve.

I'm so bored with life that two weeks ago I decided to start reading the Oxford English Dictionary from cover to cover. I'm past caring.

What word is always pronounced incorrectly?
Incorrectly.

I had a near-death experience. I looked up "dearth" in the dictionary.

A dictionary is the only place where divorce comes before marriage.

What's another word for synonym?

So what if I can't spell "armageddon"? It's not the end of the world.
Stewart Francis

Why is "bra" singular and "panties" plural?

If actions speak louder than words, why can't you hear mime artists?

What is an extravaganza?
The spare vaganza you put aside in case you ever run out of vaganzas.

What is the opposite of woe?
Giddy up!

A talent for anagrams is often latent.

She said: "You're deformed, twisted, misshapen and bow-legged." I said: "Don't bandy words with me!"

There are two words in a person's life that will open a lot of doors for them – PUSH and PULL.

"Virus" is a Latin word used by doctors that means "your guess is as good as mine".

Why is "abbreviation" such a long word?

I'm struggling to finish my word-search puzzle on Victorian villains. I can't see Hyde nor Hare.

Did you know they've taken the word "gullible" out of the dictionary?

Is the top of a mountain called the summit because nobody could think of a name for it?

Whose cruel idea was it to put an "s" in the word "lisp"?

When people with lisps say "bithneth", you know they mean business.

The word "replica" is a replica of the word "replica". *Peter Serafinowicz*

What is a synonym?
A word you use when you can't spell the other one.

Tautology causes me to worry, stress out and tense up.

When push comes to push, I'll buy a thesaurus.

When I was young, I asked my mum what a couple was. She said: "Two or three." And she wonders why her marriage didn't last!

When someone tells you that something defies description, you can be pretty sure he's going to try anyway.

Mike: "Is there a word in the English language that contains every vowel?"
Marty: "Unquestionably."

Where do people who say "Darn" and "Sugar" go to?
Heck.

How subtle is the "b" in "subtle"?

What two words have the most letters?
Post Office.

Why isn't "phonetic" spelt the way it sounds?

I always confuse the words "exotic" and "erotic", which made for an awkward conversation at the pet store.

Is it possible to be gruntled?

The first rule of Thesaurus Club is you do not talk about, mention, speak of, discuss or chat about Thesaurus Club.

Rats are under rated. Just check your dictionary.

Why is "insomniacal" not a word? It's keeping me awake at night.

My nine-year-old is good at spelling bees. He's hopeless with any other words though.

Don't use a big word when a diminutive one will suffice.

Why does the word "monosyllabic" have five syllables?

Did you hear about the man who looked up synonyms for "death" in a thesaurus? He found himself at words for a loss.

To vacillate or not to vacillate, that is the question. Or is it?

Those who say that words never hurt them never got hit on the head with a heavy dictionary.

The word "stifle" is an anagram of itself.

I once saw a forklift lift a crate of forks. It was way too literal for me.
Mitch Hedberg

There are only two four-letter words that are offensive to men – "don't" and "stop", unless they are used together.

What four-letter word ending in "k" means intercourse?
Talk.

Teacher: "Give me a sentence containing the word 'attitude'."
Little Johnny: "When I saw our dog with Billy's school cap in his mouth, I was just glad it wasn't my attitude."

Teacher: "Give me a sentence containing the word 'fascinate'."
Little Johnny: "I have nine buttons on my shirt, but I can only fascinate."

Teacher: "Give me a sentence containing the word 'ammonia'."
Little Johnny: "Tommy's mom offered me a lift after school, but I said ammonia short way from home."

Teacher: "Give me a sentence containing the word 'propagate'."
Little Johnny: "Dad knocked down the old wooden fence, and now we've got a propagate."

Teacher: "Give me a sentence containing the word 'benign'."
Little Johnny: "It's my birthday next week, and I'll benign."

Teacher: "Give me a sentence containing the word 'centimetre'."
Little Johnny: "Aunt Maisie arrived last night, and I was centimetre at the train station."

Teacher: "Give me a sentence containing the word 'gruesome'."
Little Johnny: "After it rained our grass got long and then it gruesome more."

Teacher: "Give me a sentence containing the word 'asbestos'."
Little Johnny: "My math homework may not have been perfect, Miss, but it was asbestos I could do."

Teacher: "Give me a sentence containing the word 'efficient'."
Little Johnny: "When my dad is hungry, he likes efficient chip supper."

Teacher: "Give me a sentence containing the word 'festival'."
Little Johnny: "I have history homework to do tonight, but festival I'm going to watch TV."

Teacher: "Give me a sentence containing the word 'avoidable'."
Little Johnny: "When you walk into a field of cattle, you should always take care to avoidable."

A man entered a newspaper pun contest. He sent in ten different puns in the hope that one would win. Unfortunately no pun in ten did.

WORK

Did you hear about the guy who got sacked from the calendar factory for taking a day off?

I used to be a lifeguard, but some blue kid got me fired.

I got fired from my job today. My boss said my communication skills were awful. I didn't know what to say to that.

I went on a staff training course last week. Mine failed, so it's still only a stick.

I was sacked from my job as a theatre designer. I tried to leave without making a scene.

Work is for people who don't know how to fish.

I quit my job at the helium factory. I didn't like being spoken to in that tone of voice. *Stewart Francis*

I never agree with my boss until he says something.

Boss: "Why do you come out in a rash every time I give you your wages?"
Employee: "I'm allergic to peanuts."

My postman keeps stopping work to tell me jokes. To be honest, his delivery is awful.

Work: it isn't just for sleeping any more.

Why did the door designer quit his job?
He was looking for a new opening.

Boss: "This is the fifth time you've been late for work this week. Do you know what that means?"
Employee: "That it's Friday?"

When you don't know what to do, walk fast and look worried.

My Scottish boss said: "You've got a wee cough." So I took it.

Assembly line: the notion that if a job is worth doing, it's worth doing 9.847 times a day.

I quit my job as a postman. They handed me my first letter to deliver, I looked at it and thought: This isn't for me.

My girlfriend does odd jobs on a tower block. Talk about high maintenance . . .

Did you hear about the woman whose husband got her a job as a human cannonball? She went ballistic.

My secretary quit. She caught me kissing my wife.

Boss: "I'm nobody's fool."
Employee: "Then maybe someone could adopt you."

I went for a job as a blacksmith yesterday. He said: "Have you ever shoed a horse?" I said: "No, but I once told a donkey to bugger off."

I got a job as a one-armed typist's second hand. It's shift work.

What's the best thing about being a watchmaker?
You're always working over time.

Boss: "Why are you late for work?"
Employee: "There are eight people in our house, and the alarm was set for seven."

Pride, commitment, teamwork: words employers use to try to get you to work for free.

I got sacked from my job at the fishing bait factory for causing trouble. It seems I opened a can of worms.

Why did the man quit his job selling computer parts?
He lost his drive.

No machine can do my job until it learns to drink.

I used to be a watchmaker. It was a great job. I could make my own hours.

Happiness is seeing your boss's face on the side of a milk carton.

A woman goes for a job at a lemon grove. The boss asks: "Have you any experience in picking lemons?" The woman says: "Well, I've been divorced three times."

I've just been offered a job by a man from the Brittle Bone Society. I snapped his hand off.

If you can keep your head while others about you are losing theirs, have you considered becoming a guillotine operator?

Rome did not create a great empire by having meetings – they did it by killing all those who opposed them.

Did you hear about the telecoms engineer who was committed to an asylum? His bosses said he had too many hang-ups.

I used to work at a vegetable canning factory until I was caught taking a pea.

Boss: "Are you able to do anything that other people can't?"
Job applicant: "Well, I can read my handwriting."

I got sacked from my job in a Salvation Army soup kitchen. All I said was: "Hurry up you lot, some of us have got homes to go to."

Tarzan came home from a hard day's work and said: "Jane, it's a jungle out there."

How do you get 20 vice-presidents in a Mini car?
Promote one, and watch the other 19 crawl up his backside.

Why did the man quit his job at the balloon factory?
He couldn't keep up with inflation.

Boss: "Why do you go for a haircut on company time?"
Employee: "It grows on company time."

A bus station is where a bus stops. A train station is where a train stops. On my desk I have a work station.

I earn a seven-figure salary. Unfortunately there's a decimal point involved.

My uncle has a job as a diamond cutter. When I asked him where he works, he said: "I mow the grass at Yankee Stadium."

My brother was a lifeguard in a car wash.

I lost my job when my lumber company downsized. They got rid of the deadwood.

The sooner you fall behind, the more time you have to catch up.

On my first day as a club bouncer, they showed me the door.

Boss to employee: "I didn't say it was your fault. I merely said I'm going to blame you."

I'd quit my job but I need the sleep.

Robinson Crusoe pioneered the 40-hour week. He had all the work done by Friday.

Boss: "How long have you worked here?"
Employee: "Ever since you threatened to sack me."

I used to run a halfway house for girls who don't go all the way.

I just read that a radical section of the woodworkers' union has broken away and formed a splinter group.

I now have so little influence in the office that the buck doesn't even slow down here any more.

Anyone can do any amount of work provided it isn't the work he is supposed to be doing.

Did you hear about the unruly circus driver? He refused to tow the lion.

I thought I wanted a career, but it turns out I just wanted paycheques.

On my first day at the flour company, I was really put through the mill.

Mike: "How many people work in your office?"
Marty: "About half."

I had a part-time job at the Samaritans. One day I phoned in sick, but they talked me out of it.

As I left for a job interview, my wife said: "Remember, first impressions are important." So I started with Donald Duck and then did Jimmy Cagney. Still haven't heard back though.

Work is for people who don't have a good Internet connection.

I used to be an investigative reporter, then I worked as a chef. A publisher asked me to write a cook book, but I wouldn't reveal my sauces.

Boss: "You start at $400 a week, and after six months it goes up to $1,000."
Job applicant: "Right, I'll come back in six months."

I try to go the extra mile at work, but my boss always finds me and brings me back.

Colleague: someone who is called in at the last minute to share the blame.

I used to work as a lumberjack, but I couldn't hack it, so they gave me the axe.

Business conventions are important because they demonstrate how many people a company can operate without.

Did you hear about the man who worked in an orange juice factory but just couldn't concentrate?

My wife keeps complaining about her nine-to-five job. I must admit, 4.51 is a strange time to start work.

On my first day at work I clumsily tripped and fell into some wet concrete. It made a bad impression.

If a project is going wrong, always blame one of your colleagues – but not an intelligent one.

Boss: "Shall we bring in a consultant or shall we screw it up ourselves?"

I lost my job as a faith healer because they said I had too much time off sick.

If you can smile when everything around you is going wrong, you're probably in the repair business.

I used to work in a shoe factory, but I didn't fit in.

Escapologists struggle to make a living.

I don't mind going to work. It's the eight-hour wait to go home that drives me crazy.

A union leader was reading his granddaughter a bedtime story: "Once upon a time and a half . . ."

If you have a shitty job, you probably shouldn't lick your fingers at lunch time.

I got a job at the zoo feeding giraffes, but I wasn't up to it.

Doing the job right the first time gets the job done. Doing the job wrong 14 times gives you job security.

I once had a job modelling for a pet cemetery. I was just a dogsbody.

Boss: "What are your strengths and weaknesses?"
Job applicant: "My main weakness would be my issues with reality; my main strength is I'm Batman."

Did you hear about the worker who received three promotions during one car journey? He careered off the road.

I used to work at the unemployment office, but I hated it because when they fired me I still had to turn up the next day.

Why did the man quit his job as a ploughman?
He was stuck in a rut.

I used to be a narrator for bad mimes. *Steven Wright*

In the office, 4.30 is to meeting as water is to boarding.

I recently quit my job as a butler at a stately home. I didn't like being ordered around in that manor.

The trouble with being punctual is that nobody's there to appreciate it.

I missed 19 calls at work last night. The crowd in that bingo hall were furious!

No one could call me a quitter – I always get fired.

Boss: "For a man with no experience, you're asking for a high wage."
Job Applicant: "Well, the work is so much harder when you don't know what you're doing."

Why did the man quit his job at a travel agency?
It was going nowhere.

They say you can tell a British workman by his hands – they're always in his pockets.

There's no "i" in team, but there are five in "individual brilliance".

At work we now have one day a week where we just leave the phones ringing and don't answer them, which is good because it really can get quite stressful at the Samaritans.

There was a tap on my door this morning. I really must get a new plumber.

I wish my brother would learn a trade, so I would know what kind of work he's out of.

I used to be a stuntman. I was very good at it. Some days I was on fire.

My friend's a morgue attendant, but he finds it boring. He phoned me the other day and said that it was really dead at work.

Why did the deli worker quit his job?
He couldn't cut the mustard.

Never ask a woman wine taster whether she spits or swallows.

A while back I got a job doing colonic irrigations. That takes it out of you. *Tim Vine*

How do you know if your office has sick building syndrome?
When it's not there one day because it has phoned in to say it has a sore throat.

Mike: "We're striking for shorter hours."
Marty: "Good idea. I've always thought 60 minutes was too long for an hour."

Out-of-office reply: Sorry to have missed you, but I am in hospital having a frontal lobotomy so that I may be promoted to management.

Out-of-office reply: I am currently out at a job interview and will reply to you if I fail to get the position. Be prepared for my mood.

Out-of-office reply: You are receiving this automatic notification because I am out of the office. If I was in, chances are you wouldn't have received anything at all.

Out-of-office reply: I am on holiday. Your email has been deleted.

Out-of-office reply: I will be out of the office for the next two weeks for medical reasons. When I return, please refer to me as "Sandra" instead of "Steve".

Why did the man sack his personal masseuse?
She rubbed him up the wrong way.

Beat the five o'clock rush. Leave work at noon.

I once had a job as an elevator operator. It had its ups and downs.

Boss: "If you could have a conversation with someone, living or dead, who would it be?"
Job applicant: "The living one."

The boss said I was a miracle worker, because it was a miracle if I worked.

Don't talk to me about unemployment. I come from a tiny fishing village in Derbyshire. *Milton Jones*

If the people who make motivational posters are so motivated, why are they still working in a poster factory?

Why did the transplant surgeon quit his job?
His heart wasn't in it.

I've been off work all week because my pet cow is sick. My boss thinks I'm milking it.

The closest to perfection a person ever comes is when he fills out a job application.

Since leaving the police force, my neighbour works as a safety officer at a children's playground. His career's on the slide.

Remember, a pat on the back is only a few centimetres from a kick in the pants.

Customer services adviser: "Do you want to speak to the manager or someone who knows what's going on?"

Wanted: Man to test for gas leaks with a lit match. Must be willing to travel.

I worked for a while as a tailor, but I wasn't suited to it: it was a sew-sew job.

Boss: "So what motivates you to look for work?"
Job applicant: "My probation officer."

I never drink coffee at work. It keeps me awake.

You should give 100 per cent at work: 15 per cent Monday, 20 per cent Tuesday, 40 per cent Wednesday, 20 per cent Thursday, and 5 per cent Friday.

I start a new job in Seoul next week. I thought it was a good Korea move.

My workmates said I was a spoilt and needed to start acting my age. They were only jealous because their nanny didn't pick them up from the office.

I got shown around an empty perfume factory. It made no scents whatsoever.

A young man strolled in to work at 10 o'clock one morning. His boss raged: "You should have been here at 9!" "Why?" said the young man. "What happened?"

I've just joined the coastguard. It should be an easy job because who's going to try to steal the coast?

To err is human, but to blame someone else shows management potential.

Why do builders have see-through Tupperware lunchboxes?
So they can tell whether they're going to work or going home.

Work is the greatest thing in the world, so make sure you save some for tomorrow.

A guy gave me a job at an information booth, no questions asked. *Jay London*

I wanted my girlfriend to try out as a stripper, but she couldn't bare it on stage.

On your curriculum vitae, at least you can put that you know a little Latin.

I was given the sack at work today, but that's what happens when you're a postman.

My sister couldn't get a job because of the large seagull she used to wear on a choker. It was like an albatross around her neck.

Why did the man quit his job in pool maintenance?
He found it too draining.

You can go anywhere you want if you look serious and carry a clipboard.

Boss: "Do you think you can handle a variety of work?"
Job applicant: "I should be able to. I've had six different jobs in the past two months."

Voluntary work: I wouldn't do it if you paid me.

I'm going to buy my boss a watch because every day he says to me: "What time do you call this?"

I've got a new job helping to compile a dictionary. I got a mate to put a word in for me.

What do you call an unemployed jester?
Nobody's fool.

I got a job answering other people's phones, but it wasn't for me.

I said at work today: "I don't answer to anyone." And so they fired me from the call centre.

When bosses talk about improving productivity, they are never talking about themselves.

My brother's in the watch business. I work and he watches.

Boss: "You're late again! Do you know what time we start work?"
Employee: "No, everyone's always hard at it by the time I get here."

I used to be a builder for 175 years, but that's just an estimate.

The great thing about teamwork is you never have to take all the blame yourself.

My boss is always moaning about me being late for work. I make up for it though by leaving early.

When you take a long time, you're slow; when your boss takes a long time, he's thorough.

When you don't do something, you're lazy; when your boss doesn't do it, he's too busy.

When you take a stand, you're being stubborn; when your boss takes a stand, he's being firm.

When doing something without being told, you're overstepping your authority; when your boss does the same thing, he's using his initiative.

When you apply for leave, you must be going for an interview; when your boss applies for leave, it's because he's overworked.

When you're out of the office, you're skiving; when your boss is out of the office, he's on business.

When you make a mistake, you're an idiot; when your boss makes a mistake, he's only human.

When you're off sick, you're always off sick; when your boss is off sick, he must be very ill.

You should always get right behind your boss – it's the only way to stab him in the back.

I used to work in concrete, but I got stressed.

My sister works as a lifeguard at the beach. She keeps the buoys in line.

At my office Christmas lunch there's no seating plan so we can sit where we like. I like to sit at home.

Interviewer: "Describe yourself in one word."
Job applicant: "John."

Why was the electrician always angry?
Because he had a short fuse.

Why did everyone laugh at the man who worked in the watch factory?
Because he spent all day making faces.

I work in a sweater factory. It's a very close-knit community.

My girlfriend said she'd got a job in a bowling alley. I said: "Tenpin?" She said: "No, it's a permanent job." *Tim Vine*

Meetings: the practical alternative to work.

After I quit my job as a cartographer, I didn't know which way to turn.

Did you hear about the guy who got a job at a paperless office? Everything was great until he needed a shit.

Boss in a government department: "Why didn't you take the leave due to you this year?"
Civil servant: "I needed the rest."

I must be a proctologist because I work with assholes.

My friend works as a technician in a sperm bank. But if anyone asks, he says he's in customer solutions.

Why did the man quit his job designing cul-de-sacs?
It was a dead-end job.

Business was so slow at the medicine factory, you could hear a cough drop.

After being out of work for a while, I've got a job at a factory making periscopes. Things are looking up.

An innkeeper was unhappy with the way the old pub had been demolished. So he got into the bulldozer himself and razed the bar to a new level.

I found my boss's watch in the washroom last week. I knew it was his watch because one hand didn't know what the other was doing.

Woman: "I hear your father was a conductor. Railroad or musical?"
Man: "Electrical. He was hit by lightning."

I did work as a cleaner until I realized I wasn't cut out for a life of grime.

I always take my work very seriously, which is probably why I'm such a lousy clown.

Interviewer to applicant: "Do you think you can come up with any other reason you want this job other than your parents want you out of their house?"

I used to have a job crushing fizzy drinks cans. It's the worst job I've ever had – soda pressing.

A boss says to an employee: "In your case I'm going to mix business with pleasure. You're fired!"

Why did the fisherman quit his job?
He could no longer live on his net income.

My new secretary can type 90 words a minute – a little slower if you want spaces between the words.

Boss: "And what qualities can you bring to the cement industry?"
Job applicant: "Well, I've always been a good mixer."

Did you hear about the show girl who was sacked by Hugh Hefner? She was not a happy bunny.

I thought about becoming a mime artist, but I talked myself out of it.

Why was the man who worked in the bean factory so good at his job? **Because he always had his finger on the pulse.**

I worked as a meteorologist for a month, but I left under a cloud.

The office is somewhere you can relax to escape from a stressful home life.

My friend's a female private investigator. Or gynaecologist, as he prefers to be known.

Boss: "You say you want a raise because three other companies are after you? Which three?"
Employee: "The gas company, the electric company and the phone company."

Did you hear about the bumper car operator who got fired? He's suing his boss for funfair dismissal.

Employee of the month is a good example of how somebody can be both a winner and a loser at the same time. *Demetri Martin*

A boss told some jokes, and everybody except one girl laughed. "What's the matter with you?" he asked. "Haven't you got a sense of humour?" "I don't have to laugh," she said. "I'm leaving Friday."

I thought about becoming a historian, but I couldn't see any future in it.

A boss gave his new secretary an expensive dress for her first week's salary. The next week, he raised her salary.

What did the gravedigger do before going away on vacation? **He asked someone to fill in for him.**

Boss: "What are your greatest qualities?"
Job applicant: "My motivational skills. At my last job, everyone always said they had to work twice as hard when I was around."

This isn't an office. It's hell with fluorescent lighting.

My first day as a chiropodist was a bit of a struggle. I guess I was still finding my feet.

Did you hear about the office worker who had used up all his sick days, so he called in dead?

Why did the man quit his job at Starbucks?
He hated the daily grind.

Don't be irreplaceable. If you can't be replaced, you can't be promoted.

Boss: "We need someone who's responsible."
Job applicant: "Then I'm your man. At my last job, whenever something went wrong, they said I was responsible."

What shift do cemetery workers like to work?
The graveyard shift.

I hated my job as an origami teacher. There was too much paperwork.

There is no substitute for genuine lack of preparation.

I used to work in a sweatshop, but I lost my job when people seemed to stop buying sweat.

Did you hear about the unemployed dwarf who did a bit of casual work? He asked to be paid under the table.

Why did the number theorist quit his job?
He was past his prime.

Boss: "I know you were skiving yesterday. You were out playing golf."
Employee: "That's a lie, and I have the fish to prove it!"

A tidy desk is a sign of an untidy desk drawer.

What did the guillotine operator receive when he was made redundant?
Severance pay.

The last place I worked was really tough. When I left, they not only made me give back my company car and company credit card, I even had to give back my ulcer.

YO MAMA: DANDRUFF

Yo Mama's got so much dandruff . . . it looks like she's permanently wearing a white bobble hat.

. . . her family uses it to stuff pillows and quilts.

. . . she needs to defrost it before combing her hair.

. . . when a fly landed on her head, it said: "I ain't seen this much snow in years!"

. . . when she shakes her head outside they have to clear the street with a snowplough.

. . . they are holding the next Winter Olympics at her house.

. . . she has more flakes than Cadbury's.

. . . there is a crisp layer beneath the soft top layer.

. . . polar bears use her hair as camouflage.

. . . she can simulate desiccated coconut with a single scratch.

. . . yo family wear snowboots whenever she combs her hair.

. . . it looks as if she's been the victim of an air raid by a squadron of pigeons.

. . . she provided the backdrop for *White Christmas*.

. . . I've seen penguins nesting in her hair.

YO MAMA: DIRTY

Yo Mama's so dirty . . . she lost two stone taking a shower.

. . . you can tell her age by counting the rings around her.

. . . she actually repels mosquitoes.

. . . even the rats shout: "Unclean! Unclean!"

. . . grass grows in her belly button.

. . . her farts register eight on the Richter scale.

. . . after you shake her hand you have to be quarantined.

. . . her tights can walk to the laundry basket by themselves.

. . . the last time she had a bath was to mark the end of Prohibition.

. . . when she went to the doctor he didn't send her for a blood test, he sent her for a soil test.

. . . even tramps won't be seen with her.

. . . mould forms on her teeth.

. . . mice go mud wrestling in her belly button.

. . . when her drill sergeant said: 'Hit the dirt', everyone started hitting her.

. . . her idea of a bubble bath is to eat baked beans for dinner.

. . . she leaves rings around the public swimming pool.

Yo Mama's house is so dirty . . . visitors have to wipe their feet before going back outside.

. . . the cockroaches ride around in dune buggies.

. . . the cockroaches check in but never check out.

. . . the mice bring napkins so they won't have to eat off of her floor.

. . . Mr Sheen killed himself.

. . . she has been appointed to keep the national collection of bacteria.

. . . the rats are consulting their lawyer.

YO MAMA: FAT

Yo Mama's so fat . . . she can't even jump to a conclusion.

. . . when she walks her butt claps.

. . . when she has sex she has to give directions.

. . . I had to take a train and two buses just to get on her good side.

. . . she could sell shade.

. . . she has her own postcode.

. . . when she walks across the living room, the radio skips.

. . . she needs a hula hoop to keep her socks up.

. . . she wears a microwave as a beeper.

. . . she has to wear a three-piece bathing suit.

. . . the back of her neck looks like a pack of hot dogs.

. . . I ran round her twice and got lost.

. . . she gets runs in her jeans.

. . . if she put on another two pounds she could get group insurance.

. . . she has more rolls than the town bakery.

. . . her belly button doesn't have lint, it has sweaters.

. . . this town really *isn't* big enough for the both of us.

. . . she has three shirt sizes: extra large, extra extra large, and "Oh my God, it's coming towards us!"

. . . the only thing attracted to her is gravity.

. . . she was baptized at Sea World.

. . . even her shadow has stretch marks.

. . . when she walks down the aisle of an airplane she causes turbulence.

. . . when she steps on the scale, it says: "One at a time, please."

. . . it takes five people to give her a cuddle.

. . . instead of Levi 501s she wears Levi 1002s.

. . . when it gets hot she smells like bacon.

. . . people gain weight just by watching her eat.

. . . she had her ears pierced by harpoon.

. . . the National Weather Agency assigns names to her farts.

. . . everyone can talk behind her back.

. . . when she fell down she rocked herself to sleep trying to get up.

. . . she has to pay excess baggage on her own body.

. . . her university graduation photo was an aerial shot.

. . . she shows up on radar.

. . . she's the same height lying down as standing up.

. . . she wakes up in sections.

. . . she's got smaller women orbiting around her.

. . . she was born with a silver shovel in her mouth.

. . . when mosquitoes see her they scream "Buffet!"

. . . she has stabilizers.

. . . when she goes to a restaurant she doesn't get a menu, she gets an estimate.

. . . she fell into the Grand Canyon and got stuck.

. . . she's once, twice, three times a lady.

. . . when her pager goes off, people think she's backing up.

. . . people exercise by jogging around her.

. . . when she goes to the zoo, elephants throw *her* peanuts.

. . . she has a part-time job as a trampoline.

. . . she hasn't seen her feet for six years.

. . . she uses a bed mattress as a maxipad.

. . . when she bends over we enter Daylight Saving Time.

. . . her cereal bowl is a satellite dish.

. . . when she crosses the street cars look out for her.

. . . when she takes a shower her feet don't get wet.

. . . it takes her two trips to go through a revolving door.

. . . her driver's licence says: "Picture continued on other side."

. . . when she goes to the beach she's the only one that gets a tan.

. . . when she wears leather pants, it looks like they're still on the cow.

. . . she can't play hide and seek, just seek.

. . . before sex yo Papa has to roll her in sawdust and search for the damp patch.

. . . she stood in front of the Hollywood sign and it just said H———d.

. . . when she dances the whole town rocks – literally.

. . . the only label she gets to wear is "Wide Load".

. . . when she wore a Malcolm X T-shirt, a helicopter tried to land on her.

. . . she has to get out of the car to change gears.

. . . they had to grease a doorframe and hold a doughnut on the other side to get her through.

. . . she doesn't have dreams, she has movies.

. . . when she cut her leg gravy dripped out.

. . . when she wears corduroy pants the ridges don't show.

. . . her blood type is Ragù.

. . . of her can be in four rooms at once.

. . . she has to put her belt on with a boomerang.

. . . she's on both sides of the family.

. . . her cereal bowl came with a lifeguard.

. . . people have been known to trip over her toenail clippings.

. . . when she was diagnosed with a flesh-eating virus, doctors gave her 30 years to live.

. . . when she went bungee jumping she took the bridge with her.

. . . I have to take three steps back just to see all of her.

. . . in some atlases she's listed as the eighth continent.

. . . her belly button's got an echo.

. . . instead of a cotton bud she uses a baseball bat to clean the insides of her ears.

. . . every time she turns around it's her next birthday.

. . . she left the house with high heels and came back with flip flops.

. . . when she jumped from a burning building and landed in the safety net she was still bouncing up and down three hours later.

. . . to put her hands in her pockets she has to take her pants off.

. . . when she gets in the car the tyres go flat.

. . . she doesn't wear a G string – she wears an A B C D E F G string.

. . . she puts on lipstick with a paint roller.

. . . she showers at the local car wash.

. . . she can pack all her belongings in her folds of skin.

. . . her last gynaecologist fell in and hasn't been seen for weeks.

. . . she's moving the Earth out of its orbit.

. . . the first time she had sex the earth didn't just move for her – it moved for the whole neighbourhood.

. . . you can pinch an inch on her forehead.

. . . they use the elastic in her underwear for bungee jumping.

. . . she doesn't have a doctor, she has a groundkeeper.

. . . her plastic surgeon uses scaffolding.

. . . when she gets in an elevator it *has* to go down.

. . . when she rested on her laurels they broke.

. . . when God said: "Let there be light," he told her to move out of the way first.

YO MAMA: GREASY

Yo Mama's so greasy . . . Texaco buys oil from her.

. . . her freckles slipped off.

. . . helping her across the road was like wrestling with a bar of wet soap.

. . . the kids in the park use her naked body as a slide.

. . . she sells her sweat to the chip shop.

. . . she keeps sliding off the bed at night.

. . . she can easily slip into something more comfortable.

. . . slugs find her trail of slime attractive.

. . . her slip-on shoes slip right off.

. . . her push-up bra couldn't stop itself.

. . . her leg warmers started frying.

. . . supermarket staff refer to her as a slippery customer.

. . . it's easier to hold on to a job than it is to hold on to yo Mama.

. . . she doesn't give blood, she gives oil.

Yo Mama's hair is so greasy . . . you could fry chicken in it.

. . . her centre parting slipped down to her ear.

. . . her slides keep sliding off.

. . . her grips won't grip.

. . . her head lice choke to death.

. . . she doesn't wash it with shampoo, she washes it with industrial detergent.

. . . when it is wet it forms slicks.

. . . you need to wear rubber gloves before running your fingers through it.

YO MAMA: HAIRY

Yo Mama's so hairy . . . her breasts look like coconuts.

. . . when she puts her arms to her side it looks like she has Don King in a headlock.

. . . you could knit her into a pair of gloves.

. . . it looks like she's got a herd of yak in her armpits.

. . . she's got afros on her nipples.

. . . when her son was born he suffered severe rugburn.

. . . you could stuff a mattress with the hair from her legs.

. . . she's got blackbirds nesting in her belly button.

. . . when she got in my car it looked like I had tinted windows.

. . . native beaters had to hack their way through to reach her thighs.

. . . when she walks the dog people stroke *her*.

. . . if she could fly she'd look like a magic carpet.

. . . Sting has announced he wants to save her forest.

. . . they filmed *Gorillas in the Mist* in her shower.

. . . she shaves with a weedwacker.

. . . she got a trim and lost ten pounds.

. . . she has dreadlocks on her back.

. . . Bigfoot took a picture of her.

. . . her breasts have sideburns.

. . . she has to braid her upper lip.

YO MAMA: LAZY

Yo Mama's so lazy . . . nothing runs in her family.

. . . her idea of cleaning the house is to sit in a corner and gather dust.

. . . she doesn't walk in her sleep – she hitchhikes.

. . . she thinks a two-income family is where yo Papa has two jobs.

. . . only her cheques bounce.

. . . she won't even raise a smile.

. . . her idea of exercise is changing channels on the TV.

. . . her nose runs more than she does.

. . . she's expected to win *American Idle*.

. . . when they asked her if she'd run for President, she said: "Hell, I ain't runnin' for nobody!"

. . . she couldn't even be moved to tears.

. . . she's like a sack of couch potatoes.

. . . she won't even exercise her human rights.

. . . even her bowels don't have movements.

. . . she's got a remote control just to operate her remote.

YO MAMA: NASTY

Yo Mama's so nasty . . . her breasts give sour milk.

. . . I talked to her over the PC and she gave me a virus.

. . . she bit the dog and gave it rabies.

. . . she puts ice down her knickers to keep the crabs fresh.

. . . her crabs use her tampon string as a bungee cord.

. . . she's got more clap than an auditorium.

. . . when she does the splits she sticks to the floor.

. . . she went swimming and made the Dead Sea.

. . . even her scabs have scabs.

YO MAMA: OLD

Yo Mama's so old . . . her birth certificate has expired.

. . . when she went to blow out the candles on her birthday cake she was beaten back by the flames.

. . . she's got hieroglyphics on her driving licence.

. . . she doesn't leave fingerprints any more.

. . . she was DJ at the Boston Tea Party.

. . . the average age of her friends is deceased.

. . . her blood type is discontinued.

. . . *Jurassic Park* brought back memories.

. . . she farts dust.

. . . the only dating she gets involved in is carbon dating.

. . . the candles cost more than the cake.

. . . her breasts squirt out powdered milk.

. . . it takes her longer to rest these days than it does to get tired.

. . . when she was in school there was no history class.

. . . her birth certificate is in Roman numerals.

. . . she was a waitress at the Last Supper.

. . . she's got more wrinkles than an elephant's scrotum.

. . . the last period she had was the Mesozoic.

. . . when she was a kid rainbows were in black and white.

. . . she got Adam and Eve's autograph.

. . . she can remember when the Dead Sea was only sick.

. . . her back goes out more than she does.

. . . she was deafened by the Big Bang.

. . . vultures constantly circle her house.

. . . when I told her to act her age she died.

. . . she uses her hot flushes to heat her cup of tea.

. . . she co-wrote the sixth commandment.

. . . all the names in her little black book are followed by MD.

. . . it was her who called the cops when David and Goliath began to fight.

YO MAMA: POOR

Yo Mama's so poor . . . burglars break into her home and *leave* money.

. . . she hangs the toilet paper out to dry.

. . . they put her photo on food stamps.

. . . she watches television on Etch-A-Sketch.

. . . she can only get to wear her best dress when the dog doesn't need its blanket.

. . . your Kinder eggs never have any surprises in them.

. . . that to save on water she washes her hair when she flushes the toilet.

. . . the last time your family had a hot meal was when your house was on fire.

. . . her favourite hat doubles up as a lampshade.

. . . a brick through her window would be considered a home improvement.

. . . she waves an ice cube around and calls it air conditioning.

. . . the bank repossessed her cardboard box.

. . . the only time she tasted meat was when she bit her tongue.

. . . she can't even afford to go to the free clinic.

. . . when I asked her what she was doing kicking a can down the street, she said: "Moving."

. . . when you ring the doorbell the toilet flushes.

. . . the only way she can watch TV is by drilling a hole through her neighbour's wall.

. . . she can't even afford to eat her words.

. . . she conserves toilet paper by using both sides.

. . . the garbage collectors give *her* a tip at Christmas.

. . . she can't even afford the last two letters, so she just calls herself "po".

. . . she's got more furniture on her porch than in her house.

. . . you know the story about the old woman who lived in a shoe? Well, yo Mama lives in a flip-flop.

. . . she tapes popcorn to the ceiling because it's cheaper than a smoke alarm.

. . . people rob her house for practice.

. . . that while for some people money talks, for yo Mama it doesn't even whisper.

. . . when yo brother started having epileptic fits she used him as a dishwasher.

. . . she uses tumbleweed as a Christmas tree.

. . . she's in debt to the blood bank.

. . . her idea of double-glazed windows is two layers of clingfilm.

. . . the only drink you get offered in her house is spit.

. . . I saw her wrestling a squirrel for a peanut.

. . . when I asked her where the toilet was, she said: "Just choose a corner."

. . . instead of using a steam iron, she sits on the laundry and farts.

. . . the only time she can put chips on yo plate is when she drops it.

. . . when someone rings her doorbell, she leans out the window and says "ding-dong".

. . . her idea of "the good china" is a paper plate.

. . . when I walked into her house and swatted a firefly, she said: "Who turned off the lights?"

. . . she uses cobwebs for curtains.

. . . when I stepped on a skateboard outside her house, she yelled: "Hey, get off the car!"

. . . instead of switching on the central heating she kicks yo Papa in the balls and warms her hands on his breath.

. . . she can't even afford to spend a penny.

. . . if you go to her home and ask to use the toilet, she says: "Sure, third tree on the right."

. . . when someone went into her living room and stood on a cigarette butt, she yelled: "Who turned off the heater?"

. . . she does drive-by shootings on the bus.

. . . when she heard about the Last Supper she thought the food stamps had run out.

. . . the rats in her house go round with begging bowls.

. . . when she cut her finger she used chewing gum as a plaster.

. . . she can't afford a mop, so she stands on her head to clean the floor.

. . . the only time she smelt hot food was when a rich man farted.

. . . she eats cereal with a fork to save milk.

. . . when you go over for dinner she just reads out the recipes.

. . . she went to the wishing well and threw in an IOU.

. . . her kids were made in Taiwan.

. . . when you asked her what was for dinner she took off her shoelaces and said: "Spaghetti."

. . . she has to take the trash *in*.

. . . when I went to use her bathroom I saw a cockroach sitting on a Pepsi can saying: "Wait your turn!"

. . . she only got married for the rice.

Yo Mama's house is so small . . . her front and back doors are on the same hinge.

. . . if she orders a large pizza we have to go outside to eat it.

. . . half of the TV is in one room and half in another.

. . . as soon as you enter it, you've just left.

. . . she can cut her front lawn with nail scissors.

. . . when she left a shoe box in the yard the council thought it was an extension.

. . . the front door is a cat flap.

. . . she and yo Papa sleep in separate rooms – but in the same bed.

. . . I stepped through her front door and fell out the back.

. . . only one bird can sit on her roof at a time.

. . . her cat complains that there's not enough room to swing a mouse.

. . . she can only use condensed milk.

. . . you have to stand on one leg in the shower.

. . . the living-room carpet is just a sample.

. . . the cockroaches are hunchbacked.

. . . you can be upstairs and downstairs at the same time.

. . . the bathroom tiles are just two books of postage stamps.

. . . the three-piece suite has to be in three different rooms.

. . . the main TV set is on a cell phone.

. . . when she drops a Kleenex she has wall-to-wall carpet.

. . . when mail goes through the letterbox it hits everyone inside.

. . . Barbie and Ken rejected it.

. . . the doormat just says WEL.

. . . you have to go outside just to change your mind.

YO MAMA: SHORT

Yo Mama's so short . . . she has to slam-dunk her bus fare.

. . . she doesn't see eye to eye with anyone.

. . . she can hang-glide on a Dorito.

. . . her head smells of her feet.

. . . she doesn't roll dice, she pushes them.

. . . she poses for trophies.

. . . when it comes to painting her house she can only reach the skirting board.

. . . she has to get a running start to get up on the toilet.

. . . she can do backflips under the bed.

. . . she's afraid to get off the carpet alone.

. . . she trips on her tampon string.

. . . when the doctor gave her a suppository she doubled in size.

. . . she does pull-ups on a staple.

. . . even close up she looks far away.

. . . she can pick mushrooms without bending down.

. . . whenever anyone goes into a bar and orders a short, the barman thinks they mean yo Mama.

. . . she doesn't know if she has a headache or a footache.

. . . she broke her leg jumping off the toilet.

. . . she wasn't born and raised, she was born and lowered.

. . . she's a teller at a piggy bank.

. . . when she and her twin sister walk down the street, people say: "Hey, it's a pair of shorts!"

. . . she looks like she went to a blood drive and forgot to say "when".

. . . she would drown by the time she realized it was raining.

. . . Dopey, Bashful and Doc see her as a kindred spirit.

. . . she can keep her feet warm just by breathing hard.

. . . you can see her whole body on her driver's licence.

. . . when she sneezes she hits her head on the floor.

. . . she can sit on a dime and swing her legs.

. . . she's a lumberjack for bonsai trees.

. . . she doesn't have legs, she has feet growing out of her ass.

YO MAMA: SKINNY

You Mama's so skinny . . . her bra fits better backwards.

. . . she only has one stripe on her pyjamas.

. . . she has to stand in the same place twice to cast a shadow.

. . . yo Papa put a pair of antlers on her head and used her as a hat-stand.

. . . she swallowed a meatball and thought she was pregnant.

. . . you could blindfold her with dental floss.

. . . her pants have one belt loop.

. . . when she wears a fake fur coat she looks like a pipe cleaner.

. . . instead of calling her your parent, you call her transparent.

. . . I've seen more meat on a vegan's plate.

. . . when she drinks a tomato juice she looks like a thermometer.

. . . when she closes one eye she looks like a needle.

. . . when she took up golf the pro called her the thin end of the wedge.

. . . the neighbour's dog buried her in the garden.

. . . she makes Olive Oyl look obese.

. . . she went missing for two days before yo Papa found her standing behind the lamp stand.

. . . 13 is unlucky for her because it's her bust size.

. . . while the rest of your family fly abroad on vacation, she goes air mail.

. . . she doesn't show up on X-rays.

. . . she was an artist's model for L. S. Lowry.

. . . she uses a Band Aid as a maxipad.

. . . when yo Papa penetrates her she looks like a hunchback.

. . . she looks like a mic stand.

. . . if she turned sideways and stuck out her tongue she'd look like a zipper.

. . . she's only held together by bacteria.

. . . she tied knots in her legs just so she could have knees.

. . . she can dodge raindrops.

. . . when she goes to the park the ducks throw her bread.

. . . her nipples touch.

. . . she could wear an onion ring as a necklace.

. . . when she farts she blows away.

YO MAMA: SLUTTY

Yo Mama's so slutty . . . her personalized car licence plate is VD1.

. . . she buys condoms in bulk.

. . . the identity of yo Papa is a multiple-choice question.

. . . when she got a new mini-skirt everyone commented on her nice belt.

. . . she's blind but seeing another man.

. . . she's entertained more soldiers than Bob Hope.

. . . her face is on posters at the sexually-transmitted-diseases clinic.

. . . she's introduced a Park and Ride scheme so that clients can leave their car outside her flat.

. . . turning off the bedroom light means shutting the car door.

. . . she walks down the street with a mattress strapped to her back, asking for volunteers.

. . . she got a job as a slot machine.

. . . when she fell down on a sidewalk by the time she'd got back up, she had made twenty dollars.

. . . when she gets poked on Facebook it uses four fingers.

. . . she has a number dispenser on her bedpost.

. . . yo Papa has to disguise himself as the postman to have sex with her.

. . . she gives out frequent-rider miles.

. . . I could have been your daddy but the guy in line behind me had the correct change.

YO MAMA: SMELLY

Yo Mama's so smelly . . . even dogs won't sniff her.

. . . her Sure deodorant is now Confused.

. . . the government makes her wear a Biohazard warning.

. . . a blind man walking by asked her: "How much for the shrimp platter?"

. . . farmers use her bathwater as liquid fertilizer.

. . . when she spread her legs yo Papa got seasick.

. . . a skunk smelled her butt and passed out.

. . . she's worse than a vegan's fart.

. . . her bedroom is like the place where whales go to die.

. . . she made Right Guard turn left.

. . . there's more crust in her knickers than on a loaf of bread.

. . . her poo is glad to escape.

. . . the coroner picked her up while she was sleeping.

. . . she hums more than a hummingbird.

. . . she turned the gas mask into a fashion statement.

. . . she should be charged with sock abuse.

Yo Mama's breath stinks so bad . . . when she burps her teeth have to duck.

. . . it made a Tic Tac run away.

. . . it could prise barnacles off a ship.

. . . rain goes back to the clouds.

. . . her mouth needs Odor Eaters.

. . . it can strip paint off the walls.

. . . people look forward to her farts.

. . . we don't know whether she needs gum or toilet paper.

. . . it kills more household germs than bleach.

. . . it must be taking karate lessons because it's really kicking.

. . . people on the other end of the phone hang up.

. . . she has to take prescription Tic Tacs.

. . . it really does seem like she's talking shit.

YO MAMA: STUPID

Yo Mama's so stupid . . . she couldn't even pass a blood test.

. . . she stood on a chair to raise her IQ.

. . . she spent two weeks in a revolving door looking for a doorknob.

. . . she bought a solar-powered torch.

. . . she was born on Christmas Day but can never remember her birthday.

. . . she thought hot meals were stolen food.

. . . she once ordered sushi well done.

. . . she invented a waterproof tea bag.

. . . she thinks private enterprise means owning your personal starship.

. . . she thinks a permutation is a surgical procedure.

. . . she orders a cheeseburger from McDonald's and says: "Hold the cheese."

. . . she studied for a dope test.

. . . she once asked: "What's the number for 911?"

. . . she thinks "Nessun Dorma" is a camper van.

. . . when yo Papa asked her to buy a colour TV, she said: "What colour?"

. . . she invented a pencil with an eraser on each end.

. . . she thought a lawsuit was something you wear to court.

. . . her fingers and toes are numbered.

. . . when her computer said "Press any key to continue", she phoned support complaining she couldn't find the "any" key.

. . . she thought Meow Mix was a record for cats.

. . . her dog teaches *her* tricks.

. . . she thinks "aperitif" means dentures.

. . . when she saw a sign saying "Wet Floor", she did.

. . . she thinks the English Channel is a TV station.

. . . she tosses breadcrumbs to helicopters.

. . . when you were born she took one look at your umbilical cord and said: "Wow, it comes with cable, too!"

. . . she plays solitaire for cash.

. . . she got locked inside a bed shop and slept on the floor.

. . . she planted a dogwood tree and expected a litter of puppies.

. . . when she found out she was pregnant she asked: "Who's the mother?"

. . . she failed a survey.

. . . she thinks zebras have stripes so that lions can barcode them before having them for dinner.

. . . she thinks Thailand is a men's clothing shop.

. . . she once fell *up* the stairs.

. . . when she went to the game she thought a quarterback was a refund.

. . . it takes two of her to listen to music.

. . . she called it quits when her fourth child was born because she read that every fifth child born is Chinese.

. . . she ought to carry a warning label on her forehead.

. . . the only time she gets the point is when she sits on a drawing pin.

. . . she thinks a polygon is a dead parrot.

. . . she considers mould to be a superior life form.

. . . she put her watch in the bank to save time.

. . . she thinks Moby Dick is a kind of venereal disease.

. . . her brain cells are on the endangered-species list.

. . . she thinks Sherlock Holmes is a housing project.

. . . she calls people to ask them their phone number.

. . . she uses two hands to eat with chopsticks.

. . . she asked for a refund on a jigsaw puzzle because she thought it was broken.

. . . she thinks Condoleezza Rice is a Mexican side dish.

. . . she cooks with Old Spice.

. . . it took her a week to get rid of a 24-hour virus.

. . . she needs an operating manual for a screwdriver.

. . . she climbed a glass wall to see what was on the other side.

. . . she sat in a tree house because she wanted to be a branch manager.

. . . she used to think Johnny Cash was a pay toilet.

. . . she lost a finger and now can't count past nine.

. . . she lost her position at the hairdresser's because she kept getting "blow dry" and "blow job" mixed up.

. . . she thinks innuendo is an Italian suppository.

. . . she couldn't see that her ass was on fire with a flashlight and a three-way mirror.

. . . she told me to meet her at the corner of Walk and Don't Walk.

. . . she thought menopause was a button on the stereo.

. . . she hasn't bought an electric toothbrush because she doesn't know if her teeth are AC or DC.

. . . that if you put a lens in each of her ears, you'd have a telescope.

. . . when she wanted to tighten the clothes-line she moved the house.

. . . she has to reach inside her bra to count to two.

. . . she took a doughnut back to the shop because it had a hole in it.

. . . she thinks her twin lives in the mirror.

. . . she thinks the St Louis Cardinals are appointed by the Pope.

. . . on her job application where it says "emergency contact", she put "911".

. . . when she gets amnesia she gets smarter.

. . . when everyone went to a fancy-dress party as an item of food, yo Papa told her to go as a strawberry fool.

. . . she took an umbrella to see *Rain Man*.

. . . she thinks K-Y jelly goes with ice cream.

. . . she was three before she got a birthmark.

. . . it took her seven hours to look up "wolverine" in the dictionary because she didn't realize it was in alphabetical order.

. . . she never misses an episode of her screensaver.

. . . she called the drugs hotline to order some.

. . . blondes tell jokes about *her*.

. . . she tried to wake up a sleeping bag.

. . . when she went into a think-tank she almost drowned.

. . . she could qualify as a houseplant if she learned to photosynthesize.

. . . she bought herself an electric toothbrush and an electric blanket and now she's saving up for an electric chair.

. . . she invented a new type of parachute that opens on impact.

. . . she tried to drop acid but the car battery fell on her foot.

. . . she got locked out of a convertible car with the top down.

. . . when airport customs officers asked her if she had anything to declare she was arrested after saying: "Only the crack up my ass."

. . . her shoes say TGIF – toes go in front.

. . . she got stabbed in a shootout.

. . . she refused to buy sponge, tinned fruit and jelly because she didn't want to be trifled with.

. . . she puts on a wetsuit to surf the Internet.

. . . she managed to lose her shadow.

. . . when her computer says "You've got mail" she runs outside to wait for the postman.

. . . she went to the 24-hour convenience store and asked what time they closed.

. . . she invented a silent car alarm.

. . . when she got hit by a cup she told the police that she'd been mugged.

. . . she sold her car for gas money.

. . . she stopped making ice cubes because she forgot the recipe.

. . . she once put a stamp on a fax.

. . . she jumped off a tower block in an attempt to fly because she'd read her maxipad had wings.

. . . when yo Papa told her Christmas was just around the corner she went looking for it.

. . . when she saw the headline "Knife Attack On Bus" she said: "Who'd want to stab a bus?"

. . . she tried to drown herself in a carpool.

. . . she climbed on the roof because she heard drinks were on the house.

. . . she tried to steal a free sample.

. . . she'd have to be twice as smart to be a half-wit.

. . . she thinks Christmas wrap is Snoop Dogg's holiday album.

. . . she took a ruler to bed with her to see how long she slept.

. . . she got hit by a parked car.

. . . she took the Pepsi challenge and chose Cif.

. . . I saw her in the frozen-food section of the supermarket with a fishing rod.

. . . she took a spoon to the Superbowl.

. . . when a job application said "sex" she wrote: "Monday, Wednesday and sometimes Saturday".

. . . she went to Gap to get her teeth fixed.

. . . when I told her I was reading a book by Homer she asked if I'd got anything written by Bart.

. . . she used to stand in front of the mirror with her eyes closed so that she could see what she looked like asleep.

. . . she threw a rock at the ground and missed.

YO MAMA: TEETH (BAD)

Yo Mama's teeth are so yellow . . . I can't believe it's not butter.

. . . cars slow down when she smiles.

. . . when she drinks water it turns into lemonade.

. . . when she walked into church everybody cried out: "I see the light!"

. . . when she smiles you can see Dorothy skipping across them.

. . . she got a job at the cinema spitting on popcorn.

Yo Mama's teeth are so black . . . you'd think she had eaten coal for dinner.

Yo Mama's teeth stick out so much . . . it looks like her nose is playing the piano.

Yo Mama's teeth are so rotten, when she smiles they look like dice.

Yo Mama's teeth are so crooked . . . when she smiles it looks like her tongue is in jail.

. . . she needs a map to find her tongue.

Yo Mama's teeth are so ugly . . . she got pulled over by the cops for not having dental insurance.

Yo Mama's teeth are so big . . . it looks like her mom had an affair with Mr Ed.

. . . when she sneezed she bit a hole in her chest.

. . . her dentist charges her by the tooth.

YO MAMA: UGLY

Yo Mama's so ugly . . . she has to creep up on her make-up.

. . . her family had to tie a steak round her neck so the dogs would play with her.

. . . when she stands on the beach the tide won't come in.

. . . when she was born the doctor looked at her ass then her face and said: "Twins!."

. . . when she walks into a bank they turn off the surveillance cameras.

. . . her dentist treats her by mail order.

. . . even her shadow won't be seen with her.

. . . her birth certificate was a letter of apology from the condom factory.

. . . her shrink makes her lie face down on the couch.

. . . they knew what time she was born because her face stopped the clock.

. . . she could scare the moss off a rock.

. . . when she gets up in the morning, the sun goes down.

. . . she could make an onion cry.

. . . it's seven years' bad luck just to look at her.

. . . the only way she could ever get more than one date was by buying a calendar.

. . . when she walks out of a pet store, the alarm goes off.

. . . it looks like she ran the 100-metre dash in a 90-metre gym.

. . . yo Papa had it written into their wedding vows that they would only have sex doggie-style.

. . . she practises birth control by leaving the light on.

. . . she has to fake orgasms when she masturbates.

. . . it looks like she's wearing her face inside out.

. . . her husband takes her to work with him just so he doesn't have to kiss her goodbye.

. . . vampires are too scared to suck her blood.

. . . even the tide wouldn't take her out.

. . . people go as her for Hallowe'en.

. . . she pretends she's someone else when she's having sex.

. . . if her face were her fortune she'd get a tax rebate.

. . . when she went to see *The Elephant Man* at the cinema, the audience thought he was making a personal appearance

. . . yo Papa made her convert to Islam just so she could wear a burka.

. . . her pillows cry at night.

. . . when she moved into the street all the neighbours chipped in for curtains.

. . . her face could scare a hungry wolf off a meat truck.

. . . in strip joints they pay her to put her clothes *on*.

. . . it looks like her face caught fire and they put it out with a fork.

. . . when she visited a haunted house, they offered her a job.

. . . at her wedding everybody kissed the groom.

. . . when she was born the doctor smacked her face.

. . . she has to get her vibrator drunk first.

. . . she made a blind man cry.

. . . even the toilet flushes when it sees her.

. . . when she went for a sex change the surgeon had to flip a coin.

. . . kids trick-or-treat her over the phone.

. . . Rice Krispies won't talk to her.

. . . when a wasp stings her it shuts its eyes.

. . . her mother fed her by catapult.

. . . when she worked for a dentist none of the patients needed anaesthetic.

. . . the last time she heard a whistle she got hit by a train.

. . . even Jehovah's Witnesses don't call on her.

. . . when she threw a boomerang it refused to come back.

. . . they printed her face on airline sick bags.

. . . when she looks in a mirror her reflection throws up.

. . . that if you look up "ugly" in the dictionary there's a picture of her.

YOUTH

I always remember I spent one wonderful summer in my youth rolling down hills in a large tyre. It was a Goodyear.

Every woman should hang on to her youth – except when she's driving.

I overhead my teenage daughter saying she was going to some seedy club to watch her friends in a wet T-shirt competition. I thought: I'll be the judge of that . . .

A teenager is always too tired to hold a dishcloth, but never too tired to hold a phone.

I'm not sure whether growing pains are something teenagers have – or are.

Adolescence is a time of rapid change. Between the ages of 12 and 17, a parent can age as much as 20 years.

Teenagers are incredibly well informed about any subject they don't have to study.

What's the best way to keep a teenage boy out of hot water?
Put some dishes in them.

Adolescence is that time when a girl's voice changes from no to yes.

When your kids are teenagers, it's important to have a dog so that someone in your house is happy to see you.

A teenager is someone whose hang-ups don't include clothes.

You're only young once. After that you have to think up some other excuse.

There's nothing wrong with teenagers that reasoning with them won't aggravate.

Adolescence is that short period between hopscotch and real scotch.

Studies show that one in five teens doesn't know how to peel an orange. It's a good job they've all got knives then! *Jack Dee*

How did the teenager know he had bad acne?
His dog called him Spot.

The best advice on contraception a mother can give her daughter is simply to use her head.

It's not what a teenager knows that bothers his parents: it's how he found out.

How do you make teenage boys more interested in history?
Teach them how to delete it.

My son is 21. He'll be 22 if I let him.

What's the best way to recapture your youth?
Take the car keys off him.

Cats and teenagers do not improve anyone's furniture.

I went off the rails when I was younger – I guess I just wasn't cut out to be a train driver.

I gave my son a hint. On his room door I put a sign: "Checkout time is 21."

ZOOS

I went to the zoo the other day. There was only a dog in it. It was a shih tzu.

What's the difference between a redneck zoo and a northern zoo?
A redneck zoo has a description of the animal on the front of the cage, along with a recipe.

Two idiots went to the zoo and heard the lion let out a mighty roar. "Let's get out of here!" said one. "You can go if you want," said the other, "but I'm staying for the whole movie."

How did the zoo split up a pair of gay penguins?
By giving them only one ticket to *Mamma Mia*.

I said to my girlfriend: "Have you ever been to a zoo – I mean as a visitor?"

Why don't you see many koala bears in zoos?
They can't afford the admission.

Me and my brother inherited some furniture from the local zoo. I'm glad to say I got the lion's chair. *Tim Vine*

Mike: "Why don't you take your son to the zoo?"
Marty: "No. If they want him, they can come and get him."

Little Johnny's school class went to the Natural History Museum. When he got home, his mother asked him whether he had enjoyed it. "Yes," he said, "but it was weird going to a dead zoo."

Why are there no zebras in Czech zoos?
Stripes and Czechs don't mix.

Visitor: "What's the new baby hippo's name?"
Zoo keeper: "I don't know. He won't tell me."

I read in the paper: "Rare White Tiger Kills Zoo Keeper". That's why I prefer my tigers medium to well done.

Did you hear about the man who had a job at the zoo circumcising elephants? The wages were poor but the tips were huge.

A leopard clone was found slain at the city zoo. Police suspect a copycat killer.

When a lion escapes from a zoo in Africa, how do they know when they've caught the right one?

Zoo owner: "You idiot! You left the door of the lions' cage open all night!"
Keeper: "What's the big deal? Who's going to steal a lion?"

What did the lion eat after the zoo dentist fixed its tooth?
The zoo dentist.

A man walked into a zoo and said: "I want to borrow two giraffes for a magazine photo shoot in 10 minutes." The zoo manager said: "That's a tall order."

My granddad has the heart of a lion, and with it a lifetime ban from London Zoo.